WITHDRAWN

# A Gathering of Recipes from Great Texas Cookbooks

Edited by Terry Thompson-Anderson

SHEARER PUBLISHING

Fredericksburg, Texas

Shearer Publishing
406 Post Oak Road
Fredericksburg, Texas 78624
Toll-free: 800-458-3808
Fax: 830-997-9752

www.shearerpub.com

Library of Congress Cataloging-in-Publication Data

Lone star eats : a gathering of recipes from great
Texas cookbooks /
Terry Thompson-Anderson, editor.
    p. cm.
  Includes index.
  ISBN 978-0-940672-76-5 (pbk.)
  1.  Cooking, American--Southwestern style.
  2.  Cooking—Texas. 3. Cookbooks.
  I. Thompson-Anderson, Terry, 1946-
  TX715.2.S69L65 2011
  641.59764—dc23

                            2011014679


ISBN 978-0-940672-76-5

Printed in China

# Contents

# Introduction

The food we eat in Texas is legendary. Texas has such a rich heritage of food, which has been preserved in small ethnic towns and communities and, in many instances, merged to create what we today call our own Texas Cuisine.

The two most widely known ethnic groups that brought their foods and culture to Texas were the Mexicans and the Germans. Hispanic peoples were living in Texas by the early 1700s, firmly establishing their culture in the Texas terra firma. Early Texas settlers were a mixed blend of European heritage traveling westward to seek new fertile land to farm. In the mid-1800s there was a huge influx of Germans who settled in the Texas Hill Country and the surrounding Central Texas regions, bringing their culture and food. The German schnitzel, a veal or pork steak that is battered and pan-sautéed, was the early prototype of the dish that is near and dear to the hearts of Texans—the chicken-fried steak, or CFS, as it is often called.

After the Civil War a few larger-than-life Texans began to acquire vast parcels of land in South and West Texas. It was land that everyone else thought worthless, with poor soil, rocky terrain, and sparse rainfall and water. But on those vast stretches of land were the cattle that had been brought by the Spanish missionaries and kept on the missions they established. When the missions were abandoned, the cattle became feral and proved themselves to be hearty enough to flourish on the harsh lands. The early ranchers rounded up the cattle, creating the first herds of Texas longhorn cattle. To market the cattle the ranchers drove huge herds of thousands of cattle to the markets in the Midwest. This era in Texas history fostered a number of traditions that are still a part of our culture today—the cattle ranch, the

Texas cowboy, and our love of beef. With the newfound love of beef, barbecue originated, first cooked in hand-wrought pits where it was slow-smoked over hardwood fires. In Texas the standard barbecue cut is the beef brisket. Many of the early African American churches began to sponsor barbecues as both a way of producing income and to feed the members. Then the German meat markets in the central regions of the state began to smoke their hand-made sausages and added brisket and pork. We also discovered the gustatory pleasures of slapping a well-marbled, thick-cut steak on the grill, and a whole new facet of Texas cuisine was born.

Today Texas is a rich hodge-podge of ethnicity in the big cities like Houston and Dallas, but with many small towns still remaining true to their original ethnic roots. The way we eat in Texas reflects the sum of all of our parts. We have a great love of fish and shellfish from the many lakes and rivers in the state and, of course, the vast resources of our coastal waters. Gulf Coast oysters are shipped all over the country. Texas is rich in agricultural endeavors, from rice farming in the southeast to our major citrus industry in the Rio Grande Valley. Farming in the central and southern regions provides the state with fresh seasonal vegetables and fruit. We have a bounty of farmer's markets, with more being established every year. The Texas Department of Agriculture devotes great resources to spreading the important message of the need to eat local, so that we know where our food comes from and who grew it.

In the Texas Hill Country we have a bountiful peach-growing region, and fresh blackberries and strawberries are available at many pick-your-own farms. Two of the newest groups of farming pioneers are the olive growers, who are growing thousands of olive trees in the southern regions of Central Texas, producing excellent-quality olive oils and olives, and lavender farmers who are growing lavender for culinary use as well as health and beauty products.

We have a growing number of organic farms and grass-fed beef, lamb, and buffalo growers. And, of course, any Texan will brag about our relatively new wine industry, which is producing wines that are beating out contenders from around the world in international competitions.

In compiling this cookbook, I scoured the state for Texas cookbooks, collecting an entire six-shelf bookcase full of them! Many were old books put together by small community organizations, churches, or junior leagues. Some were slick cookbooks authored by some of our state's leading chefs, who are famous worldwide. After much time spent poring over the recipes, often taking the books to bed, I selected those recipes that best represent the way we eat in Texas today. (Regrettably, I was unable to obtain permission for all the recipes that I wanted to include.)

There are great recipes in this book. I sincerely hope that you'll discover new favorites to add to your own culinary repertoire from among them.

We do things in a big way in Texas, and we love to eat! Take a Texan away from Texas for very long and you can bet there are four things he or she is bound to miss: barbecued brisket, Tex-Mex food, a chicken-fried steak with cream gravy, and a good grilled rib-eye steak.

Terry Thompson-Anderson
Editor

# Appetizers

No doubt about it, Texans love to party! Why, we'll throw a party at the drop of a hat, or for no reason at all. And nothing's more essential to the success of a party than great food. There are recipes for party nibbles that are legendary in Texas, with each host or hostess guarding his or her recipe as if it were a secret treasure. Each new happening brings the challenge for new and different finger foods.

Winter brings the holiday season, when we all love to get together with good friends. Plan a menu around warm or hot finger foods. Try lots of hot seafood dips in chafing dishes or flavored meatballs in slow cookers served with artisan breads or gourmet crackers. Individual filled tarts are time-consuming, but so very chic! Sometimes I like to have a soup station with a nice wintery soup—like cream of mushroom and some small mugs, so folks can mingle while sipping their soup.

Spring is my favorite party season. I love to get the flower beds spruced up and arrange some flowering shrubs in pots around the deck or patio. I like chilled dips—especially seafood-based, served with my favorite crackers, chips, or tortilla chips, or cheese platters with sliced breads. For spring, an iced crock of a nice chilled gazpacho with small mugs would be a nice touch.

Summer is great time for parties beside the pool, if you happen to have one, or out on the patio. Perfect summer party fare consists of salsas (tomato and fruit-based) and chile con queso, served with good-quality corn tortilla chips; chilled spinach dips with crackers; or pasta salads served with sliced French bread.

In the fall I like to serve somewhat of a hodgepodge of the most popular munchies from all the seasons. If it's a slightly cool fall day or evening, build a fire in the fire pit or *chimenea* on the patio and enjoy a last chance to entertain outdoors before the onset of winter.

In this chapter I've collected some of my old personal favorites as well as some really good new discoveries from the bounty of Texas cookbooks. So pick those that are to your liking and get out the guest list to schedule an event at your place. Remember, of course, that many of these dishes also make excellent first courses.

# Spinach and Three-Cheese Dip

1½ tablespoons unsalted butter, softened

3 tablespoons flour

2 cups half-and-half

½ cup (2 ounces) grated Parmesan cheese

1½ teaspoons kosher salt

1 tablespoon Tabasco sauce, or to taste

1 (16-ounce) package frozen chopped spinach, thawed and drained well

1 cup (4 ounces) shredded Cheddar cheese

1 cup (4 ounces) shredded mozzarella cheese

Melt the butter in a saucepan and stir in the flour, blending well. Cook, stirring constantly for about 2 minutes. Add the half-and-half, Parmesan cheese, salt, and Tabasco sauce. Stir until creamy and thickened. Remove from heat and set aside to cool.

Add the spinach to the cooled sauce and stir to blend well. Stir in the Cheddar cheese and mozzarella cheese. Spoon into an ovenproof serving dish.

Bake at 350 degrees for 10 minutes. Remove from oven and stir thoroughly. Return to oven and bake an additional 5 minutes. Serve hot with tortilla chips. You may spoon 1 cup of sour cream onto the center of the dip and place 1 cup chopped red onion on one side and 1 cup crumbled crisp-cooked bacon on the other side. Serves 10 to 15.

*Dining without Reservations*

# Spiced-Up Corn Dip

16 ounces cream cheese, softened

¼ cup freshly squeezed lime juice

1½ to 3 teaspoons ground cumin (optional)

1 teaspoon salt

1 teaspoon black pepper

1 teaspoon cayenne pepper, or to taste

1 (7-ounce) can whole-kernel corn, drained well

1 cup walnuts, chopped

1 (4-ounce) can diced green chiles, drained

2 green onions, chopped

Beat the cream cheese in a mixing bowl until smooth and creamy. Add the lime juice, cumin, salt, black pepper, and cayenne pepper and mix well. Stir in the corn, walnuts, green chiles, and green onions. Chill, covered, until ready to serve. Serve with chips. Serves 10 to 15.

*Dining without Reservations*

# Ruby's Hot Tamale Dip

1 (15-ounce) can chili

2 cans tamales, shucked and mashed

½ pound Cheddar cheese, grated

Cayenne pepper, salt, and Worcestershire sauce to taste

Combine all ingredients in double boiler and cook until cheese melts. Stir until thoroughly blended and heated. Serve in chafing dish to keep warm. Good with Fritos or tortilla chips. Makes 1½ quarts.

Mary Lindsey
*Flavors of Fredericksburg*

# Paula's Dill Dip

⅔ cup real mayonnaise

⅔ cup sour cream

1 (½-inch-thick) slice of a medium onion

Leaves and tender top stems from 5 parsley sprigs

1 tablespoon dried dill, or 3 tablespoons minced fresh dill

2 teaspoons Spice Islands Beau Monde Seasoning

Combine all ingredients in work bowl of food processor fitted with steel blade. Process until smooth and well blended. Transfer to a bowl and cover tightly. Refrigerate, covered, until ready to serve. Should be well chilled. Serve with your favorite crackers, plain potato chips, or corn tortilla chips. Makes about 1⅓ cups.

Paula Fisher, Lafayette, Louisiana
*Cajun-Creole Cooking*

# Jezebel Sauce

1 (18-ounce) jar pineapple preserves

1 (18-ounce) jar apple jelly

1 small can Coleman's dry mustard

1 small jar prepared horseradish

Combine all ingredients in food processor; process until smooth. Put into jars and refrigerate. Will keep indefinitely. Pour over cream cheese and serve with wheat crackers.

Carol Dean, Houston
*License to Cook, Texas Style*

# Jalapeño Bean Dip

1 small onion, chopped

Butter or margarine

1 (16-ounce) can refried beans

¼ to ½ pound Cheddar cheese, shredded

1 (4-ounce) can jalapeño chiles, drained and chopped

Salt and freshly ground black pepper to taste

Sauté onions in butter; add other ingredients and stir over low heat. Thin with milk, if desired. Serve warm with corn chips or tostados.

*Seasoned with Sun*

# High's Hummus

4 cups canned chickpeas, rinsed and drained

1 tablespoon minced garlic

½ teaspoon red (cayenne) pepper

½ teaspoon ground cumin

½ teaspoon paprika

1 teaspoon kosher salt

2 tablespoons minced flat-leaf parsley

¼ cup fresh lemon juice

2 tablespoons tahini paste

Olive oil

Toasted pita wedges

Greek olives, chopped tomatoes, additional olive oil, and minced parsley as garnishes

Combine all ingredients except olive oil in work bowl of food processor fitted with steel blade. Add just enough olive oil through the feed tube to get the mixture turning in the bowl (this is important for achieving a very smooth blend). Scrape down sides of bowl. As the mixture becomes smooth, slowly add more olive oil to achieve a silky smooth consistency. Process for about 2 to 3 minutes, almost "whipping" the hummus. Serve with toasted pita toasts, Greek olives, and chopped tomatoes. Drizzle olive oil on top and garnish with minced parsley.

High's Café and Store, Comfort, Texas
*The Texas Hill Country*

# Blue Heron Inn's Hot Crabmeat Dip

**8 ounces regular lump crabmeat**

**1 (8-ounce) package cream cheese, softened**

**3 tablespoons mayonnaise**

**1 tablespoon prepared horseradish**

**2 teaspoons Worcestershire sauce**

**6 ounces toasted, sliced, skin-on almonds**

Carefully pick through crabmeat to remove any bits of shell or cartilage. Set aside. Melt the cream cheese in a heavy 2-quart saucepan over medium-low heat. Stir in mayonnaise, horseradish, and Worcestershire sauce, blending well. Fold in the crabmeat. When ready to serve, transfer the dip to a chafing dish to keep warm. Scatter the toasted almonds over the top. Makes about 3 cups.

Blue Heron Inn, Rockport, Texas
*Texas on the Plate*

# Shrimp Dip

**1 (8-ounce) package cream cheese, softened**

**1 cup Kraft Thousand Island Dressing**

**½ cup mayonnaise**

**1 cup chopped green onions**

**3 to 6 teaspoons Tabasco sauce**

**1 tablespoon seasoned salt**

**1 tablespoon horseradish**

**Diced pimiento**

**1 pound cooked shrimp, chopped**

Cream the cream cheese with dressing and mayonnaise. Stir in remaining ingredients. Chill and serve with chips or crackers.

Shirley Crooks
*Flavors of Fredericksburg*

# Hot Crab and Cheese Dip

1 (8-ounce) package cream cheese

2 tablespoons milk

1 (6-ounce) can crabmeat

Pinch of salt

1 teaspoon grated onion

1 tablespoon horseradish

1 tablespoon Worcestershire sauce

Tabasco sauce to taste

1 teaspoon lemon juice

Sliced skin-on almonds

Preheat oven to 375 degrees.

Cream together the cream cheese and milk. Add crabmeat, salt, onion, horseradish, Worcestershire sauce, Tabasco sauce, and lemon juice. Pour into buttered casserole and scatter almonds over the top. Bake for 30 minutes. Serve hot with your favorite crackers.

Dean Ingram
*Kickin' Back in the Kitchen Cookbook*

# Hot Crawfish and Crab Dip

1 pound fresh mushrooms, cleaned and sliced

1 cup (2 sticks) butter

2 bunches green onions with tops, chopped

1 bunch parsley, chopped

1 pound crawfish tails, chopped

4 tablespoons flour

4 cups evaporated milk

½ pound grated Swiss cheese

½ pound grated sharp Cheddar cheese

1 pound lump crabmeat, flaked

4 tablespoons vermouth

1 teaspoon ground cayenne pepper

1 teaspoon salt

1 teaspoon black pepper

Hot sauce (optional)

Sauté the mushrooms in butter. Add green onions and parsley. Cook until onions are transparent. Add the crawfish and cool until tender. Add flour and blend well. Add evaporated milk, Swiss cheese, and Cheddar cheese. Heat over hot water, stirring until cheese melts. Fold in crabmeat. Add vermouth, cayenne pepper, salt, and pepper. Stir in hot sauce, if desired. Serve the dip on toast rounds in a chafing dish, or fill small baked puff pastry shells with it.

This is a great filling for mushrooms, as well as a dip. Wash and remove stems from large mushrooms. Brush mushroom caps with olive oil and fill with mixture. Bake at 350 degrees for 12 to 15 minutes. Yields 6 to 10 servings.

*Seasoned with Fun*

# Cheese-Crab Dip

½ bottle blue cheese salad dressing

½ bottle Thousand Island salad dressing

1 (3-ounce) package cream cheese, softened

2 tablespoons mayonnaise

1 small garlic clove, minced

1 teaspoon lemon juice

1 cup crabmeat

Combine all ingredients, chill, and serve. Can be made the day before. Serves about 8.

Mrs. Norman Smith
*The Dallas Junior League Cookbook*

# Chile con Queso

1 pound hot or mild pork sausage

½ onion, chopped

2 pounds Velveeta cheese

1 (12-ounce) can tomatoes and green chiles

7 ounces green chiles, chopped

Sauté the sausage and onion together in a skillet until done; drain off excess grease and set aside. Melt the Velveeta slowly in the top of a double boiler over simmering water; add tomatoes and chiles, stirring to blend well. Stir in the cooked sausage and onion mixture; cook just until heated through. This dip needs to be served in a chafing dish and kept hot. Serve with crisp tortilla chips. Leftovers can be frozen and reheated. Serves 20.

*Texas Cowboy Cooking*

# Pancho Villa's Birthday Cake

Make two layers of each of the following ingredients on a round serving dish.

**2 large cans jalapeño bean dip**

**1 pound ground beef, browned, with 1 package taco seasoning added**

**5 large avocados, mashed with 1 teaspoon lime juice**

**3 large tomatoes, chopped**

**1 small can sliced ripe black olives**

**2 cups grated Cheddar or Monterey Jack cheese**

**8 ounces sour cream**

Finish the dip with the sour cream spread on top to resemble icing on a cake. Serve with plenty of tortilla chips.

*The San Antonio Tex-Mex Cookbook*

# Onion Fritters

**3 large onions**

**2 teaspoons salt or to taste**

**Vegetable oil for deep-frying**

**½ cup chickpea flour**

**¼ teaspoon cayenne pepper or more to taste**

Cut onions in half from tip to stem, then thinly slice with the grain. Place in a bowl. Sprinkle with salt and work it into onions with the fingers. Set aside for 30 minutes to allow onions to sweat and soften.

Meanwhile, heat oil in deep skillet to 375 degrees.

Drain off any onion juice that accumulated in bowl. Sprinkle ¼ cup of the chickpea flour over onions and rub lightly with the fingers. Continue adding chickpea flour by the tablespoon until onions begin to hold together in a clump.

Drop clumps into hot oil and fry in batches, without crowding, until crisp and golden, 4 to 5 minutes. Remove with slotted spoon and drain on paper towels. Serve hot with the chutney of your choice.

*Easy Indian Cooking*

**TIPS:** The secret to these ethereal nibbles is no water in the batter. Lightly rubbing the chickpea flour into the softened onion shreds, using the onion juices produced by salting and draining off the excess onion moisture, is what makes these so crisp and crunchy.

# Fried Wontons

## Filling

1 green onion

2 paper-thin slices peeled ginger

Seasoning sauce (1 teaspoon cornstarch,
1 tablespoon soy sauce, 1 tablespoon
dry sherry, 1 tablespoon water, 1
teaspoon sesame oil)

1 tablespoon cooking oil

½ pound lean ground pork

1 package frozen wonton wrappers,
thawed

4 cups cooking oil for deep-frying

## Mustard and Sweet and Sour Sauce

1 tablespoon dry mustard

2 tablespoons sugar

3 tablespoons white vinegar

3 tablespoons bottled plum sauce

2 tablespoons ketchup

To make the filling, chop green onion and mince ginger. Combine the ingredients of the seasoning sauce in a bowl.

Heat 1 tablespoon of the cooking oil in a wok over high heat. Add green onion and ginger, then pork. Stir-fry until the pork loses its red color. Remove excess fat, if any. Add seasoning sauce to wok, stirring constantly until thickened. Remove to a dish and cool to room temperature.

Make the Mustard and Sweet and Sour Sauce by whisking all ingredients together in a bowl; set aside.

To assemble, have the wrappers, the filling, and a small bowl of water within easy reach.

Put about 1 teaspoon of filling in the center of each wrapper. Fold the wrapper away from you, forming a triangle. Flip the upper points of the triangle toward you. Bring the left and right corners together to create a groove around the mound of filling. With your fingertip, moisten one corner with water and place the other corner on top, pinching together firmly. Repeat until all are assembled.

Heat 4 cups of oil in a wok to 375 degrees. Add about 15 wontons to the hot oil. Fry until golden brown. Remove with a strainer. Drain on a dish lined with paper towels. Repeat with remaining wontons. Serve with Mustard and Sweet and Sour Sauce. Makes 45 wontons.

**HELPFUL TIPS:** Wontons can be frozen after being assembled. Thaw before deep-frying. They can also be deep-fried first and then frozen.

Fried wontons can be kept warm in an oven at 200 degrees for 30 minutes or reheated at 425 degrees for 3 to 5 minutes. If frozen, allow 6 to 7 minutes.

*Chinese Cuisine Made Simple*

# Hickory-Smoked Bacon Tarts

12 frozen mini-tart shells (puff pastry or phyllo dough)

5 slices Smokehouse Bacon

3 green onions, chopped

8 ounces Swiss cheese or smoked Baby Swiss, shredded

2 eggs, slightly beaten

8 ounces sour cream

Dash of salt

¼ teaspoon cayenne pepper

Bake the mini-tarts according to directions on package.

In a large skillet, fry bacon until crisp and drain on paper towels, reserving 2 tablespoons of drippings. Sauté onions in the drippings until tender and drain.

Fold together the onions, Swiss cheese, eggs, sour cream, salt, and cayenne pepper until thoroughly mixed.

Spoon mixture into the mini-tarts and place on a baking sheet. Sprinkle the crumbled bacon on top, then bake at 375 degrees for 15 to 18 minutes, or until cheese melts. Serve immediately. Serves 6.

**EDITOR'S NOTE:** Smokehouse Bacon is a New Braunfels Smokehouse product.

*New Braunfels Smokehouse*

# Stuffed Grilled Doves

16 dove breast halves, boned and skinned

32 jalapeño slivers

32 thin mozzarella cheese strips

Seasoned salt to taste

16 bacon slices

Rinse the doves and pat dry. Pound between 2 sheets of waxed paper or plastic wrap with a meat mallet until flattened. Place 2 jalapeño slivers and 2 cheese strips in the center of each dove breast; roll to enclose. Sprinkle with seasoned salt, Wrap each dove breast with a slice of bacon; secure with a wooden pick. Grill over hot coals for 10 minutes, or until the bacon and dove breasts are cooked through. Yields 16 servings.

*Texas Ties*

# Crab-Filled Tomatoes

½ pound regular lump crabmeat

1 tablespoon mayonnaise

2 tablespoons crème fraîche or sour cream

1 tablespoon minced fresh tarragon

Salt and pepper to taste

30 small cherry tomatoes

1 bunch chives, chopped (reserve several whole sprigs for garnish)

Rinse crabmeat and drain. Wrap in a clean tea towel and wring to remove any remaining moisture. Transfer to a bowl. Mix mayonnaise and crème fraîche, adding crabmeat and tarragon. Add salt and pepper to taste.

Remove top third of each tomato, then top with a portion of the crabmeat mixture. Chill up to 2 hours. Let sit at room temperature for 30 minutes before serving. Transfer to a serving platter and garnish with chive sprigs. You can arrange the platter with sprigs of chives in a cheery checkerboard pattern. Serves 6 to 8.

Bénédicte Rhyne, Delaney Vineyards,
Grapevine and Lamesa, Texas
*Under the Texan Sun*

# Hoisin Crab Pot Stickers

½ pound fresh lump crabmeat

5 mushrooms, finely chopped

⅔ cup sliced green onions

1 teaspoon grated fresh ginger

3 tablespoons hoisin sauce

1 tablespoon dark sesame oil

1 (12-ounce) package wonton wrappers

2 tablespoons vegetable oil, divided

1 cup chicken broth, divided

Soy sauce (optional)

Drain and flake the crabmeat, removing any bits of shell. Combine crabmeat, mushrooms, green onions, ginger, hoisin sauce, and sesame oil, blending well. Place 1 teaspoon crabmeat mixture in center of each wonton wrapper; moisten edges of wrapper with water. Fold wrappers in half, forming triangles; pinch edges to seal. Stand pot stickers on folded edge; press down to flatten slightly.

Pour 1 tablespoon vegetable oil into a large nonstick skillet; place over medium-high heat until hot. Fry half of the pot stickers in hot oil, about 3 minutes, or until golden brown on both sides.

Add ½ cup chicken broth; reduce heat to medium. Cover and cook 8 minutes until tender. Repeat procedure with remaining pot stickers. Serve with soy sauce, if desired. Yields 4 dozen pot stickers.

*Seasoned with Fun*

# Crabmeat Quesadillas with Pico de Gallo

12 ounces lump crabmeat

3 cups (12 ounces) shredded Monterey Jack cheese

4 green onions, chopped, including green tops

1 (4-ounce) can diced green chiles, well drained

⅓ cup sliced ripe olives

½ cup chopped pickled jalapeños

1 tablespoon minced cilantro

9 (9-inch) flour tortillas

Vegetable oil

### Pico de Gallo

4 large Roma tomatoes, cut into ¼-inch dice

1 small red onion, finely chopped

4 serrano chiles, seeds and veins removed, minced

1 heaping tablespoon minced cilantro

2 tablespoons fresh lime juice

Salt to taste

Make the Pico de Gallo by combining all ingredients in a nonaluminum bowl and stirring to blend. Refrigerate until ready to serve.

Carefully pick through the crabmeat to remove any bits of shell or cartilage. Place in bowl and add all remaining ingredients except tortillas and vegetable oil. Stir to blend well, taking care not to break up the lumps of crabmeat. Divide the crabmeat mixture among the tortillas, spreading it on half of each tortilla. Fold the tortillas over, pressing down around the edges to seal.

Heat about 1 tablespoon of the vegetable oil in a heavy 12-inch skillet over medium heat. Fry 2 or 3 of the folded tortillas at a time, turning once. Cook just until the cheese is melted and bubbly, about 2½ minutes per side. While the quesadillas are cooking, press down on them frequently with a flat spatula to make sure the halves stick together. Place on a baking sheet in a warm oven while cooking the remaining quesadillas. To serve, cut each folded tortilla in half, forming 2 wedges, or into fourths, depending on the desired portion size. Serve with a bowl of the Pico de Gallo. Yield: 18 pieces.

*Texas on the Plate*

# Seafood Tarts

1 loaf very thin white bread

½ cup (1 stick) butter, melted

1 cup mayonnaise

3 ounces crabmeat

3 ounces deveined, peeled, boiled shrimp

⅓ cup each freshly grated Parmesan cheese and shredded Swiss cheese

⅓ cup chopped onion

½ teaspoon Worcestershire sauce

2 to 3 drops of Tabasco sauce

Paprika to taste

Trim the crusts from the bread and flatten slightly with a rolling pin. Cut rounds from the centers of each slice with a 3-inch round cutter. Dip each round into the butter. Press the rounds into miniature muffin cups. Bake at 400 degrees for 10 minutes.

Combine the mayonnaise, crabmeat, shrimp, Parmesan cheese, Swiss cheese, onion, Worcestershire sauce, and Tabasco sauce in a food processor. Pulse slightly or just until mixed. Spoon into prepared muffin cups. Sprinkle with paprika. Bake for 10 minutes. Serve immediately. Makes 25 tarts.

*Austin Entertains*

# Salmon Ball

1 (16-ounce) can red salmon, drained

11 ounces cream cheese, softened

1 tablespoon chopped onion

2 teaspoons freshly squeezed lemon juice

1½ teaspoons prepared horseradish

1 teaspoon Worcestershire sauce

¼ teaspoon liquid smoke (optional)

Chopped parsley (optional)

Mix all ingredients and shape into a ball. Sprinkle parsley on top, if desired. Refrigerate. Serve with assorted crackers.

Mrs. Jack Dempsey (Estelle)
*Lone Star Legacy*

# Cucumber Rounds with Salmon Mousse

2 medium cucumbers, peeled and sliced
    ½ inch thick

3 ounces smoked salmon

5 ounces cream cheese

3 ounces sour cream

1 teaspoon fresh dill weed

½ teaspoon lemon-pepper seasoning

Paprika as garnish

Scoop out a small well in the middle of each cucumber slice. Place remaining ingredients in work bowl of food processor; process until smooth. Place mixture in a pastry bag fitted with a star tip and pipe a portion of the filling into the well in each cucumber slice. Sprinkle tops with paprika. Makes 8 to 10 servings.

Christian Chavanne, Corpus Christi Yacht Club
*¡Viva! Tradiciones*

# Tequila-Cured Salmon Tostados

4 (6-ounce) salmon fillets, skin and bones
    removed

½ cup chopped cilantro

Fine-grain sea salt

1 cup silver tequila

6 to 7 large flour tortillas

2 (8-ounce) packages cream cheese,
    softened

1 teaspoon minced chives

24 to 32 small pieces of pimiento

24 to 32 thin half-moon slices of white
    or red onion (about ¼ of a medium
    onion)

Lemon zest for garnish (optional)

Put each salmon fillet into a nonreactive container; sprinkle both sides with cilantro and sea salt. Add up to ¼ cup tequila to each container. Seal and refrigerate for at least 24 hours. (The salmon will keep for up to 2 weeks.)

When ready to assemble the tostados, preheat oven to 250 degrees. Using a 2½-inch round cookie cutter, cut cocktail-size rounds out of the large flour tortillas, about 4 or 5 per tortilla. Spray a baking sheet with nonstick cooking spray and place the rounds on the baking sheet. Bake in preheated oven until crisp and golden, about 45 minutes. Set aside.

In a medium mixing bowl, combine the cream cheese with the chives. Set aside.

Remove fillets from the marinade and pat dry. Using a very sharp paring knife, cut each fillet crosswise into 6 to 8 wafer-thin slices.

Spread about 1 tablespoon of the cream cheese mixture onto each tostada. Curl the strips of salmon into rosettes and gently stuff a piece of pimiento into the center of each rosette. Place a rosette in the center of each tortilla round and garnish with an onion slice and a sprinkling of lemon zest. Serves 8 (3 or 4 tostados per person).

*Guadalupe Rivera Martin, Mexico City*
*Fonda San Miguel*

# Crawfish Cakes with Cilantro-Lime Cream

**1 pound crawfish tails, cooked and peeled**

**3 cups soft bread crumbs, divided**

**½ cup mayonnaise**

**½ cup chopped green onions**

**2 garlic cloves, minced**

**1 tablespoon lemon juice**

**1 tablespoon Worcestershire sauce**

**1 teaspoon Cajun seasoning**

**¼ teaspoon ground cayenne pepper**

**1 large egg, lightly beaten**

**3 tablespoons vegetable oil**

**Fresh cilantro sprigs, lemon and lime slices (optional)**

**Cilantro-Lime Cream (see recipe below)**

Stir together crawfish, 2 cups bread crumbs, mayonnaise, green onions, garlic, lemon juice, Worcestershire sauce, Cajun seasoning, cayenne pepper, and egg. Shape into 12 patties and coat with remaining cup of bread crumbs.

In a large skillet, cook the patties in batches in hot vegetable oil until lightly browned, about 3 to 4 minutes, turning once. Drain on paper towels and arrange on platter. Surround the cakes with cilantro sprigs and round lemon and lime slices, if desired. Serve with Cilantro-Lime Cream. Serves 10 to 12 as appetizer.

## Cilantro-Lime Cream

*(Yields ½ cup.)*

**½ cup sour cream**

**2 tablespoons minced cilantro**

**1 tablespoon lime juice**

**¼ teaspoon salt**

Stir together all ingredients, blending well.

*Seasoned with Fun*

# Crawfish Cheesecake with Creole Mustard Sauce

1 cup (4 ounces) grated Parmesan cheese

1 cup bread crumbs

½ cup (1 stick) unsalted butter, melted

1 tablespoon olive oil

1 cup chopped onion

½ cup finely chopped carrots

½ cup finely chopped red bell pepper

Salt and pepper to taste

28 ounces cream cheese, softened

4 eggs

½ cup heavy cream

1 cup (4 ounces) shredded smoked Gouda cheese

1 pound crawfish tails, coarsely chopped, about 2 cups

Creole seasoning to taste

Creole Mustard Sauce (see recipe below)

## Creole Mustard Sauce

½ cup Creole mustard

½ cup horseradish sauce

1 teaspoon Champagne vinegar

1 tablespoon water

Salt and pepper to taste

Combine the Parmesan cheese, bread crumbs, and butter in a bowl and mix well. Press into a 9-inch springform pan.

Heat the olive oil in a large, heavy-bottomed sauté pan over high heat. Add the onion, carrots, and bell pepper. Sauté for 3 to 5 minutes, or until onion is wilted and transparent. Season with salt and pepper; set aside.

Beat the cream cheese and eggs in a large mixing bowl for 4 minutes, or until thick and creamy. Beat in the cream. Stir in the Gouda cheese, sautéed vegetables, and chopped crawfish, blending well. Season with Creole seasoning. Pour into prepared pan. Bake at 350 degrees for 1¼ hours, or until firm. Let stand for 30 minutes before cutting.

Make the Creole Mustard Sauce. Whisk the Creole mustard, horseradish sauce, vinegar, water, salt, and pepper in a bowl until well blended. Add additional water if needed for the desired consistency.

To serve, spoon the Creole Mustard Sauce into a squeeze bottle. Squeeze the sauce onto individual serving plates in the desired design. Arrange a slice of the cheesecake over the sauce. Serve additional sauce on the side. Serves 12 to 16.

*Dining without Reservations*

# Calamares *(Fried Squid)*

1 quart vegetable oil, or enough so that oil is 2 inches deep in a Dutch oven or deep fryer

6 to 8 ounces squid, cleaned and cut into ¼-inch rings

½ cup all-purpose flour, seasoned with 1 teaspoon sea salt, ½ teaspoon ground black pepper, and ½ teaspoon cayenne pepper, or to taste

2 lemon wedges

2 sprigs parsley

## Chipotle Mayonnaise

*(Makes 1¼ cups.)*

1 cup Hellmann's mayonnaise

2 chipotle chiles in adobo sauce

1 garlic clove, minced

Zest and juice of 1 lime

Sea salt and ground black pepper to taste

Prepare the Chipotle Mayonnaise. Combine all ingredients in a blender and pulse until smooth. Refrigerate until ready to serve.

To prepare the squid, heat oil to 375 degrees in a heavy Dutch oven or deep fryer. Toss a few of the squid rings in the seasoned flour and coat well; shake off excess using a small sieve or strainer. Drop the pieces of squid into the oil; do not allow them to touch. Fry 10 to 15 seconds (don't overcook) and remove the fried pieces of squid using a slotted spoon. Drain on paper towels and keep in a warm oven while frying the remaining batches. Make sure the oil returns to 375 degrees before adding each batch. Serve hot with lemon wedges, parsley sprigs, and Chipotle Mayonnaise.

*Shirley King, Fish: The Basics*
*Fonda San Miguel*

# Chilled Shrimp with Spicy and Cool Dipping Sauce

3 canned chipotle chiles in adobo sauce

1 tablespoon adobo sauce from the chiles

½ of a medium cucumber (about 5 ounces), peeled, pulp and seeds discarded

1½ cups sour cream

¼ cup minced cilantro

3 tablespoons fresh lime juice

1½ teaspoons salt

2 pounds chilled, boiled shrimp, peeled and deveined with tail section left intact

Combine all ingredients except shrimp in work bowl of food processor fitted with steel blade and process until smooth. Refrigerate, covered, until ready to serve.

Transfer the dip to a serving bowl set in the center of a platter; arrange the boiled shrimp around the bowl. Makes 2 cups.

*Texas on the Plate*

# Shrimp Wrapped in Bacon with Jalapeño

30 wooden picks

15 thin slices lean bacon, cut into halves

30 peeled and deveined large (16- to 20-count) shrimp

1 fresh jalapeño chile, seeds and veins removed, and sliced into the largest pieces you can stand

Soak the wooden picks in a bowl of water for 10 minutes. Preheat the grill. Preheat the oven to 350 degrees. Wrap 1 bacon slice around 1 shrimp and 1 slice of jalapeño chile. Secure with a wooden pick.

Arrange the bacon-wrapped shrimp on an oiled grill rack and grill each side just until the shrimp are no longer gray. You may prepare the shrimp up to this point and store in the refrigerator until just before serving or freeze them for future use. Arrange the shrimp on a baking sheet and bake until the bacon is crisp and the shrimp are pink. Makes 30 appetizers.

Wendy Krispin, Dallas
*Dallas Dish*

# Shrimp Nachos

12 ounces shrimp, boiled, peeled, and deveined

1½ cups shredded Cheddar cheese

½ cup diced green chiles, drained

⅓ cup sliced green onions

¼ cup sliced black olives, drained

½ cup mayonnaise

6 dozen round tortilla chips

Chop the shrimp coarsely. Combine the shrimp, cheese, chiles, green onions, and olives in a bowl and mix well. Stir in the mayonnaise. Arrange the chips on a baking sheet. Spoon 1½ teaspoons of the shrimp mixture on each chip. Bake at 350 degrees for 5 minutes, or until the cheese melts. Yields 24 servings.

*Texas Ties*

# Smoked Shrimp Quesadillas with Peppered Jack Cheese and Flying Avocado Slices

4 flour tortillas

1 avocado, peeled, quartered, and sliced lengthwise

12 shrimp (21- to 25-count), peeled and deveined

1 (4-ounce) log goat cheese

¼ cup grated Monterey Jack cheese

1 tablespoon minced garlic

2 tablespoons sour cream

¼ teaspoon each dried herbs: basil, oregano, thyme, and tarragon

2 tablespoons olive oil

1 teaspoon salt

### Shrimp Rub

1 cup paprika

⅓ cup onion powder

⅛ teaspoon cayenne pepper

½ teaspoon ground white pepper

2 teaspoons dark chili powder

3 tablespoons brown sugar

½ cup granulated garlic

1 teaspoon curry powder

½ teaspoon ground black pepper

¼ cup kosher salt

Begin by smoking the shrimp. Prepare the rub by combining all ingredients and tossing well with a fork to blend. Coat the shrimp with the rub, covering all sides. Heat a smoker to 180 degrees and smoke the shrimp for about 20 to 30 minutes. They will not be completely cooked. Refrigerate the shrimp and finish cooking them when they go into the quesadillas.

Combine goat cheese, grated Monterey Jack, garlic, sour cream, and herbs in a stainless steel bowl. Place bowl over simmering water. Heat to release herb flavors and stir together until smooth. Remove from heat and slather generously over each tortilla.

Lay 3 slices of avocado over top half of slathered tortillas and place warmed smoked shrimp between each slice. Fold the top half of the tortillas over the shrimp and avocado and press to seal.

Heat olive oil in a large sauté pan (nonstick works best) over medium heat. When hot, the oil will begin to shimmer; or throw in any leafy vegetable, or a blade of grass for that matter, and it will sizzle and crackle when the oil is ready. Add quesadillas and cook 2 minutes until browned. Flip and cook an additional 2 minutes to brown the other side. Cut each quesadilla into thirds and serve at once. Makes 12 pieces.

*Cooking Fearlessly*

# Creamy Shrimp Crostini

40 (½-inch-thick) diagonal French
 baguette slices

2 tablespoons olive oil

8 ounces cream cheese, softened

½ cup mayonnaise

2 tablespoons Dijon mustard

1 pound cooked, peeled, and deveined
 shrimp, chopped

½ cup minced green onion

1½ tablespoons chopped fresh dill

1 teaspoon grated lemon zest

Salt and freshly ground pepper to taste

Chopped fresh parsley (optional)

Brush 1 side of each baguette slice with the olive oil. Arrange on a baking sheet. Broil for 1 minute, or until lightly toasted. Set aside.

Beat the cream cheese, mayonnaise, and Dijon mustard in a large mixing bowl until smooth. Fold in the shrimp, green onions, dill and lemon zest. Season with salt and pepper. Spread 1 tablespoon of the shrimp mixture on each toasted bread slice. Arrange on a baking sheet. Broil for 2 to 3 minutes, or until the mixture begins to brown. Garnish with chopped parsley, if desired. Makes 40 crostini.

*Dining without Reservations*

# Jalapeño-Lime Marinated Shrimp

1 pound shrimp, shelled and deveined

1 cup chopped or julienned red bell
 pepper

1 cup coarsely chopped white onion

½ cup lime juice

¼ cup olive oil

¼ cup chopped fresh cilantro

2 garlic cloves, thinly sliced

1 jalapeño pepper, thinly sliced

1½ teaspoons salt

1 teaspoon sugar

½ teaspoon crushed Mexican oregano

¼ teaspoon black pepper

Grill or broil the shrimp and let it cool.

In a bowl, mix the other ingredients and taste for seasoning. Add the shrimp and toss. Cover and refrigerate for 2 to 3 hours before serving. Makes 3 to 4 servings.

*Matt Martinez MexTex*

# Shrimp Diablo

1½ pounds medium peeled and deveined shrimp

1 pound bacon, cut into 2-inch strips

6 jalapeño peppers, seeded and sliced lengthwise

Wrap each shrimp and a slice of jalapeño with bacon. Place on skewers and grill or broil until bacon is done and shrimp are cooked through.

For a different taste, baste with Worcestershire sauce. Quail or dove can be substituted for the shrimp, using the breasts of the birds. Wrap the pepper sliver inside the breast and wrap breast with bacon. Seal with toothpicks and grill.

*Texas Peppers*

# Shrimp Toast

1 pound raw peeled and deveined shrimp

1 (5-ounce) can water chestnuts, drained

¼ cup chives or green onions, sliced thin

2 teaspoons salt

1 teaspoon sugar

1 beaten egg

15 slices extra-thin bread, crusts removed

Fine dry bread crumbs

Process shrimp, water chestnuts, and chives in food processor. Add salt, sugar, and egg, mixing well. Spread mixture on the prepared bread slices and scatter bread crumbs on the tops. Slice each bread slice into four triangles. Fry the toasts in 1 inch of oil heated to 400 degrees, shrimp side down first. Turn and fry other side until crisp. Drain on a wire rack set over a baking sheet. Shrimp toasts may be frozen. To heat, place frozen toasts in preheated 400 degree oven for 5 to 7 minutes. Serve hot. Makes 60 toasts.

Mrs. Norman Smith
*The Dallas Junior League Cookbook*

# Texas Gulf Shrimp Toasts

50 (¼-inch-thick) French-style baguette slices

12 tablespoons unsalted butter, melted

1 teaspoon salt

1 tablespoon minced fresh thyme

8 ounces peeled, boiled shrimp, minced

¼ cup Italian-seasoned bread crumbs

6 ounces shredded Emmenthal or Gruyère cheese

½ cup mayonnaise

½ teaspoon red (cayenne) pepper

¼ teaspoon additional salt, or to taste

Radish slices

Preheat oven to 350 degrees. Arrange the bread slices on baking sheet and set aside. Combine the melted butter, 1 teaspoon salt, and thyme. Using a pastry brush, brush each toast with some of the butter mixture, making sure that each toast gets some of the herb. Bake the toasts in preheated oven until lightly browned, about 5 minutes. Cool on wire racks.

Combine the remaining ingredients, except radish slices, blending well. Spread a portion of the mixture on each baked toast. Arrange toasts on baking sheet and bake in preheated oven for 7 minutes, or until mixture is slightly bubbly. Do not overcook. Garnish each toast with a radish slice. Serve warm or at room temperature. Makes 50 toasts.

*Texas on the Plate*

# Texas Shrimp Nachos

4 chalupa shells

1 cup mashed pinto or black beans

¼ pound cooked shrimp, thinly sliced

1 cup (4 ounces) shredded American, Monterey Jack, or Cheddar cheese

Break chalupa shells in half. Spread beans on each half with a spoon or knife. Top with shrimp and cheese. Place on a baking sheet. Bake for 4 to 4½ minutes at 450 degrees, or broil for 2 minutes on the middle rack. Check your broiler to prevent burning. A little charring on the cheese is really good. Garnish with pico de gallo, sour cream, and hot sauce of your choice. Serves 4.

*Matt Martinez MexTex*

# Shrimp-Stuffed Mushrooms

12 to 20 large mushrooms

1 garlic clove, minced

1 small onion, minced

3 tablespoons olive oil, divided

¾ teaspoon salt

½ teaspoon pepper

½ cup tiny cocktail shrimp

1 slice white bread, soaked in milk and drained

1 tablespoon minced fresh parsley

1 egg, beaten

¼ cup Italian-seasoned bread crumbs

Clean mushrooms. Remove the stems and mince them. Sauté garlic, onion, and mushroom stems in 2 tablespoons of the olive oil. Add shrimp and parsley; continue to cook. Remove from heat and add salt, pepper, soaked bread slice, and egg. Stir to blend well. Fill mushrooms with mixture, rounding the tops. Scatter bread crumbs over the top and put about 3 drops of olive oil on each mushroom. Bake 20 minutes at 400 degrees or until toasted. Serve hot.

Laura Lee Planche Graber
*Lagniappe*

# Stuffed Mushrooms with Crabmeat

1 pound very large mushrooms

½ cup butter

1 teaspoon soy sauce

8 ounces crabmeat

2 tablespoons chopped chives

Salt and pepper to taste

¼ cup bread crumbs

Mayonnaise

Parmesan cheese

Remove mushroom stems and chop them. Sauté the mushroom caps in butter and soy sauce just until barely tender. Remove from pan and cool. Add the crabmeat to the same skillet along with the chopped chives, salt, and pepper. Sauté for 3 minutes. Remove from heat and add bread crumbs and chopped mushroom stems. Stir to blend and stuff into mushroom caps. Place mushrooms on a baking sheet with shallow rim; spread mayonnaise on top of each and top with a scattering of Parmesan cheese. Broil until lightly browned. Serve immediately. Serves 6.

Mrs. Don Bradford (Melinda)
*Lone Star Legacy*

# Mushroom Croustades

36 slices thin wheat bread, cut into 3-inch rounds

¼ cup butter

⅓ cup finely chopped green onions

8 ounces white mushrooms, finely chopped

2 tablespoons flour

1 tablespoon minced fresh parsley

½ teaspoon salt

⅛ teaspoon cayenne pepper

1 pound sausage, browned and drained

1 cup whipping cream

2 teaspoons fresh lemon juice

3 tablespoons freshly grated Parmesan cheese

Carefully fit bread rounds into lightly greased miniature muffin tins, pressing gently into sides to form cups. Bake in preheated 400-degree oven for 8 to 10 minutes, or until lightly browned and firm. Turn out onto wire rack to cool.

In a large, heavy-bottomed skillet, melt butter over medium heat. Add green onions and sauté for 3 to 4 minutes. Stir in mushrooms and cook, stirring frequently, for 10 to 15 minutes, or until most of the liquid is evaporated. Stir in flour, parsley, salt, and cayenne, blending well. Add sausage and cream and bring to a low boil. Reduce heat to low and simmer until mixture thickens, about 10 minutes. Stir in the lemon juice and remove pan from heat. Let cool slightly.

Spoon filling evenly into the bread cups. Scatter a portion of the Parmesan cheese over each. Place on a baking sheet and bake in preheated 350-degree oven for 8 to 10 minutes, or until cheese melts. Serve warm. Makes 36 croustades.

**HINT:** Croustades may be frozen before they are baked.

*Texas Blossoms*

# Mushroom Caviar

3 tablespoons butter

½ pound mushrooms, chopped

4 shallots, chopped

2 tablespoons chopped green onions

1 garlic clove, minced

2 tablespoons white wine

1 to 2 tablespoons sour cream

1 tablespoon chopped fresh dill, or 1 teaspoon dried dill

Salt and pepper to taste

2 teaspoons cornstarch (optional)

2 tablespoons pine nuts or chopped walnuts

Toast points

Chopped parsley

Sauté mushrooms, shallots, onions, and garlic in butter over high heat, being careful not to burn.

Add wine, sour cream, and seasonings. If needed, thicken juices with cornstarch dissolved in small amount of water. Add nuts. Taste for seasoning. Serve warm on toast points, garnished with chopped parsley. Serves 6 to 8 as appetizer, 4 to 6 as first course.

*Southern Herb Growing*

# Stuffed Jalapeños

12 whole pickled jalapeños

2 cups (8 ounces) shredded Monterey Jack or American cheese

1 cup flour

2 cups buttermilk

2 cups cracker meal or seasoned bread crumbs

Oil of your choice for deep-frying

Slit open one side of each jalapeño and discard all of the seeds and membranes. Rinse jalapeños in cold water and pat dry. Stuff with cheese. Roll the peppers in flour, dunk them in the buttermilk, and then roll in the cracker meal. Place in the freezer for about 2 to 3 hours, or until they are completely frozen.

Using enough oil to give you about 1 inch in depth, fry the peppers to a golden brown at 350 degrees. Hold in a warm oven for 10 to 15 minutes before serving. Serves 4 to 6.

*Matt Martinez MexTex*

# Cheese and Bacon Puffs

1 cup mayonnaise

1 teaspoon Tabasco sauce

½ cup (2 ounces) shredded sharp Cheddar cheese

2 to 3 teaspoons horseradish, drained

½ cup crumbled crisp-cooked bacon

1 loaf party rye bread

Combine the mayonnaise, Tabasco sauce, cheese, horseradish, and bacon in a bowl and mix well. Spread on the bread slices and place on a baking sheet. Broil until golden brown. Serves 10 as finger food.

**NOTE:** This recipe can be doubled or tripled. Feel free to increase the amounts of bacon, cheese, and horseradish to taste. Chop the bacon before cooking for more even browning.

*Settings Sunrise to Sunset*

# Baked Cheese Puffs

6 ounces cream cheese, softened

8 ounces sharp Cheddar cheese, shredded

1 cup (2 sticks) butter, softened

Dash cayenne pepper

4 egg whites, beaten

Cayenne pepper or paprika

1 loaf French bread, cut into 1-inch cubes

Combine cheeses, butter, and cayenne pepper in a double boiler to melt. Fold a small amount of the hot mixture into egg whites. Slowly add remaining mixture. Dip bread cubes into cheese mixture with a fork, coating each completely. Arrange on a baking tray, not touching. Sprinkle with cayenne pepper or paprika. Freeze or refrigerate overnight.

Bake at 400 degrees for 10 to 12 minutes. If frozen, bake 12 to 15 minutes. Serve hot. Makes about 8 dozen.

*Necessities and Temptations*

# Abilene Cheese Balls

1 pound mild bulk pork sausage

1 pound shredded Cheddar cheese

1 medium pickled jalapeño, seeded and
   chopped

3 cups biscuit mix

¼ to ½ cup water

Mix all ingredients together and form into bite-size balls. Bake at 375 degrees for 10 to 15 minutes, or until golden brown. Allow to cool before serving.

*Texas Peppers*

# Aspen Artichoke Appetizer

2 (6-ounce) jars marinated artichokes, drained (marinade liquid reserved) and finely chopped

1 small yellow onion, finely chopped

1 garlic clove, pressed

4 eggs

¼ cup bread or cracker crumbs

¼ teaspoon black pepper

¼ teaspoon dried oregano

¼ teaspoon Tabasco sauce

½ pound sharp Cheddar cheese, shredded

2 tablespoons minced fresh parsley

¼ teaspoon salt

Heat the reserved artichoke marinade and cook the onion and garlic in it until transparent and wilted. Beat the eggs; add the crumbs and seasonings. Add the cheese, onion mixture with the pan juices, and chopped artichokes. Pour into a well-buttered 7 × 11-inch baking dish. Bake at 350 degrees for approximately 30 minutes, or until you press it with your finger and it feels softly set. Cool the pan before cutting into 1½-inch squares. It may be served warm or at room temperature, but cool it to cut into squares before warming it again. Freezes well. Serves 8 to 10.

Mrs. Hubert M. Cook
*The Dallas Junior League Cookbook*

# Artichoke Nibbles

2 (6-ounce) jars marinated artichoke hearts

1 small onion, finely chopped

1 garlic clove, minced

4 eggs, beaten

¼ cup fine bread crumbs

¼ teaspoon salt

⅛ teaspoon pepper

⅛ teaspoon dried oregano

⅛ teaspoon Tabasco sauce

2 cups (8 ounces) grated sharp Cheddar cheese

2 tablespoons minced parsley

Drain marinade from one jar of artichoke hearts into a medium skillet. Drain second jar and discard marinade. Chop artichoke hearts and set aside. Heat the marinade; add onion and garlic; sauté until onions are limp, about 5 minutes. Combine eggs, bread crumbs, salt, pepper, oregano, and Tabasco. Fold in cheese and parsley. Add artichokes and sautéed onion mixture, blending well. Pour into a 9-inch-square glass baking dish. Bake at 325 degrees for 30 minutes. Allow to cool briefly before cutting into 1-inch squares. Can also be served cold. This dish may be prepared ahead of time and reheated for 10 to 12 minutes.

Mrs. Don Panter (Carolyn)
*Lone Star Legacy*

# Green Chile Pie

2 (7-ounce) cans green chiles, halved and seeded

10 bacon slices

1 pound grated Cheddar cheese

½ pound grated Swiss cheese

6 eggs, beaten

Salt and pepper to taste

½ cup shredded Muenster cheese

Line bottom of a 2-quart casserole with green chiles. Cook bacon until crisp and drain; crumble into small bits and scatter over the chiles. Mix Cheddar and Swiss cheeses and combine with beaten eggs, salt, and pepper. Pour the mixture over the bacon. Top with the shredded Muenster cheese. Bake at 325 degrees for 45 to 50 minutes. Cut into squares to serve. Serves 8 to 10.

*Lagniappe*

# Cocktail Rarebit

¼ pound American cheese

3 tablespoons milk

2½ tablespoons mayonnaise

2 teaspoons Worcestershire sauce

¾ teaspoon prepared mustard

½ onion, finely grated

Dash of cayenne pepper or Tabasco sauce

Grate cheese and combine with remaining ingredients. In a double boiler, heat mixture over boiling water until melted and smooth. Serve hot with potato chips or corn chips. Serves 4.

*Down-Home Texas Cooking*

# Lady Bird Johnson's Cheese Wafers

1 cup (2 sticks) butter

1 pound sharp Cheddar cheese, grated

1 teaspoon cayenne pepper

Dash salt

2 cups flour

2 cups plain Rice Krispies

Place butter in bowl and mix with grated cheese to soften at room temperature. When softened, add cayenne and salt to flour. Add flour mixture to cheese mixture. This can be done with a food processor or mixer, but add Rice Krispies by hand. Drop by small rounds on a greased cookie sheet. Press with the back of the spoon to flatten. Bake at 350 degrees for 10 to 12 minutes, or until lightly browned. Makes 60 wafers.

*Texas Cookoff*

# Sesame-Parmesan Toasts

1 loaf very thinly sliced white bread, crusts removed

1 cup butter, softened

1 cup Parmesan cheese

½ cup sesame seeds

1 teaspoon seasoned salt

¼ teaspoon cayenne pepper

Preheat oven to 350 degrees. Cut bread slices in half diagonally. Combine remaining ingredients and spread generously on bread, covering completely. Place on cookie sheets. Reduce oven temperature to 250 degrees and bake for about 1 hour, or until bread is completely dry and crisp. Cool on racks. Can be made ahead and stored in tins. Yields 40 to 50 toasts.

**NOTE:** These are delicious in place of chips or crackers with cold buffets or with soups or salads.

*Whitehall Club, Chicago*
*¡Viva! Tradiciones*

# Jalapeño Cheese Log

¾ cup grated very sharp Cheddar cheese

¾ cup creamed pimento cheese

¾ cup creamed English cheese

6 ounces cream cheese

1 tablespoon grated onion

3 canned jalapeño chiles, chopped

1 garlic clove, minced

1 cup chopped pecans

Leave Cheddar cheese and cream cheeses at room temperature until each is soft. Blend all ingredients, except nuts, well. Stir in nuts and form into a log. Seal in wax paper and refrigerate for 2 days. Remove from refrigerator 3 hours before time to serve.

**EDITOR'S NOTE:** English cheese is a prepared cheese that can be found in soft plastic tubes in the sliced cheese section of the supermarket.

*Of Magnolia and Mesquite*

# Greek Cheese

1 garlic clove, minced

8 ounces cream cheese, softened

¼ cup plain yogurt or sour cream

2 ounces crumbled feta cheese

1 tablespoon fresh lemon juice

¼ cup chopped parsley

¼ cup chopped green onion

1 tablespoon chopped fresh mint

2 teaspoons chopped fresh oregano

Pinch each of nutmeg and cinnamon

Salt as needed

Bring all ingredients to room temperature and combine in mixer (not blender or food processor). Taste for salt. Allow time for flavors to blend. Serve with crackers, toast, or hot bread. Serves 12.

*Southern Herb Growing*


# Eggplant Relish *(Caponata)*

½ cup olive oil

1 medium eggplant, skin left on, cut into ½-inch dice

2 cups diced celery (¼-inch dice)

1 large onion, cut into ¼-inch dice

2 tablespoons tomato paste

2 large tomatoes, peeled, seeded, and diced

⅓ cup red wine vinegar

1½ teaspoons sugar

1 cup water

Kosher salt and freshly ground black pepper to taste

¼ cup pitted Calamata olives, cut in half

¼ cup pitted green olives, cut in half

1 tablespoon capers

2 tablespoons pine nuts, toasted

1 cup chopped fresh Italian (flat-leaf) parsley

2 tablespoons chopped fresh oregano

In a large sauté pan, heat the olive oil on high until it sizzles, about 3 minutes. Reduce the heat to medium, add the eggplant, and leave on side to cook for 4 minutes. Then stir the eggplant around and cook another 4 minutes until it's very tender. Remove the eggplant from the pan, saving the oil, and set aside.

Add the celery and onion to the same pan and add a little more oil if necessary. Sauté the onion and celery until tender, about 5 minutes. Return the eggplant to the pan with celery and onion.

Add the tomato paste, tomatoes, vinegar, sugar, water, salt, and pepper. Cook over medium heat for another 5 minutes. Remove from the heat and add the Calamata and green olives, capers, pine nuts, parsley, and oregano. Transfer to a bowl and refrigerate overnight.

To serve bring the caponata to room temperature. Serve on or with slices of toasted rustic bread. Serves 6 to 8.

*Ciao Y'All*

# Sun-Dried Tomato Spread

**11 ounces goat cheese, crumbled**

**4 ounces cream cheese, softened**

**½ cup finely chopped sun-dried tomatoes**

**½ cup chopped pitted kalamata olives**

**3 tablespoons finely chopped fresh basil**

**2 tablespoons olive oil**

**1 tablespoon balsamic vinegar**

**1 tablespoons drained small capers**

Mix the goat cheese and cream cheese in a bowl and form the cheese mixture into small rounds. Arrange on a serving platter.

Combine the sun-dried tomatoes, olives, basil, olive oil, vinegar, and capers in a bowl and mix well. Spoon the tomato mixture over the cheese rounds and serve with assorted party crackers and/or sliced baguettes. Serves 12.

*Dallas Dish*

# Susan's Spicy Olive Spread

**6 ounces cream cheese, softened**

**½ cup mayonnaise**

**⅛ teaspoon freshly ground black pepper**

**1 teaspoon Tabasco sauce**

**½ cup toasted chopped pecans**

**2 tablespoons finely chopped jalapeño-stuffed olives**

**1 cup finely chopped pimiento-stuffed olives**

Combine cream cheese, mayonnaise, black pepper, and Tabasco in work bowl of food processor fitted with steel blade. Process until smooth. Add the remaining ingredients and use the pulse feature to blend them into the cream cheese mixture. Do not overprocess. The olives and pecans should still have some identity. Refrigerate until ready to serve. Serve with wheat crackers. Makes about 2¼ cups.

*Texas on the Plate*

# Anticuchos

5 pounds beef tenderloin

3 aji, jalapeño, or other hot peppers

2 garlic cloves, minced

½ teaspoon comino seed

1 Anaheim pepper, or another long green pepper

1 teaspoon pepper

1 teaspoon salt

1 cup red wine vinegar

2 tablespoons melted butter

Cut meat into 1½-inch cubes. Chop all dry ingredients thoroughly; add vinegar. Marinate meat overnight in this mixture. When ready to cook, place 2 or 3 pieces of meat on a skewer, and repeat until all meat has been skewered. Reserve marinade. Grill over hot coals to desired doneness, basting with a mixture of the reserved marinade and melted butter. An extra aji pepper may be added to the marinade, but the dish will be really hot. For a variation, try substituting pork, fish, or shrimp for the beef.

**NOTE:** This *anticucho* recipe was brought back from Peru and is now served regularly at A Night in Old San Antonio celebrations. These are a favorite at cocktail parties in the American Embassy in Peru, and now they are a cocktail favorite in many Texas homes.

Jack McKay
*Lone Star Legacy*

# Barbecued Meatballs

1 pound ground beef

½ pound bulk pork sausage

½ cup bread crumbs

1 egg, slightly beaten

1 (10¾-ounce) can onion soup

1 (10¾-ounce) can tomato soup

2 tablespoons cornstarch

2 large garlic cloves, minced

¼ cup red wine vinegar

3 tablespoons brown sugar

1 tablespoon Worcestershire sauce

⅛ teaspoon hot sauce

Combine meat, sausage, bread crumbs, and egg in a bowl; blend well. Form into balls and brown in a small amount of oil. Drain on paper towels. Mix all other ingredients and heat on low heat. Put meatballs in sauce and simmer about 30 minutes. Serve hot.

Bessie Fisher Chisum
*Lagniappe*

# Little Smokies in Whiskey Sauce

1 cup Jack Daniel's whiskey

1 cup Heinz bottled chili sauce

1½ teaspoons Tabasco sauce

1 cup firmly packed light brown sugar

2 pounds smoked cocktail-size sausages

Combine the whiskey, chili sauce, Tabasco, and brown sugar in a 4-quart saucepan over medium heat. Stir to blend, then simmer for 15 minutes, or until slightly thickened. Add the sausages and cook until they are heated through, about 10 minutes. When ready to serve, transfer to a chafing dish. Place wooden picks nearby for spearing the sausages. Serves 25 to 30 as finger food.

*Texas on the Plate*

# Sweet and Sour Sausage Balls

1 pound mild bulk pork sausage

1 pound hot bulk pork sausage

2 eggs, slightly beaten

¾ cup Italian-seasoned bread crumbs

Vegetable oil

1½ cups ketchup

6 tablespoons light brown sugar

¼ cup red wine vinegar

¼ cup soy sauce

Combine the sausage, eggs, and bread crumbs in a medium bowl, mixing well. Shape into small balls. In a large skillet, sauté the sausage balls in vegetable oil until browned. Drain. In a large saucepan, combine ketchup, brown sugar, vinegar, and soy sauce. Stir to blend well and cook, stirring often, until sugar has dissolved and sauce is smooth. Add the sausage balls and simmer for 30 minutes. Serve hot. May be frozen. Serves 25 to 30.

*Texas Blossoms*

# Longhorn Caramel Corn

1 cup butter

2 cups brown sugar

½ cup light corn syrup

1 teaspoon salt

½ teaspoon baking soda

1 teaspoon vanilla extract

6 quarts air-popped popcorn

Combine butter, brown sugar, corn syrup, and salt in a heavy-bottomed 4-quart saucepan. Bring to a boil. Boil gently, without stirring, for 5 minutes. Remove from heat and stir in baking soda and vanilla.

Remove all unpopped kernels from the popcorn. Pour the popcorn into a large roasting pan. Pour the syrup over the popcorn and toss to coat well. Bake at 250 degrees for 1 hour, stirring every 15 minutes. When cool, store in airtight container. Makes a great holiday gift. Yields 10 to 12 cups.

*Necessities and Temptations*

# Beverages

Good beverages are an integral part of Texas hospitality. Whether the beverage is as simple as a cold Shiner Bock pulled from the fridge or a special bottle of Texas red wine, a punch, or a really good glass of iced tea, Texans always have a beverage on hand to offer guests.

When setting up your liquor cabinet, keep in mind the personal favorites of your closest friends. They will love you for keeping their beverage of choice on hand. Bourbon, scotch, vodka, gin, tequila, and rum would be my first choices for stocking the hard stuff in the cabinet. A selection of liqueurs, like triple sec, Cointreau or Grand Marnier, a coffee-based liqueur, dry vermouth, an anise-flavored liqueur, and perhaps a bottle of Bailey's Irish Cream for serving over ice or in after-dinner coffee, would be good additions.

A bottle of angostura bitters and Worcestershire sauce, both of which last forever, are good to have on hand for making Bloody Marys and some of the other old classic cocktails.

When you plan an event at which you will be serving cocktails, you'll want to have some olives on hand for those martinis (try jalapeño- and garlic-stuffed olives for a spirited change of pace) as well as kosher salt for rimming those margarita glasses. You'll need fresh lemons and limes for both garnishes and flavorings and a selection of juices—generally fresh lime juice, pineapple juice, grapefruit juice, orange juice, and V-8 juice or Bloody Mary mix. Coke, 7Up, tonic water, and club soda or sparkling water will round out the bar.

Some hints for beverages as you entertain during the seasons include red wine in winter to pair with the heartier appetizers normally served then, or perhaps some hot buttered rum and spiked hot chocolate. In spring serve crisp white wines, like a good Texas sauvignon blanc or slightly sweeter Texas chenin blanc. A big pitcher of margaritas with a tray of salt-rimmed glasses is always a winner in Texas. Ideal summer beverages include rosé wines, blush wines, and a crisp, dry chardonnay or a good Texas viognier. If you're looking for an economical beverage, look no further than sangria. You can make it in any of several flavors, and it's always a crowd pleaser in the heat of summer. Wine choices for the fall are wide open— anything from sweet or dry reds to dry or sweet whites. If you're looking for a pitcher-type drink, try Bloody Marys or perhaps a great milk punch.

I love to drink and serve wine. For everyday wine drinking and for parties, I select a reasonably priced "house wine." Select your favorite, both a red and a white, and keep two or three bottles of each on hand for those times when friends drop by. When I'm having guests for dinner, however, I select wines that will pair well with the individual courses of the meal. In this case, I purchase wines that are generally of a higher quality. And, you never know when there'll be an occasion for celebrating with a toast, so I always like to have a chilled bottle of decent champagne at the ready! When purchasing wine, figure on four servings per bottle.

Remember to always be a responsible host or hostess. If you serve alcohol in your home and a guest has overimbibed, don't let him or her drive. Offer a bedroom for the night or call a cab. You'll be doing your part to keep Texas roads safe.

# Orange Frosty

1 (6-ounce) can frozen orange juice concentrate

1 cup whole or skim milk

1 cup water

⅓ to ½ cup sugar, or an equivalent amount of sugar substitute

1 teaspoon vanilla extract

12 ice cubes, cracked

Combine the orange juice concentrate, milk, water, sugar, and vanilla in a blender and process at medium speed until blended. Add the ice gradually, processing constantly at high speed until slushy. Pour into glasses and serve immediately. Serves 4.

*Dallas Dish*

# Frosty Texas Citrus Refresher

2 Texas Rio Star grapefruit

2 cups sliced fresh strawberries

1 cup pineapple sherbet

1 to 2 tablespoons honey

Grapefruit wedges for garnish

Juice grapefruit; measure 1⅓ cups juice. In a blender, combine juice, strawberries, sherbet, and 1 tablespoon honey. Blend until smooth. Sweeten with more honey, if desired. Pour into glasses and garnish with grapefruit wedges. Makes four 8-ounce servings.

TexaSweet Citrus Marketing
*License to Cook, Texas Style*

# Michilata

1 whole lime

½ lemon

4 dashes Tabasco sauce

Dash salt

Dash Lawry's Seasoned Salt

2 pinches pepper

Dash Worcestershire sauce

Tomato juice

Tecate or other Mexican beer

In a chilled pilsner glass with a salted rim, squeeze in juice of lime and lemon. Add Tabasco, salt, seasoning salt, pepper, and Worcestershire. Fill glass ¼ full with tomato juice. Fill the rest of the glass with beer. Garnish with lime wheel or wedge. Serves 1.

Emily and Bill Lafrance, Louisiana
*Kickin' Back in the Kitchen Cookbook*

# Killer Coffee

1 shot brandy

1 shot orange curaçao

1 shot Kahlúa

2 cups freshly brewed strong coffee

Whipped cream

Mix alcohols and divide between 2 coffee mugs. Fill with fresh brewed coffee and top with whipped cream. Makes 2 drinks.

*¡Viva! Tradiciones*

# Mint Cappuccino

1 cup very strong hot coffee

1 (1-ounce) package instant chocolate mix

2 teaspoons brandy

2 teaspoons Vandermint, or other chocolate-mint liqueur

2 teaspoons crème de cacao

Whipped cream

Mix the coffee, chocolate, and liqueurs together. Top with whipped cream and serve while hot. Serves 1.

Mrs. John Perkins (Sandy)
*Lone Star Legacy*

# Bellinis

2 cups white wine

2 cups Champagne

1 cup peach Schnapps

3 (12-ounce) cans peach nectar

1 cup rum

½ cup powdered sugar

Combine all ingredients, stirring until sugar is dissolved. Place in freezer overnight. Remove from freezer and stir. Mixture should be slushy. Makes 10 drinks.

*¡Viva! Tradiciones*

# Orange Sangria

1 medium orange

2 cups freshly squeezed or reconstituted frozen orange juice

1 bottle (⅘ quart) dry red wine

½ cup Cointreau

¼ cup sugar

Ice

Slice orange into thin slices. Combine orange juice, red wine, Cointreau, sugar, and orange slices. Cover and chill. Serve in a bowl or pitcher over ice.

*It's a Long Way to Guacamole*

# White Sangria

1 orange, quartered

1 lime, quartered

½ cup sugar

½ gallon dry white wine

½ cup frozen lemonade concentrate

2 fresh peaches, peeled, pitted, and sliced, or 2 unpeeled apples, cored and sliced

½ lemon, sliced thin

2 quarts club soda or sparkling water

Squeeze the orange and lime quarters into a large pitcher and add the sugar. Mix well. Add wine, lemonade concentrate and fruit, mixing well. Just before serving, add the club soda or sparkling water.

*It's a Long Way to Guacamole*

# Red Sangria

Juice of 2 lemons

Juice of 2 oranges

½ cup sugar

½ gallon Burgundy or any dry red wine

2 unpeeled apples, cored and sliced

1 lime, sliced thin

2 ounces brandy (optional)

½ gallon (2 quarts) club soda or sparkling water

Combine the lemon and orange juice with the sugar. Add the dry red wine, sliced fruit, and brandy, if desired. Chill well. Just before serving, add the club soda or sparkling water.

*It's a Long Way to Guacamole*

# Cadillac Bar's Ramos Gin Fizz

1 ounce dry gin

Juice of 1 lemon

1 teaspoon powdered sugar

1 egg white

3 ounces whipping cream

6 drops orange flower water

Combine all ingredients in blender and blend until smooth and frothy. Serve over crushed ice in a tall glass. Makes 1 drink.

Mrs. Denman Smith (Sandra)
*Lone Star Legacy*

# Bourbon Slush

2 cups strong tea

2 cups sugar

7 cups hot water

1 (12-ounce) can frozen orange juice

1 (12-ounce) can frozen lemonade

2 cups bourbon

7Up, Perrier water, or club soda

Make the tea using 2 cups water and 3 tea bags. Dissolve sugar in 7 cups hot water. Add remaining ingredients except carbonated beverage. Freeze in a 13 × 9-inch pan. To serve, chop up coarsely and fill glasses. Add 7Up, Perrier water, or club soda to fill the glasses. Makes 20 drinks.

*Gruene General Store Cookbook*

# Bahama Mama

4½ ounces rum (dark and/or light)

1½ ounces Tia Maria

1½ ounces grenadine syrup

1½ ounces freshly squeezed lemon juice

2 ounces cream of coconut

6 ounces freshly squeezed orange juice

6 ounces pineapple juice

Mix all ingredients and serve in tall glasses over lots of crushed ice. Great summer drink. Makes 4 drinks.

Wanda Jones Hanszen
*Lagniappe*

# Mojito *(Rum and Mint Cocktail)*

1 heaping tablespoon superfine sugar

8 fresh mint leaves

2 or 3 lime wedges

1½ ounces light rum

Crushed ice

Club soda

Sprig of mint for garnish

Sugar cane strip (optional)

Combine sugar, mint leaves, and lime wedges in a tall glass and muddle with a cocktail spoon or the handle of a wooden spoon. Add the rum and fill the glass with crushed ice. Top with a cocktail shaker and shake to a Latin beat. Pour the mixture into a fresh glass, add splash of club soda, and stir gently. Garnish with fresh mint and a long, thin strip of sugar cane, cut to look like a straw. Serves 1.

**VARIATION:** For a Raspberry Mojito, muddle 4 or 5 fresh raspberries with the sugar, mint leaves, and lime wedges. If desired, substitute a raspberry-flavored rum for the light rum and garnish with several additional fresh raspberries.

*Fonda San Miguel*

# Pinkerton Hot Buttered Rum

1 tablespoon brown sugar

Dash cinnamon

Dash freshly grated nutmeg

Dash allspice

1 cup apple juice

¼ cup cranberry juice

1 jigger (1½ ounces) rum

1 jigger (1½ ounces) Cointreau

1 tablespoon butter

Put brown sugar, cinnamon, nutmeg, and allspice into a mug. Add Cointreau and rum. Boil apple juice and cranberry juice together. Pour into mug. Add butter and stir to melt. Serve hot. Serves 1.

*Sue Matthews Weller*
*Lagniappe*

# Poco Loco Smashes

1 cup rum

1 cup coconut rum

1 cup apricot liqueur

2 cups orange juice

2 cups pineapple juice

Combine all ingredients and pour into glasses filled with crushed ice. Makes 7 cups.

*¡Viva! Tradiciones*

# Border Bloody Mary

1 celery stalk with leaves, coarsely chopped

1 whole chipotle chile in adobo sauce

1 (46-ounce) can tomato juice, chilled, divided

1 garlic clove, thinly sliced

½ cup orange juice, chilled

½ cup fresh lemon juice

2 tablespoons Worcestershire sauce

2 tablespoons horseradish

1 teaspoon black pepper

1 teaspoon salt

White tequila, such as Sauza Silver

Add celery, chipotle pepper, 2 cups tomato juice, and garlic to a blender; cover and puree. Pour into a large pitcher; add the remaining tomato juice and all other ingredients. Stir well. Adjust salt and pepper to taste. Refrigerate until chilled.

To serve, salt half of rim of a 6-ounce glass. Add 1 ounce chilled tequila to 4 ounces chilled Bloody Mary mixture; stir. Serve with a lime wedge and garnish with finely chopped cilantro. Serves 8 to 10.

*Matt Martinez MexTex*

# Cosmopolitan

3 ounces vodka

1 ounce Cointreau

Splash lime juice

½ ounce cranberry juice

Shake together with crushed ice and strain into a chilled glass. Makes 1 drink.

Jeri-Lynn Sandusky, Utah
*Kickin' Back in the Kitchen Cookbook*

# Lemon Drop from the Citrus Booth

4 ounces lemon vodka

1 tablespoon powdered sugar

1 ounce Tuaca

1 ounce simple syrup

Shake in a cocktail shaker with ice. Serve in a frozen cocktail glass rimmed with sugar and garnished with a lemon slice. Makes 1 cocktail.

> **EDITOR'S NOTE:** To make simple syrup, combine 2 cups sugar and 1 cup water in a 3-quart saucepan. Bring to a boil, stirring. Boil for 5 minutes. Cool before using. To store, pour into a jar with a tight-fitting lid. Refrigerate until needed.

Margarita Lobo
*Perennial Favorites*

# Perini Martini

2 jiggers Tito's Texas Vodka, or vodka of your choice, or even gin

1 teaspoon dry vermouth

1 teaspoon brine from the olives

1 large green olive, stuffed with jalapeño

Fill a large martini glass with ice cubes and a little water and let chill. In a shaker, combine the vodka, vermouth, brine, and a scoop of ice; shake vigorously. Empty the glass and strain vodka mixture over the jalapeño-stuffed olive. Makes 1 drink.

*Texas Cowboy Cooking*

# Fresh Lime Margaritas

**5 lime wedges**

**Coarse salt**

**1 cup silver tequila**

**½ cup Cointreau**

**½ cup fresh lime juice**

**Splash of simple bar syrup, if desired (1 part sugar to 2 parts water, boiled 5 minutes and cooled)**

**Ice cubes**

Rub one of the lime wedges around the rim of 4 martini glasses, dip the rims in coarse salt, and set aside. Combine tequila, Cointreau, lime juice, and syrup in a shaker and add a handful of ice cubes. Shake well and strain into the prepared glasses. Garnish each glass with the remaining lime wedges. Serves 4.

*Fonda San Miguel*

# Mesquite-a-Rita

**1 jigger Cuervo Gold Tequila**

**½ jigger Grand Marnier**

**1 jigger Triple Sec**

**1 jigger freshly squeezed lime juice**

**Lime wedges, to rim glasses**

**Coarsely ground salt**

Rub rim of an old-fashioned glass with a fresh lime, quartered. Dip rim in coarsely ground salt. Combine ingredients in shaker; shake well and pour over ice. Garnish with a lime wheel. Makes 1 drink.

*Texas Cowboy Cooking*

# Silver Coin Margarita

1½ ounces Watermelon-Infused Tequila
(see below)

¾ ounce Cointreau

⅓ ounce fresh lime juice

Crushed ice

Wedge of watermelon rind for garnish

## Watermelon-Infused Tequila

*(Makes about 3 quarts.)*

Half of a 12-pound watermelon, cut into
chunks (about 8 cups)

1 (1-liter) bottle Herradura Silver Tequila

Prepare the Watermelon-Infused Tequila. Combine watermelon chunks and tequila in a 1½- to 2-gallon nonreactive container and use a whisk or potato masher to break up the fruit. Cover and refrigerate for 48 hours. Push the mixture through a fine sieve, pressing on the watermelon to extract all juice. Dispose of pulp and seeds.

To prepare the cocktail, combine Watermelon-Infused Tequila, Cointreau, and lime juice in a cocktail shaker with a handful of crushed ice. Shake and strain into a glass. Serve straight up, garnished with a wedge of watermelon rind. Serves 1.

Zócalo, New York
*Fonda San Miguel*

# Breads & Pastries

Texas has a rich history of fine breads and pastries. I've selected a good cross section of recipes for this chapter that offer several options for breakfast rolls, biscuits, and other pastries. To provide the perfect complement to whatever you're having for dinner, there's a wide variety of breads from which to choose.

Although making breads and pastries from scratch is time-consuming, the rewards are great, and the product much superior to store-bought. As consumers, we've become so much more aware of what goes into the foods that we eat and feed our families than we have ever been. Therefore, it makes sense that the more of your food which you make from scratch, the better control you have over what goes into it!

Breads and pastries freeze beautifully. So when you find yourself with a spare day, bake like crazy and stock the freezer with homemade breads and baked goodies. You'll be glad that you did.

I usually find the best results with freezing breads and pastries are obtained if you wrap your breads and pastries tightly in aluminum foil as soon as they are completely cool, then label and freeze them. When you're ready to serve them, take them directly from the freezer, without opening the foil, and place in a preheated 350-degree oven for 15 minutes. If it's bread, after the 15 minutes, open the foil and place the bread directly on the oven rack for an additional 5 minutes to recrisp the crust. Guaranteed to be just like freshly baked!

# Pretzels

1 package active dry yeast

1 cup lukewarm water

3 cups flour, divided

1½ tablespoons butter

½ teaspoon salt

½ teaspoon sugar

4 cups water

5 tablespoons baking soda

Coarse salt

Dissolve yeast in lukewarm water. Add 1½ cups flour and the butter, salt, and sugar. Beat for 4 minutes in electric mixer. Knead in the remaining flour until dough is no longer sticky. Cover and let rise. Punch down and divide into 10 pieces. Roll into 20-inch lengths and loop each into twisted pretzel shape. Place on greased baking sheet and let rise until doubled in size.

Preheat oven to 475 degrees. Bring 4 cups of water and soda to a boil. Using a slotted spoon, carefully lower pretzels into water. When they rise to the top, return them to greased baking sheet. Sprinkle with coarse salt. Bake for about 10 minutes, or until browned. Makes 10 pretzels.

*Great German Recipes*

# Pepper Bread Sticks

4 ounces puff pastry

1 egg blended with 2 tablespoons water

1 ounce freshly grated Parmesan cheese

1 pickled jalapeño, finely chopped

Roll out pastry sheets ⅛ inch thick and cut into 10 × 1-inch strips. Brush with egg-water mixture, then sprinkle with cheese and pepper. Twist each strip 4 to 6 times to make a spiral. Line a cookie sheet with parchment paper, then place strips on paper. Bake at 350 degrees for 15 minutes, or until light golden brown. Let cool before serving.

*Texas Peppers*

# Sweet Potato Biscuits

| | |
|---|---|
| 2 medium sweet potatoes, baked | 1 tablespoon baking powder |
| ⅓ cup Crisco or other shortening | 1 teaspoon salt |
| 2 tablespoons sugar | ½ cup (or less) buttermilk |
| 2 cups all-purpose flour | |

Peel and mash the sweet potatoes, then blend in the shortening. Add the sugar and blend together. Stir in the flour, baking powder, and salt. Mix thoroughly. Slowly add the buttermilk to form a soft dough. Turn out onto work surface and knead gently until of a consistency to roll out. Roll dough out to a thickness of ¾ inch and cut with a biscuit cutter. Bake at 400 degrees for about 15 minutes. Watch closely, as bottoms can scorch easily. Makes about a dozen large biscuits.

Karen Tripp, Houston
*License to Cook, Texas Style*

# Sweet Potato Biscuits II

| | |
|---|---|
| 2 cups self-rising flour | 2 tablespoons butter, softened |
| ¼ cup sugar | 1 cup cooked, mashed sweet potato |
| ¼ teaspoon ground cinnamon | ⅓ cup milk |
| 3 tablespoons shortening | 1 tablespoon melted butter |

Combine the first 3 ingredients; cut in shortening and butter with a pastry blender until mixture resembles coarse meal. Add sweet potato and milk; stir until dry ingredients are moistened. Turn dough out onto lightly floured surface; knead 3 or 4 times. Roll dough to a thickness of ½ inch; cut with 2-inch biscuit cutter. Place on greased baking sheets.

To store before baking, cover tightly and freeze for up to 1 week.

To serve, bake biscuits, uncovered, at 425 degrees for 12 to 14 minutes (if unfrozen) or for 18 to 20 minutes (if frozen), or until light golden brown and cooked through. Brush tops with melted butter. Makes 24 biscuits.

*And Roses for the Table*

# Sour Cream Biscuits

2 cups self-rising flour

1 (8-ounce) carton sour cream

1 stick butter

Melt butter, stir in sour cream, add flour, and mix thoroughly. Drop from a mixing spoon into hot buttered muffin tins. Bake at 375 degrees until puffy and lightly browned. Makes 12 biscuits.

Doris Smith
*Flavors of Fredericksburg*

# Cheddar Chive Biscuits

2 cups flour

1 tablespoon baking powder

1 teaspoon salt

½ cup shortening

1¼ cups plain yogurt

4 ounces Cheddar cheese, grated

¼ cup chopped fresh chives

Preheat oven to 450 degrees. In a large bowl, combine flour, baking powder, and salt; blend well. Add the shortening, cutting in with a fork or pastry blender until mixture resembles coarse crumbs. Add yogurt, cheese, and chives, stirring until moist. Drop by tablespoonfuls onto greased cookie sheets. Bake in preheated oven for 9 to 12 minutes. Serve warm. Great with seafood.

*And Roses for the Table*

# Cheese Biscuits

2 cups all-purpose flour

2 teaspoons salt

Dash cayenne pepper

Dash freshly ground black pepper

1 teaspoon dry mustard

1 cup butter, softened

2 cups grated, firmly packed very sharp Cheddar cheese

Mix flour, salt, pepper, and mustard. Add butter and cheese; blend until dough is smooth. Form dough into rolls about 1 inch in diameter. Refrigerate or freeze until ready to use. To bake, cut rolls into thin slices and put onto ungreased baking sheets. Bake at 375 degrees for 12 to 15 minutes. Cool before removing from baking sheets. Makes 75 to 100 biscuits.

*Of Magnolia and Mesquite*

# Cheesy Onion Pan Biscuits

2½ cups biscuit mix

¼ cup grated Parmesan cheese

⅔ cup milk

2 teaspoons instant minced onion

Melted butter

Preheat oven to 450 degrees.

Mix all ingredients except melted butter until a dough forms. Stir 30 seconds. Roll dough out to a thickness of ½ inch and cut into 16 squares. Grease an 8-inch-square pan and press the biscuit squares into the pan. Bake at 450 degrees for 10 to 12 minutes, or until golden brown. Brush with melted butter and cool for 10 minutes before serving.

Jan Whittaker, California
*Kickin' Back in the Kitchen Cookbook*

# Jalapeño Cerveza Biscuits

3 cups biscuit mix

¼ teaspoon salt

1 teasppon sugar

1 pickled jalapeño pepper, chopped

1½ cups bock-style beer

Mix all ingredients and spoon into 12 greased muffin cups. Bake 15 minutes at 425 degrees, or until golden brown.

*Texas Peppers*

# Mayonnaise Biscuits

1 cup sifted, self-rising flour

3 tablespoons mayonnaise

½ cup milk

Preheat oven to 450 degrees. Combine all ingredients and stir until moistened. Spoon into well-greased muffin tins. Fill ⅔ full. Bake 10 to 15 minutes. Butter tops and insides. Makes 6 to 8 biscuits.

*Of Magnolia and Mesquite*

# Banana Praline Muffins

### Muffins

1 egg, slightly beaten

½ cup sugar

¼ cup canola oil

3 small bananas, mashed

1½ cups pancake mix

### Topping

3 tablespoons brown sugar

1 tablespoon sour cream

⅓ cup chopped pecans

Preheat oven to 400 degrees. Grease 12 muffin tin cups. Combine the egg, sugar, and oil, beating to blend well. Stir in the bananas and pancake mix, blending well. Combine topping ingredients in a separate bowl. Fill muffin cups ⅔ full with batter. Drop ½ tablespoon topping on each muffin. Bake for 12 to 15 minutes in preheated oven.

Betty Ann Sheffloe, Nebraska
*Kickin' Back in the Kitchen Cookbook*

# Sweet and Spicy Ham Muffins

2 (8-ounce) cans pineapple tidbits, drained, syrup reserved

20 maraschino cherries

8 eggs

6 pounds (10 cups) ground cooked ham

8 cups soft bread crumbs

1 cup firmly packed brown sugar

½ cup chopped green bell pepper

½ cup chopped onion

1 cup liquid (pineapple syrup plus milk to total 1 cup)

4 tablespoons prepared mustard

### Glaze

6 tablespoons butter

2 tablespoons water

⅔ cup firmly packed brown sugar

Preheat oven to 350 degrees. Generously grease 40 muffin cups. Arrange pineapple tidbits and cherries in cups. In a large bowl, beat eggs; stir in remaining ingredients. Spoon over pineapple and cherries, packing lightly. Bake for 30 to 40 minutes. Cool in pans for 5 minutes; invert onto a large serving platter. In a small saucepan, melt butter in water. Remove from heat; stir in ⅔ cup brown sugar until dissolved. Brush over ham muffins. Allow 2 per person. Serves 20.

*Of Magnolia and Mesquite*

# Olympic Lights Blueberry Scones

2 cups flour

2 tablespoons sugar

2 teaspoons baking powder

½ teaspoon baking soda

½ teaspoon salt

6 tablespoons cold butter

½ cup frozen blueberries

2 eggs

½ cup buttermilk, half-and-half, or heavy cream

Additional buttermilk and sugar for topping

In large bowl, sift together flour, sugar, baking powder, baking soda, and salt. Cut in butter. Stir in blueberries. In a small bowl beat together the eggs and buttermilk. Combine dry and wet ingredients. Mix as little as possible. Turn dough onto floured surface. Pat into a ½-inch-thick round and cut into 12 scones. Brush with buttermilk and sprinkle with sugar. Place on ungreased cookie sheet. Bake in top third of a 450-degree oven for 12 minutes.

**NOTE:** Instead of blueberries, ½ cup diced dried apricots can be used. If using apricots, add 1 tablespoon apricot preserves to the buttermilk. Brush the tops and sprinkle with sugar.

Olympic Lights Bed & Breakfast, Friday Harbor, Washington
*Gruene General Store Cookbook*

# Sour Cream Coffee Cake

1 stick butter

1½ cups sugar

2 eggs

2 teaspoons vanilla

8 ounces sour cream

2 cups flour

1 teaspoon baking powder

½ teaspoon baking soda

## Topping

2 tablespoons sugar

2 teaspoons cinnamon

½ cup finely chopped pecans

With mixer, cream butter and sugar until light and fluffy. Add eggs, vanilla, and sour cream. Sift flour, baking powder, and soda; add to creamed mixture. Combine the topping ingredients in a small bowl. Pour half of the batter into a well-greased 10-inch tube pan. Scatter half the topping over the batter. Add remaining batter and sprinkle with the rest of the topping. Bake at 350 degrees for 40 minutes.

Shirley Crooks
*Flavors of Fredericksburg*

# Sour Cream Coffee Cake II

## Batter

½ pound (2 sticks) butter

½ cup sugar

3 eggs

1 teaspoon vanilla extract

2½ cups flour

2 teaspoons baking powder

1 teaspoon baking soda

1 cup sour cream

## Streusel

½ cup granulated sugar

¾ cup brown sugar

1 teaspoon cinnamon

6 tablespoons melted butter

3 tablespoons flour

1 cup nuts, coarsely chopped

Make batter by creaming butter and sugar together. Add eggs one at a time, beating well and scraping down sides of bowl after each addition. Add vanilla and sift dry ingredients together; add to batter alternately with sour cream, beginning and ending with flour mixture.

Combine all Streusel ingredients in a separate bowl and work with hands until all are mixed to a crumbly texture.

Spread half of batter in a well greased 9 × 13-inch baking dish. (Batter will be very thick.) Sprinkle with half the Streusel mixture, then repeat, adding a second layer and ending with Streusel mixture. Bake at 350 degrees for 50 minutes. Cut into squares to serve. Keeps well in the refrigerator.

Judy Talkington
*Through Our Kitchen Door*

# Apple Cheddar Walnut Bread

2 cups self-rising flour

⅔ cup sugar

½ teaspoon cinnamon

½ cup coarsely chopped walnuts

1½ cups chopped, peeled Granny Smith
    apples

½ cup melted butter

½ cup shredded sharp Cheddar cheese

¼ cup milk

2 eggs, lightly beaten

Combine the flour, sugar, and cinnamon in a large bowl and mix well. Stir in the walnuts. Combine the apples, butter, cheese, milk, and eggs in a separate bowl and mix well. Add to the flour mixture, stirring until mixed; batter will be lumpy. Spoon into a buttered and floured 5 × 9-inch loaf pan. Bake at 350 degrees for 60 to 70 minutes, or until the loaf tests done. Cover with foil during the last 15 minutes of the baking time if needed to prevent overbrowning. Invert onto a wire rack to cool. Yields 1 loaf.

*Texas Ties*

# Texas Peach-Pecan Bread

| | |
|---|---|
| 2 cups unsifted all-purpose flour | 1½ cups sugar |
| 2 teaspoons baking powder | 2 eggs |
| ½ teaspoon ground nutmeg | ¼ cup sour cream |
| ½ teaspoon salt | 1 cup peeled, mashed fresh peaches |
| ⅔ cup butter or stick margarine | 1 cup chopped pecans |

In a small bowl, stir together flour, baking powder, nutmeg, and salt. In a large mixing bowl, cream butter and sugar. Add eggs and sour cream; beat 1 to 2 minutes or until light. Stir in flour mixture alternately with peaches. Stir in pecans. Pour into a greased 9 × 5 × 3-inch loaf pan and bake at 350 degrees for 50 to 60 minutes, or until knife inserted in center comes out clean. Cool 10 minutes in pan. Remove from pan to wire rack and cool completely. Yields 1 loaf.

*Cooking with Texas Highways*

# Emily Stone's Persimmon Bread

| | |
|---|---|
| 2 cups sifted all-purpose flour | 2 eggs, beaten |
| ¾ cup sugar | ½ cup canola oil |
| 1 teaspoon baking soda | 1 cup pureed pulp from peeled persimmons |
| 1 teaspoon baking powder | ½ cup golden raisins |
| ½ teaspoon salt | ½ cup chopped pecans |

Preheat oven to 325 degrees. Lightly butter a 9 × 5 × 3-inch loaf pan; set aside. Combine all dry ingredients in a bowl; toss with a fork to distribute ingredients well. Combine remaining ingredients in bowl of electric mixer. Beat at medium speed until well blended. Add dry ingredients in thirds, scraping down sides of bowl after each addition. Beat just to blend; do not overbeat.

Turn batter out into prepared loaf pan and bake in preheated oven for 1 hour and 15 minutes, or until a metal skewer inserted in the center comes out clean. Turn loaf out onto wire rack and cool before slicing. Makes 1 loaf.

*Texas on the Plate*

# Toasted Cheese Bread

1 loaf French bread

10 ounces Monterey Jack cheese, shredded

5 ounces mozzarella cheese, shredded

5 ounces Cheddar cheese, shredded

1½ cups mayonnaise

1½ to 3 teaspoons garlic powder

Paprika to taste

Preheat the oven to 350 degrees. Cut the bread loaf horizontally in half and arrange the halves cut side up on a baking sheet. Mix the three cheeses in a bowl. Stir in the mayonnaise and granulated garlic, blending well.

Spread the cheese mixture on the cut sides of the bread halves and sprinkle with paprika. Bake for 20 minutes, then broil for 2 minutes, or until brown and bubbly. Slice each bread half into 6 to 8 slices and serve immediately. Makes 12 to 16 slices.

*Dallas Dish*

# Twice-Baked Bread

1 loaf French bread

1 (8-ounce) package Swiss cheese slices, cut into triangles

4 bacon slices, partially cooked and cut into very small pieces

8 tablespoons butter, softened

¼ cup finely chopped onions

1 tablespoon prepared mustard

Partially slice the bread diagonally into 16 pieces, but do not cut through the bottom crust. Place a portion of the partially cooked bacon bits in between each slice along with the cheese. Place the bread on a foil-covered baking sheet. Combine the butter, onions, and mustard in a small bowl and mix well. "Ice" the bread on top and sides with mixture. Bake in preheated 400-degree oven for 20 minutes and serve hot.

*Texas Blossoms*

# Chuckwagon Bread

2 medium onions, chopped

3 tablespoons butter

1 (10-ounce) package refrigerated home-style or buttermilk biscuits

1 egg, slightly beaten

1 cup sour cream

½ teaspoon salt

1 teaspoon poppy seeds

Preheat oven to 375 degrees. Sauté onions slowly in butter until softened. Separate biscuits; place in a single layer in ungreased 8-inch layer cake pan, pressing together to cover bottom completely. Blend egg, sour cream, and salt. Add to onion mixture and pour over biscuits. Sprinkle with poppy seeds. Bake 30 minutes, or until topping is set. Slice in wedges; serve warm. Serves 8.

*Seasoned with Sun*

# Garlic Bread

1 freshly baked French baguette

½ cup grated Parmesan cheese

2 tablespoons minced fresh garlic

1 teaspoon chopped fresh parsley

1 teaspoon salt

10 tablespoons unsalted butter, melted

Preheat oven to 450 degrees. Split loaf of bread lengthwise.

In a small bowl, blend cheese, garlic, parsley, and salt; reserve. Brush cut sides of loaf with butter; sprinkle generously with reserved cheese mixture. Place bread on a baking sheet; bake 5 to 7 minutes, or until golden brown. Remove from oven; cut into pieces of desired size. Serves 10.

**CHEF CARL WALKER'S TIP:** Substitute 1 teaspoon garlic powder for fresh garlic.

*Brennan's of Houston in Your Kitchen*

# Hush Puppies

1¾ pounds high-gluten flour (bread or baker's flour)

1½ pounds cornmeal

1 tablespoon granulated garlic or garlic powder

1 tablespoon onion powder

½ cup sugar

2 teaspoons salt

1 tablespoon baking powder

1 medium onion, finely chopped

4 green onions with tops, chopped

About ⅓ cup whole milk

Vegetable oil

Combine dry ingredients. Stir in onions. Add milk slowly until mixture holds together well (mixture should roll between fingers with little sticking.)

Carefully drop batter by teaspoonfuls into deep hot oil (350 degrees) and fry about 3 minutes on each side or until brown. Drain on paper towels. Yield: 25 to 35 hush puppies.

Scott McLean, Country Kitchen and Bakery, Lampasas, Texas
*Cooking with Texas Highways*

# Cajun Corn Bread

1 cup all-purpose flour

1 tablespoon baking powder

½ teaspoon salt

2 tablespoons sugar

1 cup yellow cornmeal, preferably stone ground

2 eggs, beaten

¼ cup bacon drippings, melted

1 cup milk

½ cup finely chopped onion

3 canned or fresh jalapeño chiles, seeds and veins removed, minced

Preheat oven to 425 degrees. Generously grease a 10-inch cast-iron skillet. Place skillet in preheated oven for 20 minutes while preparing batter. (For a crispy outside crust, the batter should sizzle and hiss when spooned into the skillet.) Sift flour, baking powder, salt, and sugar into a large bowl. With a fork, blend in the cornmeal. Add remaining ingredients and stir just until all dry ingredients are moistened. Do not overbeat. Pour batter into skillet and bake in preheated oven until top springs back when pressed with fingertips, about 20 minutes. Cut into wedges and serve hot. Makes 8 to 12 wedges.

*Cajun-Creole Cooking*

# Husky Corn Bread

2 eggs

1 (8-ounce) carton sour cream

½ cup corn oil

1 cup cream-style corn

1 cup cornmeal

3½ teaspoons baking powder

1 teaspoon salt

Combine first 4 ingredients. Add cornmeal, baking powder, and salt. Pour into a 9-inch greased skillet. Bake at 350 degrees for 35 to 40 minutes. Yields 6 to 8 servings.

*¡Viva! Tradiciones*

# Skillet Sage and Peppered Corn Bread

6 bacon slices

1¼ cups cornmeal

¾ cup white flour

½ teaspoon salt

3 teaspoons baking powder

½ teaspoon crushed dried red chile pepper

¼ teaspoon ground white pepper

1 teaspoon paprika

1¼ cups buttermilk

1 egg

2 tablespoons molasses or honey

3 generous tablespoons freshly chopped sage

2 tablespoons chopped green onions

2 tablespoons freshly grated Parmesan cheese

Preheat oven to 425 degrees. In a 9- or 10-inch cast-iron skillet, fry bacon until crisp; reserve fat. Crumble bacon; set aside.

In a medium bowl, mix the cornmeal, flour, salt, baking powder, peppers, and paprika; blend with a fork.

In a small bowl, mix buttermilk, egg, and molasses or honey, then mix with dry ingredients. Add the chopped sage, onions, Parmesan, and crumbled bacon.

In skillet, heat ¼ cup of the reserved bacon fat to near smoking, and pour into the cornmeal mixture. Immediately return to the hot, greased skillet and bake in preheated oven for 20 to 25 minutes, until golden brown on top. Do not overcook!

**NOTE:** Use leftovers to make corn bread stuffing—delicious in baked onions, tomatoes, or pork chops.

*The Herb Garden Cookbook*

# Iron Skillet Corn Bread

1¾ cups plus 3 tablespoons cornmeal

1½ cups plus 1 tablespoon all-purpose flour

¼ cup sugar

1½ tablespoons baking powder

2 teaspoons salt

¼ teaspoon garlic powder

1½ cups buttermilk

¾ cup (1½ sticks) butter, melted

¼ cup maple syrup

3 eggs

2 jalapeño chiles, seeded and minced

About 2 tablespoons shortening

Place a 10-inch cast-iron skillet in the oven and preheat the oven to 400 degrees. Combine the cornmeal, flour, sugar, baking powder, salt, and garlic powder in a bowl and mix well. Whisk the buttermilk, butter, maple syrup, and eggs in a separate bowl until blended. Stir in the jalapeño chiles. Add the buttermilk mixture to the cornmeal mixture and stir just until combined.

Remove the hot skillet from the oven and coat with the shortening. Pour the batter into the prepared skillet and bake for 45 minutes, or until a wooden pick inserted in the center comes out clean. Invert onto a wire rack and cut into wedges. Serve immediately. Serves 4 to 6.

*Dallas Dish*

# Mama's Butter Rolls

1½ cups flour

½ teaspoon salt

½ cup shortening

¼ cup water

½ cup (1 stick) butter

1 cup sugar

1½ teaspoons cinnamon

1 cup half-and-half

½ cup sugar

1 teaspoon vanilla

Mix flour and salt in a bowl. Cut in shortening with pastry blender or two knives, as for pie crust. With a fork, mix in water, stirring until dough holds together. Turn out onto floured surface and knead lightly for two or three turns. Roll dough out to a thickness of ⅛ inch. Melt butter. Add sugar and cinnamon, mixing until well blended. Spread mixture over dough. Roll in jelly-roll fashion and cut into 1½-inch slices. Place in a well-greased pan. Bake at 375 degrees for 20 minutes. While rolls are baking, make a sauce of the half-and-half and sugar, mixed together in a saucepan. Cook over low heat, stirring, for 10 minutes. Remove from heat; add vanilla. After rolls have baked for 20 minutes, remove from oven, pour sauce over, and return to a 400-degree oven for an additional 10 minutes.

Loura Robertson
*Of Magnolia and Mesquite*

# Onion-Cheese Bread

½ cup chopped onion

1 tablespoon vegetable oil

1 egg, beaten

½ cup milk

1½ cups biscuit mix

1 cup shredded sharp processed American cheese, divided

2 tablespoons chopped parsley

2 tablespoons butter, melted

Cook onion in oil until tender but not brown. Combine eggs and milk; add to biscuit mix, stirring only until moistened. Add onion, ½ cup cheese, and parsley. Spread dough in greased 8" × 1½" round cake pan. Sprinkle with remaining cheese. Drizzle melted butter over. Bake at 400 degrees for 20 minutes, or until toothpick comes out clean. Yields 6 to 8 servings.

Mrs. Joe (Susan) Womack
*Flavor Favorites*

# Onion-Cheese Bread II

½ cup chopped onions

1 tablespoon butter

1 beaten egg

½ cup milk

1½ cups Bisquick baking mix

1 cup grated cheese

1 tablespoon poppy seeds

1 tablespoon melted butter

Sauté onions in butter until tender. Combine egg and milk. Add to Bisquick and stir only until dry ingredients are just moist. Add onion and half of the cheese. Spread dough in greased 8-inch round pie pan. Scatter remaining cheese and poppy seeds over the dough. Drizzle melted butter over all. Bake in preheated 400-degree oven for 20 to 25 minutes. Serve hot.

*Of Magnolia and Mesquite*

# Pan de Campo

4 cups all-purpose flour

5 teaspoons baking powder

2 teaspoons salt

¾ cup shortening

1½ cups milk

Mix flour, baking powder, and salt. Blend in shortening with a fork. Add milk and mix well. Let rest for 10 minutes. Divide dough in half and roll out each half in a 10-inch circle. Place in a greased Dutch oven and bake at 400 degrees until browned. (The traditional way to bake this bread is on hot coals in a Dutch oven.) Makes 2 (10-inch) loaves.

*The San Antonio Tex-Mex Cookbook*

# Pesto Bread with Cheese and Pine Nuts

2 eggs

3 tablespoons sugar

⅓ cup oil

¾ cup cream

2 cups self-rising flour

½ teaspoon baking powder

1½ teaspoons sweet basil flakes

⅓ cup grated Parmesan cheese

¼ cup pine nuts, lightly toasted

Beat together eggs, sugar, oil, and cream. In a separate bowl, combine flour, baking powder, basil, and Parmesan cheese. Add dry ingredients to egg mixture. Stir until dry ingredients are blended. Do not overmix. Stir in pine nuts.

Spread the batter in a greased 8 × 4-inch loaf pan. Place pan on a cookie sheet and bake at 350 degrees for 45 minutes, or until a toothpick inserted in the middle comes out clean. Allow the bread to cool in the pan for 15 minutes, then remove from pan and continue cooling on a wire rack.

Use a serrated bread knife to cut into slices. Yields 1 loaf.

**NOTE:** If you are using all-purpose flour, increase baking powder to 3 teaspoons and add a pinch of salt.

*Seasoned with Fun*

# Sausage Bread

1 cup raisins

1 pound hot bulk country sausage

1½ cups brown sugar

1½ cups granulated sugar

2 eggs

1 cup pecans, chopped

3 cups flour

1 teaspoon ground ginger

1 teaspoon pumpkin pie spice

1 teaspoon baking powder

1 cup cold coffee

1 teaspoon baking soda

Cream cheese

Simmer the raisins in enough water to cover for 5 minutes; drain. Mix sausage, sugars, and eggs together. Stir in nuts and raisins. Mix flour, spices, and baking powder together. Stir baking soda into coffee. Blend coffee mixture and flour mixture into sausage mixture. Pour into a greased and floured 9-inch tube pan. Bake at 350 degrees for 1½ hours. Serve with cream cheese.

Timmermann Sisters, Geronimo, Texas
*Gruene General Store Cookbook*

# Vintage House Focaccia Bread

1 ounce active dry yeast

3 cups warm water

½ cup honey

½ cup olive oil

⅔ cup chopped fresh rosemary

1½ tablespoons salt

3½ pounds bread flour or all-purpose flour

In a mixing bowl, dissolve yeast in water; let stand for a few minutes. Add honey and oil; let stand until yeast starts to foam. Add rosemary and salt. Slowly add flour. Dough should be soft and elastic; add additional water or flour, a little at a time, until you've reached the right consistency.

Transfer dough to an oiled bowl; brush oil on top of dough. Cover with plastic wrap and place in a warm area. Once dough has risen to double its size, remove from bowl and roll into desired shapes, working with a small amount of dough at a time.

Wrap again with plastic wrap and place in a warm place. Once dough has risen to almost twice its size, place on a baking sheet. Bake at 350 degrees until golden brown. Brush with oil. Serve warm or allow to cool. Serves 12 to 16.

*Vineyard Cuisine*

# Focaccia

10 pieces soft sun-dried tomatoes (about ⅓ cup)

½ cup boiling water

1 cup milk

2 tablespoons butter

3½ to 4 cups bread flour, divided

2 (¼-ounce) packages active dry yeast

2 tablespoons sugar

2 teaspoons salt

1 large egg

3 tablespoons chopped chives

Vegetable or olive oil

¼ cup additional olive oil, divided

¼ teaspoon dried oregano, crumbled

¾ teaspoon minced fresh rosemary

Combine tomatoes and boiling water in a small saucepan. Let stand for 30 minutes. Remove tomatoes from liquid (reserving liquid), finely chop, and set aside. To reserved liquid, add milk and butter, and heat mixture to 120 to 130 degrees.

In large bowl of electric mixer, combine 1½ cups flour, yeast, sugar, and salt. Gradually add the liquid mixture to flour mixture, beating at low speed until blended. Add egg and beat 3 minutes at medium speed. Stir in chopped tomatoes, chives, and enough remaining flour to make a soft dough. Turn dough out onto a lightly floured surface and knead for 5 minutes. Place in a large bowl oiled with vegetable or olive oil, turning to coat all sides of dough. Cover with plastic wrap and let rise for about 1 hour, or until doubled in size.

In a small bowl, combine ¼ cup olive oil, oregano, and rosemary; set aside.

Punch dough down. Divide dough in half and shape each portion into a 10-inch round. Place on lightly greased baking sheets. Brush both loaves with half of the olive oil mixture. Cover and let rest for 10 minutes. Bake in a preheated 350-degree oven for 15 minutes. Brush with remaining olive mixture and bake 5 to 10 minutes longer, or until lightly browned. Bread should sound hollow when tapped on bottom of loaf. Cool slightly on wire racks. Serve warm with olive oil for dipping. Makes 2 loaves.

*Texas Blossoms*

# Homemade Pizza Crust

½ package yeast

¼ cup warm water (105 to 115 degrees)

2 tablespoons olive oil

¼ cup milk

1½ cups all-purpose flour

½ teaspoon salt

⅛ teaspoon white pepper

Dissolve yeast in warm water and mix with olive oil and milk. Add flour until dough is smooth. Knead 4 minutes. Form into ball; place in greased bowl and allow to rise for 1½ hours. When double in bulk, punch down. Allow to rest for 10 minutes. Spread on greased pizza pans and top with favorite meats, cheese, vegetables, and sauce. Bake for 20 to 30 minutes at 425 degrees, or until cheese is melted and crust is crisp.

Barbara Nees Quinn
*Lagniappe*

# Cream Cheese Crescents

½ pound (8 ounces) cream cheese

½ pound (2 sticks) butter

1½ cups all-purpose flour

### Filling

½ cup granulated sugar

½ cup brown sugar

1 heaping teaspoon cinnamon

¼ cup raisins

¼ cup chopped nuts

Cream the cheese and butter together until fluffy. Add flour and blend well. Knead to form a smooth dough. Divide the dough into 5 small portions, flatten into disks, and roll lightly in flour. Wrap in plastic wrap and refrigerate overnight.

The next day combine all filling ingredients in a bowl and blend well; set aside. Roll out the dough on a lightly floured surface into thin rounds. Scatter the filling over the dough rounds. Using a pastry cutter or sharp knife, cut each round into 4 triangles and roll up, starting at the outside edge. Place crescent on baking sheet, pointed tip down and bake at 350 degrees for about 25 minutes. Cool on wire rack. Makes 20 crescents.

Mrs. Rex Corey (Robyn)
*Through Our Kitchen Door*

# Hilltop Wheat Bread

1 cup milk

½ cup shortening

1 cup cold water

½ cup brown sugar

1½ tablespoons salt

2 packages (2 tablespoons) dry yeast

1½ tablespoons wheat germ

2 tablespoons soy flour

1 teaspoon ground cumin

1 teaspoon toasted and ground coriander seed

1 teaspoon ground fennel seed

½ teaspoon ground caraway seed

3 cups whole wheat flour (preferably stone-ground), divided

2 eggs

3 cups bread flour

¼ cup butter

Scald milk with shortening added. In a medium bowl, combine milk, shortening, and cold water; using thermometer to test, cool to 130 degrees by setting pan in cold water. Test with thermometer. In bowl of electric mixer, combine brown sugar, salt, yeast, wheat germ, soy flour, ground seeds, and 2 cups whole wheat flour. Mix these dry ingredients, then add cooled milk and shortening. Beat 1 minute at medium speed. Add eggs and beat 2 minutes at high speed.

Add and mix by hand, if necessary, the remaining 1 cup whole wheat flour and the bread flour. Place in greased bowl, covered, and refrigerate for 2 hours. Remove and shape into 2 loaves; place in greased loaf pans. Cover with towel and place in warm area. Let rise until doubled in bulk. Bake 40 to 45 minutes at 350 degrees. Remove and brush tops with melted butter or soft butter while hot. Cool completely before slicing. Store in refrigerator or freezer. Makes 2 loaves.

**NOTE:** Ground caraway seed is not usually available but may be ground in a clean coffee bean grinder or pepper mill.

*Southern Herb Growing*

# Muenster Bread

### Bread

2 packages active dry yeast

¼ cup warm water

1 cup warm milk

1½ tablespoons sugar

1½ teaspoons salt

½ cup butter, melted

3½ cups bread flour

### Filling

2 pounds shredded Muenster cheese

1 egg, beaten

3 tablespoons butter, melted

Dissolve yeast in warm water; set aside. Combine milk, sugar, salt, and melted butter in a large bowl. Stir in yeast and add flour 1 cup at a time until dough is workable. Turn dough out onto a lightly floured surface and knead until smooth and elastic, about 8 minutes. Place in a greased bowl, turn to coat, and let rise in warm place until doubled in size, about 1½ hours.

Punch dough down and let rise 30 minutes more. For filling, combine cheese, egg, and butter. Punch dough down again and let rest for 15 minutes. On lightly floured surface, roll dough into a 24- to 26-inch round. Fold dough in half and place on large pizza pan. Unfold and carefully push dough circle onto outer edges of pan. Mound the cheese filling in middle of dough and bring up edges of dough, pleating around the filling. Gather dough at top and twist into a knob. If dough tears, pinch together. Let rest for 15 minutes. Bake in preheated 375-degree oven for 1 hour. Cool on wire rack for about 40 minutes, or until cheese has cooled. Do not cut until cheese is cooled. Makes 10 to 12 servings.

*¡Viva! Tradiciones*

# Pan Dulce

## Dough

**1 package yeast**

**1 teaspoon sugar**

**⅓ cup lukewarm water**

**4 cups all-purpose flour**

**½ cup sugar**

**2 tablespoons butter or shortening**

**1 teaspoon salt**

**5 eggs, beaten**

## Topping

**1 stick butter**

**1 cup all-purpose flour**

**1 cup powdered sugar**

**1 teaspoon vanilla**

**1 tablespoon cocoa**

**¼ teaspoon cinnamon**

Dissolve yeast and sugar in warm water. Combine 3 cups of the flour, sugar, butter, salt, and eggs in a large mixing bowl and mix well. Add remaining 1 cup flour and mix thoroughly. The dough should be elastic and slightly sticky. Let dough rise in a greased, covered bowl for 1½ hours, or until double in size.

For the topping, blend all of the ingredients in a food processor or blender. Remove and shape into a ball. Refrigerate the topping while the dough is rising.

Punch dough down and shape into 16 to 24 balls, depending on the size. Place on a greased cookie sheet 2 inches apart.

Shape topping into 2-inch balls. Flatten with hands into a circle. Place topping circle on top of each ball of dough, covering the dough. Mark an X on top of each with a sharp knife. Let rise until doubled in bulk, about 1½ hours.

Bake at 350 degrees for 12 to 15 minutes, or until lightly browned. Makes 16 to 24 rolls.

*The San Antonio Tex-Mex Cookbook*

# Jalapeño-Cheese Loaf

1 package dry yeast

1 cup warm water (105–115 degrees)

1 egg, beaten

2 tablespoons butter, melted

4 to 4½ cups bread flour, divided

1 tablespoon sugar

¾ teaspoon salt

¼ teaspoon garlic salt

3 small canned or fresh jalapeño chiles, seeded and chopped

1 cup (4 ounces) shredded sharp Cheddar cheese

1 (4-ounce) jar diced pimiento, well-drained

¼ cup minced onion

Dissolve yeast in warm water in a large bowl; let stand for 5 minutes. Combine yeast, egg, and butter; mix well.

Combine 3 cups bread flour, sugar, salt, and garlic salt. Gradually add flour mixture to yeast mixture, beating at medium speed of electric mixer until smooth. Beat in jalapeños, cheese, pimiento, onion, and enough of the remaining flour to form a soft dough.

Turn dough out onto a well-floured surface and knead 5 to 10 minutes, or until smooth and elastic. Place dough in a greased bowl, turning to grease top. Cover and let rise in a warm place (85 degrees), free from drafts, for 1 hour, or until doubled in bulk. Punch dough down.

Turn dough out onto a well-floured surface and knead for 1 minute. Shape dough into a loaf; place in a greased 9 ×5 × 3-inch loaf pan. Cover and let rise in a warm place (85 degrees), free from drafts, for 30 minutes, or until doubled in bulk. Bake at 400 degrees for 40 to 45 minutes, or until loaf sounds hollow when tapped. Remove from pan; let cool on wire rack. Yields 1 loaf.

*Of Magnolia and Mesquite*

# Sopapillas

3 cups flour

2 teaspoons baking powder

1 teaspoon salt

2 tablespoons shortening

1 cup milk

Salad oil for deep-drying, heated to 350 degrees

Sift flour, baking powder, and salt into bowl. Cut in shortening until mixture resembles coarse meal. Add enough milk to make a thick, stiff dough. Roll out to a thickness of ¼ inch and cut into 3-inch squares. Fry in preheated oil until brown on one side, then turn and brown on other side. Drain on paper towels. Serve warm, dusted with powdered sugar or cinnamon-sugar mixture. Honey is usually served with this pastry.

*Texas Cookoff*

# Breakfast & Brunch

In Texas, folks are known for working hard and playing hard. So whatever a particular day may hold in store, Texans know the value of eating a good, hearty breakfast. The practice began with our ancestors, who were farmers and ranchers. They needed those big, bread- and meat-laden morning meals to stock up enough calories to tackle the hard work ahead.

Although we don't generally need all those calories today, eating a good breakfast is essential to get the brain functioning for the day! If your morning time is limited, there's a Texas breakfast tradition that's quick and easy to make for the whole family—the breakfast taco.

On weekends, breakfast tends to be a more leisurely meal and is generally eaten a bit later, around mid-morning. There are dozens of great brunch dishes, many of which are casserole-type concoctions that can be assembled the night before and baked whenever you're ready to serve them.

I love to invite friends for a weekend brunch. I usually serve several dishes, perhaps buffet-style, and always include some fresh fruit. A lovely option is to serve champagne, or mimosas (half champagne, half orange juice), or Bloody Marys. It's a great, relaxed way to reconnect around the table. Even if it's just your immediate family, you'll sometimes be amazed at what everybody's been doing since the weekend before!

# Eggs Migas

1 tablespoon vegetable oil or unsalted butter

1 pound andouille or spicy smoked sausage, cut into ⅛-inch-thick slices

12 eggs, slightly beaten

Salt and black pepper to taste

6 tablespoons chopped tomato

3 tablespoons thinly sliced green onion

1 cup grated pepper Jack cheese

2 cups corn tortilla chips, broken into bite-size pieces

Sour cream and pico de gallo for garnish

Heat oil in a large skillet over medium heat. Cook sausage until it begins to brown and fat is rendered. Add eggs, salt, and pepper; stir. Fold in tomato, onion, and cheese. Cook until eggs are almost set. Toss in tortilla chips and cook mixture until set. To serve, garnish with sour cream and pico de gallo.

*Brennan's of Houston in Your Kitchen*

# Migas

4 bacon slices

4 corn tortillas, crumbled or cut into strips

6 eggs, beaten

¼ cup chopped purple onion

2 tomatoes, chopped

1 jalapeño pepper, seeded and minced

½ cup shredded Cheddar cheese

Sauté bacon in pan until crisp. Remove bacon and drain on paper towels. Fry tortillas in bacon drippings until crisp. Add remaining ingredients and cook until eggs are set. Crumble bacon and add to the eggs. Serve with warmed flour tortillas and refried beans. Serves 4 to 6.

*The San Antonio Tex-Mex Cookbook*

# Gold Rush Brunch

1 (5½-ounce) box frozen hash brown
  potatoes with onions

4 tablespoons butter

¼ cup flour

2 cups milk

½ teaspoon salt

1 cup sour cream

⅛ teaspoon pepper

2 tablespoons minced parsley

8 (¼-inch) slices Canadian bacon

8 eggs

Prepare potatoes as directed. Make sauce with flour, milk, butter, salt, and pepper; remove from heat and stir in sour cream, parsley, and cooked hash browns. Turn into a 13 × 9-inch baking dish. Arrange the Canadian bacon slices down the center and bake uncovered at 350 degrees for 20 minutes. Make 4 depressions on each side of bacon and slip eggs into depressions.

Return to oven and bake for 10 to 15 minutes, or until eggs are set. Serves 4 to 6.

Mrs. Stephen D. Trowbridge (Judy)
*Through Our Kitchen Door*

# Green Chile Strata

1 loaf French bread

1½ cups (6 ounces) shredded Monterey
  Jack cheese

1½ cups (6 ounces) shredded Cheddar
  cheese

8 ounces cream cheese, chopped

8 bacon slices, crisp-fried and crumbled

3 to 5 roasted fresh green chiles, peeled,
  seeded, and chopped

10 eggs

2 cups milk

½ teaspoon dry mustard

Cayenne pepper to taste

Cut the crust from the French bread and tear the bread into pieces. Spread in a greased 9 × 13-inch baking dish. Layer the Monterey Jack cheese, Cheddar cheese, and cream cheese over the bread. Top with the bacon and green chiles.

Beat the eggs in a bowl and whisk in the milk, dry mustard, and cayenne pepper. Pour over the layers. Bake at 350 degrees for 55 to 60 minutes, or until set and golden brown. Let stand for 10 minutes before serving. Serves 8.

*Lone Star to Five Star*

# Mexican Egg and Chorizo Casserole

3 to 4 medium boiling potatoes, peeled

3 tablespoons olive oil, divided

1 medium onion, chopped

2 pounds Mexican chorizo, removed from casing

1 (16-ounce) can diced tomatoes

2 garlic cloves, minced

2 tablespoons chile powder

1 teaspoon ground cumin

8 eggs

1½ cups half-and-half

1 teaspoon salt

1 teaspoon Tabasco sauce

Preheat oven to 450 degrees. Slice the potatoes into ¼-inch slices. Coat with about 1 tablespoon of oil; sprinkle with salt. Layer the potatoes on the bottom of a 9 × 13-inch casserole dish. Bake to form a crust, about 20 minutes. Sauté the onion in 2 tablespoons of the oil until transparent and wilted. Add the chorizo and cook until lightly browned. Spread this mixture on top of the potato layer. Lower oven temperature to 325 degrees.

Prepare the tomato sauce by combining the canned tomatoes, garlic, and spices in a saucepan. Cook for about 20 minutes. Cool slightly and puree in a blender. Spread 1 cup of the tomato sauce over the sausage layer.

Beat the eggs with the half-and-half, salt, and Tabasco. Pour over the top of the casserole. Bake at 325 degrees for 40 minutes, or until eggs are set. Serve with remaining tomato sauce.

*It's a Long Way to Guacamole*

# Sunday Morning Egg and Cheese Casserole

8 eggs, slightly beaten

6 slices bread, cubed

1 cup shredded Longhorn cheese

1 pound cooked sausage or bacon, well drained and crumbled

2 cups milk

1 teaspoon salt

1 teaspoon dry mustard

1 (4-ounce) can chopped green chiles, drained

Mix all ingredients. Pour into greased 9 × 13-inch baking dish. Place in refrigerator overnight. Next morning, remove casserole from refrigerator; preheat oven to 350 degrees. Bake casserole for 30 minutes. Let stand at room temperature a few minutes. Cut into squares and serve with fresh fruit compote and muffins. Serves 10 to 12.

*Seasoned with Sun*

# Sausage and Potato Breakfast Tacos

½ pound chorizo (Mexican sausage) or pork sausage

3 tablespoons oil

1 large potato, diced

½ to ¾ cup picante sauce

6 eggs, beaten

6 flour tortillas

Shredded Cheddar or Monterey Jack cheese (optional)

Remove sausage from casing. Brown in skillet, crumbling with a fork. Drain and remove to a paper towel.

Heat oil in skillet. Add potato and picante sauce. Cook until potatoes are tender. Add sausage and eggs and cook until eggs are done.

Warm tortillas individually on a clean skillet and fill with potato mixture. Add the shredded cheese, if desired. Serves 6.

*The San Antonio Tex-Mex Cookbook*

# Breakfast Burritos

½ pound bulk pork sausage

2 large potatoes, peeled and grated

1 medium green bell pepper, chopped

½ cup chopped onion

8 eggs, beaten

8 (8-inch) flour tortillas

¼ cup butter, melted

2½ cups (10 ounces) shredded Cheddar cheese

Taco sauce

Wrap the tortillas in foil and bake at 350 degrees for 15 minutes.

Cook sausage until browned; drain, reserving drippings in skillet. Set sausage aside. Add vegetables to skillet and cook until potatoes are browned. Add eggs; cook, stirring occasionally, until eggs are firm but still moist.

Stir the reserved sausage into the mixture. Spoon an equal amount of egg mixture in center of each tortilla; roll up. Place filled tortillas in a lightly greased 13 × 9 × 2-inch baking dish; brush with butter and cover with foil. Bake at 375 degrees for 10 minutes. Scatter the cheese over the burritos, cover, and bake an additional 5 minutes, or until cheese melts. Serve with taco sauce. Serves 4.

*Of Magnolia and Mesquite*

# Shrimp Omelet

½ pound unpeeled small shrimp

3 green onions, finely chopped

2 tablespoons butter, melted

8 eggs

4 tablespoons milk

1 teaspoon salt

¼ teaspoon freshly ground black pepper

2 tablespoons butter

1 cup shredded Cheddar cheese

Peel and devein shrimp. Sauté shrimp and green onions in melted butter in a heavy skillet until shrimp turn pink; set aside. Combine eggs, milk, salt, and pepper; beat well. Heat a 10-inch omelet pan or heavy skillet until it is hot enough for a drop of water to sizzle. Add 2 tablespoons butter; rotate pan to coat bottom. Pour egg mixture into pan. As mixture starts to cook, gently lift edges of omelet with a spatula and tilt pan so uncooked portion flows underneath. Spoon shrimp mixture and cheese over half of omelet when eggs are set and top is still moist and creamy. Loosen omelet with a spatula and fold unfilled side over filling; remove from heat. Cover and let stand 1 to 2 minutes or until cheese melts. Gently slide omelet onto a serving plate; serve immediately. Serves 4.

*Of Magnolia and Mesquite*

# Crab-Zucchini Frittata

8 ounces fresh or frozen crabmeat

2 tablespoons butter

1 garlic clove, minced

⅔ cup chopped green onions

1 cup paper-thin zucchini slices

½ cup sliced fresh mushrooms

1 teaspoon salt

Pepper to taste

3 eggs

½ cup milk

½ cup Parmesan cheese

1 tablespoon minced fresh oregano, or 1 teaspoon dried

Preheat oven to 350 degrees. Drain crabmeat and pick out shell or cartilage; set aside. Melt butter and gradually add garlic, onions, zucchini, and mushrooms, cooking only until hot. Add salt and pepper.

Beat eggs, milk, and cheese together and add oregano, sautéed vegetables, and crabmeat. Pour into buttered, shallow casserole (1½-quart). Bake 20 to 25 minutes, or until firm. Serve immediately or at room temperature; will also reheat nicely in microwave. Serves 12 as appetizer or first course, 6 as main course.

*Southern Herb Growing*

# Crawfish in Sherried Cream

1 pound cooked crawfish tails, peeled

¼ cup (½ stick) butter

1 bunch green onions, chopped

½ cup chopped parsley

½ cup (1 stick) butter

3 tablespoons all-purpose flour

1 pint heavy cream

¼ cup dry sherry

1 teaspoon fresh lemon juice

Tabasco sauce or cayenne pepper to taste

Sauté the crawfish in ¼ cup butter in a skillet and set aside. Sauté the green onions and parsley in ½ cup butter in a skillet for 3 to 4 minutes. Blend in the flour to form a roux and cook for 2 to 3 minutes longer. Stir in the cream, sherry, lemon juice, and Tabasco or cayenne pepper gradually. Cook until the sauce thickens slightly, stirring constantly. Stir in the crawfish. Place in a chafing dish and serve warm on Melba toast, in pastry shells, or over hot cooked rice. Serves 4.

*Settings Sunrise to Sunset*

# Crustless Ham and Grits Quiche

½ cup water

¼ teaspoon salt

⅓ cup uncooked quick-cooking yellow grits

1 (12-ounce) can evaporated milk

1½ cups chopped cooked ham

1 cup (4 ounces) shredded sharp Cheddar cheese

1 tablespoon chopped fresh parsley

1 to 2 teaspoons hot sauce

3 eggs, beaten

Preheat oven to 350 degrees; lightly grease a 9½-inch quiche dish. Bring the water and salt to a boil in a large saucepan. Stir in the grits. Remove from the heat and let stand for 5 minutes. The mixture should be thick. Stir in the evaporated milk, ham, cheese, parsley, hot sauce, and eggs, blending well.

Spoon into prepared quiche dish or deep-dish pie plate. Bake in preheated oven for 30 to 35 minutes, or until set and golden brown. Let stand for 10 minutes before serving. Serves 4 to 6.

*Lone Star to Five Star*

# Heavenly Ham Cups

1 pound fresh mushrooms, finely chopped

¼ cup finely chopped green onions

2 tablespoons butter

½ teaspoon salt

¼ teaspoon pepper

2 tablespoons sour cream

12 slices Smokehouse Ham

12 eggs

Ground red pepper or paprika

Preheat oven to 400 degrees. Sauté onions and mushrooms in butter for about 5 minutes, or until the mushrooms are tender. Season with salt and pepper. Add sour cream. Lightly oil 12 muffin cups and place 1 slice of ham in each cup, letting the ends of the ham hang over the edges of the cups.

Evenly divide the mushroom-onion mixture among the cups. Crack 1 egg into each of the ham cups and bake for 15 to 20 minutes, until the eggs are done.

Using 2 spoons, carefully remove the ham cups from the muffin tins. Sprinkle with red pepper or paprika. Serve immediately with hot biscuits and jam. Serves 6.

**EDITOR'S NOTE:** Smokehouse Ham is a New Braunfels Smokehouse product.

*New Braunfels Smokehouse*

# Ham Soufflé

10 slices bread, cut into cubes

4 eggs, beaten

3 cups milk

2½ cups ground ham

1 cup chopped celery

½ cup mayonnaise

½ cup chopped green onions, including green tops

½ cup sour cream

1 can cream of mushroom soup

1½ cups (6 ounces) grated sharp Cheddar cheese

Place half of the cubed bread in a well-greased 9 × 13-inch baking dish. Mix eggs and milk; set aside. Combine ham, celery, mayonnaise, onion, and sour cream. Mix until well blended. Spread over bread cubes and cover filling with remainder of bread cubes. Pour the egg mixture over bread. Cover and refrigerate overnight. When ready to bake, remove cover and bake at 325 degrees for 15 minutes. Remove from oven. Whip soup with a fork until smooth, then spread over casserole. Sprinkle with cheese and return to oven for 1 hour. Let sit several minutes before cutting into squares to serve. Seafood or chicken may be used instead of ham.

*Of Magnolia and Mesquite*

# Grillades

6 pounds veal round, ¼-inch thick, cut into serving pieces

1 tablespoon salt

1 teaspoon freshly ground black pepper

¾ cup bacon drippings

½ cup flour

2 cups chopped onions

¾ cup chopped celery

6 green bell peppers, thinly sliced

3 cups chopped green onions, including green tops

3 garlic cloves, minced

3 cups chopped tomatoes

1 teaspoon thyme

4 bay leaves

Tabasco sauce to taste

Worcestershire sauce to taste

1½ cups warm water

1 cup minced parsley

Salt and pepper the veal. In a heavy Dutch oven, brown the meat in 4 tablespoons of the bacon drippings. Remove veal; keep covered and warm. Add remaining drippings and flour to Dutch oven, stirring constantly over low heat to make a dark brown roux. Add celery, peppers, green onions, and garlic. Sauté until limp. Add the chopped tomatoes, stirring to blend well. Add seasonings and stir in the water. Place meat in Dutch oven with the roux, cover, and cook slowly for 1 hour. Cool and refrigerate overnight. Reheat by adding a small amount of water and heating slowly. To serve, remove bay leaves and stir in chopped parsley. Serve over baked cheese grits for a true Creole breakfast.

*Of Magnolia and Mesquite*

# Cream Cheese French Toast

8 slices bread

3 ounces cream cheese, softened

1 pint fresh strawberries, sliced

3 eggs beaten

½ cup milk

1 teaspoon vanilla extract

2 tablespoons sugar

Cinnamon

Spread 4 slices of bread with cream cheese. Spoon strawberries over cream cheese and top with remaining slices of bread. In shallow bowl, beat eggs with milk, vanilla, and sugar. Dip each sandwich into egg mixture, coating both sides. Cook on hot griddle until brown, flip, and cook other side. Sprinkle with cinnamon and extra strawberries. Serve warm with syrup. This recipe also works well with fresh peaches. Makes 4 servings.

*¡Viva! Tradiciones*

# Overnight French Toast

8 eggs

½ cup orange juice

⅓ cup Grand Marnier

¾ cup half-and-half

3 tablespoons sugar

¼ teaspoon salt

1 teaspoon vanilla extract

Grated zest of ½ orange

¼ cup melted butter

1 loaf French bread, sliced

Beat the eggs, orange juice, Grand Marnier, half-and-half, sugar, salt, vanilla, and orange zest in a large mixing bowl until well blended. Pour the melted butter in the bottom of a shallow dish, tilting the dish to coat the entire bottom with the butter. Place the bread slices in the dish. Pour the egg mixture over the bread slices. Chill, covered, for up to 8 hours.

Cook on a hot greased griddle until puffed and brown on both sides, turning once. Serve hot with maple syrup and confectioners' sugar. Serves 8.

*Dining without Reservations*

# Peachy French Toast

## Topping

8 tablespoons coconut

2½ cups sliced peaches

¼ cup brandy

½ cup Cream of Coconut

## French Toast

1 cup milk

6 eggs

1 tablespoon vanilla

1 teaspoon cinnamon

1 teaspoon nutmeg

1 loaf French bread, slightly dry (8 diagonal slices, ¾-inch thick)

To make the topping, place coconut in shallow baking pan; toast in oven at 350 degrees until golden; set aside. Combine the peaches, Cream of Coconut, and brandy in skillet. Cook for 8 to 10 minutes; keep warm.

To make the French toast, combine milk, eggs, vanilla, cinnamon, and nutmeg in shallow bowl. Soak bread slices in milk mixture until soggy. Heat ¼ inch of oil in skillet. Fry toast until golden on both sides. To serve, spoon the peaches on top of the toast and add maple syrup. Scatter toasted coconut over the top. Makes 4 servings.

*With Love, From Cynthia*

# Fredericksburg Peach French Toast

3 fresh peaches

1 (3-ounce) package cream cheese, softened

2 tablespoons chopped pecans

12 bread slices

2 large eggs

½ cup milk

½ teaspoon ground cinnamon

¼ teaspoon vanilla extract

Butter

Chop 1 peach and slice the other 2. Stir pecans and chopped peach into cream cheese in a small bowl. Spoon 1½ tablespoons of the cream cheese mixture onto 6 bread slices, spreading evenly. Top with remaining slices of bread. Beat together the eggs, milk, cinnamon, and vanilla in a small bowl. Dip each sandwich into the egg mixture, turning to coat. Melt 1 tablespoon butter over medium-high heat in a large skillet or griddle. Cook 2 sandwiches at a time for 3 minutes per side, adding more butter as needed. Serve topped with the sliced peaches and your favorite syrup. Serves 6.

*Texas Blossoms*

# Pecan French Toast

1 loaf French bread

4 eggs

⅔ cup orange juice

⅓ cup milk

¼ cup sugar

¼ teaspoon freshly grated nutmeg

½ teaspoon vanilla extract

½ cup coarsely chopped pecans

⅓ cup butter, melted

Slice bread into 1-inch-thick slices. Lay them in a single layer in a large baking pan. Whisk the eggs, orange juice, milk, sugar, nutmeg, and vanilla together. Pour mixture over bread. Cover with plastic wrap and refrigerate overnight.

In the morning, remove casserole and let stand until it comes to room temperature. Preheat the oven to 400 degrees. Toss pecans in melted butter and scatter over the bread. Bake for 20 to 25 minutes, or until fluffy. Serve with warmed syrup or cinnamon sugar.

Liv Volland, Wisconsin
*Kickin' Back in the Kitchen Cookbook*

# Brunch Puff

16 bacon slices, cooked until crisp, then crumbled, drippings reserved

2 onions, sliced

12 slices white bread, quartered

½ pound Cheddar cheese, grated

8 eggs, beaten

4 cups milk

1½ teaspoons salt

¼ teaspoon black pepper

½ teaspoon dry mustard

Sauté onion in bacon drippings until soft. Place ½ of the bread quarters in the bottom of a greased 9 × 13-inch baking dish. Scatter half of the bacon, onions, and cheese on the bread; repeat layers. Combine the eggs, milk, and spices; pour over the layers in the baking dish. Refrigerate for at least 24 hours before cooking.

Remove from refrigerator 1 hour before baking. Bake at 350 degrees for 45 to 50 minutes. Serves 10 to 12.

Instead of bacon, try substituting one of the following: 1 pound bulk cooked sausage, 1 pound crabmeat, 1 pound shrimp, cooked Italian sausage, chopped spinach, or chopped broccoli.

Mrs. Bob Kelly (Margaret)
*Lone Star Legacy*

# Puffy Pancake with Banana-Berry Compote

4 eggs

1 cup milk

1 cup all-purpose flour

2 tablespoons sugar

¼ teaspoon salt

2 tablespoons butter

2 bananas, sliced

1 pint strawberries, sliced

1 tablespoon sugar

1 tablespoon fresh lemon juice

Confectioner's sugar for sprinkling

Heat an ovenproof 10-inch skillet in a 425-degree oven until very hot. Process the eggs, milk, flour, sugar, and salt at medium speed in a blender until smooth. Remove the skillet from the oven and maintain the oven temperature. Place the butter in the hot skillet and swirl until melted. Add the batter. Bake in oven for 15 minutes, or until puffy and golden. Combine the bananas, strawberries, sugar, and lemon juice in a bowl and toss to mix. Spoon over the pancake and sprinkle with confectioners' sugar. Cut into wedges and serve. Serves 4.

*Settings Sunrise to Sunset*

# Sweet Potato Pancakes

2 eggs, beaten

2 cups milk

1½ cups flour

1½ cups mashed sweet potatoes

1 cup chopped pecans

½ cup butter, melted

1 tablespoon baking powder

1 teaspoon sugar

1 teaspoon salt

½ teaspoon ground cinnamon

¼ teaspoon ground cloves

Mix all the ingredients together, whisking until the batter is smooth. Spoon onto a hot griddle, about 2 tablespoons at a time, for small pancakes (a large serving spoon or half of a ¼-cup scoop makes perfect small pancakes). Cook until bubbles appear and the batter sets. Flip to cook the second side. Transfer to a warm plate and keep warm until a stack is ready to serve. Makes approximately 48 "silver dollar" pancakes. Serves 8 to 10.

*Texas Cowboy Cooking*

# Jimbo's Pancakes

1½ cups cornmeal

¼ cup flour

1 teaspoon baking soda

1 teaspoon sugar

1 teaspoon salt

2 cups buttermilk

2 tablespoons cooking oil or bacon drippings

1 slightly beaten egg yolk

1 stiffly beaten egg white

Stir together cornmeal, flour, soda, sugar, and salt. Add buttermilk, oil, and egg yolk. Stir to blend well. Fold in stiffly beaten egg white. Let batter stand for 10 minutes. Bake on hot, oiled griddle, turning only once. Yields 12 pancakes.

D'Anne DeMoss McGown
*Lagniappe*

# Gingerbread Pancakes

2 eggs

4 tablespoons brown sugar

½ cup buttermilk

½ cup prepared decaf coffee

½ cup water

2 teaspoons cinnamon

2 teaspoons ground ginger

2 teaspoons freshly grated nutmeg

¼ teaspoon ground cloves

2 cups flour

4 tablespoons butter, melted

1 tablespoon baking powder

2 teaspoons baking soda

Mix eggs, sugar, buttermilk, coffee, water, spices, and flour. Add butter. Mix just until blended; add baking powder and baking soda. Mix just until blended. Cook as you would ordinary pancakes. Makes 4 large pancakes.

Kerbey Lane Cafés, Austin
*Remember the Flavors of Austin*

# Lighter-Than-Air Pancakes

1 cup sifted flour

1 tablespoon baking powder

¾ cup sugar

⅛ teaspoon salt

1 cup milk

2 rounded tablespoons sour cream

1 egg

2 tablespoons melted butter

Whipped cream for garnish

Fresh berries for garnish

Sift the flour, baking powder, sugar, and salt into a bowl and mix well. Beat the milk, sour cream, and egg in a separate bowl. Stir into the flour mixture. Add the butter, whisking until blended. May add additional milk, 1 tablespoon at a time, until of the desired consistency. Drop by small spoonfuls onto a hot buttered griddle. Bake until brown on both sides, turning once. Garnish with whipped cream and fresh berries. Yields 12 pancakes.

**NOTE:** This is a favorite recipe for weekend guests. The recipe is easily doubled and stores well overnight. Bake pancakes until bubbles appear on the surface and the underside is golden brown. Turn the pancakes over and bake just until golden brown.

*Texas Ties*

# Salsas, Relishes & Pestos

**H**ere's where you can really have some fun with your food! Salsa, relishes, and pestos allow you to spice up any dish and add a dimension of totally fresh taste.

While there are hundreds of salsas available commercially, it is so rewarding to make your own with good, fresh ingredients—and no preservatives or other additives. Salsa is a universally popular party food when served with good-quality corn tortilla chips, but it's also a great plate garnish when serving Tex-Mex foods. I also love to top grilled fish and pork with salsa or pico de gallo. This is an especially good way to serve fish or pork during the warmer months, utilizing the method of combining a hot meat with a chilled topping to create a light taste. And it's an unwritten rule in Texas that you simply must have pico de gallo if you serve fajitas!

Variations of pesto come from many different cultures, not just Italy, which takes credit for the best-known, basil pesto. Pesto can be made from a wide variety of ingredients, including chiles. Pesto is great when tossed with pasta for a light summer or spring dish. Pesto is also delicious when served on grilled or broiled lamb or fish fillets, especially salmon.

So think beyond the bowl of tortilla chips and use these culinary creations to add some freshness and/or spice to your meals.

# Avocado Salsa

2 avocados, peeled and chopped

2 tomatoes, chopped

1 tablespoon fresh lime juice

1 tablespoon fresh lemon juice

2 teaspoons minced garlic (about 3 cloves)

1 tablespoon minced serranos (about 3 peppers)

1 tablespoon minced cilantro

1 teaspoon ground cumin

½ teaspoon salt

Combine ingredients and refrigerate for at least 1 hour. Yields 2 cups.

*Cooking with Texas Highways*

# Salsa de Tomatillos *(Tomatillo Salsa)*

¾ pound fresh tomatillos, dry outer husks removed, cut into quarters

2 medium serrano chiles, stems and seeds removed, finely chopped

3 tablespoons chopped white onion

½ teaspoon minced garlic

3 tablespoons chopped cilantro

1 heaping teaspoon salt

Place all ingredients in a blender and blend just until the salsa is thick and chunky, but not pureed, about 20 to 25 seconds. Serves 4.

Ricardo Muñoz, *Verde en la cocina mexicana*
*Jim Peyton's The Very Best of Tex-Mex Cooking*

# Matt's Smoked Salsa

3 whole medium tomatoes

½ medium sweet white onion, cut in chunks

3 whole jalapeños, or 6 whole serranos (use the latter for a hotter sauce)

3 garlic cloves

¾ teaspoon salt, or to taste

1 teaspoon red wine vinegar

2 teaspoons vegetable oil

½ cup water

Combine ingredients in a heavy pot and place the pot (uncovered) in a smoker for 1½ to 2 hours, or until the vegetables are soft. (Do not allow the vegetables to become dry; add more water if needed.)

Remove pot from smoker.

Mash (do not blend) the vegetables, taking care to mash one chile at a time until salsa tastes hot enough; discard any extra chiles. (Salsa will be chunky.) Adjust the salt to taste. Store in an airtight container in refrigerator (will keep about 2 weeks.) Yields 2 cups.

> **NOTE:** For a thicker salsa, combine 1 tablespoon cornstarch with 2 tablespoons water and drizzle the mixture into the salsa while it's still hot, stirring constantly. Simmer on low heat 5 to 10 minutes, stirring occasionally, until salsa reaches the desired thickness. If it becomes too thick, simply add a bit more water.

Matt Martinez Jr. and Steve Pate, *Culinary Frontier: A Real Texas Cookbook*
*Cooking with Texas Highways*

## Fresh Watermelon Salsa

2 cups seeded and coarsely chopped watermelon

2 tablespoons chopped onions

2 tablespoons water chestnuts

2 to 4 tablespoons chopped Anaheim chiles

1 tablespoon balsamic vinegar

¼ teaspoon garlic salt

Additional balsamic vinegar

Combine first 6 ingredients; mix well. Refrigerate for 2 hours. Add more balsamic vinegar to taste. Yields 2½ cups.

*Cooking with Texas Highways*

## Monterey Jack Cilantro Salsa

1 cup (4 ounces) shredded Monterey Jack cheese

1 (4-ounce) can chopped green chiles, drained

1 (2-ounce) can chopped ripe olives, drained

3 or 4 green onions, chopped

2 tomatoes, chopped

1 bunch cilantro, trimmed and chopped

½ to ¾ cup Italian salad dressing

Combine the cheese, green chiles, olives, green onions, tomatoes, and cilantro in a bowl and mix well. Add the dressing until the desired consistency is reached and mix well.

Let stand, covered, at room temperature for 1 to 2 hours before serving. Serve with tortilla chips. Serves 4 to 6.

*Dallas Dish*

# Classic Pico de Gallo

5 Roma tomatoes, cut into tiny (¼-inch) dice

½ cup tiny-diced red onion

2 or 3 serrano chiles, seeds and veins removed, minced

½ cup chopped cilantro leaves and tender top stems

Juice of ½ large lime

Salt to taste

Combine all ingredients in a nonreactive bowl. Toss to blend well, Season to taste with salt. (Remember that salt is the ingredient in a good pico de gallo that creates harmony among the ingredients and makes them do a little two-step in your mouth, so don't be stingy with the salt.) Serve at once. Serve with corn tortilla chips, or use as a topping or garnish with meats and vegetables. Pico de gallo is an essential ingredient when serving fajitas. Makes about 2½ to 3 cups.

> **NOTES:** If you want your pico de gallo to be really spicy, leave the seeds and veins in the chiles.
> If you're making the pico de gallo more than 1 hour in advance of serving it, don't add the salt, as it will make the tomatoes "weep" and dilute the flavor. Add the salt just before serving.

Terry Thompson-Anderson

# Dried Cherry and Chipotle Relish

1 whole head garlic

3 tablespoons olive oil

1½ cups chopped red onion

1 cup firmly packed brown sugar

1 cup orange juice

¾ cup rice vinegar

¾ cup red wine vinegar

2½ cups dried tart cherries (about 10 ounces)

3 minced canned chipotle chiles in adobo sauce

½ teaspoon ground cinnamon

Preheat oven to 400 degrees. Slice the top ⅜ inch off the head of garlic. Place the garlic in a small baking dish and drizzle 1 tablespoon of the olive oil over it. Cover with foil and roast in preheated oven for about 35 to 45 minutes, or until the garlic cloves are very soft. Set aside to cool. When garlic is cool enough to handle, squeeze the pulp from the cloves and mash to a paste; set aside.

Heat remaining 2 tablespoons of olive oil in a heavy-bottomed 12-inch skillet over medium-high heat. Add the onion and sauté until lightly browned, about 6 to 8 minutes. Add sugar, orange juice, and vinegars; stir until sugar dissolves. Increase heat to high. Boil until liquid is reduced by about one-third, stirring often, about 10 minutes. Add the garlic pulp, dried cherries, chipotle chiles, and ground cinnamon. Reduce heat and simmer until liquid has been reduced to a thin syrup, stirring occasionally, about 12 minutes. Serve at room temperature or slightly warm. Makes about 2½ cups.

**NOTE:** This relish is perfect on duck and other poultry, or on pork tenderloin, pork chops, or roast pork.

*Terry Thompson-Anderson*

# Cilantro Pesto

3 large garlic cloves, peeled and trimmed

½ cup chopped cilantro

½ cup chopped basil

¾ cup chopped sun-dried tomatoes

2 jalapeños, chopped, seeds and veins removed

⅓ cup grated Parmesan cheese

½ cup chopped pecans

½ cup extra-virgin olive oil

Pulse first 5 ingredients in food processor. Add cheese and pecans; pulse again. Slowly add oil, with machine running, until pesto is smooth. Toss with cooked pasta of your choice. Also wonderful spread on slices of French bread and broiled.

*¡Viva! Tradiciones*

# Garden Pesto

4 to 6 garlic cloves

3 cups fresh basil (tightly packed), gently rinsed and dried (experiment with various kinds of basil)

½ cup pine nuts (or walnuts or pecans)

½ to ¾ cup freshly grated Parmesan

2 to 3 tablespoons freshly grated Romano cheese

⅔ cup olive oil, or more

With machine running, drop the garlic cloves through the feed tube of food processor fitted with steel blade to mince. Stop and scrape down sides of bowl. Add basil and process until well blended. Add nuts and cheese, then slowly add the olive oil. Blend to the desired consistency, adding more olive oil if desired. Spoon into small jars and seal with melted butter. (Try substituting cinnamon basil and pecan or walnuts.) Yields approximately 2 cups. Freeze half if desired.

*The Herb Garden Cookbook*

# Garlic and Cilantro Pesto with Pita Bread

4 bunches fresh cilantro, washed and
dried well

2 bunches fresh mint

⅓ cup minced raw garlic

¼ cup skin-on sliced almonds, toasted

½ cup minced jalapeño

1 cup red wine vinegar

½ teaspoon sea salt, or to taste

1 teaspoon red (cayenne) pepper

⅓ cup extra-virgin olive oil, or more
depending on consistency desired

Pita bread, cut into small wedges for
dipping

Combine all ingredients except pita bread in work bowl of food processor fitted with steel blade. Process until smooth. The mixture should be fairly stiff and spreadable. If you prefer a looser consistency, add additional olive oil. Turn the mixture out into a serving bowl and place in the center of a platter. Arrange the pita bread wedges around the spread and serve. This pesto is also great on grilled lamb chops or salmon fillets. Makes about 3 cups.

Terry Thompson-Anderson

# Sun-Dried Tomato and Olive Pesto

⅔ cup oil-packed sun-dried tomatoes

Olive oil

¾ cup packed, stemmed fresh parsley
leaves

⅔ cup canned black olives, drained

½ cup toasted pine nuts

2 green onions, coarsely chopped

2 garlic cloves, chopped

1 tablespoon red wine vinegar

Strain tomatoes into a glass measuring cup. Pour in enough olive oil to measure ¼ cup. Combine the tomatoes and oil with next 6 ingredients in work bowl of food processor. Process until well blended. If too dry, add more olive oil by spoonfuls. Season with salt and pepper. Cover and refrigerate for up to 2 days or freeze. Bring to room temperature before tossing with your favorite hot pasta. Makes 2 cups.

*¡Viva! Tradiciones*

# Salads & Salad Dressings

A good salad is an integral part of a fine meal. A salad is an excellent way to provide fibrous greens to the family diet and add filling bulk to the meal without a lot of fat or calories. Experiment with the great variety of greens available on the market today. Salad has certainly risen above the iceberg lettuce with bottled French dressing that graced many of our childhood tables! If you can't coerce your children into eating cooked spinach, make spinach salads. Uncooked spinach provides even more nutrition!

Salads can also be made from whole grains like quinoa or bulgur wheat, as in tabouli, a very nutritious salad with Middle Eastern origins.

Get in the habit of making your own salad dressings. It's breeze with the help of a food processor or blender, and you don't have to worry about all of the preservatives and stabilizers used in commercial salad dressings to keep them from separating. Who cares? Separation is natural—simply shake the container to reemulsify your homemade dressing right before serving. Use fruity extra-virgin olive oil and try aged balsamic vinegar, good red wine vinegar, or some of the excellent fruit-based vinegars on the market. Raspberry vinaigrette is a personal favorite.

Salads can be garnished with a variety of fresh ingredients: sliced tomatoes, tomato wedges, cherry or grape tomatoes, sliced cucumber, sprouts, sliced avocado, thin-sliced purple onion, and marinated artichoke hearts. Choose from the many types of olives available. Or use toasted nuts: pine nuts, toasted pecans or walnuts, sliced, skin-on toasted almonds, or pistachios.

In Texas, salad is often the whole meal, especially during our torrid summer months. There are great pasta salads, which are both filling and prepared with a minimum of hot stove time required. There are dozens of recipes for savory shrimp and crab salads using the bounty of fresh shellfish from our coastal waters. Roasted or grilled fresh vegetables make fabulous-tasting salads, especially if you scatter a bit of aged balsamic vinegar on them and add a wedge of one of the cheeses produced by Texas' many artisan cheese makers.

Plant a small bed of salad greens in early spring and fall—arugula does very well in Texas, as do most of the "wild" greens like dandelion, mâche, lamb's ear, oak leaf lettuce, and rocket (roquette), in addition to the better-known greens like leaf lettuces, spinach, and romaine. You won't believe the premium taste of greens picked fresh from your garden. And when you grow them, you know exactly where they came from and what was put on them!

# Pepper Cream Dressing

1 cup mayonnaise

2 tablespoons water

½ teaspoon freshly squeezed lemon juice

¾ teaspoon Worcestershire sauce

¾ teaspoon dry mustard

1 tablespoon freshly ground black pepper

¾ teaspoon garlic salt

¼ cup grated Parmesan cheese

Combine all ingredients in food processor and process until smooth and well blended. Cover and chill.

*And Roses for the Table*

# Madalene's French Dressing

1½ cups vegetable or olive oil

2 eggs

⅓ cup white wine

⅓ cup white wine vinegar

⅓ cup water

½ to 1 teaspoon salt

½ teaspoon freshly ground white pepper

½ teaspoon paprika

1 tablespoon lemon thyme

2 tablespoons parsley

2 tablespoons finely chopped chives

Place all ingredients in blender container and blend until well combined. Taste for sharpness; add more salt or vinegar if needed. Chill and serve over greens or vegetables.

*Southern Herb Growing*

# Zippy Coleslaw

1 small head green cabbage

½ small onion, chopped

Salt and pepper to taste

2 tablespoons red wine vinegar

3 tablespoons olive oil

5 to 6 drops Tabasco sauce

2 tablespoons capers, drained

1½ cups mayonnaise

Shred cabbage with a knife, not a food processor. It should be slightly coarse and yield approximately 4 cups. Toss with onion in a bowl; season to taste with salt and pepper. In a separate bowl, combine remaining ingredients and whisk to blend well. Pour over the cabbage and toss to moisten cabbage. Chill well before serving.

Nancy Tarvin, Texas
*Kickin' Back in the Kitchen Cookbook*

# Jalapeño Coleslaw

2 cups thinly sliced cabbage (use packaged angel hair cabbage if you can find it)

½ red bell pepper, diced

¼ cup chopped green onion

1 small ripe tomato, diced

4 or 5 pickled jalapeño slices, finely chopped

Oil and vinegar or Italian dressing

Salt and freshly ground black pepper to taste

Combine all ingredients. Toss with oil and vinegar or Italian dressing. Season with salt and pepper. Serves 4 to 6.

*Texas Cookoff*

# Luby's Chopped Slaw

1 medium head (about 2 pounds) green cabbage, chopped

½ cup grated carrots

1 cup firmly packed finely chopped spinach leaves

1 cup mayonnaise

1 tablespoon milk

1 tablespoon granulated sugar

2 teaspoons white vinegar

¼ teaspoon freshly ground black pepper

¼ teaspoon kosher salt

In a large bowl, combine cabbage, carrots, and spinach. In a small bowl, gently whisk together mayonnaise, milk, sugar, vinegar, pepper, and salt until well blended. Pour over cabbage mixture and toss lightly to coat. Refrigerate. Serve well chilled. Serves 8.

**TIP:** To avoid a bitter slaw, discard the outside leaves of the cabbage.

*Luby's Recipes & Memories*

# Old-Fashioned Coleslaw

1 medium head cabbage, shredded

1 carrot, finely grated

1 green bell pepper, chopped

1 small onion, sliced

⅞ cup sugar

**Dressing**

1 cup cider vinegar

2 tablespoons sugar

¾ cup vegetable oil

1 tablespoon salt

1 tablespoon powdered mustard

1 tablespoon celery seed

Combine cabbage, carrot, green bell pepper, and onion. Pour the ⅞ cup sugar over all, but do not stir. In saucepan, combine the dressing ingredients and bring to a rolling boil. Pour immediately over cabbage and mix. Cover and refrigerate 4 to 6 hours. Mix and serve. Better after 2 to 3 days. Keeps in refrigerator up to 3 weeks. Serves 8.

Elenora Kohlenberg
*Gruene General Store Cookbook*

# Sweet Potato Slaw

½ cup mayonnaise

½ cup sour cream

2 tablespoons honey

2 tablespoons freshly squeezed lemon juice

1 teaspoon minced lemon zest

½ teaspoon salt

¼ teaspoon pepper

3 cups peeled, shredded raw sweet potatoes

1 medium apple, peeled, cored, and chopped (Granny Smith is good)

1 (8-ounce) can pineapple tidbits, drained

½ cup chopped pecans or walnuts

In a bowl, combine first 7 ingredients; blend until smooth. In a separate large bowl, combine potatoes, apple, pineapple, and nuts. Add dressing and toss to coat. Refrigerate for at least 1 hour. Serves 6 to 8.

*Kickin' Back in the Kitchen Cookbook*

# Wilted Lettuce Salad

¼ pound bacon

¼ cup chopped onion

1 tablespoon all-purpose flour

½ cup water

½ cup vinegar

½ teaspoon salt

1 tablespoon sugar

Your favorite fancy lettuce (endive, butter, etc.)

Chop bacon and fry until crisp. Remove from pan and set aside. Add onion to drippings and cook until transparent. Add flour and stir to blend into the drippings, leaving no traces of unblended flour. Add water, vinegar, salt, and sugar to the pan. Stir until mixture thickens slightly. Pour whole mixture over lettuce just before serving and toss with bacon. Lettuce will wilt. Serve immediately.

*Seasoned with Sun*

# Red Leaf Lettuce with Creamy Vinaigrette

**1 head red leaf lettuce, washed and torn**

## Creamy Vinaigrette

**1 tablespoon sour cream**

**2 tablespoons Dijon mustard**

**1 tablespoon red wine vinegar**

**½ teaspoon salt**

**Dash freshly ground black pepper**

**2 tablespoons green onions, tops and bottom, chopped**

**½ cup olive oil**

Combine all dressing ingredients except olive oil. Mix well. Slowly whisk in the oil, continuing to beat until thickened. Pour into tightly covered container and store in refrigerator. This dressing will keep in the refrigerator several weeks.

When ready to serve, place the lettuce in a salad bowl and add the dressing. Toss to coat all lettuce leaves. Serve.

*Of Magnolia and Mesquite*

# California Salad with Raspberry Vinaigrette

**2 heads Bibb lettuce**

**1 head green leaf lettuce**

**½ cup macadamia nuts**

**4 ripe avocados**

**Creamy Raspberry Vinaigrette (see recipe below)**

## Creamy Raspberry Vinaigrette

**3 tablespoons raspberry vinegar**

**1 tablespoon Dijon mustard**

**1 tablespoon water**

**Salt to taste**

**Pepper to taste**

**1 cup canola oil**

**1 tablespoon heavy cream**

Begin by making the vinaigrette. Combine the vinegar, Dijon mustard, water, salt, and pepper in a blender. Process until smooth. Add the oil and cream gradually, processing constantly for 30 seconds or until well blended. Refrigerate, tightly covered, until ready to serve.

To assemble the salad, rinse the lettuces and tear into bite-size pieces. Wrap in paper towels and place in a sealable plastic bag. Chill until ready to serve. Arrange the macadamia nuts on a baking sheet. Toast at 300 degrees for 10 minutes. Wrap the nuts in a clean tea towel and let cool. Chop the nuts coarsely in a food processor. Combine the lettuce and nuts in a large salad bowl. Slice the avocados and add to the salad. Pour the Creamy Raspberry Vinaigrette over the salad and toss to coat. Serve immediately. Serves 6.

*Dining without Reservations*

# Perini Ranch Salad

½ head green leaf lettuce

½ head romaine lettuce

½ head iceberg lettuce

¼ cup mushrooms

20 cherry tomatoes

½ red onion, sliced

6 to 8 green onions for garnish

## Dressing

1 cup buttermilk

1 cup Texas Mayonnaise (see recipe below)

1 large garlic clove, finely minced

1 to 2 green onions, with 2 inches of green top, thinly sliced

1 teaspoon finely minced fresh parsley or ½ teaspoon dried parsley

1 teaspoon finely minced oregano or ½ teaspoon dried oregano

½ teaspoon ground black pepper

½ teaspoon salt

Combine the dressing ingredients in a large jar. Shake vigorously to combine thoroughly. If time permits, refrigerate for 30 minutes to allow flavors to blend before serving time. Toss the salad ingredients with the dressing. Serves 6 to 8.

## Texas Mayonnaise

*(Makes approximately 1⅓ cups.)*

1 egg

1 teaspoon Dijon mustard or ½ teaspoon dry mustard

3 tablespoons fresh lemon juice or vinegar

Fresh parsley, basil, or oregano leaves (optional)

½ teaspoon salt

½ teaspoon ground red pepper

½ cup corn oil

½ cup olive oil

In a blender or food processor, place the egg, mustard, lemon juice, herbs, if desired, salt, and pepper. Blend for 1 minute. With blender or processor running, slowly add oils until mayonnaise is thick. Taste and add a little more salt or pepper, if you wish. You may also wish to add more lemon juice, if you prefer a sharper flavor and thinner consistency.

*Texas Cowboy Cooking*

# Citrus Salad with Green Chile and Honey Dressing

## Dressing

*(Makes about 2½ cups.)*

**1 cup sour cream**

**¼ cup honey**

**2 tablespoons Dijon mustard**

**2 tablespoons balsamic vinegar**

**Zest and juice of 1 large lemon**

**¼ cup minced flat-leaf parsley**

**6 fresh jalapeño chiles, seeds and veins removed, minced**

**3 fresh serrano chiles, seeds and veins removed, minced**

**¼ cup finely chopped onion**

**1 teaspoon salt**

**½ teaspoon freshly ground black pepper**

## Salad

**½ head romaine lettuce, washed, dried, and torn into bite-size pieces**

**½ head escarole, torn into bite-size pieces**

**¼ cup tightly packed whole mint leaves**

**¼ cup tightly packed whole cilantro leaves**

**1 large Ruby Sweet or Rio Star grapefruit**

**2 medium navel oranges**

**1 large ripe Haas avocado, peeled, pitted, and sliced**

**Slivered red onion**

Prepare the dressing at least 8 hours before serving to allow time for the flavors to meld together. Combine all ingredients in work bowl of food processor fitted with steel blade. Process until smooth. Refrigerate.

When you're ready to put the salad together, segment the grapefruit by slicing off the rind and all of the white pith. Then cut out the segments of fruit from between the membranes. Segment the oranges likewise.

Toss the torn romaine and escarole with the mint and cilantro leaves. Arrange a bed of the lettuce mix on individual chilled salad plates. Arrange some of the grapefruit and orange segments and avocado slices on the greens. Scatter a few slices of red onion over the top. Drizzle desired portion of the dressing over the top and serve. Serves 4 to 6.

*Texas on the Plate*

# Endive, Bacon, and Pecan Salad

3 cups Boston lettuce, loosely packed

2 cups curly endive, loosely packed

1 medium red onion, sliced

¾ cup pecans, coarsely chopped and toasted

6 bacon slices

1½ teaspoons brown sugar

¼ cup red wine vinegar

¼ teaspoon salt

¼ teaspoon black pepper

Combine lettuce, endive, red onion, and pecans in a large bowl; set aside.

Cook bacon until crisp; remove bacon, reserving 2 tablespoons of drippings in skillet. Crumble bacon and set aside.

Add brown sugar, red wine vinegar, salt, and pepper to skillet; cook over low heat until thoroughly heated. Pour over lettuce; toss gently. Scatter crumbled bacon over lettuce; serve immediately. Serves 6.

*Seasoned with Fun*

# Mexican Salad with Avocado Dressing

## Avocado Dressing

1 large avocado, peeled, pitted, and mashed

¾ cup sour cream

1½ tablespoons fresh lime juice

2 garlic cloves, crushed

½ teaspoon ground cumin

¼ teaspoon salt, or to taste

¼ teaspoon cayenne pepper

2 tablespoons vegetable oil

## Salad

3 ripe tomatoes, cut into wedges

¾ cup sliced ripe olives

1 small purple onion, sliced into rings

6 cups shredded iceberg lettuce

3 tablespoons chopped cilantro

To make the dressing, combine avocado, sour cream, lime juice, garlic, cumin, salt, and pepper in work bowl of food processor. Process until smooth. With machine running, add the vegetable oil in a slow, steady stream through the feed tube. Turn out into a bowl and cover tightly. Chill for at least 3 hours.

To assemble the salad, arrange tomatoes, olives, and onions on shredded lettuce. Scatter the cilantro over the top. Drizzle the dressing over the top of the salad and serve. Serves 8.

*Texas Blossoms*

# Greek Salad

1 head romaine lettuce, cut or torn into 2-inch pieces

1 fresh cucumber, peeled and sliced

1 cup pitted kalamata olives

½ cup stemmed and diced pepperoncini peppers

1 cup halved cherry tomatoes

1 cup Greek Salad Dressing (see recipe below)

1 cup crumbled feta cheese

½ cup sliced red onions

2 cups prepared croutons

## Greek Salad Dressing

*(Makes 3 cups.)*

1 cup red wine vinegar

¼ cup fresh lemon juice

¼ cup white vinegar

1 tablespoon dried basil leaves

1 teaspoon dried oregano leaves

1½ teaspoons kosher salt

1 teaspoon freshly ground black pepper

3 tablespoons capers

¾ cup vegetable oil

¾ cup extra-virgin olive oil

Place lettuce in a large bowl with cucumber, olives, pepperoncini peppers, and cherry tomato halves. Refrigerate.

To make the dressing, in a large bowl, whisk together red wine vinegar, lemon juice, white vinegar, basil, oregano, salt, black pepper, and capers until blended. Slowly whisk in the oils.

Toss chilled salad with 1 cup of the Greek Salad Dressing. Just before serving, top with feta cheese, red onions, and your favorite croutons. Serves 8.

**TIP:** As the Greek Salad Dressing sits, the oil and vinegars may separate. The dressing is best stored in a container with a tight-fitting lid in the refrigerator. Bring it to room temperature and shake well before using.

*Luby's Recipes & Memories*

# Goat Cheese Potato Pancakes over Mixed Greens

## Vinaigrette

1 tablespoon Spanish sherry vinegar or balsamic vinegar

½ teaspoon Dijon mustard

Salt and pepper to taste

3 tablespoons extra-virgin olive oil

1 tablespoon minced shallot

1 small garlic clove, minced

2 tablespoons finely sliced fresh chives

## Potato Pancakes

1 pound baking potatoes, peeled and coarsely grated

Salt and pepper to taste

1 tablespoon olive oil

4 ounces fresh goat cheese

1 tablespoon finely sliced chives

Additional 1½ teaspoons olive oil

## Salad

4 cups (4 ounces) loosely packed mixed baby lettuce, such as oak leaf, mustard greens, Bibb, radicchio, frisée, spinach, or arugula

Salt and freshly ground black pepper to taste

To make the vinaigrette, whisk the sherry vinegar, Dijon mustard, salt, and pepper in a bowl. Whisk in the olive oil, shallot, and garlic until emulsified. Stir in the chives. The vinaigrette may be prepared in advance, but use within 1 hour, as the garlic flavor tends to become predominant.

To make the pancakes, press the moisture from the potatoes. Toss them in a bowl with salt and pepper. Heat 1 tablespoon olive oil in a large skillet over medium-high heat until hot. Spread a ¼-inch layer of the potatoes in the skillet, forming a round pancake about 2½ inches in diameter. Spread ¼ of the goat cheese over the potato layer, not quite to the edge. Sprinkle with ¼ of the chives. Cover with another thin layer of potatoes; making sure the goat cheese is completely covered. Repeat the process with the remaining potatoes, remaining goat cheese, and remaining chives to make 3 more pancakes. Cook for 3 to 4 minutes or until the potatoes are golden brown. Turn the pancakes carefully, with a spatula, and add 1½ teaspoons olive oil to the skillet. Cook for 3 minutes longer, or until golden brown; drain.

To make the salad, toss the mixed lettuce with the vinaigrette in a bowl. Season with salt and freshly ground black pepper to taste. Arrange a mound of the greens in center of each of 4 serving plates. Top each serving with a potato pancake. Serve immediately. Serves 4.

*Austin Entertains*

# Monterey Salad and Dressing

½ head leaf lettuce, washed, dried, and picked

1 jicama, peeled and julienned

2 cups fresh spinach, washed and picked

1 cup chopped red cabbage

1 red onion, sliced into rings

2 radishes, sliced thin

1 orange, peeled and sectioned

## Dressing

¾ cup unsweetened frozen orange juice concentrate

3 tablespoons balsamic vinegar

3 tablespoons canola oil

¼ teaspoon dry mustard

Black pepper and salt to taste

Make the dressing. Mix orange juice and vinegar. Whisk in oil and seasonings, blending well. Arrange vegetables and orange sections on platter. Spoon dressing over salad. Serves 8.

Billie Shingleton
*Flavors of Fredericksburg*

# Orange Almond Salad

Mixed salad greens, about 3 cups

½ cup slivered blanched almonds

2 oranges, sectioned with membranes removed

## Dressing

2 tablespoons heavy cream

¼ cup olive oil

¼ teaspoon sugar

¼ teaspoon dried dill

Pinch of salt

Pinch of black pepper

1 green onion, finely chopped

2 tablespoons apple cider vinegar

Combine greens, orange sections, and almonds in a salad bowl or on 4 salad plates. Whisk together all dressing ingredients except the vinegar. When homogenous, drizzle in the vinegar and whisk to blend. Pour over salad right before serving. Serves 4.

*The Texas Provincial Kitchen Cookbook*

# Lamar Park Salad

2 ears corn, cooked, kernels cut from cob

1 bunch arugula

1 bunch red leaf lettuce

2 bunches watercress

½ cup red wine vinegar

1 large shallot

12 sun-dried tomatoes, rehydrated

3 tablespoons balsamic vinegar

8 large fresh basil leaves

⅓ cup olive oil

Combine corn and next 3 ingredients in large bowl. Place all remaining ingredients in a blender and pulse until smooth. Toss salad with dressing. Yields 4 to 6 servings.

*¡Viva! Tradiciones*

# Mushrooms with Asparagus and Greens

1 cup extra-virgin olive oil

½ cup balsamic vinegar

1 tablespoon minced fresh basil

1 teaspoon minced garlic

1 teaspoon chopped shallot

⅛ teaspoon salt

⅛ teaspoon pepper

16 fresh shiitake mushrooms, stems removed

20 spears fresh asparagus, cut into 5-inch pieces

6 cups mixed salad greens

1 cup chopped red tomato

1 egg yolk

Whisk the olive oil, balsamic vinegar, basil, garlic, shallot, salt, and pepper in a bowl until blended. Add the mushrooms and toss gently to coat. Marinate at room temperature for 1 hour or longer. The mushrooms will absorb the vinegar before the oil. Do not refrigerate. (Refrigeration could cause the oil to solidify, preventing the marinade from being absorbed.)

Blanch the asparagus until crisp-tender in salted boiling water in a saucepan. Drain and plunge into a bowl of ice water. Let stand until cool; drain.

Arrange the salad greens on the bottom half of each of 4 salad plates. Fan the asparagus over the chopped tomato on the top halves of the plates. Drain the mushrooms, reserving the marinade. Arrange the mushrooms in the center of the plates, overlapping both the asparagus and salad greens.

Whisk the egg yolk vigorously into the reserved marinade to form a strong emulsion, adding additional balsamic vinegar if needed. Drizzle over the salad and serve at once. Serves 4.

*Austin Entertains*

# Spinach Salad with Sweet-Sour Dressing

1 (10-ounce) bag baby spinach leaves, rinsed and chilled until crisp

1 (8-ounce) can water chestnuts, drained and sliced

1 (16-ounce) can bean sprouts, drained

8 bacon strips, cooked until crisp and crumbled

4 hard-boiled eggs, sliced

### Sweet-Sour Dressing

1 cup canola oil

¾ cup sugar

¼ cup apple cider vinegar

⅓ cup ketchup

2 tablespoons Worcestershire sauce

1 medium onion, chopped

To make the dressing, combine all ingredients and whisk to blend well. Refrigerate until ready to use.

Combine all salad ingredients and toss to blend. Add enough of the dressing to moisten to your taste. Toss again and serve. Serves 6.

Ralph and Jeannine Bowles, Washington
*Kickin' Back in the Kitchen Cookbook*

# Spinach Salad with Prosciutto Dressing

### Prosciutto Dressing

6 tablespoons extra-virgin olive oil

¼ cup chopped prosciutto, about 1½ ounces

2 tablespoons minced garlic

6 tablespoons dry white wine

6 tablespoons fresh lemon juice

2 tablespoons sugar

Salt and pepper to taste

### Salad

1 (10-ounce) bag baby spinach leaves

2½ cups sliced mushrooms

½ cup chopped toasted walnuts

½ cup freshly grated Parmesan cheese

To make the Prosciutto Dressing, heat olive oil in a small skillet over medium heat. Add prosciutto and garlic. Sauté for 3 minutes; add white wine, lemon juice, and sugar. Simmer for 5 minutes. Transfer to a small bowl and season to taste with salt and pepper. Allow dressing to cool.

To assemble the salad, combine the spinach, mushrooms, walnuts, and cheese in a large bowl. Add the dressing to the bowl and toss salad to coat all ingredients well. Serves 4 to 6.

*Texas Blossoms*

# Spinach Salad with Egg and Bacon Dressing

1 cup mayonnaise

2 tablespoons buttermilk

1 tablespoon fresh lemon juice

2 hard-boiled eggs, grated

4 bacon slices, cooked until crisp,
    drained, and crumbled

Salt and pepper to taste

2 green onions, chopped, including green
    tops

1 bunch fresh spinach

Fresh mushrooms, sliced (optional)

Whisk together mayonnaise, buttermilk, and lemon juice. Add eggs, bacon, salt, pepper, and green onions. Chill. Mixture should be thick. Wash, drain, and tear spinach. Add sliced mushrooms. Just before serving, add dressing and toss. Dressing will keep for one week in refrigerator. Serves 6.

Jan McManus LeBlanc
*Lagniappe*

# Spinach and Pear Salad with Rosemary Vinaigrette

4 cups baby spinach leaves

4 teaspoons coarsely chopped pecans,
    toasted

Rosemary Vinaigrette (see recipe below)

2 ripe pears, thinly sliced

¼ cup crumbled blue cheese or
    Gorgonzola cheese

## Rosemary Vinaigrette

½ cup extra-virgin olive oil

2 tablespoons red wine vinegar

2 tablespoons rice vinegar

1½ tablespoons minced shallots

1½ teaspoons chopped fresh rosemary

Make the vinaigrette by combining the olive oil, wine vinegar, rice vinegar, shallots, and rosemary in a jar with a tight-fitting lid. Seal jar tightly and shake to mix. Store in refrigerator until ready to use. Shake well before using.

To assemble the salad, toss the spinach and pecans in a salad bowl. Add just enough of the Rosemary Vinaigrette to coat the spinach; toss gently. Divide the spinach mixture evenly among 4 salad plates and top evenly with the pears and cheese. Serves 4.

*Dallas Dish*

# Nantucket Bleu Spinach Salad

2 bunches leaf spinach, stemmed, washed, and dried well

1 pint fresh blueberries

⅔ cup blue cheese, crumbled

½ cup chopped pecans, toasted

### Nantucket Dressing

1 green onion, minced

½ pint fresh blueberries

1 teaspoon salt

3 tablespoons sugar

⅓ cup raspberry vinegar

1 cup vegetable oil

To make the dressing, combine green onion, blueberries, salt, sugar, vinegar, and oil. Pour over salad and toss. Serves 4.

*Perennial Favorites*

# Pear and Chèvre Salad

### Salad

6 cups baby greens

1 large firm pear, cored and diced

½ cup thinly sliced green onions

2 ounces goat cheese

⅓ cup toasted walnuts

### Dressing

½ cup fresh strawberries, hulled

¼ cup white wine vinegar

½ cup canola oil

1 tablespoon sugar

½ teaspoon salt

½ teaspoon pepper

Combine all dressing ingredients in blender and blend until smooth. Refrigerate dressing until ready to serve. Shake well before using.

Toss greens with pears and onions. Drop goat cheese by the ½ teaspoon into salad. Toss salad with dressing and scatter the walnuts on top. Makes 3 to 4 servings.

*¡Viva! Tradiciones*

# Pear and Feta Salad with Pecans

| | |
|---|---|
| 1 head romaine lettuce, or any mixed salad greens | 4 ripe pears, peeled and sliced |
| | 1 cup feta cheese, crumbled |

Arrange greens on individual salad plates; divide pear slices among the plates, arranging in a circular pattern; sprinkle feta cheese over the greens and pears. Dribble 1½ tablespoons of Perfect Dressing over the salads and top with a scattering of the Sugared Pecans.

## Sugared Pecans

| | |
|---|---|
| ¼ cup sugar | 2 cups pecans |
| 1 egg white | Dash of salt |

Preheat oven to 325 degrees. Beat sugar, egg white, and salt with a fork until frothy. Add pecans and mix to coat pecans with the mixture. Pour pecans onto a foil-lined cookie sheet in a single layer and bake for 20 minutes until crisp. Cool.

## Perfect Dressing

| | |
|---|---|
| 2 cups olive oil | 1 teaspoon salt |
| ¾ cup raspberry vinegar | ¼ teaspoon onion powder |
| 1 teaspoon sugar | |

Blend all ingredients in food processor until completely emulsified. This dressing is good on all types of salads, but especially on those that need a tart sweetness.

*Gruene General Store Cookbook*

# Hill Country Peach Salad
# with Peach-Lavender Vinaigrette

16 cups seasonal mixed greens

1½ cups crumbled Gorgonzola cheese

¾ cup toasted pecans

6 peaches, peeled and sliced

## Peach-Lavender Vinaigrette

1 cup rice wine vinegar

2 teaspoons culinary lavender flowers

2 tablespoons Dijon mustard

2 teaspoons salt

2 teaspoons black pepper

1 cup peach preserves

2 cups canola oil

Make the Peach-Lavender Vinaigrette. Combine all ingredients except peach preserves and canola oil in work bowl of food processor fitted with steel blade; process until smooth and well blended. Stop machine and add the peach preserves. With machine running, add the canola oil in a slow, steady stream through the feed tube. Process until only small pieces of peaches from the preserves remain.

Place seasonal greens in serving bowl, sprinkle with Gorgonzola, and add the toasted pecans and sliced peaches. Toss the salad with desired amount of dressing and serve at once. Remaining vinaigrette can be stored in the refrigerator for up to a month. Serves 6 as entrée salad, or 8 as side salad.

Silver K Café, Johnson City, Texas
*The Texas Hill Country*

# Texas Peach Salad

1 French baguette, cut into ½-inch diagonal slices

¼ cup butter, melted

¼ cup fresh cheese (from cow's milk or goat's milk), softened

1 teaspoon chopped fresh herbs (thyme, basil, and oregano)

8 ounces mixed greens (arugula, endive, and mâche)

¼ cup Candied Pecans (see recipe below)

2 Texas peaches, peeled and diced

¼ cup Texas Peach Vinaigrette (see recipe below)

## Texas Peach Vinaigrette

4 Texas peaches, peeled and diced, divided

2 tablespoons peach nectar

1 shallot, minced

2 tablespoons rice wine vinegar

¼ cup vegetable oil

Salt and black pepper to taste

## Candied Pecans

½ cup pecan halves

1 teaspoon vegetable oil

1 cup confectioners' sugar

For the vinaigrette, puree 2 peaches with peach nectar in bowl using a hand blender. Add the shallot, vinegar, and remaining diced peaches. In a slow stream, whisk in the oil to create a creamy emulsion. Adjust seasoning. Allow flavors to marry a few hours before serving.

For the nuts, toss pecans with oil. Place on a baking sheet. Bake at 350 degrees for 10 minutes, stirring every 3 minutes. Toss with confectioners' sugar. Allow to cool. Store in an airtight container until ready to use.

To plate the salad, dip baguette slices in butter. Toast or broil until golden brown. Combine the cheese and herbs; spread over bread. Broil until hot and bubbly. In a large mixing bowl, toss the greens, pecans, diced peaches, and vinaigrette. Arrange on plates and top with toast. Serves 4.

*The Kitchen Table*

# Cranberry Freeze

1 (16-ounce) can whole cranberry sauce

1 (8-ounce) can crushed pineapple, drained

1 cup sour cream

¾ cup chopped nuts

¼ cup sugar

In large bowl, combine all ingredients; blend well. Spoon into a 6-cup fluted tube pan. Freeze. Let soften slightly before serving. Serves 6.

*Of Magnolia and Mesquite*

# Cranberry Salad

1½ cups water

1½ cups granulated sugar

1 package (12 ounces) fresh cranberries

2 navel oranges, peeled, sectioned, and cubed

1 red apple, cored and sliced

1 banana, sliced

2 tablespoons chopped pecans

In a medium saucepan, combine water, sugar, and cranberries. Cook over medium heat, stirring occasionally, just until cranberries begin to open. Transfer to a large bowl. Refrigerate 2 hours. Fold in oranges, apple, banana, and pecans. Refrigerate. Serve well chilled. Serves 8.

**TIP:** To store cranberries in the freezer, wrap the original bag in foil or place it in a freezer bag. Use Gala apples for a crisp texture with a sweet taste.

*Luby's Recipes & Memories*

# Tropical Fruit Salad with Fresh Mint Dressing

## Salad

1 medium pineapple

1 kiwi, peeled and thinly sliced

1 large banana, peeled and cut into
    ½-inch chunks

2 medium peaches, peeled and sliced

1 cup whole strawberries, halved

3 tablespoons slivered almonds, toasted

## Fresh Mint Dressing

1 cup sugar

⅓ cup water

½ cup loosely packed fresh mint leaves

To make dressing, combine sugar and water in a small saucepan; bring to a boil, stirring occasionally. Remove from heat.

Combine sugar mixture and mint leaves in container of electric blender; process until leaves are finely minced. Chill 2 to 3 hours before using. Makes ⅔ cup.

To make salad, cut pineapple in half lengthwise. Scoop out pulp, leaving shells ¼ to ½ inch thick; set aside.

Cut pineapple pulp into bite-size pieces, discarding the core. Combine pineapple chunks, kiwi, banana, peaches, and strawberries; toss gently. Spoon the fruit into the pineapple shells. Sprinkle with toasted almonds. Serve with Fresh Mint Dressing.

*Of Magnolia and Mesquite*

# Sliced Tomatoes and Mozzarella with Pesto

1½ cups packed fresh basil leaves

½ cup olive oil

⅓ cup freshly grated Parmesan cheese

¼ cup pine nuts, toasted

2 garlic cloves

4 large ripe tomatoes, sliced

4 ounces smoked or regular mozzarella
    cheese, sliced

Fresh basil leaves for garnish

Puree the first 5 ingredients in food processor, stopping occasionally to scrape sides of bowl. (Pesto can be made 1 week ahead. Transfer to a container. Pour enough oil over the top just to cover; chill. Stir before using.)

Overlap the tomato and cheese slices on platter. Top with small dollops of pesto. Garnish with basil leaves.

*And Roses for the Table*

# Spicy Red Potato Salad

2½ pounds small red potatoes, halved

½ cup mayonnaise

1 tablespoon lime juice

½ teaspoon cumin

½ teaspoon Tabasco sauce

¼ teaspoon cayenne pepper

1 tablespoon Dijon mustard

1 tablespoon chopped fresh garlic

1 teaspoon kosher salt

½ teaspoon freshly ground black pepper

¼ cup sliced green onions

¼ cup diced red onions

½ cup diced tomatoes

2 tablespoons chopped fresh cilantro

¼ cup canned green chiles, diced

Place potatoes in a large saucepan and cover with cold water. Boil until potatoes are tender but not mushy. Drain into a colander and let them cool just enough to handle. Place mayonnaise, lime juice, cumin, Tabasco sauce, cayenne pepper, Dijon mustard, garlic, salt, and black pepper into a blender. Cover with lid and puree together a few seconds until smooth. In a large bowl, fold together potatoes, puree, green onions, red onions, tomatoes, cilantro, and green chiles. Refrigerate. Serve well chilled. Serves 8.

> **TIP:** The spicy flavors can be kicked up by increasing the amount of green chiles or replacing them with freshly chopped jalapeños.

*Luby's Recipes & Memories*

# Cynthia's Jalapeño Potato Salad

10 cups cubed, boiled, and peeled
  potatoes (about 5 pounds)

8 boiled eggs, coarsely chopped

10 celery stalks, diced

10 green onions, chopped

1 large yellow onion, diced

3 to 4 cups good-quality mayonnaise

½ cup chopped pickled jalapeños

2 tablespoons juice from jalapeños

¼ cup chopped parsley

2 teaspoons ground cumin

1 tablespoon black pepper

1 tablespoon salt

In a large bowl, combine potatoes, celery, and both onions. Combine remaining ingredients and add to potato mixture. Mix well and chill several hours or overnight. Serves 24.

*The Peach Tree Tea Room Cookbook*

# German Potato Salad

2½ pounds small red new potatoes (unpeeled), scrubbed and sliced into bite-size pieces

6 smoked bacon slices, fried crisp and crumbled, drippings reserved

1 medium onion, chopped

1½ tablespoons all-purpose flour

¼ cup firmly packed light brown sugar

1 teaspoon paprika

½ teaspoon celery salt

½ teaspoon freshly ground black pepper

⅓ cup apple cider vinegar

⅔ cup hot beef stock

1½ tablespoons minced flat-leaf parsley

Place potato slices in a 4-quart saucepan and add cold water to cover. Bring the potatoes to a boil, then simmer for 20 minutes, or until potatoes are tender but not mushy. Drain and place in a large bowl; set aside to keep warm.

Heat the reserved bacon drippings in a heavy 12-inch skillet over medium heat. Add the onion and cook until it is wilted and transparent, about 7 minutes. Stir in the flour all at once, blending well. Cook, stirring for 3 to 4 minutes. Add the brown sugar, paprika, celery salt, pepper, vinegar, and hot beef stock. Bring to a full boil and stir until thickened. Stir in the crumbled bacon. Pour the dressing over the potatoes, add parsley, and stir to coat the potatoes thoroughly with the dressing. Serve hot or warm. Serves 6.

*Texas on the Plate*

# Pea Salad

½ cup mayonnaise, or to taste

Juice of 1 lemon

½ jar capers

2 tablespoons caper juice

1 can Le Sueur peas, drained

1 package baby lima beans, cooked

1 small can sliced black olives, drained

1 small can sliced green olives

1 small onion, grated

Salt and pepper to taste

Mix ½ cup mayonnaise with lemon juice and caper juice. Set aside. Combine all remaining ingredients. Add mayonnaise mixture and mix well. Season to taste with salt and pepper. Chill at least 1 hour. Serves 4.

Carol Spears Harris, M. A. Tyler Ranch, Tilden, Texas
*Stolen Recipes*

# Black Bean Salad

3 (15-ounce) cans black beans

½ cup olive oil

Juice of 1 lime

3 tablespoons red wine vinegar

4 cloves garlic, minced or pressed

½ cup purple onion, chopped

¼ cup fresh cilantro, chopped fine

1 cup salsa

½ cup sliced black olives

2 cans whole-kernel corn (optional)

Drain beans and place in a bowl. Combine oil, lime juice, vinegar, and garlic; pour over beans. Add onion, cilantro, salsa, olives, and corn, if desired, and toss. Chill several hours. Serves 10 to 12.

You may also serve this as an appetizer with tortilla chips.

*The San Antonio Tex-Mex Cookbook*

# Blue Dog Black Bean Salad

⅓ cup corn oil

¼ cup fresh lime juice

3 tablespoons chopped cilantro

1 tablespoon minced pickled jalapeños

1 teaspoon minced garlic

½ teaspoon ground cumin

½ teaspoon salt

1 (16-ounce) can black beans, rinsed and drained

½ cup chopped red onion

½ cup chopped red bell pepper

½ cup chopped yellow bell pepper

In a large bowl, stir the oil, lime juice, cilantro, jalapeños, garlic, cumin, and salt. Add beans. Add onions and peppers; stir until all ingredients are well coated. Cover and refrigerate several hours or overnight. Can also be used as a dip. Serves 6.

Blue Dog Inn, New Braunfels, Texas
*Gruene General Store Cookbook*

# Johnny's Taco Salad

## Taco Meat

2 tablespoons vegetable oil

2 medium white onions, peeled and finely chopped

4 garlic cloves, peeled and minced

2 pounds ground beef chuck

2 teaspoons chili powder

1 teaspoon ground cumin

1 teaspoon dried oregano

½ teaspoon cayenne pepper

Kosher salt and freshly ground pepper

## Salad

Vegetable or peanut oil for frying tortillas

6 (8-inch) flour tortillas or 4 store-bought flour tortilla bowls

1 head iceberg lettuce, shredded

1 large tomato, cored and diced

2 cups grated Monterey Jack cheese

1 cup sour cream

2 small to medium avocados, peeled, pitted, and diced

Corn chips (optional)

To prepare the taco meat, heat the oil in a large skillet over medium heat. Add the onion and garlic, and sauté for 2 minutes, or until translucent. Add the beef and stir to break it up. Cook for about 10 minutes, or until browned.

Stir in the chili powder, cumin, oregano, cayenne pepper, salt, and pepper to taste and continue cooking for 2 more minutes. Remove from the heat and set aside.

To prepare the tortilla shells, preheat the oil to 350 degrees in a heavy 4-quart Dutch oven. You will need at least 5 to 6 inches of oil.

Use a large ladle and push each tortilla down in the oil, holding it in place with the ladle. The sides will naturally turn upward to form a bowl as long as you keep the tortilla submerged in the center with the ladle. It will take about 4 minutes until they are lightly browned.

Cool the tortillas before making the salad. You can make these shells a day ahead of time if you wish. Cool them and store in an airtight container.

To serve, place a tortilla shell on a plate. Layer first with ¼ of the shredded lettuce, diced tomato, and hot taco meat. Repeat 2 more times. Top with a little more lettuce, Monterey Jack cheese, a dollop of sour cream, avocado, and diced tomato. Serves 4 to 6.

*Ciao Y'All*

# Tabouli

⅓ cup fine-grain bulgur wheat

4 green onions, sliced thin, including green tops

1 cup minced fresh parsley

¼ cup minced fresh mint leaves

½ of a medium cucumber, peeled, seeded, and finely chopped

⅛ teaspoon ground allspice

⅛ teaspoon ground cinnamon

⅛ teaspoon freshly grated nutmeg

1½ tablespoons extra-virgin olive oil

1½ tablespoons freshly squeezed lemon juice

Salt and freshly ground black pepper to taste

2 medium tomatoes, seeded and cut into tiny dice

Green leaf lettuce leaves

Pita bread

Place the bulgur wheat in a fine-meshed wire strainer and rinse under cold water. Drain, then squeeze dry in a clean towel. Combine green onions, parsley, mint, cucumber, allspice, cinnamon, nutmeg, olive oil, and lemon juice in a medium bowl. Add the bulgur wheat and stir to blend well. Season with salt and pepper. Cover the bowl with a clean towel and allow bulgur to soften overnight, refrigerated. Before serving, stir in the tomatoes. Serve on lettuce leaves with pita bread. Makes about 2½ cups.

> **NOTE:** Bulgur wheat is made from wheat kernels that have been steamed, dried, and crushed. It comes in fine, medium, and coarse grinds and has a tender, chewy texture. It can be found in specialty markets or Middle Eastern food stores.

Terry Thompson-Anderson

# Pasta San Antonio

1 pound dried pasta (corkscrew or fusilli)

1 teaspoon olive oil

½ cup chopped red onion

1 cup chopped celery (optional)

1 red bell pepper, chopped

½ cup black olives, sliced or halved

1 cup salsa

3 tablespoons olive oil

3 tablespoons fresh lime juice

1 teaspoon dry mustard

¼ cup fresh cilantro, chopped fine

½ teaspoon dried oregano

2 garlic cloves, minced or pressed

1 teaspoon Worcestershire sauce

Cook pasta according to package directions. Drain and run under cold tap water to cool. Drain again. Toss with olive oil to prevent sticking. Add onion, celery, bell pepper, and olives; toss.

Combine remaining ingredients, blending well to make a dressing. Pour over pasta mixture and chill before serving. Serves 8 to 10.

*The San Antonio Tex-Mex Cookbook*

# Shrimp and Pasta Salad with Basil and Garlic Dressing

## Basil and Garlic Dressing

2 tablespoons red wine vinegar

1 tablespoon Dijon mustard

3 large garlic cloves, minced

½ teaspoon salt

Pinch of freshly ground black pepper

½ teaspoon Tabasco sauce

1 heaping teaspoon minced fresh basil

½ cup extra-virgin olive oil

## Salad

1 (4-ounce) jar marinated artichoke hearts, drained and chopped

½ cup sliced ripe olives

6 oil-packed sun-dried tomatoes, chopped fine

1 teaspoon crushed red pepper flakes

½ teaspoon salt

1 pound small shrimp (70–90 count), boiled, peeled, and deveined

½ pound penne rigate pasta or other tubular pasta, cooked al dente and drained

½ cup grated Parmesan cheese

Red-tipped lettuce leaves, washed and dried

Prepare the dressing by combining all ingredients except olive oil in work bowl of food processor fitted with steel blade. Process until smooth. With processor running, add the olive oil in a slow, steady stream through the feed tube until all is added. Process an additional 15 seconds to form a strong emulsion. Refrigerate until needed.

To prepare the salad, combine all ingredients, except lettuce leaves, in a large bowl. Toss to blend well. Add the dressing and stir to incorporate. Refrigerate until ready to serve.

To serve, place lettuce leaves on individual serving plates and spoon a portion of the salad on each. Serves 4 to 6.

*Texas on the Plate*

# Tangy Shrimp and Bean Salad

2 cups cooked fresh pinto beans or frozen lima beans

1 cup sliced celery

½ cup chopped green onions, with tops

¼ cup chopped pimiento or red bell pepper

½ cup pitted ripe olives, halved

¼ cup sliced radishes

¾ pound shrimp, cooked and peeled

1 garlic clove, minced

1 tablespoon chopped lemon thyme

½ teaspoon paprika

Black pepper to taste

½ cup white wine vinegar or fresh lemon juice

½ cup salad oil

½ teaspoon Tabasco sauce

Prepare vegetables and combine with shrimp in salad bowl. Set aside. Blend the garlic, thyme, paprika, pepper, vinegar, oil, and Tabasco sauce until smooth. Pour dressing over salad and chill thoroughly. Serves 8.

*Southern Herb Growing*

# Crab-Pecan Salad

1 cup mayonnaise, preferably homemade

1 tablespoon fresh lemon juice

1 teaspoon Dijon mustard

½ cup minced fresh parsley

½ cup minced fresh dill, or 2 to 3 teaspoons dried dill

½ cup fresh chives, chopped

1½ pounds lump crabmeat, broken up

⅓ cup thinly sliced celery (1 small stalk)

Tender leaves from large head of Boston lettuce, washed and well dried

½ cup (about 2 ounces) pecan halves, slivered and lightly toasted

Lemon wedges for garnish

In a small bowl, stir the mayonnaise with the lemon juice and mustard until blended.

Set aside 1 tablespoon each of the parsley and dill and 1 teaspoon of the chives for garnish. Fold the remaining parsley, dill, and chives into the mayonnaise.

In a medium bowl, toss the crabmeat with the celery; gently fold about ⅔ cup of the mayonnaise into the crab mixture (enough to moisten and flavor the salad).

Arrange the lettuce leaves on a chilled dinner plate or a large platter; loosely mound the crabmeat on the leaves. Sprinkle the reserved parsley, dill, and chives and the pecan halves attractively on top. Garnish with the lemon wedges. Serve with the remaining mayonnaise.

*Of Magnolia and Mesquite*

# Jaxon's Chicken-Pecan Salad with Curry

¼ cup sour cream

¼ cup mayonnaise

2 tablespoons cider vinegar

½ teaspoon curry powder

¼ teaspoon salt

⅛ teaspoon white pepper

1 cup finely chopped celery

1 teaspoon grated onion

2 cups cooked, chopped chicken

½ cup chopped pecans

2 avocados, peeled, seeded, and halved

Combine all ingredients except avocados. Stir to blend well. Serve mounded in avocado halves. The pecans add the crunch to this lovely luncheon salad. Serves 4.

*Seasoned with Sun*

# Chicken Salad Tujacue

4 whole chicken breasts

1 (14-ounce) can chicken broth or 1 pint chicken stock

1 teaspoon salt

¼ teaspoon pepper

1 cup Italian salad dressing

2 cups finely chopped celery

1 shallot, finely chopped

2 hard-boiled eggs, finely chopped

¼ cup toasted almond slivers

½ cup (scant) mayonnaise

¼ teaspoon mustard

Salt and pepper to taste

Simmer chicken breasts in broth or stock with salt and pepper until real tender, about 20 to 25 minutes. Allow the breasts to cool in the broth, then remove skin and bones and cut into bite-size pieces. Marinate chicken pieces in Italian salad dressing overnight. On the next day, combine the remaining ingredients, blending well. Stir into the chicken and chill. Serves 6 to 8.

Charleen Miller
*Flavors of Fredericksburg*

# Smokehouse Turkey and Bacon Salad

2 cups Smokehouse Smoked Turkey, shredded

¾ cup chopped celery

½ pound Smokehouse Bacon, cooked crisp and crumbled

¼ cup sweet pickle relish

¼ to ½ cup good-quality mayonnaise

Scatter the bacon bits over the smoked turkey and celery.

Add sweet relish and toss with enough mayonnaise to lightly coat the mixture, but not overpower the rich smoky flavor. (It's critical to add just the right amount of mayonnaise.)

Serve on sandwiches or stuff into a ripe tomato. Serves 6.

**EDITOR'S NOTE:** Smokehouse Smoked Turkey and Smokehouse Bacon are New Braunfels Smokehouse products.

*New Braunfels Smokehouse*

## Soups & Chilies

If you're looking to generate some controversy, just start arguing with a Texan about the best way to make chili. Trust me, every born and bred Texan has his or her family's passed-down chili traditions and the secretly guarded family recipe. And you won't be changing their minds about how to make chili.

There are as many varieties of chili as there are people who love it. There are the advocates of chili with beans, opposed by those would never, ever put a bean in chili. Here are folks who swear only ground beef or venison will do, and those who will use only meaty chunks of beef chuck. Chili cook-offs are big business in Texas. There are chili cooking teams that have been together for years, making the circuit of the cook-offs every year whether they ever win or not. It's all for the fun of doing it. But however you feel about the subject of chili, it's a tradition that goes back to the roots of our Texan culture. And you'd better have some good corn bread to serve alongside!

Soup is one of my favorite food categories. Sometimes nothing satisfies like a good bowl of soup with a nice glass of wine and a slice of good bread. It's one of those comfort foods that recall home and all the attendant warm fuzzy feelings. Remember when you had a really nasty cold and Mom would bring you a steaming hot mug of soup that always made you feel better? Soup can be a hearty meal like gumbo, or it can be a light creation celebrating a seasonal vegetable like cream of asparagus or spring peas.

Chilled soups hit the spot when the thermometer soars. Gazpacho, cucumber, or seasonal, fresh fruit soups can be the star of a light spring or summer luncheon when paired with a green salad, or the opener for a spring or summer dinner.

Good things from the soup pot are hard to beat.

# Cold Peach Soup

1½ pounds peaches, peeled, pitted, and sliced

2 cups sour cream

1 cup fresh orange juice

1 cup pineapple juice

½ cup dry sherry

1 tablespoon fresh lemon juice

Sugar (optional)

Puree peaches in food processor until smooth. Add all remaining ingredients except sugar (in batches, if necessary) and process until smooth. Pass soup through a fine strainer. Add sugar to taste. Serve chilled.

*Of Magnolia and Mesquite*

# Cream of Lemon Soup

⅓ cup fresh lemon juice

2 (1½-inch) strips of lemon rind

3 cups canned chicken broth (or homemade)

1½ tablespoons cornstarch, dissolved in 2 tablespoons canned chicken broth or water

½ cup crushed ice

½ cup well-chilled heavy cream

Ice water for chilling

Salt to taste

Snipped fresh chives for garnish

In a saucepan, combine the lemon juice, rind, and the broth. Bring the liquid to a boil, and boil it for 5 minutes. Discard the rind, stir the cornstarch mixture, and whisk it into the broth mixture. Cook the broth over moderately high heat, stirring, until it is thickened. Remove pan from heat and whisk in the cream. In a blender, blend the soup with ½ cup crushed ice until it is smooth; transfer it to a metal bowl. Skim the froth and chill the soup, covered, in a larger bowl of crushed ice and ice water, stirring occasionally, for 30 minutes. Season the soup with salt, then ladle it into chilled bowls. Garnish with chives. Serves 2.

*Of Magnolia and Mesquite*

# Asparagus Soup

2 tablespoons unsalted butter

½ onion, diced

2 green onions, diced

4 cups chicken stock

1 pound asparagus, washed

2 cups cream

1 teaspoon salt

½ teaspoon freshly ground black pepper

Melt butter in a skillet and sauté white and green onions until transparent. Add stock and bring to a boil. Add asparagus and cook until tender, 8 to 10 minutes. Reserving 12 asparagus tips, put the rest of the asparagus with the stock in a blender. Cover and blend until smooth. Chill asparagus puree. Stir in cream, salt and pepper, and reserved asparagus tips. Serve chilled. Serves 6.

**NOTE:** To prepare fresh asparagus, hold each end and break like a stick. The asparagus will break off at the less than wonderful end, leaving a perfect spear. No cutting!

Commander's Palace, New Orleans
*Perennial Favorites*

# Asparagus Soup II

1 tablespoon butter

1 small onion, chopped

1 tablespoon all-purpose flour

2 (14-ounce) cans chicken broth

1 pound asparagus, cut into 1-inch pieces

1 teaspoon dried summer savory

Sour cream or plain yogurt (regular or low-fat)

Melt butter in a saucepan over medium heat. Add chopped onion and cook until tender. Add flour and stir 2 minutes. Gradually mix in chicken broth. Bring to a boil and add asparagus and summer savory. Simmer until asparagus is tender. Cool slightly.

Remove asparagus with slotted spoon, reserving soup base. Puree asparagus in food processor or blender until smooth, adding a little bit of the soup base as needed to puree. Return to saucepan to warm. Season with salt and pepper. Serve in bowls, topped with sour cream or yogurt. (Can also be served chilled.)

*And Roses for the Table*

# Mariposa Soup

1 small garlic clove, peeled and crushed

½ teaspoon salt, or more to taste

2 cups peeled and chopped seedless cucumbers (about 3)

1½ cups buttermilk

¼ cup fresh mint, plus some for garnish

1 tablespoon red wine vinegar

2 ice cubes

Mash garlic and salt into paste and add to blender. Add 1½ cups cucumbers to blender (reserving the other ½ cup for garnish) along with buttermilk, mint leaves, vinegar, and ice cubes; blend until smooth. Garnish with mint leaves and the remaining ½ cup finely diced cucumbers. Serves 4.

Gay Estes
*Perennial Favorites*

# Summer Squash Soup with Lime Sour Cream

3 tablespoons olive oil

1 onion, chopped

3 to 4 garlic cloves, minced

4 cups summer squash, chopped

4 poblano chiles, roasted, peeled, and chopped

1 cup chicken broth or vegetable broth

1 cup buttermilk

Salt and freshly ground black pepper to taste

### Lime Sour Cream

½ cup sour cream

2 teaspoons freshly squeezed lime juice

½ teaspoon lime zest

1 teaspoon ground cumin

Heat the olive oil in a heavy 4-quart saucepan over medium heat. Add the onion and garlic; sauté for 3 minutes. Add the squash and cover. Cook over medium heat for 8 to 10 minutes, or until squash is tender. Add the chopped chiles. Transfer ingredients to a blender and add the chicken or vegetable broth. Blend until pureed. Add buttermilk a little at a time for the desired consistency. Serve soup chilled, topped with a dollop of the Lime Sour Cream.

To make the Lime Sour Cream, combine all ingredients in a bowl and whisk until smooth. Chill before using.

*It's a Long Way to Guacamole*

# Blanco Queso Sopa *(White Cheese Soup)*

½ large onion, finely chopped

3 tablespoons butter

1½ (4-ounce) cans mild green chiles, drained, seeded, and finely chopped

2 (14-ounce) cans plum tomatoes, drained, seeded, and finely chopped

6 ounces cream cheese, cut into pieces

1 (14-ounce) can chicken broth

1½ cups half-and-half

4 teaspoons freshly squeezed lemon juice

Cayenne pepper to taste

Salt to taste

Garlic powder to taste

Ground cumin to taste

Crisp-cooked tortilla strips

Chopped green onions

Shredded Monterey Jack cheese

Sauté the onion in the butter in a large skillet until tender. Add the green chiles and tomatoes. Cook for 8 to 10 minutes over medium heat until the liquid evaporates, stirring occasionally. Reduce the heat to low. Stir in the cream cheese. Cook until the cheese is melted, stirring often. Stir in the chicken broth, half-and-half, lemon juice, cayenne pepper, salt, garlic powder, and cumin. Cook over medium heat until soup is hot; do not boil. Ladle into bowls to serve. Top with tortilla strips, green onions, and shredded Monterey Jack cheese. Serves 12.

*Dining without Reservations*

# Green Chiles Cheese Soup

½ cup chopped onion

1 or 2 garlic cloves, minced

¼ cup butter

¼ cup flour

½ teaspoon salt

⅛ teaspoon pepper

3 cups milk

1 cup chicken broth

¼ cup chopped green chiles

1½ cups shredded Monterey Jack cheese

Ground cumin to taste

Cook chopped onion and garlic in butter until tender. Stir in flour, salt, and pepper. Add milk and broth. Stir over heat until slightly thickened and bubbly. Cook and stir 1 minute. Stir in peppers and cheese. Cook over low heat until cheese melts. For a really creamy soup, run all through the blender. Add cumin to taste and serve. Serves 6.

Jan Fritz
*Flavors of Fredericksburg*

# Caldo de Frijol y Queso *(Bean and Cheese Soup)*

1 pound bacon

2 large onions, chopped

1 (2½-pound) can tomatoes

1 can water

6 to 8 stalks celery, chopped

1 pound Cheddar cheese, shredded

2 pounds pinto beans, cooked

1 to 2 tablespoons vinegar

Cut bacon into small pieces and fry. Drain bacon and sauté onions in bacon fat. Remove onions from fat. Combine bacon and onions in large saucepan; add tomatoes and water. Add celery and shredded Cheddar cheese to tomato mixture. Simmer until cheese is melted and thoroughly mixed with other ingredients. Purée the cooked pinto beans in blender; add to tomato mixture. This will probably be very thick and can be thinned with water or tomato juice. Add vinegar; stir, and season to taste. Serves 10.

*Seasoned with Sun*

# Sopa Frijole

½ pound bacon

1 onion, chopped

2 garlic cloves, minced or pressed

1 jalapeño, seeded and minced

2 cans (14½-ounce) tomatoes, diced

1 pound pinto beans, soaked, cooked, and drained

2 cans (10¾-ounce) chicken broth

1 teaspoon ground cumin

Salt and pepper to taste

## Toppings

2 cups grated Cheddar or Monterey Jack cheese

Sour cream

Crumbled bacon

Fry bacon in a large pot; remove and crumble, reserving drippings. Sauté the onion, garlic, and jalapeño in reserved bacon drippings. Add diced tomatoes.

In a blender or food processor, puree the cooked beans. Add beans and chicken stock to tomato mixture. Season with cumin, salt, and pepper. Simmer 15 to 20 minutes.

To serve, ladle soup into bowls. Top with cheese, crumbled bacon, and sour cream. Serves 6 to 8.

**VARIATION:** You may substitute 1 can Ro-Tel tomatoes for 1 can of the tomatoes if you like a spicier dish.

*The San Antonio Tex-Mex Cookbook*

# Borracho Black Bean Soup

4 (15-ounce) cans black beans, drained
    and rinsed

6 cups chicken broth

1 bay leaf

1 tablespoon vegetable oil

1 small onion, chopped

1 fresh jalapeño, chopped

2 garlic cloves, chopped

2 teaspoons ground cumin

2 teaspoons dried oregano

½ teaspoon cayenne pepper

½ teaspoon sugar

Salt to taste

1 longneck bottle of beer

1 (15-ounce) can diced tomatoes, with
    juice

## Garnish

4 ounces Monterey Jack cheese, grated

4 ounces sour cream

4 slices Smokehouse Bacon, cooked crisp
    and crumbled

Crisp corn tortilla chips

In a large pot, simmer the beans and chicken broth with the bay leaf for 20 minutes. Remove bay leaf. Using a potato masher, mash beans.

In a skillet, sauté the vegetables in the oil until tender-crisp. Add seasonings and beer. Heat to a simmer, and add diced tomatoes. Simmer for 8 to 10 minutes before adding to the beans.

Serve the soup in warm bowls. Sprinkle with cheese, add a dollop of sour cream, and then sprinkle with crumbled bacon. Serve with crisp tortilla chips. Serves 10.

**EDITOR'S NOTE:** Smokehouse Bacon is a New Braunfels Smokehouse product.

*New Braunfels Smokehouse*

# Black Bean Soup

3 cups black beans

1 ham bone

½ pound salt pork

1 bay leaf

⅛ teaspoon dried thyme

3 quarts water

1 quart beef stock

1½ teaspoons garlic powder

2 medium onions, chopped

1 large carrot, chopped

1 tablespoon sherry

Salt and pepper to taste

Cook all ingredients except sherry, salt, and pepper until beans are very tender, about 3 hours. Remove bay leaf, pork, and ham bone. Pour soup, a little at a time, into blender and liquefy. When smooth, return soup to stove and heat. Add salt, pepper, and sherry. Cool and place in plastic containers for storing, or serve hot. Serves 8.

*Seasoned with Sun*

# Cream of Jalapeño Soup

4 tablespoons butter

1 large onion, chopped

1 large carrot, peeled and finely chopped

1 large green bell pepper, seeded and finely chopped

3 fresh jalapeños, seeded and finely minced

3 tablespoons flour

3 cups chicken broth

2 cups cream

1 cup shredded Monterey Jack cheese

1 cup shredded Cheddar cheese

In a large saucepan, melt 2 tablespoons butter and cook onion, carrot, green bell pepper, and jalapeños on low heat until tender. Set aside.

In a pot, melt remaining 2 tablespoons of butter. Stir in flour and cook, stirring constantly, 2 minutes. Gradually stir in broth and cream. Increase heat and bring to a boil, stirring occasionally. Reduce heat and simmer until thickened.

Stir in both cheeses and vegetables. Heat through until cheeses are melted. Serve immediately. Serves 4 to 6.

You may add 1 (4-ounce) can diced green chiles for a spicier version.

*The San Antonio Tex-Mex Cookbook*

# Creamy Corn Soup

¼ cup chopped onion

2 tablespoons butter

2 (14-ounce) cans corn, drained

2 cups milk or half-and-half

2 tablespoons flour

Salt and pepper to taste

1 (14-ounce) can chicken broth

½ pound shredded Monterey Jack cheese (or Pepper Jack)

Dash of Tabasco sauce

6 bacon slices, cooked until crisp and crumbled

12 tortilla chips, broken

Sauté onion in butter until transparent. Stir in corn. Add flour, salt, and pepper. Cook for 1 minute. Gradually add the broth and mix well. Slowly stir in milk or half-and-half until thickened. Add Tabasco. Add cheese. Stir over low heat until melted.

To serve, ladle soup into individual bowls. Top each serving with bacon and tortilla chips. Serves 4.

*Under the Texan Sun*

# Mrs. Dean's Corn Soup

2 bacon strips, cut into small pieces

1 small onion, finely chopped

1 (16-ounce) can cream-style corn

1 corn can of milk

¼ teaspoon paprika

Salt and pepper to taste

Chopped chives as garnish

Sauté bacon pieces in a 12-inch skillet over medium heat until done, but not crisp. Remove bacon with a slotted spoon and set aside. Sauté the onion in bacon drippings until onion is transparent. Return bacon to pan. Add creamed corn, milk, paprika, salt, and pepper. Heat just to boiling, stirring frequently. Serve hot, garnishing each bowl with chopped chives. Serves 4.

**EDITOR'S NOTE:** A 16-ounce can equals 2 cups.

Mrs. Daniel O'Donnell (Sharon)
*Lone Star Legacy*

# Butternut Squash Soup

½ cup (1 stick) unsalted butter

1 onion, chopped

1 large baking potato (about 12 ounces),
  peeled and sliced

1 sweet potato (about 10 to 12 ounces)
  peeled and sliced

3 cups peeled and diced butternut squash

2 jalapeños, seeds and veins removed,
  minced

1¼ teaspoons minced fresh ginger

½ cup all-purpose flour

1½ quarts chicken stock

2 teaspoons real maple syrup

Salt to taste

¼ teaspoon cayenne pepper, or to taste

1 cup whipping cream

Sour cream and chopped toasted pecans
  as garnish

Melt the butter in a heavy 6-quart soup pot over medium heat. Add the onion and sauté until wilted and transparent, about 5 to 6 minutes. Add the potato, sweet potato, squash, jalapeños, and ginger. Toss to coat with the butter in the pot. Add the flour all at once and stir to blend well. Cook over medium heat for 3 to 4 minutes, stirring, until all flour is blended into the butter. Add the chicken stock and maple syrup. Season to taste with salt and cayenne pepper. Bring to a boil to thicken the soup, stirring often. Cover the pan, lower heat to a simmer, and cook until all vegetables are very tender, about 30 to 45 minutes. Puree the soup in batches in food processor or blender until very smooth. Return soup to a clean pot and stir in the whipping cream. Cook just to heat the cream through.

To serve, ladle the soup into shallow soup plates; garnish each serving with a dollop of sour cream and scatter a few of the toasted pecans over the sour cream. Serves 6 to 8.

*The Texas Hill Country*

# Mushroom Soup

¼ cup butter or stick margarine

1 pound mixed fresh mushrooms, cleaned
    and sliced

1 cup peeled and sliced potatoes

1 cup sliced carrots

½ cup chopped celery

½ cup chopped onion

1 (14½-ounce) can chicken broth

¼ cup dry sherry

1 tablespoon plus 2 teaspoons cornstarch

1 teaspoon salt

¼ teaspoon white pepper

1 cup whole milk

1 cup half-and-half

Fresh chives or parsley (optional)

Melt butter in a large, heavy saucepan. Stir in mushrooms, potatoes, carrots, celery, and onion. Cook over medium heat, stirring frequently, 6 to 10 minutes, or until mushrooms are golden. Stir in chicken broth and bring to a boil. Reduce heat, stir in sherry, and simmer, covered, for 15 minutes.

Meanwhile, in a small bowl, combine cornstarch, salt, and pepper with milk and half-and-half, blending well. Add slowly to mushroom mixture, stirring constantly, and cook over low heat until mixture comes to a boil. Cook about 1 minute longer or until slightly thickened, stirring constantly. Ladle into bowls and garnish with chives or parsley. Yields 6 servings.

*Cooking with Texas Highways*

# Tomato Wine Soup

2 cups fresh or canned tomatoes

¼ cup (½ stick) butter

2 tablespoons flour

1 teaspoon salt

1 teaspoon minced lemon thyme

1 tablespoon minced fresh basil or 1 teaspoon dried

Pinch pepper

¼ teaspoon baking soda

1 cup half-and-half

½ cup dry white wine

If using fresh tomatoes, chop and simmer in a saucepan with butter until soft. Cool slightly, then puree or blend. Return to saucepan. If using canned tomatoes, blend, then place in saucepan and add butter.

Stir in flour, salt, lemon thyme, basil, and pepper. Bring to a boil. Reduce heat and simmer for 5 minutes. Stir in baking soda and half-and-half. Cook over low heat until slightly thickened. Do not boil. Stir in wine and heat to simmer. Cook 15 to 20 minutes until sharp wine taste has cooked away. Makes 6 (½-cup servings).

*Southern Herb Growing*

# Sopa de Papas *(Potato Soup)*

6 slices bacon, cut into pieces

6 medium potatoes, peeled and quartered

2 medium onions, chopped

½ cup chopped celery

1 teaspoon salt

½ teaspoon black pepper

10 cups water

2 tablespoons butter

½ cup cream or half-and-half

1 teaspoon fresh cilantro, minced

1 small can diced green chiles

In a large saucepan, combine first 7 ingredients. Bring to a boil. Cover and simmer until potatoes are tender.

Strain, reserving stock. Puree vegetables and bacon in food processor or blender with 2 cups of stock. Add back to remaining stock. Beat with a wire whisk until blended. Melt butter and stir into soup with remaining ingredients.

Reheat over a low fire until warm, being careful not to boil. Serves 8 to 10.

*The San Antonio Tex-Mex Cookbook*

# Sopa de Tortilla *(Tortilla Soup)*

6 tablespoons vegetable oil

12 small corn tortillas, cut into ¼-inch strips

2 medium tomatoes, broiled

¼ cup chopped white onion

1 garlic clove

6 cups chicken stock

Sea salt and ground black pepper to taste

2 sprigs fresh epazote, chopped, or 2 tablespoons dried epazote

6 tablespoons shredded Monterey Jack cheese

2 dried pasilla chiles, fried crisp for 10 to 15 seconds, seeded, and crumbled

Heat oil in a large, heavy Dutch oven over medium heat. Fry tortilla strips until golden brown, about 2 to 3 minutes; remove with a slotted spoon, drain on paper towels, and set aside. Pour off all but 1 tablespoon of the oil in the pan and set aside. In a blender, combine tomatoes, onion, and garlic; puree to a smooth sauce. Heat the remaining tablespoon of oil over medium heat and fry the pureed sauce until it has thickened and is reduced by about one-quarter. Add chicken stock and bring to a boil. Check seasonings, adding salt and pepper if needed. Reduce heat to simmer. Add half of the tortilla strips and the epazote. Cook an additional 5 minutes. To serve, divide the remaining tortilla strips among 6 bowls and put 1 tablespoon of the shredded cheese into each one. Ladle hot soup into the bowls and garnish with crumbled chiles. Serves 6.

Fonda El Pato, Mexico City
*Fonda San Miguel*

# Crawfish and Corn Chowder

½ cup vegetable oil

½ cup all-purpose flour

1 onion, finely chopped

1 red bell pepper, chopped

1 tablespoon minced garlic

1 (17-ounce) can cream-style corn

1 (16-ounce) can whole-kernel corn, drained

2 pounds crawfish tails

1 quart half-and-half

1 (11-ounce) can tomatoes with green chiles

1 potato, peeled and chopped

1 teaspoon salt

Black pepper to taste

Cayenne pepper to taste

Whisk the oil and flour in a heavy saucepan until blended. Cook over medium-low heat until the roux is the color of light brown peanut butter, stirring constantly. Add the onion, bell pepper, and garlic. Cook for 3 to 5 minutes, stirring constantly. Add the corn and crawfish tails and mix well.

Cook for 3 minutes, stirring frequently. Stir in the half-and-half, tomatoes with green chiles, potato, and salt. Cook over medium heat until the chowder begins to thicken and the potato is very tender, stirring occasionally. Season to taste with black pepper and cayenne pepper. Ladle into soup bowls. Serves 10 to 12.

*Dallas Dish*

# Oyster Stew

½ cup (1 stick) butter

1 quart oysters, drained

2 quarts half-and-half

2 teaspoons salt (less if using salted butter)

1 teaspoon ground white pepper

½ teaspoon paprika

6 tablespoons chopped celery leaves

Melt butter in a large saucepan. Add oysters and sauté about 3 or 4 minutes, or until the edges begin to curl. Add half-and-half, salt, and pepper. Heat to boiling, but do not allow to boil.

To serve, pour into individual soup plates or a heated tureen, sprinkle with paprika, and garnish with celery leaves. Serves 6.

*Gulf Coast Cooking*

# Seafood Gumbo

2 medium onions, coarsely chopped

2 green bell peppers, coarsely chopped

2 tablespoons minced garlic

1 tablespoon vegetable oil

2 teaspoons dried thyme

2 tablespoons shrimp base (optional)

1 (14.5-ounce) can diced tomatoes

6 tablespoons Louisiana hot pepper sauce

6 tablespoons Worcestershire sauce

4 tablespoons Creole Seafood Seasoning (see recipe below)

1 bay leaf

1 pound frozen sliced okra

1½ teaspoons filé powder

1 quart seafood stock or water

1½ cups raw shucked oysters

1 pound (36–42 count) shrimp, peeled and deveined

1 pound crabmeat or cubed fish fillets

Hot cooked rice

## Creole Seafood Seasoning

*(Yields 3½ cups.)*

¾ cup salt

6½ tablespoons finely ground black pepper

4 tablespoons cayenne pepper

7½ tablespoons garlic powder

6 tablespoons onion powder

1 cup paprika

½ cup tightly packed dried thyme leaves

7 tablespoons tightly packed dried oregano leaves

To make the Creole Seafood Seasoning, place salt, black and cayenne peppers, garlic and onion powders, paprika, thyme, and oregano in a medium bowl; mix thoroughly. Or place in food processor and pulse lightly for a finer texture. Store seasoning in a covered container and keep in a cool, dry place up to 6 months.

In a large stockpot over medium-low heat, sauté onion, bell pepper, and garlic in oil 15 to 20 minutes. Add thyme, shrimp base, tomatoes, hot sauce, Worcestershire sauce, Creole Seafood Seasoning, and bay leaf; cook 10 minutes.

Add okra and filé powder; cook 5 minutes. Add stock, oysters, shrimp, and crabmeat; simmer 15 to 20 minutes, or until seafood is cooked through. Remove bay leaf before serving over hot cooked rice. Serves 8.

*Brennan's of Houston in Your Kitchen*

# Creamy Mussel Soup
# with Spicy Jalapeño and Cilantro Pesto

## Cilantro Pesto

2 ounces pine nuts, toasted

2 to 3 jalapeños, seeded

6 garlic cloves

4 ounces olive oil

4 large bunches cilantro, 10 stems with
leaves reserved for garnish

2 tablespoons Parmesan cheese

Salt to taste

## Mussel Soup

1 cup chardonnay

¼ pound butter

½ cup minced shallots

2 quarts heavy cream

½ cup fresh lemon juice

4 dozen mussels, rinsed clean, shells and
all

All of the Cilantro Pesto

Salt and cayenne pepper to taste

Make the pesto by combining pine nuts, jalapeños, garlic, and oil in blender; puree. Add the cilantro and cheese and blend into a paste. Add salt to taste. Set aside.

To make the soup, reduce the chardonnay in a large, heavy-bottomed saucepan until it is almost dry. Add the butter and lightly sauté the shallots for 3 minutes. Add the heavy cream and lemon juice and bring to a simmer. Add the mussels. Bring back to a simmer and gently stir in all of the Cilantro Pesto. Once the soup begins to simmer, adjust the salt and cayenne pepper level to your liking. Serve with whole-leaf cilantro garnish on top. Serves 8 to 10.

*Fired Up!*

# Winter Sausage Soup

2 pounds smoked link sausage (such as sausage from Opa's Smoked Meats in Fredericksburg), sliced

1 medium onion, chopped

2 cups sliced carrots

1 (28-ounce) can whole tomatoes, chopped and undrained

1 cup chopped celery

4 cups peeled and cubed potatoes

16 cups rich beef broth

1 garlic clove, minced

1 tablespoon brown sugar

1 teaspoon pepper

4 cups shredded cabbage

Salt to taste

Chopped parsley

In a large stockpot brown the sausage. Drain off fat. Add remaining ingredients except cabbage, salt, and parsley.

Bring to a boil, reduce heat and simmer, covered, for 1 hour. Add the cabbage and cook for 15 minutes more. Taste for salt. Garnish with chopped parsley. Serves 18 to 20.

*The Peach Tree Tea Room Cookbook*

# Sicilian Meatball Soup

½ pound lean ground beef

1 egg

2 tablespoons Italian bread crumbs

8 teaspoons grated Parmesan cheese

2 to 3 sprigs parsley, minced

1 garlic clove, minced

Salt and pepper to taste

7½ cups beef stock

1 cup fresh spinach

½ pound tagliatelle ribbon noodles

Minced fresh basil and additional grated Parmesan cheese

In a bowl, combine the beef, egg, bread crumbs, Parmesan cheese, parsley, garlic, salt, and pepper; knead until smooth. Roll into balls about 1 inch in diameter.

In a saucepan or soup pot, bring stock to a boil. Add the meatballs and spinach; simmer for 5 minutes. Add the noodles; cook until tender but still firm. Serve immediately; sprinkle basil and Parmesan on top. Serves 6.

*Vineyard Cuisine*

# Steak and Big Bean Chili with Homemade Biscuits

2 pounds beef chuck steak, cut into ¼-inch cubes

½ teaspoon salt

2 tablespoons vegetable oil

1 (18-ounce) can onion soup

1 (45-ounce) can kidney beans, drained

1 (28-ounce) can tomato sauce or puree

1 (12-ounce) can cola (not diet)

1 (6-ounce) can tomato paste

1 tablespoon chili powder

2 teaspoons ground cumin

2 teaspoons baking cocoa

½ teaspoon pepper

Homemade Biscuits (see recipe below)

## Homemade Biscuits

2 cups milk

½ cup vegetable shortening

½ cup (scant) sugar

1 teaspoon salt

1 package active dry yeast

½ cup warm water

5 to 6 cups all-purpose flour

Make the chili. Season the steak with the salt and brown on all sides in the oil in a skillet. Drain and place the steak in a slow cooker. Process the onion soup in a blender for 1 minute and pour over the steak. Add the beans, tomato sauce, soda, tomato paste, chili powder, cumin, cocoa, and pepper and stir to mix well.

Simmer on low for 6 hours or on high for 2 hours, stirring occasionally. Ladle into chili bowls and serve with the Homemade Biscuits. (For Chili Mac, spoon the chili over hot cooked macaroni and top with grated Cheddar cheese and chopped onion.) Serves 4 to 6.

To make the Homemade Biscuits, scald the milk in a saucepan. Add the shortening, sugar, and salt to the scaled milk and stir until blended. Cool to 115 degrees. Dissolve the yeast in the warm water and stir. Add the yeast mixture to the cooled milk mixture and mix well. Add the flour gradually, stirring until mixture forms a ball.

Let rise, covered, in a warm environment until doubled in bulk, then turn out onto a lightly floured surface and knead well. Let dough rest for 15 minutes. Pat or roll the dough out to a thickness of ½ inch. Cut with a round cutter. Fold the rounds over and arrange in a greased round or oblong baking dish. Let rise until doubled in bulk.

Preheat the oven to 400 degrees and bake biscuits for 10 minutes, or until light brown. Serve immediately.

*Dallas Dish*

# Texas-Style Chili

6 ancho chiles, stems and seeds removed and torn into small pieces

4 chiles de arbol or japones chiles, stems and seeds removed

7 garlic cloves, peeled

½ cup chopped onion

1½ teaspoons oregano

1½ teaspoons ground cumin

1 cup water

2 tablespoons cooking oil

2 pounds skirt steak or beef stew meat, either cut into ½-inch pieces or coarsely ground (chili grind)

1 cup water

1 (8-ounce) can tomato sauce

2 teaspoons hot paprika

1 teaspoon salt, or to taste

2 tablespoons masa harina or Maseca, or substitute all-purpose flour

Water

1 cup grated mild Cheddar cheese

Place the ancho and chiles de arbol or japones chiles in a bowl, cover them with very hot tap water, and allow them to soak for 20 minutes. Drain and discard the water. Put the rehydrated chiles in a blender with the garlic, onion, oregano, and cumin. Add the first 1 cup water and blend for 2 minutes at high speed. Set aside.

Heat 1 tablespoon of the oil in a heavy pot or Dutch oven over medium-high to high heat. When oil is hot, add 1 pound of the beef and cook until browned. Remove the meat and set aside. Add the remaining tablespoon of oil and brown the remaining 1 pound of beef. Return the reserved beef to the pot. Add the second 1 cup water, the tomato sauce, paprika, salt, and reserved blended chile mixture. Stir to blend well.

Bring the chili to a simmer, cover the pot, and cook at a low simmer for 1¾ hours, or until the meat is very tender. Meanwhile, mix the masa or flour with 2 tablespoons of water and set aside.

When the meat is very tender, remove the cover and stir in about ½ of the masa mix. Continue simmering the chili, uncovered, for about 10 minutes, or until thickened, adding a little more of the masa-water mix if necessary. Serve the chili garnished with the cheese. Serves 4.

*Jim Peyton's The Very Best of Tex-Mex Cooking*

# Bloody Mary Chili

2 pounds coarsely ground chuck

2 medium onions, coarsely chopped

1 large bell pepper, coarsely chopped

2 (15-ounce) cans pinto beans

3 to 4 medium tomatoes, coarsely chopped, or 1 large can diced tomatoes

2 garlic cloves, minced

½ teaspoon cayenne pepper, or to taste

Salt and pepper to taste

1 bottle Bloody Mary mix

Shredded Monterey Jack cheese

In a large Dutch oven, brown meat with onions and green peppers until meat is no longer pink. Drain well and return mixture to Dutch oven. Add all remaining ingredients, using half of the Bloody Mary mix, and cook over low heat for 1 hour, stirring occasionally. Throughout the cooking time, add more Bloody Mary mix as needed for desired flavor and consistency. Serve smothered with Monterey Jack cheese. Serves 6 to 8.

Texas Beef Council
*License to Cook, Texas Style*

# Fish & Shellfish

Texas is richly blessed with an abundance of fish and shellfish. Our Gulf Coast stretches for hundreds of miles and supports a huge seafood industry. The coastal waters offer shrimp and oysters as well as dozens of varieties of fin fish. Our state also has over 80,000 miles of rivers, plus countless lakes and private ponds. Freshwater fish abound—from catfish to perch, crappie, bass, sunfish, stripers, rainbow trout, and many more.

Fish, as we know today, is not only delicious when prepared properly but a very healthy addition to our diet. If you're new to cooking fresh fish and shellfish, the most important thing to learn is how to buy fresh seafood. Whenever possible, make your selections from whole, uncut fish and have the market fillet and skin them for you. That way, you can really tell if the fish is fresh! Look at the fish closely. The eyes should be clear and protruding from the sockets, not clouded and sunken. The flesh should be firm to the touch and never mushy. It should not have a slimy feeling, but rather should be moist with no signs of dryness. The gills should be bright red in color. Brownish gills indicate advanced age. Of course, the fish should never smell "fishy," only "faintly marine." If the fish smells when you buy it, it will taste worse when you cook it! When buying whole fish, remember that you'll lose about 70 percent of its weight to bones, head, fins, tail, and skin, depending on the type of fish. The average serving of filleted fish is 6 to 8 ounces per person. If buying already filleted fish is your only choice, select those fillets that are firm to the touch with no signs of flaking or coming apart. Again, let your nose be your guide. The fillets should not smell overly fishy.

Always buy shrimp in their shells so you can judge the freshness. The shells should be firm with the tails firmly attached. Fresh shrimp will never have an ammonia smell. When you buy shucked oysters in their liquor (the juice contained in the oyster shell), the oysters should not be white and chalky-looking, and the liquor should be thick and rather viscous but clear. Scallops should be moist, never dry in appearance and should have a sweet, inviting aroma with never a hint of ammonia odors.

If you're an angler, always remember to gut your fish as soon as possible after taking them off the hook and get them on ice immediately. That way they'll stay perfectly fresh. Always use fresh fish within two days, or freeze them.

The secret to cooking fish and shellfish is to not overcook them. Cook fish fillets just until they turn opaque throughout. Some fish, such as salmon and of course tuna, are best cooked on the rare to medium side. Ideally, you should cook fish fillets for 5 minutes per inch of thickness for a perfectly done fish. Cooking fish until it begins to flake is overcooking it. Shrimp should be cooked just until they turn opaque and take on that nice coral-pink hue at the edges. Overcooked shrimp are rough and rubbery. When frying oysters, cook them just until the batter is crispy and golden. The oyster should actually still be almost liquid inside the crust. Scallops are the shellfish that is the most abused in terms of cooking. They should be cooked only until that exact moment when they turn opaque all the way through. Overcooked scallops have an unpleasant, rubbery texture and lose their delicate flavor.

# Oysters Patou

½ loaf day-old French bread

1 cup butter

3 medium onions, minced

1 medium bell pepper, chopped

1 celery stalk, chopped

2 garlic cloves, minced

3 pints oysters, drained, liquor reserved

1 pound medium shrimp, peeled and deveined

1 tablespoon minced fresh thyme (1 teaspoon dried)

1 tablespoon minced fresh basil

½ teaspoon Tabasco sauce

1½ teaspoons salt, or to taste

2 teaspoons cayenne pepper, or to taste

1 teaspoon ground white pepper

1 teaspoon ground black pepper

1 cup thinly sliced green onions, including green tops

1 cup minced fresh parsley

Grated Parmesan cheese

Slice bread thin and place on baking sheet. Bake at 200 degrees for about 30 minutes, or until dried and crisp. Do not brown. Place dried bread in a bowl and pour 3 cups reserved oyster liquor over the top; set aside to soak. Sauté onions and next 3 ingredients in butter until soft. Add any remaining oyster liquor and cook until liquor has evaporated. Set aside 24 oysters. Cut remaining oysters in half and set aside. Cut shrimp in thirds. Add shrimp, herbs, and Tabasco to vegetable mixture; cook 4 to 5 minutes. Mix salt and peppers together and add all but 1 teaspoon to pan. Add oyster halves to the pan and cook until oysters curl around edges. Mash bread with the oyster liquor. Add bread to pan, reduce heat to low, and cook until sauce is smooth. Remove from heat; add green onions and parsley. Refrigerate mixture for at least 2 hours. Arrange 24 oyster shells or 12 ramekins on a baking sheet. Place 1 oyster in each shell, or 2 in each ramekin. Season oysters with reserved salt and pepper mixture. Mound a portion of the dressing over oysters. Top each with a scattering of Parmesan cheese. Bake in preheated 375-degree oven for 25 to 30 minutes, or until cheese is lightly browned and dressing is bubbly. Can also be cooked in a large shallow casserole dish with whole oysters at the bottom. Serves 10 to 12.

*¡Viva! Tradiciones*

# Oysters Rockefeller

48 oysters in the shell

1 pound rock salt

½ cup (1 stick) butter

8 slices bacon, crisp-cooked, drained, and crumbled

10 ounces spinach, trimmed and chopped fine

3 tablespoons chopped fresh parsley

3 tablespoons chopped celery leaves

3 tablespoons chopped green onions

⅓ cup dry bread crumbs

½ teaspoon salt

Tabasco sauce to taste

Shredded Parmesan cheese

1 teaspoon Pernod, or other anise-flavored liqueur

Scrub and shuck the oysters, reserving the deeper shells. Place the oysters in the deep shells and arrange on a bed of the rock salt on a large baking sheet.

Melt the butter in a skillet. Add the crumbled bacon, spinach, parsley, celery leaves, green onions, bread crumbs, salt, and Tabasco sauce. Cook for 5 to 10 minutes over low heat, or until lightly cooked, stirring constantly. Adjust the seasonings to taste. Spoon over the oysters. Scatter a portion of the cheese on each oyster. Bake at 425 degrees until the edges of the oysters curl and the topping is lightly browned. Drizzle a few drops of Pernod over each oyster just before serving. Serves 4 to 6.

*Dining without Reservations*

# Dijon Deviled Crab

4 tablespoons mayonnaise

4 tablespoons Dijon mustard

6 tablespoons Worcestershire sauce or to taste

1 teaspoon Tabasco sauce

¼ teaspoon salt

2 tablespoons fine-chopped red bell pepper

2 tablespoons fine-chopped green onion tops

2 tablespoons fine-chopped celery

1 pound lump white or claw crabmeat

2 tablespoons butter

6 tablespoons fine dry bread crumbs

Mix together mayonnaise, mustard, Worcestershire and Tabasco sauces, salt, and chopped vegetables. Fold into crabmeat gently. Divide equally among 4 buttered ovenproof ramekins.

Melt butter in a small skillet and stir in bread crumbs. Top each ramekin with buttered crumbs. Broil until crumbs are golden brown and crab is heated through. Serves 4.

*Gulf Coast Cooking*

# Southwestern-Style Crab Cakes with Limes and Chiles

1 large egg

2 tablespoons mayonnaise, crème fraîche, or sour cream

2 teaspoons Dijon mustard

Pinch of cayenne pepper

½ teaspoon freshly ground white pepper

Pinch of salt

¼ teaspoon Worcestershire sauce

1 pound fresh or pasteurized precooked crabmeat (lump or back fin), flaked

¼ cup chopped parsley

¼ cup chopped green onions

8 to 10 saltine crackers, crushed, or 1 cup soft white bread crumbs

1 to 2 fresh 2-inch serrano chiles, seeded and minced

2 tablespoons unsalted sweet butter

2 tablespoons vegetable oil

Lime wedges for garnish

Mix together the egg, mayonnaise, mustard, pepper, salt, and Worcestershire sauce. Add the crabmeat, parsley, green onions, saltine crackers, and chiles. Mix thoroughly. Shape and press the mixture into 10 or 12 round patties, place on foil, cover, and chill for at least ½ hour before cooking. The recipe can be prepared ahead and refrigerated for 5 to 6 hours. Bring to room temperature before using. Heat the butter and oil in a skillet. Add crab cakes and sauté on both sides over medium-high heat a few minutes or until golden and lightly crispy. Drain on paper towels. Serve hot with lime wedges.

*Gruene General Store Cookbook*

# Chef Henry's Crab Cakes

4 tablespoons butter

¾ cup fine-chopped onion

¼ cup fine-chopped green bell pepper

¼ cup fine-chopped red bell pepper

¼ cup fine-chopped celery

3 egg yolks

1 whole egg

¼ cup mayonnaise

2 teaspoons cider vinegar

2 teaspoons lemon juice

1 teaspoon salt

½ teaspoon ground white pepper

¾ teaspoon dry mustard

3 or 4 drops Tabasco sauce, or to taste

2 teaspoons Worcestershire sauce

2 teaspoons Creole seasoning blend

2 tablespoons chopped parsley

1 cup fresh bread crumbs

1 pound regular lump crabmeat

Flour

Vegetable oil or butter

## Creole-Style Mustard Sauce

½ cup heavy cream

½ cup dry white wine

½ cup chicken stock

1 cup (2 sticks) butter (unsalted if using salted stock)

⅓ cup Creole mustard or other coarse-grained mustard

Salt to taste

Ground white pepper to taste

Melt 4 tablespoons butter in a skillet and sauté onion, bell peppers, and celery just until tender. Transfer to a mixing bowl.

Combine egg yolks, whole egg, and mayonnaise and beat well. Beat in vinegar, lemon juice, seasonings, and parsley. Mix in bread crumbs and fold in crabmeat gently.

Divide into equal portions of desired size and shape into cakes. Dust with flour and sauté in hot oil or butter, turning to brown both sides. (For a first course, make small crab cakes and allow 2 per person.) Serve hot, topped with Creole-Style Mustard Sauce.

To make the mustard sauce, combine cream, wine, and stock in a saucepan and cook over medium heat until reduced by half. Remove from heat and whisk in butter a piece at a time. Add mustard and seasonings. Keep warm.

Henry Douglas, Radisson Admiral Semmes Hotel, Mobile, Alabama
*Gulf Coast Cooking*

# Texas Jumbo Lump Crab au Gratin

2 cups dry white wine

2 cups heavy cream

¼ cup minced garlic

¼ cup minced shallots

2 limes, juiced and zested

1 jalapeño, seeded and minced (if you love the heat, leave the seeds)

½ cup diced red bell pepper (¼-inch dice)

1½ teaspoons salt

6 egg yolks

1 pound jumbo lump blue crab

1 bunch cilantro, finely chopped

½ cup soft goat cheese

1 cup grated Parmesan cheese

1 cup panko bread crumbs

In a medium saucepan over high heat, reduce white wine to 2 tablespoons of amber liquid. Add the heavy cream, garlic, and shallots. Reduce by half. Add the lime juice and zest, jalapeño, bell pepper, and salt. Return to a simmer.

In a separate bowl, whisk the egg yolks. Slowly whisk the simmering liquid into the egg yolks. It is very important that you add the liquid slowly. Otherwise the hot liquid will scramble the eggs.

Return the mixture to the saucepan and simmer for 1 to 2 minutes until sauce coats the back of a spoon. Immediately turn off the heat. Add the crabmeat and cilantro to the mixture. Transfer to an ovenproof casserole. Dot the top of the casserole with goat cheese. Evenly spread the Parmesan cheese on top. Evenly spread the bread crumbs on top. Bake at 375 degrees for 30 to 35 minutes, or until the gratin is crusty and the casserole is bubbly. Serves 4.

*Fired Up*

# Crab and Avocado Cakes

1 pound regular lump crabmeat, picked
    over

1 avocado, peeled and chopped

1 shallot, minced

1 egg, beaten

2 tablespoons butter, softened

2 tablespoons lemon juice

1 teaspoon fresh dill, minced

¾ cup bread crumbs

Salt and black pepper

Pinch of cayenne pepper

Olive oil (about ½ cup)

Mix together crabmeat, avocado, shallot, egg, butter, lemon juice, dill, ¼ cup bread crumbs, salt, black pepper, and cayenne pepper. When well mixed, form into 12 cakes.

Heat oil in a skillet. Gently dredge the crab cakes in the remaining bread crumbs, and fry in the heated oil, turning once. When golden brown, remove from pan and drain on paper towels. Serves 4 to 6.

**NOTE:** Use two spatulas to turn over delicate crab cakes. Lift up a crab cake with one spatula, then turn over onto the other spatula, then slide crab cake back into the hot oil.

*The Texas Provincial Kitchen Cookbook*

# Crabmeat au Gratin

3 tablespoons butter

3 tablespoons flour

2 cups milk

½ cup dry sherry

1 teaspoon Worcestershire sauce

1 tablespoon seasoned salt, or to taste

1 pound lump crabmeat

½ cup grated Cheddar cheese

½ cup grated Monterey Jack cheese

Paprika

Melt butter in a saucepan. Add flour and stir to mix thoroughly.

Add milk, sherry, Worcestershire sauce, and seasoned salt, stirring constantly. Bring to a boil, continue stirring, and cook for 5 minutes. Remove from heat. Sauce may be refrigerated at this point, if desired.

Mix sauce with crabmeat and divide among individual ramekins or spoon into a buttered ceramic baking dish. Top with a mixture of the two cheeses and sprinkle with paprika. Preheat oven to 350 degrees and bake about 15 minutes for ramekins or 30 minutes for one large dish. Allow additional cooking time if the sauce has been refrigerated. Serves 4 to 6.

Gaido's Seafood Restaurant, Galveston, Texas
*Gulf Coast Cooking*

# Enchiladas Suizas de Jaiba
## *(Crabmeat Enchiladas with Sour Cream Sauce)*

6 tablespoons vegetable oil

12 corn tortillas

Crabmeat Filling (see below)

Sour Cream Sauce (see below)

### Crabmeat Filling

*(Makes 3 cups and fills 12 enchiladas.)*

1¼ pounds lump crabmeat

6 tablespoons olive oil

3 tablespoons butter

3 garlic cloves, chopped

1 medium white onion, chopped

2 pickled jalapeños, chopped, with ¼ cup liquid from the jar

2 or 3 pickled carrots, chopped

2 medium tomatoes, seeded and chopped

¼ cup chopped fresh parsley

¼ cup chopped fresh cilantro

Sea salt and ground black pepper to taste

### Sour Cream Sauce

*(Makes 3¾ cups.)*

3 cups sour cream

¾ cup milk

1 teaspoon sea salt

1 teaspoon ground white pepper

Prepare the Crabmeat Filling. Pick through the crabmeat and remove any bits of shell or cartilage, taking care not to break up the lumps. In a heavy nonreactive skillet, heat the oil and butter over medium heat, add garlic and onion, and sauté until the onion is wilted and transparent. Add the jalapeños and juice, carrots, tomatoes, parsley, and cilantro and cook for about 3 minutes; season to taste with salt and pepper. Reduce heat to low and cook until mixture thickens, about 20 minutes. Add crabmeat and cook just until crabmeat is heated through. Adjust seasonings as needed. Keep warm.

Prepare the Sour Cream Sauce. Combine ingredients, whisk in a small bowl, and set aside.

In a small skillet, heat oil over medium-high heat. Soften the tortillas in the oil by holding each tortilla with tongs and dipping it into the hot oil for about 10 to 15 seconds, or until softened. Drain on paper towels. Place 3 tablespoons of the Crabmeat Filling down the center of each tortilla and roll it up. Arrange 2 enchiladas on each serving plate. Top with Sour Cream Sauce and served immediately. Serves 6 to 8.

*Fonda San Miguel*

# Scallops with Key Lime Sauce

2 pounds bay scallops (or sea scallops cut in half)

Flour seasoned with salt and white pepper

6 tablespoons butter or olive oil, divided

2 tablespoons flour

¾ cup dry white wine

2 garlic cloves, crushed

½ cup heavy cream

¼ cup Key lime juice

⅓ cup chopped fresh basil

Salt and white pepper to taste

4 very thin lime slices

Toss scallops in seasoned flour, shaking off excess. In a skillet, melt 4 tablespoons butter and sauté scallops just until they turn opaque throughout. Remove from pan.

Add remaining butter to pan and stir in flour to make a roux. Add white wine and garlic, stirring to make a smooth sauce. Add cream and stir until smooth. Stir in lime juice, basil, salt, and pepper.

Drain any liquid from scallops and return them to sauce to heat.

Serve in individual shells, ramekins, or over hot rice. Garnish with a lime slice. Serves 4 to 6.

*Gulf Coast Cooking*

# Scallop Supreme

1 pound large sea scallops

Flour seasoned with salt and pepper

⅓ cup olive oil

1 egg yolk

Juice of 1 lemon

½ cup butter, divided

3 garlic cloves, minced

½ cup half-and-half

1 tablespoon minced chives

1 tablespoon minced parsley

Grated Parmesan cheese

Dredge scallops in seasoned flour. Heat olive oil in a heavy-bottomed skillet until hot. Sauté the scallops in olive oil over medium heat for about 4 minutes, or just until they turn opaque throughout. Turn once. Remove to serving dish and keep warm. In a saucepan, whisk egg yolk and lemon juice. Add ¼ cup of the butter and the garlic. Cook over low heat until butter is melted. Do not allow the eggs to curdle. Add half-and-half and remaining butter and whisk until sauce thickens, but do not allow it to boil. Remove from heat and whisk in chives and parsley. Pour sauce over scallops, sprinkle with Parmesan cheese, and serve with crusty bread. Serves 4.

*¡Viva! Tradiciones*

# Shrimp in Garlic Sauce

½ to ¾ pound small Gulf Coast shrimp, peeled and deveined, tail section left on

Coarse salt

8 tablespoons good-quality olive oil

3 large garlic cloves, peeled and very coarsely chopped

1 dried red chile pepper, stem and seeds removed, torn into 2 pieces

½ teaspoon paprika, preferably Spanish-style

1 tablespoon minced parsley

1 loaf French or Italian bread for dipping

Dry the shrimp and sprinkle with the salt on both sides. Let stand for 10 minutes. Heat oil on top of stove in an 8-inch heatproof casserole, preferably earthenware. Add the garlic and chile pepper. When the garlic begins to turn golden, add shrimp. Cook over medium-high heat, stirring, for about 2 minutes, or until the shrimp is just done. Be careful not to overcook, or the shrimp will be tough.

Sprinkle with parsley, paprika, and additional salt to taste. Serve immediately, right in the cooking dish, and provide lots of good bread for dipping in the oil. Serves 4 as a fish course, 6 as an appetizer.

Karen and Jim Johnson, Alamosa Wine Cellars, Bend, Texas
*Under the Texan Sun*

# Shrimp Soused with Tequila

24 large shrimp, shelled (with tail sections left intact)

Salt to taste

Vegetable oil

½ cup tequila

Minced zest of 1 lime

Juice of 4 limes

24 thin slices of seeded jalapeño, or to taste

¼ heaping cup chopped green onions, including green tops

Split the shrimp lengthwise to devein and butterfly. Season with salt. Sauté in hot vegetable oil until barely done. Pour the tequila over the shrimp and flame. Remove shrimp to a dish using a slotted spoon. Mix remaining ingredients in skillet, heat, stirring often, until onions are slightly wilted. Pour over shrimp. Serve as a first course with crusty bread. Serves 4.

*Gulf Coast Cooking*

# Shrimp Paesano

## Shrimp

1 pound jumbo shrimp, peeled and
  deveined
Half-and-half
All-purpose flour for dredging
Dry bread crumbs for dredging
Olive oil

## Sauce

1 egg yolk
Juice of ½ lemon
1 stick butter, divided
2 garlic cloves, minced
Chopped fresh parsley
Chopped fresh chives

Soak shrimp in half-and-half for 10 minutes. Remove and drain shrimp, reserving half-and-half. Dredge shrimp in flour. Dip in reserved half-and-half and dredge in bread crumbs. Sauté in olive oil over medium heat for 5 minutes. Transfer to broiler and broil until golden. Drain and serve topped with sauce.

To prepare sauce, combine egg yolk and lemon juice in a heavy saucepan. Add 4 tablespoons butter and stir over low heat until melted. Add garlic and remaining 4 tablespoons butter. Stir briskly until butter melts and sauce thickens. Add parsley and chives. Serves 2 to 3.

Mary Vance Jones
*Mesquite Country*

# Shrimp Rémoulade

2 pounds shrimp, boiled, peeled, and
  deveined
¾ cup olive oil
½ cup red wine vinegar
2 tablespoons chili sauce
¼ cup Creole mustard

½ cup minced celery
½ cup minced green onions
1 bay leaf
1 teaspoon salt
½ teaspoon cayenne pepper
1 tablespoon paprika

Place shrimp in a shallow baking dish; set aside. Combine all remaining ingredients and whisk to blend well. Pour over shrimp and marinate, covered, in refrigerator for at least several hours but preferably overnight. Serve in a bowl with toothpicks for hors d'oeuvres or on shredded lettuce and sliced tomatoes as a salad. If serving as a salad, garnish with cucumber and/or avocado slices. Serves 12 as finger food; 4 as a salad.

Mrs. B. Thomas McElroy
*The Dallas Junior League Cookbook*

# Shrimp Creole

2 tablespoons canola oil, or more as needed

1 large onion, chopped

1 green bell pepper, chopped fine

4 celery stalks, chopped

2 garlic cloves, minced

1 can whole tomatoes, crushed

1 small can tomato sauce

2 pounds uncooked shrimp, peeled and deveined

5 bay leaves

Cayenne pepper

Salt and pepper to taste

4 tablespoons minced parsley

2 green onions (green portion only), sliced thin

Fry onions, bell pepper, celery, and garlic in oil until soft. Add tomatoes and tomato sauce and cook until oil begins to bubble up over the top. Add shrimp and cook for 10 minutes. Add 3 cups water and bay leaves, cayenne pepper, salt, and pepper. Simmer slowly until it reaches consistency of a medium sauce. Add parsley and green onion tops. Cook a few minutes more. Serve over rice with a green salad and crispy French bread.

> **VARIATION:** Add ¾ cup sliced okra, ⅛ teaspoon ground cloves, and a dash of thyme to tomatoes.

Jeannine Miller and Jan Peterson
*Flavors of Fredericksburg*

# Batter for French-Fried Shrimp

1 cup flour

1 egg

2 tablespoons vegetable oil

1 cup ice water

½ teaspoon salt

½ teaspoon sugar

Beat all ingredients together with electric mixer. Butterfly shrimp before dipping them in the batter. Fry in hot oil (375 degrees) until golden. Drain on a paper-towel-lined wire rack.

Mrs. Barry W. Uhr (Karen)
*Through Our Kitchen Door*

# Bacon-Wrapped Shrimp

⅓ cup Pickapeppa Sauce

⅔ cup honey

Bacon slices, partially cooked and drained

Large uncooked shrimp, peeled and deveined

Mix the Pickapeppa Sauce and honey in a small bowl. Set aside. Cut bacon strips in half. Wrap each shrimp in a half slice of bacon, securing each with a bamboo skewer. After all shrimp have been skewered, place the skewers in a large baking dish and pour the honey mixture over them. Marinate for a couple of hours. Grill until shrimp turns opaque and is cooked through.

Judy Boegler, Texas
*Kickin' Back in the Kitchen Cookbook*

# Grilled Shrimp with Spicy Garlic Paste

1 large garlic clove, minced

1 teaspoon salt

1 teaspoon paprika

½ teaspoon cayenne pepper

2 tablespoons olive oil

2 teaspoons fresh lemon juice

2 pounds shrimp in shells, brined

Lemon wedges

Preheat grill or broiler. Mix the garlic with the salt in a bowl and stir in the paprika and cayenne pepper. Add the olive oil and lemon juice to the garlic mixture and stir until the mixture has the consistency of a thin paste. Add the shrimp and toss until evenly coated. Chill up to 1 hour.

Thread the shrimp onto skewers, if desired, and grill or broil for 2 to 3 minutes per side, or until the shells turn bright pink, turning once. Serve hot or at room temperature with lemon wedges. Serves 2.

*Dallas Dish*

# Bourbon-Barbecued Shrimp

2 pounds jumbo shrimp

2 cups barbecue sauce

1 (16-ounce) bottle zesty Italian salad dressing

3 tablespoons bourbon whiskey

6 tablespoons freshly squeezed lemon juice

2 teaspoons dill weed

2 tablespoons Worcestershire sauce

Tabasco sauce to taste

Remove heads from shrimp, leaving shells on, and wash well. Chill in a glass baking dish for about 30 minutes.

Mix barbecue sauce, salad dressing, and bourbon; cook over low heat, uncovered, for about 10 minutes. Add lemon juice, dill weed, and Worcestershire sauce. Set aside to cool.

Pour cooled marinade over shrimp, stirring well to cover, and refrigerate for at least 4 hours (the longer, the better).

Remove shrimp from marinade and toss onto fine wire mesh over a hot charcoal fire. Grill for about 5 minutes, turning frequently. Do not overcook. As soon as the shell starts to separate from the tail, remove shrimp from the grill and serve.

Add Tabasco sauce to the marinade, bring to a boil, and serve with shrimp. Serves 4 to 6.

Janet Robinson, Morgan City, Louisiana
*Gulf Coast Cooking*

# Broiled Shrimp Cayenne

1 teaspoon salt

1 garlic clove, split

4 tablespoons corn oil

1½ teaspoons lemon or lime juice

1½ to 2 pounds shrimp, shelled and deveined

¼ teaspoon cayenne pepper

6 tablespoons butter, melted

Mash salt and garlic together, combine with oil and lemon juice, and pour over shrimp. Sprinkle with cayenne pepper, mix well, and allow to marinate at least 30 minutes. Arrange shrimp in a shallow baking dish, add melted butter, and stir to coat each shrimp.

Broil for 5 to 8 minutes, turning and basting so shrimp cook evenly. Serve with saffron rice and peas. Serves 6.

Raymond Huffman, Duck Key Lodge, Duck Key, Florida
*Gulf Coast Cooking*

# Doe's Broiled Shrimp

2 pounds raw shrimp, peeled

Konriko Creole Seasoning, or substitute
your favorite Cajun or Creole
seasoning blend

5 cloves minced garlic

½ stick butter

2 tablespoons olive oil

2 tablespoons peanut oil

Juice of 3 lemons

1 tablespoon Worcestershire sauce

1 tablespoon paprika

1 tablespoon Creole seasoning

½ teaspoon red pepper

Tabasco sauce to taste

Sprinkle shrimp with Creole seasoning. Make a basting sauce of the remaining ingredients. Broil the shrimp quickly on both sides, basting frequently with the sauce. Serve the remainder of the sauce with the shrimp.

Doe's Eat Place, Greenville, Mississippi
*Of Magnolia and Mesquite*

# Gulf Coast Shrimp Bake

¾ cup (1½ sticks) butter

1 large bell pepper, chopped

1 medium onion, chopped

2 large tomatoes, chopped

Juice of 1 lemon

2 tablespoons seasoning blend

¼ teaspoon garlic powder

½ teaspoon Italian seasoning

3 bay leaves

½ cup picante sauce

2 celery stalks, chopped

¼ teaspoon ground cumin

⅔ cup barbecue sauce

½ cup steak sauce

1 tablespoon chopped fresh cilantro

½ cup ketchup

1 cup water

⅔ cup dry white wine

3 pounds large shrimp, peeled and
deveined

Place butter in a baking pan and melt in a 375-degree oven. Add bell pepper, onion, and tomato and bake until softened. Add lemon juice and next 13 ingredients. Mix well. Add shrimp. Bake 30 minutes, or until shrimp are pink. Baste with pan juices about every 10 minutes. Do not overcook. Serve hot on a large platter with warm French bread. Serves 4.

Sandra Medina
*Mesquite Country*

# Gaido's of Galveston Shrimp Creole

2 pounds fresh shrimp, peeled and
  deveined

2 tablespoons lemon juice

2 tablespoons Worcestershire sauce

2 teaspoons salt

3 tablespoons butter

1 medium onion, chopped

½ green bell pepper, chopped

2 garlic cloves, minced

2 tablespoons flour

1 teaspoon sugar

¼ teaspoon black pepper

2-¼ cups chopped tomatoes

1 (8-ounce) can tomato sauce

Cooked white rice

Soak peeled shrimp in lemon juice, Worcestershire, and salt. Melt the butter and add onion, bell pepper, and garlic; sauté for 5 minutes. Blend flour, sugar, and pepper into vegetable mixture. Combine tomatoes and tomato sauce with the vegetable mixture. Simmer, covered, over low heat for 15 to 20 minutes. Add shrimp and juice and cook 5 minutes. Serve over hot buttered rice.

Pat Frase
*Gruene General Store Cookbook*

# Home-Style Rice with Shrimp

2 cups uncooked long-grain rice

2 tablespoons olive oil

½ cup finely chopped onion

3 garlic cloves, mashed

½ cup chopped bell pepper

½ cup tomato sauce

1 teaspoon salt

1 pound uncooked shrimp, shelled,
  deveined, and cut into ½-inch pieces

3½ cups chicken broth

In a large deep skillet, sauté the rice in oil over low heat for 4 to 5 minutes, or until the rice is wheat brown in color, stirring constantly. Add onion and garlic and sauté a few more seconds. Add bell pepper and tomato sauce; mix thoroughly.

Stir in the salt, shrimp, and chicken broth. Bring to a boil. Reduce heat and simmer, covered, for 15 minutes. Remove from heat and let rest for 5 minutes. Very important: Never lift the lid while dish is simmering or before it has completed the 5-minute rest period. Fluff rice with a fork and serve. Serves 4 to 6.

**VARIATION:** If you like hot rice, substitute 1 roasted and chopped poblano pepper for the bell pepper.

*Matt Martinez MexTex*

# Crawfish Etienne

1 pound crawfish tails

¼ cup (½ stick) unsalted butter

1 small bunch green onions, chopped

3 garlic cloves, minced

½ cup minced parsley

½ cup (1 stick) unsalted butter

3 tablespoons flour

2 cups half-and-half

3 tablespoons sherry

Salt, cayenne pepper, black pepper, and Tabasco sauce to taste

16 ounces fettuccini, cooked al dente and drained

Sauté the unrinsed crawfish tails in ¼ cup butter in a skillet until cooked through. In another skillet, sauté the green onions, garlic, and parsley in ½ cup butter until tender. Stir in the flour and cook, stirring, until lightly browned. Add the half-and-half gradually, stirring constantly. Stir in the sherry and crawfish tails. Season to taste with salt, cayenne pepper, black pepper, and Tabasco. Cook just until thickened. Serve immediately over the hot pasta. Serves 6.

*Dining without Reservations*

# Hazel Whitith's Crawfish Etouffée

¼ cup vegetable oil

1 cup fine-chopped onion

½ cup fine-chopped celery

½ cup fine-chopped green bell pepper

2 garlic cloves, crushed

1 tablespoon tomato paste

1 teaspoon cornstarch

¾ cup fish stock

1 pound shelled crawfish tails (or shrimp)

1 cup thin-sliced green onions

¼ cup fine-chopped parsley

½ teaspoon Tabasco sauce

¼ teaspoon salt, or to taste

Hot cooked rice

In a large skillet, heat oil over medium-high heat. Add onion, celery, bell pepper, and garlic. Cook 8 to 10 minutes, or until tender, stirring frequently. Stir in tomato paste and cook 1 minute.

In a small bowl, combine cornstarch and fish stock, stirring until smooth. Add to vegetables in skillet and bring to a boil, stirring constantly. Add crawfish, green onions, parsley, Tabasco sauce, and salt. Cook 5 minutes, or until crawfish are tender, stirring frequently. Serve over hot rice. Serves 4.

McIlhenny Company, Avery Island, Louisiana
*Gulf Coast Cooking*

# Crawfish Pie

Pastry for a double-crust 9-inch pie

1 pound peeled crawfish tails

3 cups chopped onion

2 celery stalks, finely chopped

2 tablespoons vegetable oil

½ cup (1 stick) butter

¼ cup chopped green onions

2 garlic cloves, minced

½ cup milk

½ cup seasoned bread crumbs

¼ cup tomato sauce

1 egg, beaten

¼ cup chopped fresh parsley

1 teaspoon salt, or to taste

½ teaspoon pepper

Preheat the oven to 350 degrees. Fit one of the pie pastries into a 9-inch pie plate. Chop ⅓ of the crawfish tails, leaving the remaining ones whole. Sauté the onion and celery in the oil in a skillet until tender. Stir in the butter, green onions, and garlic; sauté for 2 minutes longer. Reduce the heat to low and cook for 10 minutes, stirring occasionally. Remove from heat and stir in the crawfish tails, milk, bread crumbs, tomato sauce, egg, parsley, salt, and pepper.

Spoon the crawfish mixture into the pastry-lined pie plate and top with the remaining pastry, crimping the edge and cutting vents in the top. Bake for 1 to 1½ hours, or until the crust is golden brown. Serves 4 to 6.

*Dallas Dish*

# East Texas Catfish

4 tablespoons butter

2 teaspoons paprika

½ teaspoon cayenne pepper

¼ teaspoon black pepper

1 tablespoon minced fresh thyme

1 tablespoon minced fresh oregano

½ teaspoon salt

4 fresh catfish fillets

Heat broiler and place oven rack 5 inches below heat source.

Melt butter and combine with spices, herbs, and salt. Coat the catfish fillets with the mixture. Broil until opaque throughout, about 6 minutes per side, turning once. Serves 4.

*And Roses for the Table*

# Mustard-Fried Catfish Fingers

4 pounds skinned catfish fillets

3 cups prepared yellow mustard

5 eggs, well beaten

4 large garlic cloves, minced

2¼ teaspoons Tabasco sauce

2 cups yellow cornmeal

2 cups corn flour (sold as unseasoned fish fry)

2 cups Italian-seasoned bread crumbs

2 teaspoons salt

2 teaspoons freshly ground black pepper

2 teaspoons Hungarian paprika

2 teaspoons granulated garlic

Canola oil for deep-frying, preheated to 350 degrees

Tartar sauce, preferably homemade

Pat the catfish fillets dry on absorbent paper towels. Using a sharp knife, cut the fillets into 1-inch-wide strips across the width of the fillets; set aside.

In a large bowl, combine mustard, eggs, garlic, and Tabasco sauce. Whisk to blend well. In another bowl, combine the cornmeal and all remaining ingredients except canola oil and tartar sauce. Toss with a fork to blend well. Dredge the fish pieces in the mustard mixture, turning to coat well. Dip them in the cornmeal mixture, coating well. Shake off all excess breading. Lower the breaded pieces into the preheated oil. Do not overcrowd the oil. Fry just until golden brown and crisp, about 3 to 4 minutes. Drain on a wire rack set over a baking pan. Repeat until all fish pieces have been cooked. Serve hot with tartar sauce. Serves 6 to 8.

*Texas on the Plate*

# Rice-Paper-Wrapped Fish

4 sheets rice paper

1 red bell pepper, cut into thin julienne strips

2 tablespoons grated fresh ginger

2 sliced serrano chiles

4 (5-ounce) fillets of your favorite fish

⅛ cup canola oil

½ cup soy sauce

½ cup rice wine vinegar

1 tablespoon dark sesame oil

Soak rice paper in warm water until it softens. Place on damp towel. In middle of paper place a portion of the julienned bell pepper, ginger, and sliced serrano chile. Place fish on top of vegetables. Roll bottom corner onto back of fish and then roll sides onto fish. (Fish should sit on rice paper diagonally.)

Roll fish so rice paper completely covers fish. Repeat with remaining fish and rice paper. Heat canola oil in pan to 350 degrees. Brown packets on one side in oil, turn, and brown the other side. Place in a 375-degree oven for 5 minutes.

Mix soy sauce, rice wine vinegar, and sesame oil. Drizzle over fish and serve hot. Serves 4.

*Mars Restaurant, Austin*
*Remember the Flavors of Austin*

# Glazed Teriyaki Salmon

⅓ cup orange juice

⅓ cup soy sauce

¼ cup dry white wine

2 tablespoons vegetable oil

1 tablespoon grated fresh ginger

1 teaspoon dry mustard

1 teaspoon lemon juice

Pinch of sugar

1 garlic clove, minced

½ teaspoon freshly ground black pepper

4 (4- to 6-ounce) salmon fillets

Combine all ingredients except salmon in a shallow dish or large zip-top plastic bag. Add salmon. Cover or seal and chill for 30 minutes, turning once.

Preheat oven to 450 degrees. Remove fillets from marinade, reserving marinade. Place fillets in a 13 × 9-inch pan. Bake for 10 minutes, or until fish flakes easily with a fork. Remove from oven. Keep warm.

Bring the reserved marinade to a boil in a small heavy saucepan. Cook, stirring often, for 6 to 8 minutes, or until reduced by half. Pour over fillets and serve. Serves 4.

*Seasoned with Fun*

# Pecan Red Snapper

¼ cup flour

Salt and freshly ground black pepper

4 red snapper fillets

3 tablespoons butter

¼ cup chopped pecans

2 to 3 additional tablespoons butter

Juice of ½ lemon

1 tablespoon minced parsley

1 teaspoon chopped fresh herbs, such as
   chives or thyme

Season the flour with ¼ teaspoon salt and black pepper. Measure the thickness of each fillet. Roll in the seasoned flour. Heat 3 tablespoons butter in a hot skillet until foamy. Add 1 fish fillet. Cook for 10 minutes per inch of total thickness until brown on both sides, turning once. Remove to a heated platter. Repeat with remaining fillets. Wipe the skillet clean with paper towels. Cook the pecans in 2 to 3 tablespoons butter until the butter is nut brown and the pecans are toasted. Add the lemon juice, salt, and pepper to taste, parsley, and fresh herbs all at once. Heat quickly. Pour over the fish and serve immediately. Serves 4.

*Dining without Reservations*

# Snapper with Cilantro Pesto

2 cups lightly packed cilantro leaves

1 cup olive oil

1 tablespoon minced garlic

3 tablespoons freshly squeezed lime juice

2 tablespoons chopped onion

¼ teaspoon cayenne pepper

¼ teaspoon chili powder

½ teaspoon ground cumin

Kosher salt to taste

4 red snapper fillets

1 pound uncooked shrimp, peeled and
   deveined

Process the cilantro, olive oil, garlic, lime juice, onion, cayenne pepper, chili powder, cumin, and kosher salt in food processor until smooth. Scrape down sides of bowl as needed to process all ingredients well.

Place the fish and shrimp in a stainless steel or glass bowl. Add the pesto and toss to coat completely. Marinate in the refrigerator for 30 minutes to 2 hours.

Remove the fish from the bowl and arrange in a single layer in a baking dish that has been sprayed with nonstick cooking spray. Remove the shrimp and squeeze lightly to remove excess pesto; set aside. Spoon the pesto remaining in the bowl over the fish.

Bake fish at 375 degrees for 10 minutes per inch of thickness, or until the fish is opaque throughout.

Heat a nonstick sauté pan over medium-high heat. Add the shrimp and quickly sauté just until the shrimp turn pink.

To serve, arrange the fish on a serving platter, spooning the pan drippings over them. Top with the shrimp and serve immediately. Serves 4.

*Dining without Reservations*

# Red Snapper with Crawfish Cream Sauce

1 pound red snapper fillets

¼ cup flour

Salt and freshly ground black pepper to taste

½ cup butter

Crawfish Cream Sauce (see recipe below)

### Crawfish Cream Sauce

1 pound peeled crawfish tails

½ cup butter

½ green bell pepper, chopped

1 cup half-and-half

1 egg yolk, lightly beaten

1 bunch green onions, sliced

1 cup chopped fresh parsley

6 garlic cloves, minced

¼ cup dry sherry

1 teaspoon white pepper

½ teaspoon salt

½ teaspoon freshly ground black pepper

¼ teaspoon dried thyme

¼ teaspoon dried basil

¼ teaspoon dried oregano

Rinse the fillets and pat dry. Coat the fillets with a mixture of the flour, salt, and pepper.

Sauté the fillets in the butter for 3 to 4 minutes per side, or until the fillets are opaque throughout, turning once. Arrange on a serving platter and set aside to keep warm.

Spoon the warm Crawfish Cream Sauce over the fillets. Serve immediately. Serves 4.

To make the Crawfish Cream Sauce, rinse the crawfish and pat dry. Sauté the crawfish in the butter for 2 minutes. Add the green pepper and mix well. Stir in a mixture of the half-and-half and egg yolk; reduce heat. Add the green onions, parsley, garlic, sherry, white pepper, salt, black pepper, thyme, basil, and oregano and mix well. Cook for 5 minutes, stirring frequently.

*Texas Ties*

# Snapper Pontchartrain

½ cup chicken broth

½ cup sherry

4 pounds fresh red snapper fillets

1 tablespoon paprika

1 teaspoon garlic salt

½ teaspoon pepper

2 tablespoons butter

1 tablespoon minced parsley

6 green onions, finely chopped

10 to 15 large white mushrooms, sliced

⅓ cup butter

5 garlic cloves, minced

2 tablespoons flour

¼ cup (1 ounce) freshly grated Parmesan cheese

½ cup half-and-half

1 pound small shrimp, peeled, deveined, and cooked

Boil the chicken broth and sherry in a small saucepan until reduced by half. Remove from heat.

Season the fish fillets with paprika, garlic salt, and pepper. Dot with 2 tablespoons butter. Place in a large, shallow baking pan. Bake at 350 degrees for 15 to 20 minutes, or until almost cooked through. Remove and set aside. Preheat broiler and place oven rack 5 inches below heat source.

Sauté the parsley, green onions, and mushrooms in ⅓ cup butter in a skillet. Add the garlic. Sauté until light brown. Stir in the flour and cook, stirring constantly, for 2 to 3 minutes, or until flour is lightly browned. Add the cheese, reduced chicken broth mixture, and half-and-half. Add the shrimp and stir to blend well. Pour over the baked fish and broil for 5 minutes or until lightly browned. Serve immediately. Serves 8.

*Dining without Reservations*

# Pecan-Crusted Red Snapper with Spring Lemon Herb Sauce

## Pecan Crust Breading

1 cup bread crumbs

2 cups pecan pieces

1 teaspoon each: dried basil, oregano, whole leaf thyme, granulated garlic, granulated onion, white pepper

## Pecan-Crusted Red Snapper

6 boned red snapper fillets, 6 to 8 ounces each, about ½-inch thick

2 eggs

1 cup milk

1 cup flour

1 cup olive or canola oil

## Spring Lemon Herb Sauce

1 cup chardonnay or other dry white wine

1 shallot, minced

4 garlic cloves, minced

2 cups good chicken stock, reduced to 1 cup

1 cup mixed fresh lemon herbs: lemon balm, lemon thyme, sorrel, lemon basil, begonias

1½ teaspoons salt or to taste

½ teaspoon white pepper

1½ cups (3 sticks) butter, cut into 1-inch cubes and chilled

Pulse all breading ingredients in food processor until medium-fine. Place on a flat dish and set aside.

Prepare the snapper. Combine the eggs and milk; whisk well to create egg wash. Put flour on a flat dish. Holding the red snapper by the tail, dredge it in the flour until well dusted. Shake off excess flour.

Pass floured fillet through the egg wash, wetting the entire fillet. Place fillet in pecan meal breading mixture. Lightly press the mixture onto both sides of the fillet with the palm of your hand. Remove and shake off excess. Set aside on a dry sheet pan or cookie sheet until all fillets are breaded.

Make the herb sauce. In a saucepan, reduce wine with garlic and shallots until almost dry. Add reduced chicken stock and heat until boiling. Combine hot stock mixture and herbs in blender and turn on high. Be careful. Cover top with towel and let expanded steam release. Quickly add the butter, 3 to 4 chunks at a time, until all is in solution. Add salt and white pepper. This is a light, thin sauce that will hold for 30 minutes only.

Heat oil in a large skillet or sauté pan over medium-high heat until it shimmers. Sauté the snapper fillets until golden brown in batches of 2 or 3, so the oil doesn't cool down. Place in a single layer on a baking sheet in warm (180 degrees) oven while sautéing remaining fillets.

Place a portion of the Spring Lemon Herb Sauce on each fillet. Serve at once. Serves 6.

*Cooking Fearlessly*

# Hot and Crunchy Trout with Mango-Jalapeño Aioli

## Hot and Crunchy Trout

6 to 8 trout fillets (8 ounces each)

¼ cup almonds

¼ cup sesame seeds

2 cups cornflakes

¼ cup granulated sugar

1½ tablespoons crushed red pepper flakes

1 tablespoon salt

1 cup milk

2 eggs

1 cup all-purpose flour

6 tablespoons clarified butter

## Mango-Jalapeño Aioli—The Easy Way

Juice of 2 lemons

1 bunch cilantro, leaves only, roughly cut

½ cup Mango Jalapeño Sauce (see recipe below)

1 cup mayonnaise

2 garlic cloves, minced

Salt and pepper to taste, about ½ tablespoon

## Mango-Jalapeño Sauce— The Fearless Way

1 pound mangoes, diced

1½ cups granulated sugar

3 ounces champagne vinegar

2 tablespoons minced garlic

3 tablespoons diced red onion

4 jalapeños, seeded and sliced

½ teaspoon salt

Begin by making the Mango-Jalapeño Sauce. Combine mangoes, sugar, vinegar, garlic, and red onion in a saucepan; bring to a boil, then reduce heat to a simmer and cook for 10 minutes. Add jalapeños and salt. Serve the sauce hot or cold. If making aioli, chill completely before adding to other ingredients.

Make the Mango-Jalapeño Aioli. Combine all ingredients in a bowl and whisk until well blended. Set aside.

To fry the trout, toast the almonds and sesame seeds separately in a dry skillet until lightly toasted. Set aside to cool.

Combine cooled almonds, sesame seeds, cornflakes, sugar, red pepper flakes, and salt in food processor and pulse until coarse and crunchy, but well blended. Empty onto platter or baking sheet.

Whisk milk and eggs to make egg wash. Put flour on a flat dish. Holding the trout fillets by the tail, dredge in the flour until well dusted. Shake off excess flour.

Pass the dusted fillets through the egg wash, wetting the entire fillet. Place the fillet in the hot and crunchy mixture, lightly pressing the mixture on the fillet with the palm of your hand. Coat both sides. Set aside on a dry sheet pan or cookie sheet until all trout are breaded.

In a large, heavy sauté pan, heat 6 tablespoons clarified butter to about 325 degrees until it shimmers, or until parsley sizzles when tossed in. Lay the trout in the hot pan, skin side up. Sauté for about 3 minutes on each side. It will cook to a golden crunchy brown. Turn only once.

Place each fillet on a cookie sheet in a warm oven (180 degrees) until you have cooked all fillets. To serve, place a pool of the Mango-Jalapeño Aioli on each serving plate and lay a Hot and Crunchy Trout in the sauce. Serve at once. Serves 6 to 8.

*Cooking Fearlessly*

# Trout Meunière Amandine

1½ pounds fresh trout fillets, skinned

Salt

Milk

Flour

1 cup butter, divided

½ cup minced parsley

½ teaspoon ground black pepper

2 green onions, chopped, including green tops

2 garlic cloves, minced

1 tablespoon freshly squeezed lemon juice

1 tablespoon dry white wine

2 tablespoons butter

1 (3-ounce) package sliced, skin-on almonds

Season fish fillets with salt. Dip in milk and lightly dust with flour, shaking off all excess. Brown in ½ cup of the melted butter, turning once. Remove to heated platter and keep warm in low oven. Lightly brown remaining ½ cup butter in a small skillet. Add parsley, pepper, garlic, lemon juice, and wine. Simmer gently 3 to 5 minutes. Add green onions and cook 1 more minute. Meanwhile, toast almonds in 2 tablespoons butter in a small skillet. Add to sauce mixture and pour over browned trout. Serve immediately. Serves 4.

Jan McManus LeBlanc
*Lagniappe*

# City Grill's Gulf Redfish with Spicy Szechuan Sauce

6 redfish fillets (⅓ to ½ pound each) or
    fillets of swordfish, tuna, mahi-mahi,
    or shark

## Szechuan Marinade

1 (8-ounce) can Szechuan chili paste

1 cup dark honey

2 tablespoons rice wine vinegar

3 tablespoons Oriental sesame oil

3 tablespoons peanut oil

Juice of 1 to 2 fresh limes

## Spicy Szechuan Sauce

1 cup mayonnaise

2 tablespoons rice wine vinegar

1 tablespoon Oriental sesame oil

¼ cup Szechuan Marinade

3 to 4 tablespoons Thai basil, chopped

## Garnishes

6 Thai basil sprigs

Lime wedges

Slivered scallions

Combine marinade ingredients, blending well. Mix together the ingredients for the Spicy Szechuan Sauce and chill.

Dip the fillets in the marinade, and place presentation side down on the grill over red-hot coals. Grill until well marked by the grill, turning once (approximately 8 minutes per inch of thickness of the fish).

Serve with a generous dollop of Spicy Szechuan Sauce, either on the side or melted on the fish, and garnished with a sprig of the basil, several lime wedges, and slivered scallions. Serves 6.

City Grill, Austin
*The Herb Garden Cookbook*

# Mike Wicker's Redfish on the Half Shell

4 (12- to 13-ounce) redfish fillets,
    unscaled

1 cup Worcestershire sauce

6 tablespoons unsalted butter

Juice of 2 large lemons

Lemon-pepper seasoning

Tony Chachere's Creole Seasoning

Heat gas grill to medium. Combine Worcestershire sauce, butter, and lemon juice in a small saucepan over medium heat. Cook until butter has melted, stirring often. Place the fish fillets, skin side down, in a large baking dish. Baste liberally with the butter mixture. Save remaining butter for basting while grilling. Season the fillets to taste with lemon-pepper and Creole seasonings.

Grill the redfish, skin side down, for 15 to 20 minutes, or until meat turns opaque throughout. Baste often with the remaining butter mixture. Do not turn the fish while grilling. Do not overcook. Remove to serving plates and serve hot. Serves 4 to 6.

> **EDITOR'S NOTE:** To prepare this delicious dish you must have a fresh redfish with the skin and scales intact. It's a great example of Texas "fishermen's cooking," whereby fish is cooked within hours of being caught.

Mike Wicker
*Texas on the Plate*

# Balsamic-Glazed Tuna

### Balsamic Glaze

¼ cup fat-free chicken broth

1 tablespoon balsamic vinegar

4 teaspoons brown sugar

1 tablespoon soy sauce

½ teaspoon cornstarch

### Tuna

4 (6-ounce) tuna steaks

¼ teaspoon salt

1¼ teaspoons pepper

¼ cup sliced green onions

To prepare the glaze, combine the chicken broth, balsamic vinegar, brown sugar, soy sauce, and cornstarch in a small saucepan and whisk until smooth. Bring to a boil and cook for 1 minute, stirring constantly. Keep warm.

To prepare the fish, season the tuna steaks with salt and pepper. Spray a grill pan with nonstick cooking spray and heat over medium-high heat. Place the tuna on the grill pan and cook for 3 minutes on each side for medium-rare, or until done to taste. Remove from the heat. Place the tuna on serving plates and spoon the glaze over the top. Scatter green onions over each portion. Serves 4.

*Lone Star to Five Star*

# Camp's Grilled Tuna with Yogurt-Dill Sauce

## Yogurt-Dill Sauce

2 cups plain low-fat yogurt

1 tablespoon Dijon mustard

2 teaspoons horseradish

¼ cup fresh dill, minced

½ cup finely sliced green onion

Juice of ½ lemon

## Tuna

2 pounds fresh tuna steaks (1 inch thick)

¼ cup fresh lime juice

¼ cup olive oil

Blend all sauce ingredients. Add salt and freshly ground pepper to taste. Refrigerate. Preheat grill or broiler. Rub tuna steaks with lime juice, then olive oil. Broil or grill about 3 to 4 minutes per side, turning once. Serve with Yogurt-Dill Sauce. Serves 4 to 6.

*¡Viva! Tradiciones*

# Poultry & Game Birds

The first thing that pops into most people's minds when you mention poultry is generally chicken. While chicken is a noble, tasty meat and certainly one that is lower in fat than red meats, the world of poultry is rich with other birds.

Although they are not as popular as they once were, Cornish hens have a delicious flavor and can be roasted to make a quick, luscious meal. They're readily available, usually frozen, in the poultry section of most supermarkets.

Texas is blessed to be part of the Central Flyway for migrating birds, so we have a bounty of wild game birds that spend their winters here each year. Ducks and geese abound in the coastal marshlands, giving lucky hunters the opportunity to stock their freezers with the delicious birds.

Dove is another tasty little bird that proliferates in Texas. They're very popular with hunters and there are myriad ways to cook them and enjoy their delicate taste. Bobwhite quail are hunted in Texas, but we also are fortunate to have a growing quail-raising industry. Fresh, semiboneless quail are available in many of our specialty markets. Chefs love the delectable little birds for the grand array of dishes that can be created using them. Quail is equally delicious pan-sautéed, deep-fried, roasted, braised, or grilled. I've even seen quail used quite nicely in salads. Quail legs make a tasty party finger food, grilled with a nice glaze or deep-fried and served with a dipping sauce.

Pheasant is a regal bird that can be hunted in our Panhandle Plains region and used as the centerpiece of a special dinner.

Whenever possible, purchase organic or free-range chickens. Those who live in cities with large farmers' markets can usually find a purveyor of free-range and/or organic chickens. Many specialty grocery markets also carry them. Take care not to overcook chicken. Certainly, chicken is one critter that should be cooked until it is completely done, but if overcooked, chicken becomes dry, stringy, and tasteless. Nothing is more delicious than a perfectly roasted whole chicken, cooked for 20 minutes per pound at 350 degrees. The skin is golden brown and crisp, and the meat is juicy, tender, and so very flavorful.

# Smothered Game Birds

10 quail or 12 doves, breasts only

Enough flour, salt, and pepper to lightly coat birds

6 slices Smokehouse Bacon, cut in half

3 tablespoons flour

2 (10-ounce) cans beef broth

1 pound fresh mushrooms, cleaned and sliced

4 green onions, sliced

½ cup white wine

¼ cup chopped parsley

Dredge birds in flour seasoned with salt and pepper. Shake off excess flour. Sauté bacon in Dutch oven (or heavy pot with lid) until done, but not crisp. Remove bacon from Dutch oven and drain on paper towels.

Brown birds in hot bacon drippings. Remove and drain on paper towels. Slowly brown the flour in bacon drippings. Add beef broth, stirring constantly until thickened.

Add mushrooms and green onions. Return the birds to the Dutch oven. Top with bacon. Cover and cook in 325-degree oven for 1 hour.

Add white wine and sprinkle with parsley. Cook for another 15 minutes. Serve over brown, white, or wild rice. Serves 4 to 6.

**EDITOR'S NOTE:** Smokehouse Bacon is a New Braunfels Smokehouse product.

*New Braunfels Smokehouse*

# Doves in Sherry Sauce

12 to 15 dove breasts, boned

¼ cup seasoned flour

4 tablespoons butter

1 small onion, minced

¾ to 1 cup sherry, divided

1 (14½-ounce) can tomatoes

1 (4-ounce) jar marinated mushrooms, undrained

1 tablespoon dry chicken bouillon

1 tablespoon Worcestershire sauce

1 cup water

Dredge doves in flour. Melt butter over medium-high heat in a large saucepan or Dutch oven. Add doves and sauté. Remove doves and add onion to saucepan. Sauté until softened. Return doves to pan.

Add ¾ cup sherry and remaining 5 ingredients. Bring to a boil. Reduce heat and simmer 60 minutes, or until meat is tender. If desired, add remaining ¼ cup sherry and cook 15 minutes longer. Serve with rice or noodles.

Monica Burdette, The Inn at El Canelo, Raymondville, Texas
*Mesquite Country*

# Dove Pie

**Pastry for one 9-inch double-crust pie**

### Stock and Meat

**10 to 12 doves, cleaned**

**2 celery stalks, with leaves, chopped**

**1 carrot, chopped**

### Filling

**1 celery stalk, chopped**

**⅓ cup onion, chopped**

**1 tablespoon butter**

**1 tablespoon flour**

**1½ cups dove broth**

**½ teaspoon Worcestershire sauce**

**¾ cup fresh or frozen peas**

**¾ cup finely chopped carrots**

**1 cup sliced mushrooms**

Using enough water to cover the doves, boil the doves in a stockpot along with celery and carrot, about 30 minutes, until well cooked. Remove doves from broth, reserving 1½ cups of the broth. Allow doves to cool, then debone and shred the meat. Set aside.

Line a 9-inch pie plate with half of the pastry. Set aside. Roll out other half of the pastry for top.

Heat oven to 400 degrees. In a large skillet, heat butter and brown carrots, celery, and onions. Add flour and mix well. Add the stock and allow flour to blend completely with stock. Add Worcestershire sauce and allow mixture to thicken. Add peas, carrots, mushrooms, and dove meat. Simmer for 10 minutes.

Pour dove filling into prepared pie plate. Cover with other half of rolled-out pastry; seal and decorate edges. Bake for 35 to 40 minutes. Allow to cool slightly before serving. Serves 6.

*The Texas Provincial Kitchen Cookbook*

# Barbecued Doves

12 doves

Milk

6 canned jalapeños

6 slices bacon

Italian salad dressing

Salt and pepper

Marinate doves in milk overnight. Remove and pat dry. Place ½ jalapeño inside cavity of each dove. Wrap ½ slice bacon around each dove; secure with toothpick. Sprinkle with salt and pepper. Barbecue over slow fire with generous applications of Italian salad dressing, about 30 minutes. Serves 4.

*Seasoned with Sun*

# Barbecued Doves II

12 doves

4 cups beef broth or consommé

## Barbecue Sauce

2 cups (4 sticks) butter

1 (5-ounce) bottle A.1. steak sauce

2 tablespoons mustard

Juice of 3 lemons

2 dashes Tabasco sauce

1 tablespoon sugar

1 tablespoon salt

Garlic salt to taste

Place doves in a large saucepan and pour broth over them to cover by 1 inch; add water if needed. Bring to a boil, reduce heat, and simmer 30 to 45 minutes, or until doves are tender but not falling apart. Set aside and preheat grill. To prepare the sauce, combine all ingredients in a separate saucepan and heat slowly over low heat. Be careful not to let the sauce boil, or it will separate. Place doves on a hot grill and baste with sauce, turning frequently. Cook 8 to 10 minutes. Serve immediately with extra barbecue sauce.

Carolyn Brown, Salado Seco Ranch
*Grazing across Texas*

# Wino Quail

4 tablespoons butter

6 whole quail, or 8 quail breasts

3 tablespoons flour

¾ teaspoon salt

½ teaspoon white pepper

2 cups coarsely chopped onions

2 cups coarsely chopped mushrooms

3 garlic cloves, thinly sliced

⅛ teaspoon thyme leaves

1 cup chicken broth

1 cup dry white wine

1 cup half-and-half or heavy cream

Chopped chives or parsley for garnish

In a Dutch oven or other large pot, melt the butter over moderate heat. Dust the quail with flour, salt, and pepper, then place in the pot. Add the onions, mushrooms, garlic, and thyme. Toss and sauté the birds along with other ingredients in the pot for 3 to 4 minutes, cooking until onions are translucent.

Add the broth and wine. Cook ever so gently with the lid on for 1 to 1½ hours, watching the broth so it does not get dry. Add water as needed and occasionally scrape the bottom of the pot. If the sauce is too thick, you may also add water until you reach the desired consistency.

When the birds are tender, add cream and gently simmer for 3 to 4 minutes. Season with salt and pepper to taste. Garnish with chives or parsley. Serve over rice. Serves 4 to 6.

*Matt Martinez MexTex*

# Mom's Quail

24 quail

Crisco

2 cups apple juice

1 cup water

1 apple, cut in eighths

1 cup sherry

1 stick of butter

Wash birds, sprinkle with salt and pepper, and soak in bowl of cold water for at least 1 hour.

Shake the birds in flour and fry in Crisco in heavy skillet until brown and crisp. Remove birds and place in roaster. Add apple juice, water, and apple segments. Cook, covered, in 350-degree oven for 2 hours. During the second hour, add butter and sherry to the pan. Baste frequently.

Martin F. "Bubba" Wood, Dallas
publisher of *Grazing across Texas*

# Roast Pheasant with Caramelized Pears

3 pheasants, dressed and cleaned (about 2 to 2½ pounds each)

¼ cup honey

¼ cup Oriental hoisin sauce

1 cup canola oil

¼ cup bourbon whiskey

Freshly ground black pepper

Salt and additional freshly ground black pepper

12 applewood-smoked bacon strips

## Caramelized Pears

4 pears, peeled, cored, and sliced in half

½ cup light brown sugar

⅓ cup finely chopped pickled ginger (sushi ginger)

¼ cup chicken stock

## Chili-Coriander Sauce

⅓ cup finely minced pickled ginger

¾ cup jalapeño pepper jelly, melted and strained

¼ heaping cup whole coriander seeds, toasted

1 cup water

1 tablespoon chili paste with garlic

¼ cup sherry wine vinegar

1 bunch fresh cilantro leaves and stems

2 cups chicken stock

Tie the legs of the pheasant together with butcher's (cotton) twine and tuck the wing tips under the bodies, securing them with poultry pins. Place in a large baking dish. Combine honey, hoisin sauce, canola oil, whiskey, and black pepper, whisking to blend well. Pour the marinade over the birds, turning to coat well. Marinate in refrigerator for 8 hours or overnight.

Preheat oven to 350 degrees. Remove birds from marinade and arrange them, breast side up, in a roasting pan, not touching. Salt and pepper the birds, then cover each breast with 4 bacon slices. Cover the pan and place in preheated oven. Roast for 40 minutes, then uncover and roast an additional 15 minutes to brown the pheasants.

While birds are roasting, prepare the Caramelized Pears. Place the brown sugar in a heavy 12-inch sauté pan; heat until melted and syrupy. Add the ginger and chicken stock, stirring over medium-high heat until the sugar has melted into the stock and the mixture is smooth and thick. Add the pear halves and cook until they are lightly caramelized but still crisp and tender. Set aside and keep warm.

Prepare the Chili-Coriander Sauce. Combine the pickled ginger, jalapeño jelly, coriander seeds, water, and chili paste with garlic. Cook over medium-high heat until the coriander becomes very fragrant. Add the sherry vinegar and cilantro. Cook to reduce the liquid by half. Add the chicken stock and reduce until slightly thickened and syrupy, about 25 minutes. Strain the sauce through a fine strainer, discarding solids. Set aside and keep warm.

Remove bacon strips from pheasant and discard. Slice pheasants in half through the back and breast bones. Place a pheasant half on each serving plate and arrange 2 pear halves around each serving. Drizzle a portion of the sauce over each serving. Serve at once. Serves 4 to 6.

*Texas on the Plate*

# Country-Style Braised Wild Duck

4 large wild ducks, about 2 to 2½ pounds each, cleaned

2 yellow onions, quartered

8 large garlic cloves, peeled

¾ pound andouille sausage, cut into 1-inch slices

Canola oil for glazing

Salt and freshly ground black pepper

## Gravy

3 medium yellow onions, chopped

4 large garlic cloves, minced

1 medium green bell pepper, chopped

3 celery stalks, chopped, including leafy tops

¼ cup minced flat-leaf parsley

½ pound andouille sausage, sliced into bite-size pieces

1 pound mushrooms, sliced

1 teaspoon red (cayenne) pepper

⅓ cup Worcestershire sauce

3 fresh bay leaves, minced

2 teaspoons minced fresh thyme

2 teaspoons minced fresh sage

1 cup cabernet sauvignon

2 cups beef stock

1 (14-ounce) can artichoke hearts (not marinated), drained and quartered

Salt and freshly ground black pepper to taste

Additional beef stock as needed

Brown roux made with 3 tablespoons bacon drippings and 3 tablespoons all-purpose flour

4 green onions, chopped, including green tops

Cooked Texmati or other basmati rice

Remove and discard the tail knob from the ducks. Stuff each duck with the onion quarters, garlic, and andouille sausage. Rub ducks with canola oil and season with salt and pepper. Heat a thin glaze of canola oil over medium heat in a Dutch oven or flameproof roasting pan. When the oil is hot, place the ducks on their backs in the pan.

To prepare the gravy, scatter the onions, garlic, bell pepper, celery, parsley, ½ pound andouille sausage, and mushrooms in the pan. Combine the red pepper, Worcestershire sauce, bay leaves, thyme, sage, and cabernet sauvignon, whisking to blend well. Pour the wine mixture into the pan. Set the pan over medium-low heat and cook to reduce the wine by about half, approximately 30 minutes. Add the beef stock, cover the pan, and simmer gently for 1 hour. The juices should run light pink when the breast is pierced. Add the artichoke hearts and cook an additional 15 minutes. Remove the ducks from the pan; set aside and keep hot. Return the pan to medium heat and add 1 cup additional stock. Bring the liquid to a full, rolling boil. Add the brown roux all at once and stir to blend; cook until thickened, about 5 minutes. Stir in the green onions.

To serve, cut the ducks in half lengthwise through the breastbone, discarding the backbone. Place a portion of the cooked rice on each serving plate and arrange duck, cut side down, on the rice. Spoon vegetables and gravy from the pan over and around the ducks. Serve hot. Serves 6 to 8.

*Texas on the Plate*

# Thai-Style Barbecued Hens

4 Cornish game hens, 14 to 16 ounces each

¼ cup minced cilantro

1 tablespoon freshly ground black pepper

12 garlic cloves, minced

2 tablespoons canola oil

### Glazing Sauce

6 garlic cloves, peeled and trimmed

2 serrano chiles, seeds and veins removed, minced

3 tablespoons dark brown sugar

1 tablespoon honey

2 lemongrass stalks, white portion only, chopped

1 tablespoon grated fresh ginger

4 shallots, chopped

⅓ cup soy sauce

¼ cup minced fresh cilantro

Preheat grill to medium heat. Prepare the Glazing Sauce by combining all ingredients in work bowl of food processor fitted with steel blade. Process until smooth. Set aside.

Split the hens in half lengthwise through the breastbone and backbone. In a small bowl, combine the minced cilantro, black pepper, garlic cloves, and canola oil, stirring to blend well. Rub the mixture over the skin side of each hen. Grill hens for about 30 minutes, turning every 5 minutes for even browning. Internal temperature should read 165 degrees on an instant-read meat thermometer. For the last 10 minutes of grilling, baste the hens with the Glazing Sauce. Transfer hens to a serving platter and drizzle any remaining glaze over them. Serve hot. Serves 6 to 8.

Terry Thompson-Anderson

# Niçoise-Style Roast Cornish Hens

3 (16- to 20-ounce) Cornish game hens

7 large garlic cloves, minced

1 tablespoon plus 1 teaspoon minced fresh thyme

2 tablespoons minced fresh basil

2 teaspoons minced fresh marjoram

2 teaspoons minced fresh savory

Freshly squeezed lemon juice

2 cups all-purpose flour, seasoned with salt, black pepper, and cayenne pepper

Freshly ground black pepper

½ cup olive oil

5 anchovy fillets

1½ cups dry white wine

1 cup chicken stock

6 large Roma tomatoes, peeled, seeded, and diced

1 cup pitted niçoise olives, roughly chopped

1 tablespoon minced flat-leaf parsley

Carefully detach the skin from the breast meat of the hens, working your fingers under the skin and taking care not to tear the skin. Loosen the skin down the sides of the hens, working toward the backbone. Combine the minced garlic with the minced herbs; divide the herb mixture in half, setting half aside. Divide the remaining half among the hens, stuffing a portion under the loosened skin of each. Split each hen in half through the breastbone and backbone. Rub the surface of the hens all over with the lemon juice, coating well. Dredge each piece in the seasoned flour, coating well and shaking off all excess flour. Season each piece liberally with black pepper.

Preheat oven to 400 degrees. Heat the olive oil in a heavy-bottomed 12-inch skillet over medium heat. When the oil is hot, add 3 of the hen pieces, skin side down, and cook until golden brown. Turn the pieces over and brown the cut side. Remove to a heatproof, shallow-sided, open roasting pan, placing the hens cut side down. Repeat with the remaining hen pieces, placing them in the baking dish after browning. Reserve the pan drippings in the skillet. Roast hens in preheated oven for 30 minutes, or until juices run clear.

While the hens are roasting, grind the anchovies to a smooth paste; set aside. Pour off all oil from the skillet and return pan to medium-high heat. Add the white wine, scraping up all browned bits from bottom of pan. Cook until the wine is reduced almost to a glaze. Add the chicken stock, anchovy paste, and remaining herb and garlic mixture. Cook to reduce liquid by half. Add the diced tomatoes; cook until tomatoes have broken down and mixture has thickened, about 15 minutes, stirring often. Add the olives and cook just to heat through.

To serve, place a portion of the tomato mixture on each serving plate and top with a roasted hen half, cut side down. Scatter minced parsley over the birds and serve hot. Serves 6.

Terry Thompson-Anderson

# Roast Free-Range Chicken with Mexican Mint Marigold Butter and White Wine Sauce

2 (3½- to 5-pound) free-range chickens

½ pound (2 sticks) unsalted butter, softened

2 tablespoons minced fresh Mexican mint marigold, or substitute fresh tarragon

1 teaspoon freshly ground black pepper

1½ teaspoons salt

¼ cup dry vermouth

2 cups rich chicken stock

## White Wine Sauce

4 tablespoons (½ stick) unsalted butter

¼ cup all-purpose flour

Pan drippings from cooking chicken

3 French shallots, finely chopped

Freshly ground black pepper

4 cups rich chicken stock

⅔ cup sauvignon blanc

Salt to taste

Preheat oven to 400 degrees. Spray a shallow-sided, flameproof roasting pan with nonstick spray. Wash the chicken well and pat very dry with absorbent paper towels. Set aside. Combine the butter, Mexican mint marigold, pepper, salt, and vermouth in work bowl of small food processor fitted with steel blade. Process until smooth and well blended. Remove butter mixture to a bowl using a rubber spatula.

Using your fingers, loosen the skin of the chicken from the meat all around the breast. You will have to carefully sever the tissue attached to the middle of the breastbone, using your index finger like a hook. Separate the skin down the rib cage on the sides and all the way to the tailbone and down to the leg joint. Your hand will be completely under the skin. Take care not to tear the skin over the breast meat.

Using your hands, spread the Mexican mint marigold butter under the loosened skin of the chicken, distributing evenly. Pat the skin back into place, evening out the buttery lumps. Smear the remaining butter on the outside skin of the chicken, tie the legs together with butcher's (cotton) twine, and place in the prepared roasting pan, breast side up. Pour the 2 cups chicken stock around the chicken.

Loosely cover the chicken with parchment paper and roast for 20 minutes per pound in preheated oven. After the first 15 minutes, turn the chicken to one side and baste with pan juices, using a bulb baster or spoon. Repeat the turning and basting every 15 minutes until chicken is once again on its back. Remove the parchment paper for the last 15 minutes of roasting. Chicken should be nicely browned with crisp skin on all sides. To test for doneness, pierce the flesh of the thigh near bone with a skewer. The liquid that runs out should be clear with no traces of pink. Place chicken on cutting board and cover loosely with aluminum foil. Allow the chicken to rest for 15 minutes. Prepare White Wine Sauce while chicken is resting.

Combine the softened butter and flour in work bowl of food processor fitted with steel blade. Process until well blended, with no traces of unblended flour. Scrape out into bowl with rubber spatula and set aside. Place the flameproof roasting pan directly on burner over high heat. Add the shallots and black pepper, then sauté until shallots are wilted and transparent. Add the white wine and stir, scraping up all browned bits from bottom of pan. Cook until pan juices and wine are reduced to a glaze. Add the chicken stock and cook to reduce by half. Strain the sauce into a 2-quart saucepan. Place saucepan over medium-high heat and bring to a full, rolling boil. Whisk in the butter and flour mixture, one small chunk at a time, until desired thickness has been reached.

To serve, carve the chickens into 4 pieces each (2 breast-wing portions, 2 thigh-leg portions.) Arrange the pieces on serving platter. Pass the sauce separately in a sauceboat. Serves 6 to 8.

**NOTE:** Mexican mint marigold, also known as yerba anise, is the Gulf Coast's answer to true French tarragon, which simply will not grow in our humidity. Identical in taste to real tarragon, mint marigold is a very hardy evergreen in all but the harshest Texas winters. It will grow to gargantuan proportions and reward you with thousands of brilliant yellow blooms. (Use the flowers in salads or as a garnish.) If the herb gets "bitten" by a moderate freeze, simply cut it back to about 2 inches from the ground and wait until spring. It will come back even fuller than it was the year before.

*Texas on the Plate*

# Crispy Oven-Fried Chicken

3 quarts water

½ cup kosher salt

½ cup sugar

1 (2½- to 3-pound) chicken, cut up

3 cups cornflakes, crushed

½ cup (2 ounces) grated Parmesan cheese

1 teaspoon salt

¼ teaspoon garlic powder

¼ teaspoon pepper

½ cup (1 stick) butter, melted

Mix the water, salt, and sugar in a large bowl until sugar is dissolved and add the chicken pieces to the brining solution. Soak for 45 minutes and drain. Rinse and pat dry with paper towels. Chill the chicken in the refrigerator for up to 1 day.

Preheat the oven to 400 degrees. Toss the cornflakes, cheese, salt, garlic, and pepper in a sealable plastic bag. Dip the chicken in the butter and add to the cornflake mixture. Seal the bag tightly and shake until the chicken is well coated. Arrange the chicken in a single layer on a baking sheet and bake for 40 to 45 minutes, or until cooked through and crispy. Serves 4.

*Dallas Dish*

# Jalapeño Chicken

½ cup butter, melted

1 (6-ounce) can frozen orange juice
concentrate, undiluted

1 (8-ounce) bottle Italian salad dressing

2 (2- to 2½-pound) chickens, cut up

Sliced jalapeño peppers to taste

Combine first 3 ingredients, mixing well. Dip chicken pieces in sauce, coating well. Place in a foil-lined 3½-quart baking pan. Pour remaining sauce over chicken. Sprinkle sliced jalapeños over top. Cover with foil and bake at 350 degrees for 45 minutes to 1 hour. Remove foil; broil until browned. Serves 8 to 10.

Jan Leuschner Meeks
*Flavor Favorites*

# Loren's Chicken

1 can of beer

1 whole chicken

Paper towel

Lemon-pepper seasoning

Salt and black pepper to taste

First you drink the can of beer. Next, fill the can half full of water. Take the whole chicken and rinse the cavity and stuff a wet paper towel into the neck cavity. Then place the chicken on the beer can, neck end up and season all over with lemon-pepper seasoning, salt, and black pepper. Place the chicken on the beer can upright on the smoker and smoke until the skin really splits. This takes approximately 3 hours, depending on the size of the chicken.

Kathleen Gunn, Gunn Ranch, D'Hanis, Texas
*Stolen Recipes*

# Sugar-Fried Chicken

2 to 2½ pounds boneless chicken breasts

½ cup canola oil

2 tablespoons brown sugar

### Marinade

½ cup ketchup

½ cup water

1 small onion, chopped

3 garlic cloves, minced

1 tablespoon ground cumin

1 tablespoon Season All seasoned salt or Old Bay Seasoning

1 teaspoon pepper

1 teaspoon salt

Combine all marinade ingredients, blending well. Coat the chicken with marinade and let stand for 20 minutes. Heat the oil in a heavy skillet. Add brown sugar, stirring until melted. Add chicken and brown on both sides. Add the marinade plus 2 cups of water; bring to a boil and simmer for 20 minutes, or until chicken is cooked through. Serve with yellow rice.

**NOTE:** To make yellow rice, add 1 teaspoon turmeric to water when cooking the rice.

*Texas Cookoff*

# Best-Ever Buttermilk Fried Chicken

1 pound thinly sliced chicken breast

1 cup buttermilk, divided

¼ cup yellow cornmeal

¼ cup plus 2 teaspoons flour, divided

½ teaspoon salt

1 teaspoon coarsely ground black pepper

¼ cup vegetable oil, divided

¾ cup chicken broth

Place chicken slices in a shallow dish and pour in ½ cup of the buttermilk, turning chicken to coat well. In another dish combine cornmeal, ¼ cup flour, salt, and pepper. Dredge the chicken pieces in the cornmeal mixture, patting to coat well. In a large skillet heat 2 tablespoons of the oil over medium-high heat. Add half of the chicken and cook, turning once, until chicken is crisp and white throughout. Remove chicken and keep warm. Repeat with the remaining chicken and oil. Stir in the remaining 2 teaspoons flour and cook, stirring 1 minute. Whisk broth and the remaining ½ cup buttermilk into pan drippings, scraping up browned bits from bottom of pan. Simmer, stirring, for 2 minutes. Season with additional salt and pepper to taste. Serve gravy with the chicken. Serves 4.

*Texas Blossoms*

# Chicken Fredericksburg

2 tablespoons olive or canola oil

2 boneless, skinless chicken breasts, lightly floured

1 teaspoon minced garlic

1 teaspoon minced jalapeño, or to taste

⅓ cup caramelized onions

1 ripe peach, peeled and sliced, with its juice

2 tablespoons dry white wine

½ cup whipping cream

1 tablespoon toasted pecan pieces

## Spaetzle

2 eggs, beaten

½ cup milk

1½ cups all-purpose flour

¼ teaspoon salt

⅛ teaspoon freshly grated nutmeg

2 tablespoons butter

To make the spaetzle, combine the eggs and milk; stir in the flour, salt, and nutmeg, stirring until very smooth. Press the dough through a spaetzle maker or colander into boiling water. Boil for 2 to 3 minutes, then drain and set aside.

Prepare the chicken. Heat the oil in a heavy 10-inch skillet over medium heat. When oil is hot, sauté the chicken breasts on both sides until golden brown. Remove from pan, set aside, and keep warm. Add the garlic and jalapeño to the pan and cook until garlic is light tan. (Don't allow it to brown.) Add the onions and peach with its juice. Add the wine and deglaze the pan, scraping up browned bits from the bottom. Add the whipping cream. Return the chicken breasts to the pan and simmer until the sauce thickens, about 4 to 6 minutes.

While the sauce is thickening, finish cooking the spaetzle. Melt the butter in a heavy 10-inch skillet and sauté the spaetzle until light golden brown on the edges, about 3 to 4 minutes.

To serve, divide the spaetzle between two serving plates. Place a chicken breast on the spaetzle, top with a portion of the sauce, and garnish with toasted pecan pieces. Serves 2.

Welfare Café & Biergarten, Welfare, Texas
*The Texas Hill Country*

# South-of-the-Border Chicken with Tomatillo Sauce

6 boneless, skinless chicken breasts

6 tablespoons soy sauce

¼ teaspoon ground ginger

6 tablespoons Italian salad dressing

¼ teaspoon garlic powder

4 teaspoons toasted sesame seeds

4 teaspoons freshly squeezed lemon juice

4 ounces cream cheese

Tomatillo Sauce (see recipe below)

## Tomatillo Sauce

1½ pounds fresh tomatillos

1 cup water

Salt to taste

2 garlic cloves, peeled

2 jalapeño chiles, seeds and veins removed, chopped

¼ cup chopped cilantro

⅓ cup chopped onion

3 tablespoons canola oil

Make the Tomatillo Sauce. Remove the paperlike outer skin from the tomatillos. Combine tomatillos, water, and salt in a saucepan. Bring to a boil and boil, covered, for 5 minutes. Drain the tomatillos, reserving ½ cup of the cooking liquid. Combine tomatillos, reserved cooking liquid, garlic, jalapeños, cilantro, onion, and canola oil in work bowl of food processor. Process until smooth. Reheat the sauce gently before serving.

To prepare the chicken, place the breasts in a sealable plastic bag. Combine the soy sauce, ginger, salad dressing, garlic powder, sesame seeds, and lemon juice in a bowl; whisk to blend well. Pour the mixture over the chicken and seal the bag. Marinate in the refrigerator for 8 to 12 hours. Drain the chicken, discarding the marinade. Arrange chicken on preheated grill rack.

Grill until a meat thermometer inserted in the thickest portion registers 170 degrees, turning twice. Serve each chicken breast with a portion of the cream cheese and Tomatillo Sauce. Serves 6.

*Dining without Reservations*

# Sesame Chicken

1 pound boneless, skinless chicken breasts

1 teaspoon white sesame seeds

1 teaspoon black sesame seeds

4 cups cooking oil for deep-frying

1 cup tapioca starch

1 tablespoon cooking oil

6 dried red chile peppers

1 tablespoon chopped garlic

2 green onions, cut into 1-inch pieces

Cilantro sprigs for garnish

## Marinade

⅛ teaspoon freshly ground pepper

1 tablespoon cornstarch

1 tablespoon soy sauce

1 tablespoon dry sherry

1 tablespoon water

## Seasoning Sauce

1 teaspoon cornstarch

2 tablespoons rock sugar, crushed

1 tablespoon dark soy sauce

1 tablespoon soy sauce

4 tablespoons water

Slice chicken across the grain into pieces ¼ inch thick. Transfer chicken slices to a mixing bowl. Add marinade ingredients and toss to coat thoroughly. Let stand for 15 minutes or longer in the refrigerator.

Combine Seasoning Sauce ingredients together in a small bowl.

Toast the white and black sesame seeds together in a small skillet over medium heat until the white ones turn lightly brown. Remove and set aside.

Heat 4 cups of oil in a wok to 375 degrees. Sprinkle tapioca starch over chicken slices and coat well. Deep-fry half of the chicken until golden brown. Remove with a strainer and drain on paper towels. Repeat the deep-frying process for the other half of the chicken.

Remove hot oil to a heatproof container. Clean and dry the wok. Add 1 tablespoon oil to the wok over high heat. Add chile peppers and garlic, stirring for a few seconds.

Add chicken to the wok. Pour in seasoning sauce and add green onions. Reduce heat to medium and stir until the liquid is almost gone.

Remove to a serving platter. Sprinkle sesame seeds on top. Garnish with cilantro and serve.

*Chinese Cuisine Made Simple*

# Peanut-Chicken Dijon

¼ cup butter or margarine, divided

5 tablespoons Dijon mustard, divided

6 boneless, skinless chicken breasts, pounded thin

1½ cups finely chopped roasted peanuts, divided

¼ cup peanut oil

1 cup sour cream

2 to 3 tablespoons chopped parsley

¼ teaspoon salt

¼ teaspoon white pepper

In a saucepan over medium heat, melt 2 tablespoons butter. Add 3 tablespoons mustard and whisk until smooth. Remove from heat. Brush chicken with mustard mixture, then coat using 1 cup chopped peanuts. Set aside.

Melt remaining butter in a large skillet (large enough to cook all chicken breasts at the same time) over medium heat and stir in oil. Add chicken and sauté 3 minutes on each side, or until done. Remove chicken, set aside, and keep warm.

Discard butter, oil, and any dark peanuts from skillet. Add sour cream, remaining mustard, parsley, salt, and pepper to skillet; stir until smooth and heated through. Spoon a portion of the sauce over each chicken breast and garnish with remaining peanuts. Yields 6 servings.

*Cooking with Texas Highways*

# Chicken Saltimbocca

6 boneless, skinless chicken breast halves

6 thin slices boiled ham

3 slices Mozzarella cheese, halved

½ cup chopped tomato

1½ teaspoons minced fresh sage, or substitute ½ teaspoon crushed dried sage

⅓ cup fine dry bread crumbs

2 tablespoons grated Parmesan cheese

2 tablespoons minced parsley

4 tablespoons melted butter

Wrap chicken breast halves in plastic wrap and pound lightly into 5-inch squares. Remove plastic. Place a ham slice and a half slice of cheese on each piece of chicken. Top with tomato and sage to taste. Tuck in sides and roll up, jelly-roll style. Secure with toothpicks. Combine bread crumbs, Parmesan cheese, and parsley. Dip the chicken rolls in melted butter, then in bread crumb mixture. Place in a shallow baking pan. Bake at 350 degrees for 40 to 45 minutes. Serves 6.

Wendy Tarpley
*Lone Star Legacy*

# Parmesan Chicken Alfredo

8 boneless, skinless chicken breasts, 5 to 6 ounces each

## Parmesan Breading

2 cups panko (Japanese) bread crumbs

2 cups (8 ounces) shredded Parmesan cheese

2 tablespoons dried parsley flakes

1 tablespoon granulated garlic

1 teaspoon kosher salt

1 teaspoon freshly ground black pepper

2 cups all-purpose flour

2 extra-large eggs

1 cup milk

## Chicken

¼ cup extra-virgin olive oil

2 tablespoons butter

2 cups prepared Alfredo sauce

Place a large piece of plastic wrap over a cutting board. Lay chicken breasts down on plastic wrap, separating them by 2 inches. Cover breasts completely with another piece of plastic wrap. Using a meat mallet, pound each breast until ¼ inch thick. Refrigerate until ready for breading.

To make Parmesan Breading, mix together in a large bowl bread crumbs, Parmesan cheese, parsley, garlic, salt, and pepper. Set aside. In a shallow bowl, place flour. In another bowl, whisk eggs and milk. Dredge chicken breasts, one at a time, in flour, pressing firmly and coating both sides. Remove from flour, shake off excess flour, and place into egg mixture, coating both sides. Remove and place into Parmesan mixture, pressing firmly to coat both sides completely. Place breaded breasts on a tray.

To cook the chicken, in a large skillet over medium-high heat, add olive oil and butter. Place breaded breasts in pan and cook 2 to 3 minutes on each side, or until nicely browned and crisp. Remove to a serving platter. Garnish with extra Parmesan cheese and serve with a creamy Alfredo sauce. Serves 8.

**TIP:** All the pounding and breading steps can be done well ahead of time, and the final cooking only takes a few minutes to complete. Try serving this flavorful dish with crispy garlic bread and a pesto-sauced pasta side dish.

*Luby's Recipes & Memories*

# Chicken Parmesan

4 chicken breast halves, skinned and boned

Salt, pepper, garlic powder, and flour

2 tablespoons olive oil

1 tablespoon butter

4 slices provolone or mozzarella cheese

2 cups prepared or homemade tomato pasta sauce

½ cup grated Parmesan cheese

Pound the chicken breasts between two sheets of plastic wrap or parchment paper to flatten them. Season and flour lightly. Brown the chicken lightly on both sides in a skillet with oil and butter. Cover each piece of chicken with a slice of the cheese. Place breasts in shallow casserole and cover with pasta sauce. Scatter Parmesan cheese over the top. Bake at 350 degrees for 15 to 20 minutes. Serves 4.

Taylor Miller and Tom Alt
*Flavors of Fredericksburg*

# Grilled Honey-Cilantro Chicken Sandwiches

2 tablespoons vegetable oil

2 tablespoons honey

Juice of 1 lime

½ bunch fresh cilantro, trimmed and chopped

1 teaspoon ground cumin

4 boneless, skinless chicken breasts

Cajun seasoning to taste

Butter, softened

4 to 6 hamburger buns

Lettuce

Sliced fresh tomatoes

Thinly sliced red onion

Combine the oil, honey, lime juice, cilantro, and cumin in a sealable plastic bag. Rub the chicken with Cajun seasoning and add the chicken to the bag. Seal tightly and turn to coat chicken breasts well. Marinate in the refrigerator for 30 to 60 minutes, turning often.

Preheat the grill. Grill the chicken until a meat thermometer inserted in the thickest part of the chicken registers 170 degrees, turning occasionally. Several minutes before the chicken is done, spread butter on the cut sides of the buns and lightly grill. Slice the chicken in half or serve whole on the grilled buns, topped with lettuce, tomatoes, and red onion. Makes 4 to 6 sandwiches.

*Dallas Dish*

# Chicken Breasts in Phyllo

1½ cups mayonnaise

1 cup green onions, chopped

⅓ cup lemon juice

2 teaspoons dry tarragon

2 garlic cloves, minced

12 chicken breast halves, boned and skinned

Salt and pepper to taste

24 sheets phyllo dough

⅓ cup butter, melted

⅓ cup freshly grated Parmesan cheese

Combine first 5 ingredients to make a sauce. Lightly sprinkle chicken breasts with salt and pepper. Keep package of phyllo dough covered with a slightly damp cloth. Place a sheet of phyllo on a work surface. Quickly brush with melted butter (about 2 teaspoons). Place second sheet on top of first; brush with butter. Spread about 1½ tablespoons of the sauce on each side of breast (about 3 tablespoons in all). Place breast in one corner of buttered phyllo sheet. Fold corner over breast, then fold sides over and roll breast up in the sheets to form a package. Place in an ungreased 9 × 13-inch baking dish. Repeat with remaining breasts and phyllo. Brush the packets with rest of butter and sprinkle with Parmesan cheese. At this point, the dish may be refrigerated or frozen (tightly sealed). Thaw completely before baking. Bake at 375 degrees for 30 to 40 minutes, or until golden. Serve hot. Serves 12.

Kay Broaddus
*Hullabaloo in the Kitchen II*

# Lemon Chicken Cutlets

⅓ cup all-purpose flour

1 tablespoon Cavender's All-Purpose Greek Seasoning

Salt and black pepper to taste

Dash of paprika

4 or 5 boneless chicken breasts

2 tablespoons butter

1 tablespoon vegetable oil

3 tablespoons butter

1 tablespoon Tony Chachere's Instant Brown Gravy Mix

1 bunch green onions, chopped

2 tablespoons fresh lemon juice

1 (10-ounce) can chicken broth

1 tablespoon capers

1 tablespoon chopped parsley

Slivered almonds

2 tablespoons butter

Mix the flour, Greek seasoning, salt, black pepper, and paprika together. Pound the chicken with a meat mallet until thin. Coat the chicken in the flour mixture, shaking off the excess and reserving the remaining flour mixture. Melt 2 tablespoons of butter in the oil in a large skillet. Add the chicken and sauté over medium-high heat until brown and cooked through, turning once. Place the chicken in a baking dish sprayed with nonstick cooking spray, reserving the drippings in the skillet.

Melt the 3 tablespoon of butter in the reserved drippings. Add a mixture of the gravy mix and reserved flour mixture and cook to form a roux, stirring constantly. Add the green onions, lemon juice, and chicken broth. Cook for 1 minute or until thickened, stirring constantly. Add the capers and chopped parsley and stir to mix well. Pour over the chicken and bake at 350 degrees for 1 hour.

Sauté the almonds in 2 tablespoons butter in a skillet until brown and toasted. Sprinkle over the top of the chicken mixture when ready to serve. Serves 4 or 5.

*Settings Sunrise to Sunset*

# Lemon Chicken

1 pound boneless, skinless chicken breasts

3 cups cooking oil for deep-frying

2 tablespoons carrot shreds as garnish

## Marinade

⅛ teaspoon pepper

1 tablespoon cornstarch

2 tablespoons soy sauce

1 tablespoon dry sherry

## Batter

¼ teaspoon salt

2 teaspoons baking powder

¼ cup cornstarch

½ cup flour

3 tablespoons cooking oil

⅔ cup water

## Lemon Sauce

1 tablespoon cornstarch

3 tablespoons sugar

¼ cup fresh lemon juice

½ cup chicken broth

1 teaspoon sesame oil

Lemon slices from 1 lemon

Slant a cleaver at a 45-degree angle to the cutting board and slice chicken across the grain into ¼ × 1 × 2-inch-thick pieces. Add marinade to chicken and toss to coat thoroughly. Let stand for 15 minutes or longer in the refrigerator.

Mix batter ingredients in a bowl and whisk until smooth. Combine Lemon Sauce ingredients in a small saucepan.

Heat 3 cups oil in a wok over high heat to 375 degrees. Add chicken to batter and mix to coat well. Add half the chicken pieces one by one to the hot oil. Deep-fry 3 to 5 minutes, or until golden brown and cooked inside. Remove with a strainer to a cookie sheet lined with paper towels. Deep-fry the rest of the chicken the same way.

Bring Lemon Sauce to a boil over high heat, stirring occasionally.

Transfer chicken to a serving platter. Pour sauce over chicken. Garnish with carrot shreds.

*Chinese Cuisine Made Simple*

# Basil-Stuffed Chicken with Caper Sauce

6 bacon slices

2 cups chopped fresh basil

1 small garlic clove, peeled and trimmed

¼ cup extra-virgin olive oil

½ teaspoon fresh lemon juice

Salt to taste

4 boneless, skinless chicken breasts, cut
    in half vertically

Freshly ground black pepper to taste

1 cup all-purpose flour

2 eggs, lightly beaten

1 cup bread crumbs

Caper Sauce (see recipe below)

## Caper Sauce

1 cup low-salt chicken broth

½ cup dry white wine

2 tablespoons drained capers

3 tablespoons unsalted butter

Preheat the oven to 375 degrees. Cook the bacon in a skillet until brown and crisp; drain. Crumble the bacon and process with the basil and garlic in a food processor until pureed. Add the olive oil gradually, processing constantly until incorporated. Spoon into a bowl and mix in the lemon juice. Season to taste with salt. Set aside.

Make a horizontal slit in the side of each breast portion to form a pocket. Stuff 1 tablespoon of the basil mixture in each pocket and sprinkle the surface of the chicken with salt and pepper.

Coat the chicken with the flour and dip in the eggs. Coat with the bread crumbs and arrange in a single layer in a greased baking dish. Bake for 20 to 30 minutes, or until the chicken is cooked through. Drizzle with the Caper Sauce. Serves 4.

To make the Caper Sauce, combine the broth and wine in a heavy saucepan. Bring just to a boil over medium-high heat and cook until the mixture is reduced by one-fourth, stirring occasionally. Stir in the capers and simmer. Remove from heat and add the butter, whisking vigorously until well blended and thickened. Do not reheat the sauce.

*Dallas Dish*

## EDITOR'S NOTE ON REDUCING LIQUIDS

How many times have you been vexed by a recipe that tells you to reduce liquids by two-thirds or by half? Worse yet are the ones that want you to reduce 4 cups to ½ cup. How do you "eyeball" that? Those reductions, however irritating, are vital steps in a recipe and will affect its final flavor. Not reducing the liquids in a recipe that tells you to do so will result in a lame, wimpy flavor—nothing like what its creator had in mind! Reducing liquids *intensifies* their flavor: it makes chicken broth more "chickeny," beef broth "beefier." Wine achieves a greater depth of flavor (red wine can actually become syrupy when drastically reduced), herbs and seasonings in the liquid are more pronounced, tomatoes more "tomatoey," as in good pasta sauces that simmer for an hour, or chili that cooks for a couple of hours.

But take heart! There is an easy trick that makes reducing liquids in a recipe a piece of cake. It requires a wooden spoon and a small knife. Let's say the recipe tells you to reduce a soup or sauce to ½ cup. Easy. Take the pan in which you will cook the dish (very important) and pour in ½ cup of water. Place the handle of the spoon on the bottom of the pan so that the spoon is darkened by the water level of ½ cup. Take the small knife and cut a notch at the top of the water line. As the liquid is reducing, simply use that notch as your guide to the amount left!

Now, if a recipe tells you to reduce something by one-half or two-thirds, again select the pan in which you will cook the dish and add water in the total amount of liquid that will be used in the recipe. Put the handle of the wooden spoon on the bottom of the pan and measure the total depth of the water. Let's say it's 6 inches. Then make your notch at 3 inches for reducing by half, 2 inches for reducing by two-thirds, etc. This technique takes away the guesswork and makes you look like a pro, not to mention that the recipe is being prepared accurately and will most assuredly be wonderful!

# Capered Lemon Chicken

2 tablespoons olive oil

4 boneless, skinless chicken breasts

1 cup chopped onion

4 garlic cloves, crushed

1 cup sliced mushrooms

2 cups dry white wine, such as chardonnay

1 teaspoon Italian herb seasoning

1 dash black pepper or cayenne

1 to 2 tablespoons small capers, drained

2 lemons, sliced very thin

1 cup chopped fresh Italian (flat-leaf) parsley

In a large heavy-bottomed skillet, sauté the chicken in olive oil until brown on both sides. Remove and set aside. In same skillet, sauté onion, garlic, and mushrooms for 3 minutes. Add wine, Italian seasoning, and pepper. Replace chicken and simmer for 3 minutes. Add capers, lemons, and parsley. Cover and simmer for 6 to 8 minutes, or until chicken is done. Serves 4.

*¡Viva! Tradiciones*

# Chicken Breasts with Orange Sauce

2½ cups chicken broth

12 boneless, skinless chicken breast halves

2 tablespoons butter

2 tablespoons all-purpose flour

½ cup reserved chicken broth

½ teaspoon salt

2 teaspoons sugar

Grated zest of 1 orange

½ cup orange juice

1 tablespoon lemon juice

Pinch of white pepper

Parsley

Simmer the breasts in the chicken broth for about 30 to 40 minutes. Do not boil. Reserve ½ cup of the broth. Set breasts aside and keep warm.

In a saucepan, melt the butter. Add the flour and stir to blend well. Cook for 2 to 3 minutes. Add the reserved chicken broth and blend. Bring to a simmer to thicken. Add all remaining ingredients except parsley. Cook for 3 to 4 minutes. Pour the sauce over chicken breasts and garnish with parsley. Serves 12.

*Necessities and Temptations*

# Chicken with Forty Cloves of Garlic

2 or 3 heads of garlic

2 tablespoons olive oil

1 tablespoon unsalted butter

4 chicken breasts

Salt and pepper to taste

½ cup dry white wine

1 bay leaf

½ teaspoon thyme

1 cup chicken broth

1 tablespoon unsalted butter

Peel the papery outer skin from the garlic heads and discard. Separate into 40 cloves. Heat the olive oil and 1 tablespoon butter in a large skillet over medium-high heat. Add the chicken breasts. Season with salt and pepper. Cook, turning once, just until chicken is lightly browned on both sides. Arrange the garlic cloves around the chicken. Add the wine, bay leaf, and thyme. Cover tightly and reduce the heat to low. Cook for 25 to 30 minutes, or until the chicken is cooked through. Remove the chicken and garlic to a serving platter, cover with foil, and set aside; keep warm. Discard bay leaf. Drain the skillet, reserving 1 tablespoon of the dripping in the pan.

Return skillet with the reserved drippings to medium-high heat and add the chicken broth. Bring to a boil and cook until the liquid is reduced by half. Remove from heat and stir in the 1 tablespoon butter. Spoon the sauce over the chicken. To benefit from the full garlic experience, squeeze the soft pulp from the cooked garlic and eat with the chicken. Serves 4.

*Dining without Reservations*

# Chipotle Chicken Breast

## Oven-Roasted Tomatoes

**1 pound ripe Roma tomatoes, cut into ¼-inch slices**

**2 teaspoons kosher salt**

**1 teaspoon freshly ground black pepper**

## Chicken

**1 tablespoon kosher salt**

**1 teaspoon freshly ground black pepper**

**2 cups all-purpose flour**

**8 boneless, skinless chicken breasts (7 to 8 ounces each)**

**4 tablespoons olive oil**

**¼ cup (½ stick) butter**

**1 cup prepared chipotle pesto or chipotle salsa**

**16 slices white American cheese (found at deli counter)**

**3 tablespoons chopped fresh cilantro**

To make Oven-Roasted Tomatoes, preheat oven to 350 degrees. Place tomato slices on a lightly oiled, foil-lined baking sheet. Blend salt and pepper together and sprinkle on tomato slices. Place in oven and roast about 30 minutes, or until edges of slices are slightly browned and roasted. Remove slices from oven and let cool.

To make the chicken, in a shallow bowl, mix salt, pepper, and flour. Coat each chicken breast, shaking off excess flour. Place a large skillet on medium-high heat and add olive oil and butter. Put 2 or 3 chicken breasts in skillet at a time to cook 4 to 6 minutes on each side, or until chicken is nicely browned and juices run clear. Remove cooked chicken breasts and place on a foil-lined baking sheet. Top each cooked chicken breast with 1 tablespoon of chipotle pesto, 2 or 3 slices of Oven-Roasted Tomatoes, and 2 slices of white American cheese. Place breasts in oven 2 minutes, or until cheese melts. Remove from oven and place on a serving platter; garnish with chopped fresh cilantro. Serves 8.

**TIP:** You can make the Oven-Roasted Tomatoes well ahead of time for quick and easy preparation.

*Luby's Recipes & Memories*

# Chicken, Sausage, and Ham Jambalaya

½ cup vegetable oil

1½ cups chopped onions

1 cup chopped green bell peppers

¾ cup chopped celery

1 teaspoon salt

1 teaspoon cayenne pepper, or to taste

1 tablespoon minced garlic

1 pound andouille sausage, cut into bite-size slices

1½ pounds chicken breasts, cut into 1-inch cubes

1 additional teaspoon salt

1 additional teaspoon cayenne pepper, or to taste

3 bay leaves

12 ounces ham, cut into cubes

3 cups uncooked white rice

6 cups chicken stock

½ cup chopped green onions

Minced fresh parsley

Dash of Tabasco sauce

Heat the oil in a large Dutch oven over medium-high heat. Add the onions, bell peppers, celery, 1 teaspoon salt, and 1 teaspoon cayenne pepper. Sauté for 5 to 6 minutes, or until the vegetables are tender. Add the garlic. Sauté for 30 seconds. Add the sausage and sauté for 5 minutes.

Season the chicken pieces with additional 1 teaspoon salt and cayenne pepper. Add the chicken and bay leaves to the sausage mixture. Sauté for 6 minutes, or until chicken is browned. Add the ham and cook for 2 minutes. Stir in the rice and chicken stock. Cook, covered, over low heat for 25 to 30 minutes, or until all of the liquid is absorbed and rice is tender. Discard the bay leaves. Stir in the green onions and parsley. Season with Tabasco. Serve at once. Serves 10 to 12.

*Dining without Reservations*

# Chicken Vindaloo

⅓ cup white wine vinegar

5 large garlic cloves, peeled

3 tablespoons freshly grated ginger

1½ tablespoons curry powder

2 teaspoons ground cumin

¾ teaspoon ground cardamom

¼ teaspoon ground cloves

¼ generous teaspoon dried crushed red pepper

2 tablespoons yellow mustard seeds

2 pounds skinless, boneless chicken thighs

4 tablespoons olive oil

2½ cups chopped onions

1 can (14- to 16-ounce) diced tomatoes in juice

1 cinnamon stick

½ cup chopped fresh cilantro

Place first 8 ingredients in blender. Add 1 tablespoon mustard seeds and blend until smooth. Transfer spice mixture to large bowl. Add chicken and 2 tablespoons oil and toss to coat well. Heat remaining 2 tablespoons of oil in a large, heavy pot over medium-high heat. Add onions and sauté until golden, about 5 minutes. Add chicken mixture and stir 3 minutes to blend flavors. Add tomatoes with their juice and cinnamon stick. Bring to a boil and reduce heat. Cover and simmer until chicken is tender, stirring occasionally, about 30 minutes. Season chicken mixture to taste with salt and pepper. Mix in remaining 1 tablespoon mustard seeds. Simmer uncovered until liquid is slightly thickened, about 8 minutes. Stir in cilantro and serve over basmati rice. Serves 6.

*Esther Glover*
*Perennial Favorites*

# Sindhi Chicken Curry

12 skinless boneless chicken thighs, about 4 pounds

1 cup plain nonfat yogurt at room temperature

1 teaspoon cornstarch

2 tablespoons vegetable oil

2 cups finely chopped onions

1 tablespoon minced peeled ginger

1 tablespoon minced garlic

1 tablespoon minced green chiles, preferably serranos

1 tablespoon ground coriander

1½ teaspoons ground cumin

¾ teaspoon turmeric

¾ teaspoon cayenne pepper

1 (28-ounce) can diced tomatoes, including juice

½ cup minced cilantro

2 teaspoons salt, or to taste

1½ teaspoons garam masala

¼ cup chopped cilantro, divided

Rinse chicken and pat dry. Stir together the yogurt and cornstarch until smooth; set aside.

In a large saucepan with a tight-fitting lid, heat oil over medium-high heat. Add onions and sauté until beginning to color, 6 to 8 minutes. Reduce heat to medium and sauté until dark golden, 10 to 12 minutes longer.

Stir in the ginger, garlic, and chiles. Sauté for 2 minutes. Increase heat to medium-high. Add chicken and brown well, 6 to 8 minutes.

Reduce heat to medium. Add coriander, cumin, turmeric, and cayenne pepper. Mix well and cook for 2 to 3 minutes. Add the tomatoes, yogurt mixture, ½ cup cilantro, and salt. Mix well. Cover and bring to a boil.

Reduce heat to low and simmer until chicken is no longer pink inside, about 25 minutes. Remove from heat. Stir in garam masala and 3 tablespoons cilantro.

Garnish with the remaining cilantro before serving. Serve with rice or Indian bread.

*Easy Indian Cooking*

# Cajun Deep-Fried Turkey

1 (10- to 12-pound) turkey

Creole seasoning to taste

1½ cups melted butter

¼ cup onion juice

¼ cup garlic juice

¼ cup celery juice

¼ cup lemon juice

¼ cup Worcestershire sauce

¼ cup Tabasco sauce

2 tablespoons liquid smoke

8 gallons peanut oil for deep-frying

Rinse the turkey and pat dry. Rub the turkey with Creole seasoning; wrap with plastic wrap. Marinate in the refrigerator for 24 hours.

Combine the butter, onion juice, garlic juice, celery juice, lemon juice, Worcestershire sauce, Tabasco sauce, and liquid smoke in a saucepan 1 hour before the planned time for cooking the turkey. Cook over low heat just until heated through, stirring occasionally. Fill a syringe designed for injecting turkeys with the warm mixture. Inject the turkey all over until it is bloated and can hold no more of the mixture; use all the mixture. Chill for 1 hour.

Heat the peanut oil in a 60-quart Cajun pot to 350 to 375 degrees. Place the turkey in a fryer basket. Submerge the basket slowly into the oil. Deep-fry for 3½ to 4 minutes per pound, or until cooked through; drain. Wrap the turkey in parchment paper. Chill for 20 minutes before slicing. Serves 8.

**NOTE:** This is, without a doubt, the best turkey ever! The preparation is worth the mess as the turkey is extremely moist and flavorful. Do several at a time.

**EDITOR'S NOTE:** A deep-fried turkey is indeed a delicious and succulent bird. You must exercise a great deal of caution, however, when frying turkeys. Be certain that your pot has at least a 60-quart capacity to avoid spillover of the oil when the turkey is added to the pot. This could cause a grease fire or severe burns. Be sure to use heavy-duty potholders to remove the turkey after it has cooked. Before you remove the turkey, be certain to turn off the flame under the pot so that any dripping oil does not ignite.

*Texas Ties*

# Meat & Game

Texas has long been associated with the copious consumption of red meats. Stands to reason, since our state is known for producing fine beef cattle and for having great numbers of wild game.

The early settlers in Texas counted on wild game to provide a great deal of their meat. Even today, the families of hunters rely on wild game as a supplement to the meats they purchase. Wild game meat is lean, so it's healthier for us than beef. But because it's so lean, it requires care when cooking so that it's not dry and tough. Follow recipes carefully.

Pork was a popular meat with our German ancestors in Texas, and the tradition remains today. We love pork in all forms—from pork chops to juicy pork roasts to those finger-lickin'-good, slow-smoked baby back ribs. You'll find some pork dishes in this chapter that are sure to become favorites at your table.

Raising free-range lamb is a growing industry in Texas, as Texans discover the great taste of the meat. Nothing beats a roasted leg of lamb as a spectacular entrée for a special occasion.

I've included a bevy of recipes for the beef lovers, too, including the Broken Spoke's recipe for CFS (chicken-fried steak to foreigners) as well as the ultimate CFS—a chicken-fried rib eye!

Whatever your cooking mode might be on a given day—slow-smoking, grilling, pan-sautéing, deep-frying, braising, broiling, or roasting—there's a recipe here for you.

# Barbecue Dry Rub

¼ cup chili powder

1 teaspoon crushed bay leaf

2 tablespoons ground cayenne

¾ cup paprika

½ cup freshly ground black pepper

½ cup salt

½ cup sugar

3 tablespoons garlic powder

Thoroughly mix all ingredients. Store in the refrigerator and use as needed. Rub on the surface of meat to be cooked. Great on ribs, chicken, beef, or pork. Makes about 2 cups.

*License to Cook, Texas Style*

# Barbecue Mop Sauce

2 teaspoons hot sauce

¾ cup Worcestershire sauce

⅓ cup cider vinegar

¼ cup corn oil

1 (12-ounce) can beer

1 tablespoon lemon juice

2 teaspoons dry mustard

2 teaspoons chili powder

3 teaspoons paprika

2 garlic cloves, minced

⅓ cup finely chopped onion

Combine all ingredients and mix well. Mop meat or chicken frequently with the sauce as you barbecue. Store leftover sauce in refrigerator. Makes about 3 cups.

**EDITOR'S NOTE:** Pour a portion of the sauce into a bowl to use so that you don't contaminate the entire batch with raw or partially cooked meat juices. Do not save any of the sauce in which you have dipped a brush used on raw or cooking meat.

*License to Cook Texas Style*

# Doc Bridgeford's Rib Sauce

1 cup honey

Tabasco sauce to taste

½ bottle Louisiana Red Hot Sauce

1 tablespoon mustard

1 bottle ketchup

½ cup vinegar

1 cup brown sugar, dissolved in water

¼ cup Worcestershire sauce

2 sticks butter

Heat ingredients in a saucepan and baste pork ribs as they are cooking on the grill.

Perry Arledge Smith, Arledge Ranch, Seymour, Texas
*Stolen Recipes*

# Steak Diane

12 ounces beef tenderloin, very thinly sliced

Salt and pepper

Butter

Beat tenderloin slices with meat mallet to flatten. Sprinkle with salt and pepper. In hot skillet, brown meat in enough butter to keep pieces from sticking to pan. Remove to platter and keep warm.

## Sauce

½ cup chopped green onions, including tops

½ cup sliced fresh mushrooms

4 tablespoons butter

1½ tablespoons Worcestershire sauce

2 tablespoons port wine

Brown onions and mushrooms in butter until soft. Add Worcestershire sauce and wine. Pour over meat and serve. Serves 2.

*Seasoned with Sun*

# Pepper Steak España

3 pounds beef tenderloin, sliced thin

¼ to ½ cup butter

1 pound white mushrooms, sliced

3 green bell peppers, sliced into strips

3 to 4 tomatoes, quartered

1 (6-ounce) can tomato paste

1 teaspoon dried oregano

Seasonings—salt, garlic powder, and
    freshly ground black pepper to taste

¼ cup high-quality Texas port-style wine

Steamed rice

Brown the meat in 2 tablespoons butter. Add seasonings and cook over low to medium heat until meat is tender. Set aside.

In a separate skillet, melt 2 tablespoons butter and sauté the green pepper, mushrooms, and tomatoes for 5 minutes. Add vegetables to meat skillet. Mix in tomato paste. Heat thoroughly and let simmer until green peppers are cooked, not more than 15 minutes. Add the port, stir, and serve at once over steamed rice. Serves 4.

*Under the Texan Sun*

# Simply Elegant Steak

1½ pounds tenderized boneless beef
    round steak

1½ tablespoons vegetable oil

2 large onions

¼ teaspoon ground ginger

1 tablespoon soy sauce

1 (4-ounce) can sliced mushrooms,
    drained, liquid reserved

1 (10¾-ounce) can condensed cream of
    mushroom soup

½ cup dry sherry

1½ teaspoons garlic salt

3 cups hot cooked rice

Cut steak into thin strips. Slice onions ½ inch thick and separate into rings. In a large skillet, brown meat in oil over high heat. Remove meat from skillet. In the same skillet, add onions to the remaining oil, and sauté until tender-crisp. Stir in ginger and soy sauce. Blend soup, sherry, liquid from mushrooms, and garlic salt. Stir in mushrooms. Return steak to sauce. Reduce heat; cover, and simmer for 1 hour, or until steak is tender. Serve over rice. Serves 6.

Phyllis Gray Bjerke
*Lagniappe*

# Mesquite-Grilled Frontier Sirloin

2 tablespoons prepared mustard

2 tablespoons vegetable oil

6 garlic cloves, dry-roasted until soft

½ teaspoon Worcestershire sauce

½ teaspoon crumbled dried whole sage

8 green onions

2 boneless top sirloin strip steaks, 18 to 20 ounces each and 1 inch thick

Salt

Freshly ground black pepper

Mesquite chips

4 serrano chiles, halved lengthwise

Combine first 5 ingredients in a food processor or blender. Rub steaks and onions with mixture, season with salt and pepper, and let sit at room temperature for 45 minutes.

On an outdoor grill, fire up enough charcoal to form a single layer of coals. Place a few handfuls of mesquite chips or pods in water to soak. When charcoal is covered with gray ash, scatter mesquite over it and place steaks directly over fire. Place onions and serranos on a small piece of aluminum foil, a little off to the side of the fire, where heat is lower. Grill steaks on one side about 4 to 5 minutes, covering partially with grill lid (vents open) to trap some of the mesquite smoke. Turn steaks, again cover grill partially, and cook to desired doneness, about 4 more minutes for medium-rare. When you turn steaks, also turn onions and serranos, removing them when soft. Top steaks with onions and serranos; serve immediately. Yields 4 servings.

Cheryl Alters Jamison and Bill Jamison
*Cooking with Texas Highways*

# Chunks of Sirloin

4 pounds lean, boneless sirloin

½ cup olive oil

½ stick butter, melted

Juice of ½ lemon

4 to 6 tablespoons Worcestershire sauce

½ cup chopped fresh parsley

Freshly ground black pepper, lemon pepper, and salt to taste

Have your butcher cut a sirloin 4 inches thick. Combine the remaining ingredients and rub into the beef. Let sit at room temperature for 1 hour.

Grill the beef for approximately 10 minutes, turn and repeat. Remove from grill and let sit for 5 or 10 minutes before carving. With a sharp knife, slice into ¼-inch slices and serve immediately. Serves 8 to 10.

XL Ranch, Potter County, Texas
*Texas Cowboy Cooking*

# Texas Rib-Eye Steaks with Sautéed Onions

2 tablespoons olive oil

1 small white onion, coarsely chopped

1 small purple onion, coarsely chopped

3 green onions, chopped

½ cup chopped green bell pepper

2 jalapeño peppers, seeded and chopped

¼ cup sugar

1 tablespoon cider vinegar

1 teaspoon Worcestershire sauce

¼ teaspoon salt

⅛ teaspoon freshly ground black pepper

Dash of ground cloves

4 rib-eye steaks, cut 1 inch thick

Heat oil in a large saucepan over moderate heat. Add onions and peppers; sauté until tender, stirring occasionally. Stir in next 6 ingredients; reduce heat to low. Stirring occasionally, cook for 20 minutes, or until liquid has cooked in. Season steaks with pepper and place on grill over hot coals. Cook 4 minutes on each side or to desired doneness. Spoon some of the onion mixture over each steak. Serves 4.

*Cooking with Texas Peppers*

# Texas Chicken-Fried Rib-Eye with Tabasco Cream Gravy

4 to 6 trimmed rib-eye steaks, cut ⅝ inch thick, approximately 7 to 8 ounces each

3 cups all-purpose flour, seasoned with 2 teaspoons each: salt, black pepper, granulated garlic, onion powder, paprika, cayenne pepper

Egg wash made from 3 eggs well beaten with 4 cups milk

4 cups Japanese (panko) bread crumbs, seasoned with 2 teaspoons salt and 2 teaspoons Chef Paul's Meat Magic Seasoning, or other Cajun-style seasoning blend

Canola oil for deep-frying, heated to 350 degrees

### Tabasco Cream Gravy

½ cup bacon or sausage drippings

½ cup all-purpose flour

½ teaspoon black pepper

2 teaspoons chicken base paste, or 2 chicken bouillon cubes

4 cups whole milk, or more as needed

2 tablespoons Tabasco sauce

Salt to taste

Pat the steaks dry using absorbent paper towels. Place each steak between two sheets of plastic wrap and pound to about half their thickness with a meat-tenderizing mallet. Dredge the steaks in the seasoned flour, coating well and shaking to remove all excess flour. Dip steaks in the egg wash, coating well. Press the steaks into the seasoned bread crumbs, coating well on both sides and shaking off excess crumbs. Refrigerate steaks until you are ready to fry them.

Make the Tabasco Cream Gravy. Heat the drippings in a heavy cast-iron skillet over medium heat. When the drippings are hot, add the flour all at once and whisk to blend well. Cook, whisking constantly, for 3 to 4 minutes. Add the pepper and chicken base paste, stirring to blend well. Add the milk and whisk until smooth. Bring the gravy to a full boil to thicken; boil for about 1 minute. Lower heat and season to taste with salt and additional black pepper, if desired. Stir in Tabasco sauce. Thin gravy with additional whole milk as needed.

Deep-fry the breaded steaks in the preheated oil. Cook only until the crust is crisp and medium golden brown, about 4 minutes, turning once. Be sure not to crowd the oil. You will probably have to fry the steaks in two batches. Do not overcook the steak; they should be served medium-rare to medium so they are fork-tender. Place the steaks on individual plates and top with a liberal amount of the gravy. Serves 4 to 6.

*Texas on the Plate*

# Ranch-Roasted Rib Eye

**1 (12-pound) boneless prime rib**

Trim excess fat from meat and cover completely with lots of Rib-Eye Rub. Place meat on pit and roast 3 hours at 325 degrees, or until it reaches an internal temperature of 125 degrees (rare). Turn meat every hour. Remove from heat and let rest for at least 40 minutes before serving. Serve with Perini Ranch Horseradish Sauce.

### Rib-Eye Rub

**1 cup coarsely ground salt**

**2 cups coarsely ground black pepper**

**⅓ cup flour or cornstarch**

**⅓ cup garlic powder**

**⅓ cup dried oregano**

Combine all ingredients and rub over the surface of the meat.

### Perini Ranch Horseradish Sauce

**2 ounces prepared horseradish**

**8 ounces sour cream**

**1 teaspoon finely chopped fresh parsley (optional)**

Mix the horseradish and sour cream. Refrigerate immediately. Garnish with parsley, if desired. Great with prime rib, peppered beef tenderloin, and on beef sandwiches.

*Texas Cowboy Cooking*

# Rib-Eye Steak in a Bock Beer Marinade

### Rib-Eye Steak

6 rib-eye steaks, 14 to 16 ounces each

### Shiner Bock Marinade

1 (12-ounce) Shiner Bock, or your local or
   homemade dark beer

2 tablespoons chopped garlic

2 tablespoons finely diced red onion

2 tablespoons Worcestershire sauce

4 shakes Tabasco sauce

Juice of 2 limes

¼ cup brown sugar, firmly packed

1 tablespoon coarse brown mustard
   (Creole-style is good)

2 tablespoons olive oil

2 teaspoons salt

Make the marinade by combining all marinade ingredients except salt. Place the steaks in a large plastic zip-sealing bag and pour the marinade over the steaks. Place bag on a platter or baking sheet and refrigerate for 4 hours or overnight.

Remove the steaks from the bags and drain well. Cook the steaks on a gas grill over medium-high heat about 4 minutes on each side for medium-rare to medium. Season with salt to taste after cooking. Serves 6.

*Cooking Fearlessly*

# Cowboy Coffee Steak

½ cup finely ground coffee

¼ cup packed brown sugar

¼ cup kosher salt

½ cup coarsely ground pepper

4 rib-eye steaks (12 to 14 ounces each)

2 tablespoons vegetable oil

Preheat oven to 450 degrees. Mix the ground coffee, brown sugar, kosher salt, and pepper in a small bowl. Press evenly over both sides of the steaks. Heat the vegetable oil until smoking in a skillet (preferably cast-iron) large enough to hold all of the steaks without crowding. Add the steaks and sear for 2 to 3 minutes on each side. Remove to a baking sheet.

Roast the steaks in preheated oven for 5 to 10 minutes for medium-rare, or until done to taste. Let stand at room temperature for 5 minutes or longer before serving. Serves 4.

*Lone Star to Five Star*

# Stuffed Bell Peppers

6 large, uniformly shaped green bell peppers

1 pound lean ground beef

1 onion, diced

2 or 3 celery stalks, diced

1 can tomato sauce

1 teaspoon Gebhardt's Chili Powder

1½ cups cooked rice

Salt and pepper to taste

Grated cheese (optional)

Buttered bread crumbs (optional)

Wash peppers; cut tops off. Remove seeds and white membranes; set aside.

Make the filling. Brown the meat in a skillet until cooked through. Add onion and celery; continue cooking until onions are limp. Add tomato sauce and chili powder, mixing well. Add cooked rice. Season with salt and pepper. Fill each pepper with meat and rice mixture; stand upright in a baking dish. Add hot water to baking dish to a depth of ½ inch. Top each pepper with grated cheese or buttered bread crumbs. Bake 30 to 40 minutes in a 375-degree oven. Makes 6 servings.

*Tales from Texas Tables*

# Baboti

2 onions, chopped

2 to 4 cups chopped apples

2 tablespoons butter, melted

2 bread slices

½ cup milk

2 pounds ground chuck

2 tablespoons curry powder

2 tablespoons sugar

2 tablespoons vinegar

1 egg, slightly beaten

2 teaspoons salt, or to taste

¼ teaspoon black pepper

1 teaspoon turmeric

1 to 1½ cups raisins

Sauté onion and apple in butter until tender. Soak bread in milk; drain. Combine sautéed mixture, bread, and remaining ingredients; mix well. (Mixture will be very moist.) Shape into a loaf on the rack of a broiler pan. Bake at 350 degrees for 1¼ hours. Yields 6 to 8 servings.

Janet Painter
*Flavor Favorites*

# Meat and Potato Patties

1 pound all-purpose potatoes (about 3)

1 pound lean ground beef or ground lamb

1½ teaspoons powdered allspice

¾ teaspoon turmeric

¾ teaspoon cayenne pepper

1¼ cups very finely minced red onion (about 1 large)

½ cup chopped cilantro

½ cup fresh mint, finely chopped, or 1 tablespoon dried mint

2 teaspoons grated peeled ginger

2 teaspoons garlic paste or very finely minced garlic

2 tablespoons freshly squeezed lemon juice

2 teaspoons salt, or to taste

¾ cup dry bread crumbs

1 cup vegetable oil

In a saucepan of boiling water, cook the whole potatoes with skins on until tender, 20 to 25 minutes. Drain. When cool enough to handle, peel and mash. Set aside.

In a skillet over medium heat, sauté ground meat, breaking up any lumps, until no longer pink, 4 to 5 minutes. Let cool to room temperature.

Combine meat with potatoes, allspice, turmeric, cayenne pepper, onion, cilantro, mint, ginger, garlic, lemon juice, and salt. Mix together by hand, kneading to a smooth doughlike consistency. Adjust seasonings.

Divide the mixture into 16 portions and form each portion into a meat patty about ½ inch thick, making sure sides are smooth and free of cracks. Dip in bread crumbs, pressing to coat.

Heat 2 tablespoons of the oil in a skillet over medium heat. Add 3 to 4 patties and sauté, turning once, until golden on both sides, 3 to 4 minutes. Drain on paper towels. Repeat with remaining patties and oil in batches, heating oil and skillet in between batches. Serve hot with chutney of your choice. Makes 16 patties.

*Easy Indian Cooking*

# Black Forest Beef and Onions

3 pounds beef chuck, cubed

8 tablespoons butter

¼ cup flour

¼ cup minced parsley

1 teaspoon thyme

1 bay leaf

2 tablespoons wine vinegar

2 cups beer

3 onions, sliced

1 teaspoon sugar

1 teaspoon salt

½ teaspoon black pepper

Cooked egg noodles

Flour the beef and brown it in 4 tablespoons of the butter. Add parsley, thyme, bay leaf, wine vinegar, and beer. Bring to a boil, then lower heat and simmer 1 hour, covered, or until meat is tender. Sauté onions in the rest of the butter; add sugar and cook until glazed. Add to beef. Season with salt and pepper. Serve over cooked egg noodles.

*Gruene General Store Cookbook*

# Holiday Beef Tenderloin

1 (2-pound) beef tenderloin

2 tablespoons soy sauce

Pepper to taste

2 tablespoons olive oil

2 garlic cloves, minced

3 shallots, minced

⅓ cup dry red wine

2 tablespoons Dijon mustard

1 cup beef broth

¼ cup heavy cream

Trim any excess fat from the beef. Pour the soy sauce over the meat in a pan and season with pepper. Marinate for at least 30 minutes. Heat the olive oil in a large heavy-bottomed skillet over medium-high heat. Add the tenderloin and cook until brown on all sides. Place in an ovenproof skillet. Bake at 450 degrees for 40 minutes for medium-rare, turning once. Remove to a cutting board and keep warm. Drain the drippings from the skillet. Over medium heat, add the garlic and shallots and sauté until golden brown. Add the red wine, Dijon mustard, beef broth, and cream. Simmer for 8 minutes, or until reduced and thickened. Slice the beef into ¼-inch-thick slices and spoon the sauce over the meat. Serves 6.

*Dining without Reservations*

# Herbed Rib Roast

3 tablespoons whole black peppercorns

6 bay leaves

3 tablespoons kosher salt

9 garlic cloves, minced

1 tablespoon minced fresh thyme

2 tablespoons minced fresh rosemary

1 tablespoon olive oil

1 (7- to 8-pound) standing rib roast, fat trimmed

2 cups beef broth

1 small sprig fresh rosemary

1 small sprig fresh thyme

1 garlic clove, minced

Salt and black pepper to taste

Grind the peppercorns, bay leaves, and kosher salt in a spice grinder. Add the 9 garlic cloves and the chopped thyme and rosemary; mix well. Stir in the olive oil. Rub the paste over the roast. Place the meat in a large Dutch oven. Chill, covered, for 24 hours.

Bake, uncovered, at 450 degrees for 20 minutes. Reduce the oven temperature to 350 degrees. Cover and bake for 1½ to 2 hours. Remove the roast to a large platter, reserving the pan juices. Let stand for 25 minutes before carving. Skim off the fat from the pan juices. Add the remaining ingredients. Simmer over medium heat to deglaze the pan, scraping up browned bits from the bottom of the pan. Pour into a small saucepan, adding the juices that have collected on the platter. Simmer for 10 minutes. Skim any fat that has collected on the top. Season with salt and pepper, strain to remove herb sprigs, and serve with the roast. Serves 8.

*Dining without Reservations*

# Italian Braised Beef

3 to 4 pounds beef chuck roast

1 large onion, chopped

2 tablespoons olive oil

3 (8-ounce) cans tomato sauce

4 ripe tomatoes, chopped, or 1 (28-ounce) can Italian plum tomatoes, chopped

1 cup water

½ teaspoon ground allspice

2 tablespoons chopped fresh marjoram

1 tablespoon chopped fresh sage

2 teaspoons chopped fresh thyme

6 garlic cloves, minced

¼ cup chopped parsley

½ pound fresh mushrooms, sliced

Salt and pepper to taste

In a large Dutch oven or deep ovenproof skillet, slowly brown meat and onion in olive oil on top of stove or in oven at 450 degrees. Turn over to brown both sides of meat.

Add tomato sauce, tomatoes, water, allspice, marjoram, sage, thyme, garlic, and parsley (reserve some parsley for garnish.) Cover and cook on top of stove over low heat or in oven at 300 degrees for 1½ to 2 hours. Meat should be very tender. Add more water if necessary.

When meat is tender, skim off any excess fat. Add mushrooms and continue to simmer for 15 to 20 minutes. Remove meat from pan and let rest 10 to 15 minutes.

Slice meat and serve with sauce over macaroni, rigatoni, or rice. Garnish with reserved parsley. Serves 6 to 8.

**NOTE:** Substitute Chianti or zinfandel for 1 cup of water for extra flavor in sauce.

*Southern Herb Growing*

# Malaysian Beef Satay

## Spicy Peanut Sauce

**1 tablespoon butter**

**1 small onion, finely chopped**

**1 garlic clove, minced**

**¼ cup smooth peanut butter**

**¼ cup water**

**2 drops of Tabasco sauce**

**2 teaspoons sugar**

**½ teaspoon ground coriander**

## Beef Satay

**⅓ cup soy sauce**

**⅓ cup peanut oil or vegetable oil**

**2 onions, finely chopped**

**2 garlic cloves, crushed**

**3 tablespoons toasted sesame seeds**

**2 pounds sirloin steak, cut into 1-inch cubes**

**1 teaspoon fresh lemon juice**

**2 teaspoons ground cumin**

**Salt and pepper to taste**

To prepare the sauce, melt the butter in a saucepan and add the onion and garlic. Sauté until light brown. Add the peanut butter, water, Tabasco, sugar, and coriander and mix well. Cook until thickened, stirring constantly. (You may prepare in advance up to this point and store, covered, in the refrigerator. Reheat before serving.)

To prepare the satay combine the soy sauce, peanut oil, onions, garlic, and sesame seeds in a large bowl and mix well. Add the beef and toss to coat. Marinate, covered, in the refrigerator, for 3 hours. Drain the beef, reserving the marinade. Thread the beef onto skewers and brush with the lemon juice. Sprinkle with the ground cumin, salt, and pepper. Place on a grill rack and grill for 10 minutes, basting with the reserved marinade and turning occasionally. Serve with the Spicy Peanut Sauce for dipping. Serves 4 to 6.

*Settings Sunrise to Sunset*

# Slow-Smoked Brisket
# with Hellfire and Brimstone Sauce

10- to 12-pound beef brisket, untrimmed

Sliced yellow onions

Hamburger-sliced dill pickles

## Dry Rub

*(Makes 1 cup.)*

⅓ cup light brown sugar

1 tablespoon plus 1 teaspoon salt

1 tablespoon plus 1 teaspoon granulated
garlic

1 tablespoon plus 1 teaspoon granulated
onion powder

1 tablespoon plus 1 teaspoon celery salt

2 tablespoons plus 2 teaspoons paprika

1 tablespoon medium-hot chili powder

2 teaspoons finely ground black pepper

1 teaspoon lemon-pepper seasoning

1 teaspoon dry mustard

1 teaspoon dried thyme

¼ teaspoon ground red (cayenne) pepper

## Big Yellowback Basting Sauce

*(Makes about 1 quart.)*

1 cup Italian salad dressing

1 cup apple cider vinegar

1 cup yellow mustard

1 tablespoon freshly squeezed lime juice

2 teaspoons pureed garlic

2 teaspoons pureed onion

½ teaspoon crushed red pepper flakes

2 teaspoons medium-hot chili powder

2 teaspoons ground cumin

¼ cup Worcestershire sauce

1½ teaspoons freshly ground black
pepper

¼ teaspoon salt

## Hellfire and Brimstone
## Barbecue Sauce

*(Makes 2 quarts.)*

½ stick unsalted butter

4 green onions, minced, including green
tops

2 tablespoons granulated garlic

¼ cup dark red chili powder

1 tablespoon finely ground black pepper

6 cups tomato ketchup

⅓ cup prepared mustard

⅓ cup firmly packed light brown sugar

½ cup granulated sugar

1 cup apple cider vinegar

¾ cup beer

⅓ cup dry red wine

1½ teaspoons dried Mexican oregano

1 teaspoon red (cayenne) pepper

½ cup Worcestershire sauce

2 tablespoons Tabasco sauce

Begin by preparing the fire. Build a charcoal or wood fire in firebox of barbecue pit. When the coals are glowing red, add soaked hardwood chunks. Allow the fire to cook down until temperature in the cooking chamber is around 220 degrees.

While the fire is cooking down, prepare the Dry Rub by combining all ingredients and blending well; set aside.

Make the Big Yellowback Basting Sauce by combining all ingredients and whisking to blend well. Set aside.

Rub the Dry Rub into the meat, coating it well on all sides. Let meat sit at room temperature until the temperature in the pit is right. Place meat on cooking rack in pit, fat side up, and baste with the Big Yellowback Basting Sauce. Cook the meat for about 12½ to 15 hours, depending on size of brisket. Turn and baste often. Maintain a temperature of 220 degrees in the pit, adding more charcoal and wood chunks as needed. For the last hour of cooking, wrap the brisket tightly in aluminum foil.

While the brisket is cooking, make the Hellfire and Brimstone Barbecue Sauce. Combine all ingredients in a 4-quart soup pot. Stir over medium heat until butter has melted. Simmer, covered, for 1 hour. Cool and store in refrigerator until ready to use. Never use the barbecue sauce on the meat while it is cooking. It will cause the "bark," or outside crust, of the meat to char and have a bitter taste.

When ready to serve the meat, unwrap it and trim off the surface fat. Cut the nose end loose from the layer of fat under it and cut out the fat layer. Slice the meat across the grain into thin slices. (Thin slices are tenderer than thick ones.) Serve hot with sliced onions and hamburger pickles. Pass the hot barbecue sauce separately. Serves 10 to 12.

*Texas on the Plate*

# Oven-Roasted Beef Brisket

2 tablespoons chili powder

2 tablespoons salt

1 tablespoon garlic powder

1 tablespoon onion powder

1 tablespoon ground black pepper

1 tablespoon sugar

2 teaspoons dry mustard

1 bay leaf, crushed

4 pounds beef brisket, trimmed

1½ cups Beef Stock

### Beef Stock

*(Makes 4 quarts)*

3 to 4 pounds meaty beef bones

1 large onion, coarsely chopped

2 to 3 carrots, coarsely chopped

3 to 4 stalks celery, coarsely chopped

Fresh herbs to taste: parsley, thyme, rosemary

1 tablespoon salt

1 tablespoon ground black pepper

Water

To make the Beef Stock, roast the bones in a 400-degree oven for approximately 45 minutes. Place the roasted bones in a large stockpot and add the vegetables and herbs. Add 2 cups of water to the roasting pan, scraping up the browned bits stuck to the pan; add the broth to the stockpot. Cover the bones and vegetables with salt, pepper, and 1 gallon of water. Bring to a boil and skim any foam on the surface. Simmer for about 4 hours, adding water as needed to keep the bones covered. Remove from heat and let cool. Remove any fat from the surface, add salt and pepper, and strain bones and vegetables. Pour into freezer-safe containers and freeze until needed.

Make a dry rub by combining chili powder, salt, garlic and onion powders, black pepper, sugar, dry mustard, and bay leaf. Season the raw brisket on both sides with the rub. Place in a roasting pan and roast, uncovered, for 1 hour at 350 degrees.

Add beef stock and enough water to yield about ½ inch of liquid in the roasting pan. Lower oven to 300 degrees, cover pan tightly, and continue cooking for 3 hours, or until fork-tender.

Trim the fat and slice meat thinly across the grain. Top with juice from the pan. Serves 10.

**NOTE:** The brisket can be mopped with mop sauce during cooking. To make the mop sauce, combine 1 part cooking oil, 1 part water, and 1 part vinegar; add chopped onions, lemon, and garlic and cook until thickened.

*Texas Cowboy Cooking*

# South Dallas Short Ribs

2 to 3 pounds beef short ribs

**Baking Sauce**

1 (14-ounce) bottle chili sauce or catsup

1 (12-ounce) can Coca-Cola

4 tablespoons Worcestershire sauce

1 teaspoon black pepper

1 teaspoon celery salt

2 tablespoons Louisiana Hot Sauce

Make baking sauce by combining all ingredients. Cook short ribs in boiling water about 5 minutes. (This removes excess fat.) Drain and place in baking dish. Pour sauce over meat and cover. Cook at 325 degrees, basting often. Cook for about 2 hours, or until meat is falling off the bones.

Serve with cooked turnip greens, sweet potato custard, and corn bread on the side.

*Texas Cookoff*

# Broken Spoke's Chicken-Fried Steak

1 large egg

1 cup buttermilk

Salt to taste

Pepper to taste

½ cup all-purpose flour

½ cup cracker meal

1 (3- to 5-ounce) beef cutlet, hand tenderized

Vegetable shortening

Broken Spoke's Cream Gravy (see recipe on page 222)

Whip together egg, buttermilk, salt, and pepper in a large bowl; set batter aside.

Blend together flour and cracker meal in another bowl. Place cutlet in cracker mixture and cover both sides well. Submerge cutlet in egg batter, then place it back in cracker mixture, patting both sides again evenly to coat. Place shortening in a deep fryer or cast-iron skillet and heat to 325 degrees. Place cutlet in fryer and fry until it floats and turns golden brown. Remove steak from fryer; drain well, reserving ½ cup drippings for gravy. Place steak on plate and keep warm while preparing cream gravy. Spoon gravy generously over steak. Yields 1 serving.

### Broken Spoke's Cream Gravy

½ cup reserved drippings or shortening

¼ cup all-purpose flour

1 quart milk

Salt to taste

Pepper to taste

Place drippings in a 10- to 12-inch cast-iron skillet and heat until hot. Gradually add flour and cook over low heat until mixture turns brown, stirring constantly to prevent scorching. Add remaining ingredients and cook, stirring constantly, until thick. If gravy gets too thick, thin to desired consistency with water. Yields enough gravy for 6 to 8 steaks.

*James White and Annetta White, The Broken Spoke, Austin*
*Cooking with Texas Highways*

# Paprika Cream Schnitzel *(Paprika-Rahmschnitzel)*

4 bacon slices

1½ pounds veal cutlets, cut into individual portions ½ inch thick

2 tablespoons chopped onion

2 tablespoons sweet Hungarian paprika

Salt to taste

1 cup sour cream

½ cup tomato sauce

Cook bacon until crisp; remove from skillet, crumble, and reserve. Brown the veal in the bacon drippings; add onion and cook until lightly browned. Season with paprika and salt. Stir in the sour cream and tomato sauce, blending well. Cover and simmer for 20 minutes on medium-low heat until veal is tender. Do not allow the gravy to boil. Sprinkle with the crumbled bacon. Great with egg noodles or rice. Serves 4.

*Medeline Schuerer Schulte, Brick Haus Restaurant, Amana, Iowa*
*German-Style Recipes*

# Marinated Ham

2 slices cooked ham

½ cup red wine

¼ cup plum jelly

In a small saucepan, melt the jelly, then add wine. Pour over ham slices in covered glass dish. Refrigerate overnight. Serve at room temperature.

*Of Magnolia and Mesquite*

# Grilled Mushroom Pork

## Bourbon Mushrooms

**2 pounds fresh mushrooms, sliced**

**1 cup extra-virgin olive oil**

**2 tablespoons chopped fresh garlic**

**½ cup diced yellow onions**

**¼ cup Kentucky bourbon**

**¼ cup A.1. steak sauce**

**2 teaspoons kosher salt**

**1 teaspoon freshly ground black pepper**

## Pork Chops

**8 boneless pork chops (7 to 8 ounces each)**

**½ cup Blackened Seasoning (see recipe below)**

**1 tablespoon chopped fresh parsley**

## Blackened Seasoning

**½ cup paprika**

**3 tablespoons seasoned salt**

**4 teaspoons granulated or powdered garlic**

**4 teaspoons granulated or powdered onion**

**2 teaspoons dried oregano leaves**

**2 teaspoons dried thyme leaves**

**4 teaspoons cayenne pepper**

**2 teaspoons freshly ground black pepper**

To make Blackened Seasoning, combine paprika, seasoned salt, garlic, onion, oregano, thyme, cayenne, and black pepper in a small bowl. Mix well. Store in airtight container.

To make Bourbon Mushrooms, in a large bowl, toss together mushrooms, olive oil, garlic, and onions. Add mixture to a large skillet and cook 3 to 4 minutes over medium-high heat without stirring. Then stir and cook an additional 3 to 4 minutes. Gather mushrooms into center of pan and add bourbon, steak sauce, salt, and pepper. Cook mushrooms another 3 to 4 minutes, or until liquids reduce into a syrup, glazing mushrooms. Remove glazed mushrooms from skillet. Keep warm for topping pork.

To make Pork Chops, season both sides of pork chops with Blackened Seasoning. Pat down each chop firmly in a few spots to flatten them. Place seasoned chops into a lightly oiled large skillet over medium-high heat. Cook 3½ to 4 minutes on each side until nicely browned and cooked thoroughly. Remove chops and place on a serving platter. Add Bourbon Mushrooms to skillet and sauté until heated; place mushrooms over chops and garnish with chopped fresh parsley. Serves 8.

**TIP:** Bourbon Mushrooms can be prepared well ahead of time and refrigerated. Simply warm them prior to serving. Try Bourbon Mushrooms with your favorite steak or burger.

*Luby's Recipes & Memories*

# Lone Star Pork Chops

1 cup Italian salad dressing

½ cup tomato sauce

1 tablespoon chili powder

½ teaspoon cayenne pepper

1 jalapeño pepper, seeded and diced

½ teaspoon dry mustard

4 pork chops, about 1½ inches thick

In a bowl, combine all ingredients except pork chops. Pour half of the marinade into a large baking dish. Reserve and refrigerate remaining marinade. Add pork chops to the dish, turning to coat both sides. Cover and marinate in the refrigerator for 3 to 24 hours, turning occasionally. Remove chops; discard marinade. Grill or broil chops, turning once, until done. In a saucepan, bring the reserved marinade to a boil. Pour over cooked pork chops. Serves 4.

*Texas Peppers*

# Creole Chops

5 tomatoes, chopped

1 (15-ounce) can beef bouillon

1 (15-ounce) can tomato sauce

1 onion, chopped

½ cup apple cider vinegar

1 tablespoon minced garlic

1 teaspoon crushed red pepper

Minced fresh basil or dried basil to taste

8 pork or venison chops

Vegetable oil

Combine the tomatoes, bouillon, tomato sauce, onion, vinegar, garlic, red pepper, and basil in a saucepan and mix well. Simmer for 20 minutes, stirring occasionally.

Preheat the oven to 325 degrees. Brown the chops on both sides in a small amount of oil in a skillet. Remove the chops to a baking dish and pour the tomato mixture over the top. Bake, covered, until the chops are cooked through. Serves 8.

Caroline Rose Hunt, Rosewood Hotels & Resorts, Dallas
*Dallas Dish*

# Boneless Pork Chops with Ancho Cream Sauce

4 boneless pork loin chops, ½ inch thick

¼ teaspoon salt

¼ teaspoon black pepper

4 bacon slices

Vegetable cooking spray

¼ cup Ancho Base (see recipe below)

¾ cup whipping cream

Sprinkle pork loin chops with salt and pepper. Wrap a bacon slice around each chop; secure with wooden picks, if desired. Coat grill rack with vegetable cooking spray; place the rack on grill over medium coals. Place chops on rack and cook, covered with grill lid, 8 minutes on each side or until done.

Combine the Ancho Base and whipping cream in a saucepan, stirring with a wire whisk until smooth. Bring to a boil over medium heat, whisking constantly, 5 minutes or until thickened. Spoon Ancho Cream Sauce onto individual serving plates, top each with a pork chop. Serve immediately. Serves 4.

## Ancho Base

*(Yields 2¼ cups.)*

3 dried ancho chiles

4 ounces sun-dried tomatoes

3 tablespoons minced garlic

½ cup chopped onion

4 beef-flavored bouillon cubes

1 tablespoon dried oregano

1 tablespoon brown sugar

2 tablespoons Worcestershire sauce

¼ cup tomato paste

1½ cups water

Combine all ingredients in a saucepan. Bring to a boil over medium heat. Reduce heat and simmer, stirring occasionally, for 10 minutes. Cool about 15 minutes.

Position knife blade in food processor bowl; add mixture. Process until smooth, stopping often to scrape down sides of bowl. Refrigerate up to 1 week or freeze up to 3 months.

*Seasoned with Fun*

# Grilled Pork Chops

3 tablespoons hoisin sauce

1 tablespoon hot mustard

1 tablespoon chopped shallot

1 tablespoon minced garlic

1 tablespoon grated fresh ginger

1 tablespoon chopped fresh jalapeño chile

1 tablespoon chopped scallion

1 tablespoon chopped fresh cilantro

4 pork chops, butterflied

Salt and pepper to taste

Preheat the grill. Process the hoisin sauce, mustard, shallot, garlic, ginger, jalapeño, green onion, and cilantro in a blender until pureed and of a sauce consistency.

Season the pork chops with salt and pepper. Grill for 10 minutes and turn. Liberally baste chops with the sauce and grill for 10 minutes longer, or until cooked through. Serves 4.

*Dallas Dish*

# Country-Style Ribs

3 to 4 pounds country-style pork spareribs

¼ cup prepared mustard

¼ cup soy sauce

2 tablespoons prepared horseradish

2 tablespoons honey

¼ teaspoon ground ginger

Cover spareribs with unsalted water in large pot. Simmer, covered, for 1 hour and drain well. Stir together mustard, soy sauce, horseradish, honey, and ginger. Brush over ribs. Grill over hot coals, turning frequently and brushing often with mustard mixture. Ribs can be put on cookie sheet and baked in 350-degree oven for 30 to 45 minutes, turning twice and basting each time with sauce. Serves 4.

D'Anne DeMoss McGown
*Lagniappe*

# Sweet Jalapeño BBQ Ribs

3 pounds country-style pork ribs

½ teaspoon granulated garlic

½ teaspoon each salt and pepper

1 (10½-ounce) jar red jalapeño jelly

1 medium onion, chopped

1 (5-ounce) bottle A.1. steak sauce

2 jalapeño chiles, seeded and minced

Season ribs with granulated garlic, salt, and pepper. Place ribs on a rack in a broiler pan. Broil 5½ inches from heat source for 18 to 20 minutes, or until well browned, turning once. While ribs are broiling, combine jelly, onion, steak sauce, and minced jalapeños in a saucepan. Cook over low heat until jelly melts. Simmer for a few minutes; remove from heat. When ribs are browned, remove them to a baking dish. Lower heat to 350 degrees. Pour sauce over ribs, cover, and return to oven for about 1 hour, or until meat is fork-tender.

Jeri-Lynn Sandusky, Utah
*Kickin' Back in the Kitchen Cookbook*

# Cactus Juice Spareribs

1 rack of pork spareribs, about 3 pounds

Salt

Freshly ground black pepper to taste

1 cup olive oil

Juice from 4 large limes

½ cup gold tequila

1 onion, finely chopped

2½ tablespoons minced garlic

3 jalapeño peppers, seeded and minced

2 tablespoons minced cilantro

Season the ribs with salt and pepper. In a small mixing bowl, whisk the olive oil, lime juice, tequila, onions, garlic, jalapeño peppers, and cilantro. Season with more salt and pepper. Place the ribs, meat side down, in a glass baking dish. Pour the marinade over the ribs, coating each side completely. Cover and refrigerate at least 12 hours, turning every couple of hours. Remove from the refrigerator and bring the ribs to room temperature. Preheat the grill to low. Place the ribs meat side down, and grill, turning and basting with marinade every 15 minutes. Cook for about 1½ to 2 hours, or until the ribs are very tender.

*Texas Peppers*

# Chuckwagon Pork Roast with Tangy Sauce

## Pork Roast

½ teaspoon salt

½ teaspoon garlic salt

½ teaspoon chili powder

1 (4-pound) pork loin

## Tangy Sauce

1 cup apple jelly

1 cup ketchup

2 teaspoons vinegar

2 teaspoons chili powder

Combine salt, garlic salt, and chili powder and rub into pork. Roast at 325 degrees for 2 hours, or until a meat thermometer inserted in the center registers 160 degrees.

To make the sauce, combine all ingredients in a saucepan. Bring to a boil and simmer 2 minutes. About 15 minutes before pork is done, brush with sauce. Add ½ cup of pan drippings to remaining sauce and serve with pork. Serves 12.

**VARIATION:** Substitute other pork cuts, if desired. Pork tenderloin should roast 30 minutes, and baby back ribs need to cook 20 minutes.

Catering by Don Strange, San Antonio
*Mesquite Country*

# Alsatian Pork Roast

## Rub

1 cup salt

½ cup white pepper

1 tablespoon paprika

1 teaspoon garlic powder

1 teaspoon onion powder

1 teaspoon allspice

## Roast

1 (3-pound) center-cut pork loin roast

8 bacon slices, diced

2 cups sliced mushrooms

1 large carrot, peeled and sliced

1 celery stalk, sliced

2½ cups white wine

1½ cups heavy cream

1 tablespoon tarragon mustard

½ cup small capers, drained

1 tablespoon horseradish

1 cup basic white sauce

Preheat oven to 400 degrees. Combine all rub ingredients in a jar. Rub roast with spice mixture; reserve leftover rub. Lay bacon, mushrooms, carrot, and celery in bottom of Dutch oven. Place roast over vegetables. Bake for 15 minutes. Pour half of the wine over the roast and reduce heat to 375 degrees. Bake for an additional 40 to 50 minutes. Remove roast from pan and keep warm. Place Dutch oven on stove top over medium heat. Add remaining wine and all remaining ingredients. Simmer, stirring, until thickened. Season with salt and pepper as needed. Slice roast and serve with sauce and vegetables. Splendid served cold the next day. Serves 4 to 6.

Bruno and Frederika Courtin, Windows on the Bay, Corpus Christi, Texas
*¡Viva! Tradiciones*

# Mamma's Pork Pot Roast

1 bone-in pork shoulder (3 to 4 pounds)

8 large garlic cloves, peeled and cut into thick slices

24 to 30 Italian parsley leaves

Kosher salt and freshly ground black pepper

2 to 3 tablespoons vegetable oil

All-purpose flour

1 carrot, peeled and coarsely chopped

1 celery stalk, coarsely chopped

1 small yellow onion, peeled and coarsely chopped

4 large garlic cloves, peeled and coarsely chopped

2 cups boiling water

½ cup Italian parsley leaves

Preheat oven to 325 degrees. Pierce meat all over with a paring knife. Insert a piece of garlic and a few parsley leaves into the pierce marks. Season meat very well with salt and pepper, rubbing seasoning into the meat evenly. Let seasoned meat sit for 30 minutes.

Heat the oil in a large roasting pan over medium-high heat. Meanwhile, flour the meat all over. Add the meat to the pan and brown on all sides, being careful not to scorch it.

About halfway through the browning process, add the carrot, celery, onion, and coarsely chopped garlic. Brown the vegetables.

When the vegetables and meat are brown, add the water and the parsley to the pan and cover. Place the pan in the oven and roast for 3 to 4 hours, turning the meat every hour until tender.

Remove roast from oven. Remove cover and let roast cool for about 1 hour.

Heat gravy and strain to remove vegetables. Refrigerate roast and gravy.

Slice cold and arrange in a 9 × 13-inch baking pan. Remove the hardened fat from the gravy while it's still cold. (This roast is best if made the day before.)

Spoon the defatted gravy over the roast, cover with foil, and heat in a 325-degree oven until warm. Arrange the meat on a platter and pour the gravy over the top. Serves 6 to 8.

*Ciao Y'All*

# Bourbon-Spiced Pork Tenderloins

2 (1-pound) pork tenderloins, trimmed

¼ cup bourbon

½ cup soy sauce

¼ cup Dijon mustard

¼ cup packed brown sugar

¼ cup olive oil

2 tablespoons grated ginger

2 teaspoons Worcestershire sauce

4 garlic cloves, minced

Arrange the pork tenderloins in a nonmetallic dish. Combine the bourbon, soy sauce, Dijon mustard, brown sugar, olive oil, ginger, Worcestershire sauce, and garlic in a blender or food processor container. Process until smooth. Pour over the pork tenderloins, turning to coat. Marinate, covered, in the refrigerator for 8 to 10 hours. Drain, reserving the marinade.

Sear the tenderloins on all sides over hot coals, turning with tongs. Do not pierce the pork. Reduce the temperature to medium. Grill for 20 minutes or until cooked through, basting frequently with the reserved marinade. Let stand for 10 minutes before slicing. Cut into ½-inch slices. Serves 6.

*Texas Ties*

# Chili-Spiced Barbecued Pork Tenderloin

2 pieces pork tenderloin, about
   2½ pounds total

2 tablespoons chili powder

1 tablespoon ground cumin

2 teaspoons dried Mexican oregano

4 large garlic cloves, minced to a paste

1 tablespoon freshly squeezed lime juice

Olive oil

Build a smoky fire in the barbecue pit, using hardwood chunks that have been soaked in water for 1 hour. Trim all fat and silverskin from the meat; set aside.

In a small bowl, combine the remaining ingredients, except olive oil, and blend well. Stir in just enough olive oil to form a loose, spreadable paste. Spread the paste on all sides of the meat.

Place the meat on the cooking rack of barbecue pit and cook until an instant-read thermometer inserted in the thickest part of the meat registers 145–150 degrees, about 30 to 45 minutes. Remove the meat and set aside, covered loosely with foil, to rest for 10 minutes before slicing. Slice the meat on a baking sheet with sides (or on a meat carving board with a juice well). Slice about ½ inch thick. Fan slices out on serving plates and drizzle a portion of the drippings from the baking sheet over each serving. Serve hot. Serves 4 to 6.

*Texas on the Plate*

# Pork Tenderloin in Lime Cream Sauce

2 tablespoons vegetable oil

1¼ pounds pork tenderloin

2 tablespoons butter

2 tablespoons onion, chopped

2 tablespoons shallots, chopped

¼ cup white table wine

1 can (10¾-ounce) chicken broth

½ cup beef broth

1 cup heavy cream

2 tablespoons freshly squeezed lime juice

Preheat oven to 400 degrees. Heat oil in large, heavy ovenproof skillet over high heat. Add pork and brown on all sides, turning frequently. Transfer skillet to oven until pork is cooked through, about 20 minutes.

Meanwhile, melt butter in large, heavy skillet over medium heat. Add onion and shallots; sauté 3 minutes. Add wine and boil until liquid is reduced by half, stirring occasionally, about 5 minutes. Add both stocks and boil until liquid is reduced to 6 tablespoons, stirring frequently, about 13 minutes. Add whipping cream and boil until sauce is reduced to 1 cup, stirring often, about 7 minutes. Mix in fresh lime juice and season to taste with salt and pepper.

Cut pork diagonally into ¼-inch slices. Spoon sauce on plates, fan pork atop sauce, and serve. Serves 4.

*And Roses for the Table*

# Southwestern Pork Tenderloins with Cumin Mayonnaise

1½ tablespoons ground cumin

1 tablespoon chili powder

¾ teaspoon salt

¼ teaspoon freshly ground pepper

2 (1-pound) pork tenderloins

4 additional teaspoons ground cumin

1 cup mayonnaise

2 teaspoons freshly squeezed lime juice

3 tablespoons chopped fresh cilantro leaves

Mix 1½ tablespoons ground cumin, chili powder, salt, and pepper in a small bowl. Rub on the pork to coat well. Place on a rack in a roasting pan. Roast at 450 degrees for 12 to 18 minutes, or until a meat thermometer inserted in thickest portion registers 160 degrees. Cool before serving.

Heat a small skillet over medium heat. Add 4 teaspoons ground cumin. Cook for 2 minutes, or until slightly darkened, stirring constantly. Remove from heat and combine with the mayonnaise, lime juice, and cilantro in a bowl; mix well. Serve with the pork. Serves 8 to 10.

*Dining without Reservations*

# Pork Medallions in Mustard Sauce

3 tablespoons vegetable oil

1 tablespoon coarse-grained mustard

½ teaspoon salt

½ teaspoon black pepper

2 (¾-pound) pork tenderloins

¼ cup dry white wine

Mustard Sauce (see recipe below)

Fresh basil sprigs (optional)

Combine vegetable oil, mustard, salt, and pepper, stirring well. Rub mixture over pork tenderloins; place in a heavy-duty zip-top plastic bag. Refrigerate for 8 hours.

Place pork tenderloins on rack in a shallow roasting pan. Insert meat thermometer in thickest part of meat. Bake at 375 degrees for 25 minutes, or until meat thermometer registers 160 degrees, basting every 10 minutes with white wine.

Slice pork tenderloins into ¾-inch-thick slices and arrange on each dinner plate. Spoon Mustard Sauce around pork on each plate. Garnish with a fresh basil sprig, if desired. Serves 4.

## Mustard Sauce

*(Yields 1¼ cups.)*

1¾ cups whipping cream

¼ cup coarse-grained mustard

¼ teaspoon salt

¼ teaspoon white pepper

Heat whipping cream in a heavy saucepan until reduced to 1¼ cups, about 5 minutes. Do not boil. Stir in the mustard, salt, and white pepper; heat 1 minute.

*Seasoned with Fun*

# Marinated Grilled Leg of Lamb

½ cup Dijon mustard

2 tablespoons soy sauce

1 teaspoon minced fresh rosemary or thyme

Dash garlic powder

¼ teaspoon ginger

2 tablespoons olive oil

1 leg of lamb (6 to 8 pounds), all fat trimmed away

Blend all ingredients together except the olive oil and lamb. Beat in the oil by drops. Paint the marinade onto the lamb with a spatula. To have the leg of lamb ready for an 8:00 p.m. dinner, put the marinade on it before noon and put it in the oven at 4:00 p.m. Cook a 6- to 8-pound leg of lamb for 3 to 4 hours at 350 degrees.

*Of Magnolia and Mesquite*

# Butterflied, Grilled Leg of Lamb

1 leg of lamb (4 to 7 pounds), boned and butterflied

## Marinade

6 to 8 garlic cloves, finely minced

⅓ cup finely chopped rosemary leaves (6 to 8 sprigs)

1 tablespoon Dijon mustard

1 tablespoon ground black pepper

Juice of 1 lemon

Grated zest of 1 lemon

1 tablespoon salt

2 tablespoons olive oil

Combine the marinade ingredients. Place the lamb in a large zip-lock plastic bag. Add the marinade. Turn and squeeze the plastic bag to be sure all surfaces of the meat come in contact with the marinade. Refrigerate for 2 to 4 hours.

Grill over hot coals, approximately 8 to 10 minutes per side. This will leave it a delicious medium-rare. If you must, cook it a few more minutes, but don't overcook. Serve with mint jelly. Serves 8 to 10.

*Texas Cowboy Cooking*

# Meatball Curry

## Koftas (Meatballs)

2 pounds ground beef or lamb

½ cup chopped onion

3 tablespoons chopped cilantro

2 teaspoons minced green chiles, preferably serranos

1 teaspoon peeled, minced ginger

1 teaspoon minced garlic

1½ teaspoons ground coriander

1 teaspoon garam masala

¾ teaspoon ground cumin

½ teaspoon cayenne pepper

1 teaspoon salt, or to taste

## Curry

2 tablespoons vegetable oil

1½ cups chopped onion

1 cup water

1 tablespoon peeled, minced ginger

1 tablespoon minced garlic

1 tablespoon minced green chiles, preferably serranos

2 teaspoons ground coriander

1 teaspoon ground cumin

½ teaspoon turmeric

½ teaspoon cayenne pepper

1 (28-ounce) can tomatoes, pureed with juice

¼ cup chopped cilantro

1½ teaspoons salt, or to taste

1 teaspoon garam masala

2 tablespoons chopped cilantro for garnish

Make the Koftas  In a bowl, combine ground meat, onion, cilantro, chiles, ginger, garlic, ground coriander, garam masala, cumin, cayenne pepper, and salt. Mix by hand. (Do not use a food processor.) Form into 30 to 35 walnut-size balls. Use a light touch; do not compact, or the meatballs will be too hard. Place on baking sheet. Set aside.

Make the Curry  In a large, deep skillet with a tight-fitting lid, heat oil over medium-high heat. Sauté the onions until beginning to color, 6 to 8 minutes. Reduce heat to medium and sauté until browned, 8 to 10 minutes longer. Pour in the water.

Place baking sheet with meatballs on top of skillet, making sure the skillet is covered completely. Reduce heat to low and simmer until onions are very soft, 8 to 10 minutes, or until water has evaporated. The meatballs will "set" because of the steam from the skillet, which will prevent them from breaking while browning.

When onions are soft and there is no more liquid in the skillet, carefully lift meatballs from baking sheet and arrange on top of onions, turning them bottom side up when transferring from baking sheet. Cover pan to allow meatballs to set, 1 to 2 minutes. Uncover, increase heat to medium-low, and cook until meatballs are firm enough to turn gently with spoon and all the meat juices have been absorbed, 6 to 8 minutes. Gently stir meatballs to brown, taking care not to break them.

Scatter ginger, garlic, chiles, coriander, cumin, turmeric, and cayenne pepper over top. Reduce heat to low and continue to brown for 2 minutes longer. If spices stick to pan, add 2 tablespoons water to deglaze and mix well.

Stir in tomatoes, ¼ cup chopped cilantro, and salt. Increase heat to medium. Cover and return to a gentle boil. Reduce heat to low and simmer, covered, stirring occasionally, until gravy is thickened, 20 to 30 minutes. Remove from heat and sprinkle garam masala over top. Cover and let stand for 5 minutes. Stir mixture. Garnish with 2 tablespoons of cilantro before serving. Serve with rice or an Indian bread. Serves 6.

**TIP:** The gravy may appear to be too soupy. This is the way Indians like it, because it is spooned on top of rice and absorbed. If served with an Indian bread, the bread is used to dunk in the gravy—considered by some to the best part of the dish. If you prefer, reduce to desired thickness by simmering uncovered.

*Easy Indian Cooking*

# North Indian–Style Lamb Curry on Bread

1 cup plain nonfat yogurt at room temperature

1 teaspoon cornstarch

2 tablespoons vegetable oil

4 cups finely chopped onions (3 to 4)

4 teaspoons peeled minced ginger

4 teaspoons minced garlic

1 tablespoon minced green chiles, preferably serranos

3 pounds boneless leg of lamb, cut into bite-size pieces

4 teaspoons ground coriander

2 teaspoons ground cumin

¾ teaspoon turmeric

½ teaspoon cayenne pepper

2 teaspoons salt, or to taste

2 (28-ounce) cans diced tomatoes

1 teaspoon garam masala

¼ cup chopped cilantro

1 loaf soft French bread, sliced 1 inch thick

Thin slices onions or green onions for garnish

3 tablespoons chopped cilantro for garnish

Juice of ½ lime

Stir together yogurt and cornstarch until smooth; set aside.

In a large skillet, heat oil over medium-high heat. Sauté onions until beginning to color, 6 to 8 minutes. Reduce heat to medium and sauté until browned, 15 to 20 minutes longer. Stir in the ginger, garlic, and chiles. Sauté for 3 to 4 minutes. Increase heat to medium-high. Add lamb and brown until meat and onions are a dark rich brown, 10 to 15 minutes. Add water, 1 tablespoon at a time, if necessary to prevent burning.

Add coriander, cumin, turmeric, cayenne pepper, and salt. Reduce heat to medium. Sauté for 3 to 4 minutes. Add tomatoes and yogurt mixture and return to a boil.

*(Continued)*

Reduce heat to maintain a gentle boil. Cover and cook, stirring occasionally, until meat is tender, about 1 hour. Remove from heat. Sprinkle with garam masala and ¼ cup cilantro. There should be a lot of gravy.

To serve, arrange bread in single layer on a large serving platter. Top with lamb and spoon gravy evenly over top to soak into bread. (Assemble 10 minutes before serving to allow bread to soak up gravy.) Garnish with onions and 3 tablespoons chopped cilantro. Sprinkle with lime juice. Serves 8.

**TIP:** The gravy should be slightly runny to soften the bread. If it has cooked down too much, add a little hot water and simmer to incorporate.

*Easy Indian Cooking*

# Pasta

I don't recall ever meeting anyone who didn't like pasta. Pasta dishes can be as simple as your favorite cooked pasta tossed with warm extra-virgin olive oil, garlic, and quickly wilted spinach with a bit of grated Parmesan cheese scattered on top. Toss in some small cooked shrimp perhaps and add a salad. Voilà! A quick, easy, and healthy meal. Or your pasta can be topped with a slow-simmered marinara sauce. You can add meatballs, Italian sausage, chicken, etc. You can top your sauced pasta with grated Parmesan or Romano cheese or with shredded Asiago cheese. And what child won't tell you that one of his or her favorite foods is macaroni and cheese, which is best, of course, when made from scratch.

Keep in mind a few pointers about cooking pasta. First and foremost is that pasta must be cooked in a very large pot of vigorously boiling water. For example, 1 pound of pasta should be cooked in a 10-quart pot in about 7 quarts of boiling water. Always add salt to the pasta water, but never oil, which will prevent your sauce from coating the pasta. Cook pasta to the al dente stage, which means, literally translated, "to the tooth," or with a tiny bit of crunch left to the strands. Overcooked, mushy pasta is not altogether palatable. Drain pasta immediately into a large strainer, shaking out excess water. Save a bit of the pasta cooking water to thin your sauce, if needed. Generally, pasta is then tossed with the sauce you wish to serve and topped with meats and a cheese, if desired.

# Mr. B's Crawfish and Fettuccine

1 cup (2 sticks) cold unsalted butter, cut into tablespoon-size pieces

⅔ cup chopped mixed red and green bell peppers

⅔ cup chopped onion

2 cups cooked and shelled crawfish tails

½ teaspoon Brennan's Creole Seasoning, or substitute other Creole-style seasoning for fish

⅛ teaspoon crushed red pepper flakes

⅔ cup chopped peeled tomatoes

4 tablespoons sliced green onions

1 pound fettuccine, cooked and drained

4 whole boiled crawfish as garnish

Melt 2 tablespoons butter in a large sauté pan. When hot, sauté bell peppers and onion for 1 minute. Add crawfish tails, Creole seasoning, and crushed red pepper. Sauté 2 to 3 minutes. Add tomatoes and green onions and sauté 1 minute. Add remaining pieces of cold butter, 2 at a time, swirling the pan and stirring with a fork. When butter has been incorporated, taste to correct seasonings.

Divide cooked fettuccine into 4 portions and place each in the center of a warm plate. Spoon crawfish mixture around pasta and garnish with a whole boiled crawfish. Serves 4.

Mr. B's Bistro, New Orleans
*Gulf Coast Cooking*

# Shrimp Fettuccine

3 quarts water

1½ pounds spinach fettuccine

¾ cup vegetable or olive oil, divided

1 pound medium shrimp, shelled and deveined

4 cloves garlic, crushed

½ cup brandy

1½ cups heavy cream

Salt and ground white pepper to taste

1 cup freshly grated Parmesan cheese

In a large pot, bring water to a boil. Add fettuccine and return to a boil for 3 minutes, or until the pasta is cooked but still firm (al dente). Drain, rinse with cold water, and drain again. Transfer to a large warm bowl, add ¼ cup oil, and toss gently. Cover and set aside.

Pour remaining oil in a large skillet and place over medium heat. When hot, add shrimp and sauté 1 minute. Add garlic and brandy and sauté for 2 minutes. Add cream, cooked fettuccine, salt, and pepper. Simmer for 5 minutes. Remove from heat and sprinkle with cheese, tossing well. Serve at once. Serves 4 to 6.

Henry Douglas, Radisson Admiral Semmes Hotel, Mobile, Alabama
*Gulf Coast Cooking*

# Linguine with Shrimp

12 ounces linguine

Salt to taste

Olive oil to taste

1 cup sliced mushrooms

2 garlic cloves, minced

¾ teaspoon minced rosemary

2 tablespoons olive oil

2 pounds shrimp, peeled and deveined

1 cup bottled clam broth

⅔ cup whipping cream

½ teaspoon freshly ground pepper

Cook the pasta in boiling salted water in a large pan using package directions; drain. Toss with just enough olive oil to coat in a bowl. Set aside. Sauté the mushrooms, garlic, and rosemary in 2 tablespoons olive oil in a skillet for 2 minutes. Add the shrimp. Cook just until the shrimp turn pink, stirring constantly; do not overcook. Stir in the clam broth, whipping cream, and pepper. Simmer until thickened and slightly reduced, stirring constantly. Pour over the pasta, tossing to mix. Serve immediately. Serves 4.

*Texas Ties*

# Shrimp with White Wine and Dill Sauce

3 tablespoons butter

3 tablespoons all-purpose flour

1½ cups half-and-half

¾ teaspoon dried dill weed

½ teaspoon salt

2 tablespoons butter

1 tablespoon chopped onion

¾ cup dry white wine

2 teaspoons fresh lemon juice

1 pound medium shrimp, peeled and deveined

Hot cooked angel hair pasta or fettuccine

Heat the 3 tablespoons of butter in a medium saucepan. Add the flour gradually, stirring constantly, until well blended. Cook until of a paste consistency, stirring constantly. Add the half-and-half gradually, stirring constantly. Stir in the dill weed and salt; simmer over medium-low heat until thickened and of a sauce consistency, stirring frequently. Remove from the heat and cover to keep warm.

Heat 2 tablespoons of butter in a large saucepan over medium-high heat. Add the onion and cook for 3 to 4 minutes, or until tender. Stir in the wine and lemon juice and bring to a boil. Add the shrimp and cook for about 4 minutes, or until the shrimp are pink and cooked through; do not overcook the shrimp.

Add the dill sauce to the shrimp and stir to blend well. Reduce the heat to low and simmer until thickened, stirring frequently. Spoon over hot cooked pasta on a serving platter. Serves 2 to 4.

*Dallas Dish*

# Pasta with Asiago Cheese and Artichoke Marinara Sauce

¼ cup extra-virgin olive oil

1 medium onion, cut into tiny dice

3 large garlic cloves, minced

1 tablespoon minced fresh basil

2 (6-ounce) jars marinated artichoke hearts, well drained and chopped

1 heaping tablespoon tomato paste

½ teaspoon kosher salt or sea salt

½ teaspoon freshly ground black pepper

1 (28-ounce) can crushed tomatoes

1 (15-ounce) can diced tomatoes and their liquid

1 cup (4 ounces) shredded Asiago cheese

Pasta of choice, cooked al dente and drained well

Grated or shaved imported Parmesan cheese

Heat the olive oil in a heavy, deep-sided 10-inch skillet over medium heat. When oil is hot enough to make a few onion pieces sizzle, add the onion, garlic, basil, and artichoke hearts. Sauté until the onion is wilted and transparent, about 7 minutes, stirring often. Add the tomato paste, salt, and pepper; stir to blend well. Cook until the tomato paste is darkened to a rich, brick-red color, stirring constantly, about 4 minutes. Add the crushed tomatoes and diced tomatoes and their liquid; stir to blend well. Lower heat, cover pan, and simmer for 30 minutes, stirring occasionally. Stir in the Asiago cheese. Cook just until cheese is melted and heated through. Serve over al dente pasta of your choice. Top with a liberal scattering of freshly grated or shaved Parmesan cheese. Serves 4 to 6.

Terry Thompson-Anderson

# Cheese Ravioli with Sun-Dried Tomatoes

9 ounces fresh cheese ravioli

½ cup (1 stick) butter

4 garlic cloves, minced

2 cups light cream

1 cup freshly grated Parmesan cheese

½ cup oil-packed sun-dried tomatoes, roughly chopped

Freshly ground pepper to taste

¼ cup vodka (optional)

Cook the ravioli using package directions; drain. Cover to keep warm. Heat the butter in a skillet over medium heat until melted. Add the garlic. Cook until light golden brown, stirring constantly. Add the light cream, whisking constantly. Bring to a simmer, whisking constantly; do not boil. Remove from heat. Add the cheese, tomatoes, and pepper; stir to mix well. Return to medium heat and cook until thickened, stirring constantly. Stir in the vodka. Cook just until heated through. Remove from heat. Add the ravioli, tossing to coat. Serve immediately. Serves 2.

*Texas Ties*

# Lasagna with Sausage and Spinach

1 pound sweet Italian sausage, removed from casings

1 (15-ounce) container ricotta cheese

2 cups shredded mozzarella cheese

2 eggs

1¾ cups grated Parmesan cheese

2 (16-ounce) jars Classico Tomato Basil pasta sauce

12 lasagna noodles, cooked al dente

2 (10-ounce) packages frozen chopped spinach, thawed and pressed in strainer to remove moisture

1 (14-ounce) jar sun-dried tomato Alfredo sauce

Preheat oven to 350 degrees.

Fry the sausage, breaking up any lumps with the back of a spoon. Drain and set aside. Combine the ricotta, mozzarella, eggs, and ¼ cup of the Parmesan cheese. Set aside.

Pour 1½ cups of the pasta sauce into a lasagna pan. Add a layer of lasagna noodles. Add a layer of spinach, then the cheese mixture; top with crumbled sausage and another layer of the pasta sauce. Repeat layers, ending with sauce. Pour the Alfredo sauce over the lasagna. Top with the remaining 1½ cups Parmesan cheese. Bake, covered, for 45 minutes. Uncover and bake for an additional 15 minutes. Let stand for 15 minutes before cutting.

Margaret Purkey
*Kickin' Back in the Kitchen Cookbook*

# Gourmet Chicken Spaghetti

3 pounds chicken

8 ounces thin spaghetti

4 tablespoons butter

4 tablespoons flour

1 cup heavy cream

1 cup chicken broth

1 cup mayonnaise

1 cup sour cream

1 cup Parmesan cheese

2 tablespoons freshly squeezed lemon juice

⅓ cup dry white wine

½ teaspoon garlic powder

½ teaspoon cayenne pepper

1 teaspoon dry mustard

1 teaspoon salt

8 ounces sliced mushrooms

4 tablespoons butter

Additional Parmesan cheese for topping

Boil chicken in water to cover until tender, about 45 minutes. Drain, reserving broth, then cool and bone. Break spaghetti into thirds and boil in the reserved broth until al dente. Drain and set aside.

In a skillet, melt butter; add flour and cook until bubbly, stirring constantly. Add the cream and chicken broth, stirring and cooking until thickened. Add mayonnaise, sour cream, Parmesan, lemon juice, wine, and seasonings; set aside.

In a small skillet, sauté mushrooms in butter. Place mushrooms, chicken, and spaghetti in a 3-quart casserole. Pour the sauce over the top and scatter top with paprika and additional Parmesan cheese. Bake at 350 degrees for 30 to 40 minutes. May be made ahead of time and frozen. Serves 8 to 10.

Sally Kendall Bundy
Gadelle McMahon Todd
*Lagniappe*

# Tony's Fedelini al Bucaniera

2 garlic cloves, chopped

1 teaspoon crushed red pepper flakes

7 tablespoons olive oil, divided

1 pound tomatoes, peeled and chopped

¾ cup shelled and deveined shrimp (about ½ pound)

½ cup fresh shelled clams

Salt and pepper to taste

1 pound fedelini or thin spaghetti

¼ cup mixed chopped fresh parsley and basil

½ pound lump crabmeat

Sauté garlic and red pepper flakes in half the olive oil. Add tomatoes and cook for 15 minutes. Set aside.

In a separate pan, sauté shrimp and clams in remaining oil. Cook just until shrimp are done, then add reserved tomato sauce. Season with salt and pepper and set aside.

In a large pot of boiling water, cook fedelini just until done (al dente). Drain, sprinkle with parsley and basil, and mix with reserved sauce. Add crabmeat and heat through. Serve at once. Serves 4 to 6.

Tony's Restaurant, Houston
*Gulf Coast Cooking*

# Macaroni and Cheese

2 cups (8 ounces) dry elbow macaroni

4 tablespoons nonfat dry milk

2 tablespoons all-purpose flour

1 tablespoon butter or margarine, melted

1¼ cups boiling water

3 cups (12 ounces) shredded American cheese

¼ teaspoon kosher salt

Preheat oven to 350 degrees. Cook macaroni 1 to 2 minutes longer than package directions so pasta is soft but not mushy. Drain. In a large bowl, combine dry milk, flour, and butter. Whisking constantly, gradually add in boiling water. Add 1 cup of the cheese and continue whisking until smooth and creamy, about 2 to 3 minutes. Fold in macaroni, 1 additional cup of cheese, and salt. Transfer to a lightly greased 11 × 7-inch casserole dish and cover with foil. Bake 25 to 30 minutes, or until sauce in center of casserole is thick and creamy. Remove foil and sprinkle remaining 1 cup cheese evenly over top. Return to oven until cheese melts. Serves 6.

*Luby's Recipes & Memories*

# Mexican Lasagna

1 pound lean ground beef, browned

1 (16-ounce) can refried beans

2 teaspoons dried oregano

1 teaspoon ground cumin

¾ teaspoon garlic powder

12 uncooked lasagna noodles

2½ cups water

2½ cups picante sauce or salsa

1 (16-ounce) carton sour cream

¾ cup finely sliced green onions

1 (4-ounce) can sliced black olives

1 cup (4 ounces) shredded Monterey Jack cheese

Combine beef, beans, oregano, cumin, and garlic powder. Place 4 of the uncooked lasagna noodles in the bottom of a 13 × 9 × 2-inch baking dish. Spread half of the beef mixture over the noodles. Top with more noodles and the remaining beef mixture. Cover with remaining 4 noodles. Combine water and picante sauce. Pour over the lasagna. Cover tightly with foil; bake at 350 degrees for 1½ hours, or until noodles are tender. Combine sour cream, onions, and olives. Spoon over the lasagna, then top with the cheese. Bake, uncovered, for an additional 5 minutes, or until cheese has melted. Serves 12.

Dorothy Russell
*Flavors of Fredericksburg*

# Tex-Mex

Tex-Mex food is the one by which Texas cuisine has long been identified by the majority of "foreigners" (those unfortunate folks who don't live in the Lone Star State.) It's a cuisine that has evolved over the centuries since the Spanish conquered Mexico, then ventured north to explore the vastness of Texas. Mexicans settled in regions that are now Texas, bringing with them their heritage of cooking, which had then become a fusion of indigenous food blended with the foods of the Spanish, along with a newfound love of beef from the cattle brought by the Spanish explorers. In Texas, they were likewise influenced by indigenous foods and culture, and Tex-Mex cooking was born. It's a rich blend of cooking styles relying on fresh ingredients and lots of spicy chiles, both fresh and dried.

Tex-Mex is the second most popular restaurant food in Texas, surpassed only by American cuisine. In 2008 Tex-Mex restaurants in Texas grossed $3.5 billion. And I'd wager there are more Tex-Mex restaurants in the state than burger franchises! Even in small Texas towns, it's not unusual to see three Mexican restaurants—and often not a single McDonald's.

There's a definite art to cooking good Tex-Mex food—and many skills that must be learned by doing. If you're new to Texas and you want to learn how to make the legendary Tex-Mex tamales, then befriend a Hispanic cook and ask them to teach you the process. Making enchiladas might seem to be a simple process of putting a filling on a corn tortilla, rolling it up, and baking a pan of them, topped with a sauce and some cheese. But first that corn tortilla has to be softened in a small amount of hot fat, or it will crack and tear when you try to roll it. A great way to add flavor to enchiladas is to boil dried chiles in water and puree them with some of the cooking water. Dip the tortillas first in the chile "sauce," then soften them in the hot fat. The chile is seared on the tortillas, adding another dimension of flavor to the enchiladas.

To cook Tex-Mex, you'll want to learn about the many varieties of chiles used in the cuisine. Jalapeño and serrano chiles are fresh (as opposed to dried) chiles, which are used uncooked in salsas and pico de gallo and cooked in many of the Tex-Mex stews, or guisadas. You can moderate the heat of fresh chiles by removing the seeds and the whitish veins inside the chiles before using them. Poblano chiles, another fresh chile, are always blistered and peeled before they are used. The poblano chile is most recognizable as the chili that is stuffed with either a meat picadillo or cheeses, then battered and fried to make classic chiles rellenos. When the poblano chile is dried, it is called an ancho chile and is used to make rich sauces and to flavor other dishes. Jalapeño chiles are dried and smoked to become chipotle chiles, which are also used to create rich, spicy, smoky sauces and as an ingredient in many dishes. Other dried chiles that are used in Tex-Mex cooking are gaujillo, mulatto, pasilla, cascabel, and morita, to name just a few.

Tex-Mex is a fascinating and challenging cuisine to learn, but the tastes are well worth the effort.

# Serrano Chile Guacamole

3 serrano chiles, seeds and veins removed, coarsely chopped

4 large cilantro sprigs (stems and leaves), coarsely chopped

1 small white onion, peeled and coarsely chopped

4 very ripe Haas avocados, peeled, seeds removed, and cut into coarse chunks

Salt to taste

Shredded lettuce and tomato wedges as garnish

Place serrano chiles, cilantro, and onion in work bowl of food processor fitted with steel blade. Process until vegetables are pureed and smooth. Add the avocado chunks and process to desired consistency. (Some people like their guacamole real smooth, or you can leave some small chunks of the avocado if you prefer.) Turn the mixture out into a bowl and stir in the salt. Don't be stingy with the salt, or your guacamole will have a flat, boring taste.

An old trick for storing guacamole before serving is to place the seeds from the avocados on the surface of the mixture and push them in slightly. Cover tightly with plastic wrap and refrigerate until ready to serve. The seeds will prevent a drastic color change for about 4 hours.

To serve, arrange the shredded lettuce in the center of a serving platter and turn the guacamole out onto the lettuce. Place tomato wedges around the edge of the guacamole. Yields about 4 cups.

**EDITOR'S NOTE:** There's a quick and easy way to remove the soft pulp from a properly ripened avocado. First, using a chef's knife, cut the avocado in half lengthwise, cutting as deeply as possible until you reach the seed, but be sure to cut all the way around the avocado. Using both hands, twist the avocado in half. Lightly whack the seed with the blade of the knife, then gently twist the knife to remove the seed; discard the seed. Use a large spoon to scoop out the pulp in one piece. To dice the avocado, using a small paring knife, score the flesh into cubes, then use a large spoon to scoop the diced pulp from the skin.

*Texas on the Plate*

# Crispy Beef Tacos

1½ pounds lean ground beef

1 teaspoon salt

1½ tablespoons flour

1½ tablespoons chili powder

1½ cups water

½ teaspoon ground cumin

1 garlic clove, minced or pressed

Oil for frying tortillas

12 corn tortillas

**Toppings**

1 cup shredded Cheddar cheese

½ cup chopped onion

1 cup shredded lettuce

1 tomato, chopped

Salsa or bottled picante sauce

Brown ground beef in a large skillet, crumbling with a spoon while cooking. Drain.

Add salt, flour, chili powder, water, cumin, and garlic. Stir until blended. Simmer over medium heat until thickened, stirring occasionally. Set aside.

Heat ½ inch of oil in skillet. Hold a tortilla with tongs and dip one side in the oil until browned. Then dip the other side in the oil and brown, holding the edges apart to form a pocket. Drain on paper towels.

Fill individual taco shells with meat filling. Top with your choice of toppings. Serves 6.

*The San Antonio Tex-Mex Cookbook*

# Frito Pie

2 cups small Fritos

1 (15-ounce) can Wolf Brand Chili

Shredded Cheddar cheese

Chopped onions

Place 1 cup Fritos into each of 2 soup or cereal bowls. Heat chili in a small saucepan; pour over Fritos, dividing evenly. Top with cheese and onions. Yields 2 servings.

*Cooking with Texas Highways*

# Meat-Filled Chiles Rellenos

1 pound beef stew meat or boneless chicken breast

4 cups water

1 teaspoon salt

2 teaspoons ground coriander

½ teaspoon ground cloves

2 garlic cloves, minced or pressed

½ onion, chopped

1 cup raisins

1 to 2 tablespoons olive oil

8 to 10 poblano peppers, or canned green chiles

1 cup flour

½ cup cornmeal

1 teaspoon baking powder

½ teaspoon salt

2 eggs, beaten

1 cup milk

Oil or shortening for frying

Poach meat in water until tender. Drain and chop in food processor. Add seasonings, garlic, onion, and raisins. Sauté in olive oil.

Roast fresh chiles at 400 degrees for 20 minutes, or until skin blisters. Place in bowl and cover with plastic wrap. Let steam in bowl for 20 minutes. Peel chiles, leaving stems on. (Roasting and peeling is not necessary if using canned chiles.) Slit and remove seeds. Stuff chiles with meat mixture. Mix remaining ingredients, except oil, to make a batter. Stir well.

Heat 2 or more inches of oil in frying pan to 375 degrees. Dip the chiles in the batter. Place gently into oil and fry until golden brown. Drain on paper towels and serve immediately with salsa or green tomatillo sauce. Serves 4 to 6.

**VARIATION:** You can make this recipe without frying by layering the ingredients in a greased casserole as follows: ½ batter mixture, poblano chiles, meat mixture, and remaining batter mixture. Bake until set.

*The San Antonio Tex-Mex Cookbook*

# Cheese Enchiladas

24 corn tortillas

2 medium onions, chopped

1½ pounds cheese, grated (Longhorn

Cheddar or Monterey Jack or a combination)

1 recipe Enchilada Sauce (see recipe below)

Preheat oven to 350 degrees.

Soften the tortillas in hot oil for about 10 seconds each to make them pliable (so they won't crack when rolled). Fill each tortilla with 1 generous heaping tablespoon of the cheese and ½ tablespoon of the onions. Roll. Place, open edge down, in a 9 × 13-inch casserole. Pour the Enchilada Sauce over the top just before baking and top with the remaining cheese. Bake at 350 degrees for 20 to 30 minutes. Serves 8.

**NOTE:** You can also top the cheese enchiladas with leftover chili and grated cheese.

## Enchilada Sauce

2 teaspoons vegetable oil

1 medium onion, chopped

2 large garlic cloves, crushed

2 (16-ounce) cans whole tomatoes

3 tablespoons chili powder

½ teaspoon ground cumin

¼ teaspoon dried Mexican oregano

1 teaspoon salt

Sauté the onion and garlic in oil. Add remaining ingredients. Cover and simmer for 30 minutes. If a smooth sauce is desired, cool and puree in blender. Reheat to serve. Use this for cheese or beef enchiladas. Makes about 4 cups of sauce, enough for 24 enchiladas.

*It's a Long Way to Guacamole*

# Enchiladas Suizas

2 tablespoons vegetable oil

1 medium onion, chopped

1 garlic clove, minced

2 cups tomato sauce

2 (4-ounce) cans chopped green chiles

3 cups chicken, cooked and chopped

16 corn tortillas

6 chicken bouillon cubes

3 cups half-and-half, heated

½ pound Monterey Jack cheese, shredded

Heat oil in a large skillet. When oil is hot, sauté the onion until wilted and transparent. Add garlic, tomato sauce, green chiles, and chicken. Simmer 10 minutes and add salt if needed. Soften the tortillas in microwave for 1½ minutes on high. Dissolve bouillon cubes in hot half-and-half. Dip the softened tortillas in the bouillon mixture. Fill with seasoned chicken. Roll tortillas and place, seam side down, in a 9 × 13-inch casserole. Pour the remaining cream over the enchiladas and cover with cheese. Bake at 350 degrees for 30 minutes. Serves 8.

*It's a Long Way to Guacamole*

# Enchiladas Ranchero

## Ranchero Sauce

**1 medium onion, chopped**

**1 garlic clove, minced or pressed**

**2 tablespoons olive oil or bacon drippings**

**1 (10-ounce) can diced tomatoes and green chiles**

**½ teaspoon salt**

**¼ teaspoon dried oregano**

**¼ teaspoon ground cumin**

## Enchiladas

**Oil to soften tortillas**

**12 corn tortillas**

**1 pound grated white Mexican cheese (Monterey Jack, fresco, asadero, or quesadilla)**

**2 cups cooked, chopped chicken or ground beef (optional)**

Sauté onions and garlic in oil or bacon drippings until clear. Add tomatoes, green chiles, and seasonings. Simmer 10 minutes. Adjust seasonings.

Heat ¼ inch of oil in a small skillet. Dip each tortilla in the oil to soften. You can also dip each tortilla in the warm sauce to soften. This will save calories.

Place 2 tablespoons of grated cheese at one end of each tortilla to fill (or use 1 tablespoon cheese and 1 tablespoon meat). Roll each tortilla tightly and place in a 9 × 13-inch greased casserole dish, seam side down. Pour Ranchero Sauce over the top and sprinkle with the remaining cheese.

Bake at 350 degrees for 30 minutes, or until bubbly and cheese has melted. Serves 6.

*The San Antonio Tex-Mex Cookbook*

# Tomatillo Chicken Enchiladas

⅓ cup half-and-half

6 ounces cream cheese, softened

2 cups shredded cooked chicken

¾ cup finely chopped onion

½ teaspoon salt

Vegetable oil

12 (8-inch) corn tortillas

Tomatillo Sauce (see recipe below)

¾ cup (3 ounces) shredded Cheddar cheese

¾ cup (3 ounces) shredded Monterey Jack cheese

Shredded lettuce

Chopped tomatoes

Sliced ripe olives

Sour cream

## Tomatillo Sauce

24 tomatillos, husked

4 to 6 serrano chiles, stemmed and seeded (leave some seeds to add spice, if you wish)

3 cups chicken broth

2 tablespoons cornstarch

2 tablespoons chopped fresh cilantro

1 teaspoon salt

Begin by making the Tomatillo Sauce. Bring the tomatillos, serrano chiles, and broth to a boil in a saucepan and boil for 7 to 10 minutes. Dissolve the cornstarch in a small amount of cold water in a bowl and add to the boiling tomatillo mixture, along with the cilantro and salt; blend well. Boil for 5 minutes longer, stirring occasionally. Remove from heat and cool slightly. Process in a blender or food processor until pureed. Set aside.

Preheat the oven to 350 degrees. Beat the half-and-half and cream cheese in a mixing bowl until smooth and fluffy. Add the chicken, onion, and salt; mix until combined. Heat a small amount of oil in a skillet until hot. Dip the tortillas in the hot oil to soften, or microwave the tortillas in a buttered microwave-safe dish for 1½ minutes.

Spread a thin layer of the Tomatillo Sauce in a 9 × 13-inch baking dish. Spread a thin layer of the Tomatillo Sauce on each tortilla. Spoon about ¼ cup of the chicken mixture down the center of each tortilla and roll to enclose the filling.

Arrange the enchiladas, seam side down, in the prepared baking dish. Spoon the remaining Tomatillo Sauce over the top and cover with foil. Bake for 20 minutes and remove the foil. Scatter the mixed cheeses over the enchiladas and bake for 5 minutes longer, or until the cheese is melted. Serve with shredded lettuce, tomatoes, olives, and sour cream. Serves 4 to 6.

*Dallas Dish*

# Aji de Gallina

## Chicken and Broth

1 (4½ pound) chicken or hen

1 quart water

1 leek

1 onion

1 carrot

Salt to taste

## Entrée

¾ cup vegetable oil, divided

1 onion, finely chopped

1 garlic clove, crushed

½ teaspoon cumin seed

2 cups soft bread crumbs

1 cup evaporated milk

3 tablespoons pureed hot chile pepper

1 cup grated cheese

½ cup chopped nuts

2 pounds white potatoes, peeled and boiled

Combine chicken and next 5 ingredients in a saucepan. Bring to a boil and cook until chicken is tender. Remove chicken, skin and debone, and shred meat. Strain broth and reserve.

To prepare entrée, heat ½ cup oil in a skillet. Add onion, garlic, and cumin seed and sauté until browned. Soak bread crumbs in milk. Add to onion mixture and simmer 15 minutes. Place in a blender and blend until creamy. Return to skillet. Fry chile pepper in remaining ¼ cup oil in a separate skillet. Add chile pepper, shredded chicken, cheese, and nuts to onion mixture. Simmer 10 minutes, thinning with reserved broth and adding salt as needed. The sauce should be thick. Garnish with potatoes and serve with rice. Serves 6.

Rosanna Robalino
*Mesquite Country*

# Guisado de Pollo *(Chicken Stew)*

## Chicken

1 whole chicken, about 3 pounds

1 onion, quartered

1 to 2 tomatoes, quartered

2 whole serrano chiles

2 garlic cloves, peeled

Salt to taste

## Sauce

Water

1 pound fresh tomatoes, or 1 (14-ounce) can whole tomatoes

2 garlic cloves, peeled

1 onion, finely chopped

2 tablespoons canola oil

Pinch of ground cumin

2 serrano chiles, minced

Salt to taste

Boil chicken in water to cover with onion, tomatoes, chiles, garlic, and salt until meat is tender and beginning to come away from the bones, about 40 minutes. Remove chicken from broth; strain and reserve broth for another meal.

When chicken is cool, separate the meat from the bones and skin. Discard bones and skin. Shred chicken fine by rubbing pieces between fingers to separate fibers.

For the sauce, combine garlic and tomatoes in a blender. Add just enough water to facilitate blending, then puree; set aside.

In a heavy-bottomed, deep-sided skillet, add oil and sauté onions until translucent. Add pureed tomatoes, cumin, and serrano chiles. Simmer about 5 minutes, then add shredded chicken. Simmer for 20 minutes, or until liquid is reduced and thickened. Add salt to taste. Serves 6.

*The Texas Provincial Kitchen Cookbook*

# Carne Guisada *(Stewed Beef)*

2 pounds round steak, cut into 1-inch chunks

4 tablespoons all-purpose flour

2 tablespoons vegetable oil

½ large white onion, sliced

2 garlic cloves, chopped

2 medium tomatoes, chopped

½ cup chopped cilantro leaves

2 poblano chiles, roasted, peeled, seeded, and cut into ¼-inch strips, or 4 serrano chiles, chopped (or fewer for milder taste)

1 cup beef broth

1 teaspoon sea salt, or to taste

Flour tortillas

Dredge meat chunks in flour, coating well. In a heavy, deep-sided 12-inch skillet or Dutch oven, heat the oil over medium heat and brown the meat thoroughly, stirring often, about 6 to 10 minutes. Add the onion, garlic, tomatoes, cilantro, and chiles; sauté for 3 to 4 minutes. Add beef broth, reduce heat to low, cover. and cook for 1 hour to 1 hour and 20 minutes, or until the beef is tender and the mixture has cooked down to a thick sauce. Add salt. Serve in individual serving bowls with flour tortillas. Serve with refried beans and Mexican rice, if desired. Serves 6 to 8.

*Fonda San Miguel*

# Joe Padilla's Fajitas

4 pounds beef fajita meat (skirt steak), or substitute tenderized flank steak

Juice of 8 to 12 Mexican limes

2 garlic cloves, minced

2 onions, sliced

2 serrano chiles, minced

2 large handfuls cilantro leaves, chopped

Mexican beer

Salt to taste

Trim off excess fat from the meat and remove the muscle fibers. Each strip of fajita meat should be ½ inch to ¾ inch thick in order to cook evenly.

Place one layer of fajita meat in the bottom of a large Pyrex roasting pan. Pour the lime juice over the meat. Add some of garlic, onion, serrano chiles, and cilantro. Add another layer of meat and continue until all ingredients have been used. Pour enough beer over the fajitas to fill the pan halfway. Cover with plastic wrap and marinate in refrigerator for 6 hours, basting occasionally.

Build a mesquite fire in your grill and let it burn until the coals are extremely hot but not flaming. Lay the meat across the grill and cover. Turn the meat only once as it cooks. When done, remove the meat from the grill, slice across the grain in ½-inch strips, and season with salt to taste. Serves 6 to 8.

**EDITOR'S NOTE:** Serve with warm flour tortillas, sour cream, guacamole (optional), and pico de gallo.

Joe Padilla, Padilla Ranch, Victoria, Texas
*Stolen Recipes*

# Elemental Arracheras *(Fajitas)*

2 to 2½ pounds skirt steak, trimmed of membrane and fat

Juice of 6 to 7 limes

2 to 3 pickled jalapeños, minced

6 garlic cloves, minced

Salt to taste

1 to 2 medium onions, thickly sliced

Vegetable oil

Lime wedges

Flour tortillas (preferably thick), warmed

Place steaks in a shallow glass container. Combine next 3 ingredients and pour mixture over steaks. Refrigerate for at least 6 to 8 hours, turning occasionally.

Remove steaks from refrigerator and drain. Sprinkle salt over steak and let sit at room temperature for about 45 minutes. Coat onions with oil and place on a piece of foil.

On an outdoor grill, fire up enough charcoal to form a single layer of coals. When coals are covered with gray ash, place steaks directly over the fire; place onions a little to the side, where they'll get less heat. Grill steaks to medium-rare, about 5 to 6 minutes per side; remove from grill. Turn onions occasionally, removing when soft (some edges will be brown and crispy). Allow steaks to sit for 5 minutes before slicing diagonally across the grain into finger-length strips.

Pile meat, onions, and lime wedges on a platter; serve with tortillas. Yields 6 generous servings.

Cheryl Alters Jamison and Bill Jamison
*Cooking with Texas Highways*

# Puerco en Pipian *(Pork in Pumpkin Seed Sauce)*

6 pounds pork loin

**Sauce**

½ cup lard

½ pound raw unsalted pumpkin seeds

¼ pound raw peanuts

½ cup sesame seeds

6 serrano chiles

1 onion, peeled and sliced

6 tomatillos, husked, washed, and boiled

3 garlic cloves, peeled

2 lettuce leaves

¼ cup chopped cilantro

2 radishes with tops

1 to 2 cups water

Salt to taste

Heat 1 to 2 tablespoons of the lard in a heavy-bottomed skillet. Fry the pumpkin seeds, peanuts, and sesame seeds for about 5 minutes. Transfer nut and seed mixture to a separate bowl. Add a bit more lard to the skillet. Fry the chiles, onion, and tomatillos for about 5 minutes. Add garlic and fry for another 1 minute. Place the nut and seed mixture and the fried chili mixture in a blender. Add the lettuce leaves, cilantro, and radish leaves (reserve radishes for garnish) and enough water to facilitate blending. Puree mixture well. (If your blender seems overloaded, you may need to puree in batches.)

Heat remaining lard in a fresh skillet. Add pureed sauce. Simmer for 20 minutes until slightly reduced. (The sauce tastes better if made one day in advance. If this is what you wish to do, then cool sauce and store in refrigerator or freezer at this point until ready to use.)

Trim excess fat from the pork and cut into bite-size pieces. Place raw meat in a pot, cover with water, and boil until cooked, about 25 to 30 minutes.

Heat the sauce in a large Dutch oven, adding in some of the pork broth to thin sauce to desired consistency. Add cooked pork and allow to simmer for 15 minutes before serving. Arrange radish slices on top of pipian before serving. Serves 8.

*The Texas Provincial Kitchen Cookbook*

# Carnitas

**2½ tablespoons olive oil**

**2 pounds boneless country-style pork ribs, cut into ¾-inch chunks**

**1¼ cups milk**

**1 teaspoon dried thyme**

**3 garlic cloves, minced**

**Salt to taste**

Heat the olive oil in a large pot over medium heat. Add the pork and cook, stirring every 30 seconds, until the meat is browned all over, about 5 minutes. Add the milk, thyme, and garlic and bring the milk to a bare simmer.

Continue simmering the meat, stirring about every 5 minutes, until all of the liquid has evaporated and adjusting the heat as necessary to keep the simmer very low, for about 1¾ hours. The milk will appear curdled, but don't worry.

When all of the liquid is gone and the meat begins to sizzle in the rendered fat, turn the heat slightly higher and continue cooking, stirring often, until each piece of meat is golden brown, about 10 minutes, but do not allow it to scorch. Season with salt and serve the carnitas with corn tortillas, guacamole, and salsa, or coarsely chop and use it as a filling for tacos. Serves 4.

*Jim Peyton's The Very Best of Tex-Mex Cooking*

# Refried Beans

**2 tablespoons peanut oil or other vegetable oil**

**½ onion, finely chopped**

**1 garlic clove, minced**

**3 cups cooked pinto beans and broth**

**Salt to taste**

In a medium skillet, heat the oil over medium heat. Add the onion and sauté for 4 minutes, or until translucent. Add the garlic and sauté for 3 minutes longer. Add the beans and broth and mash with a potato masher. The beans should be partially crushed and thick. It isn't necessary to mash them completely smooth. If the beans are too pasty, add more broth. Season to taste with salt. Serves 4.

**Bacon Bean Refrito:** Use any kind of cooked beans. Chop 4 slices of bacon and fry in the skillet until crispy. Remove the bacon with a slotted spoon and drain on paper towels. Proceed as directed, using the bacon fat in place of the oil. Add the crumbled bacon to the beans just before serving.

**White Bean Refrito:** Use cooked white navy beans. Add ½ teaspoon ground cumin and ¼ teaspoon paprika to the sautéed onion and garlic and proceed as directed. Add ½ cup chopped fresh cilantro after making the beans.

*Nuevo Tex-Mex*

# Mexican-Style Beans or Refried Beans

Dried pinto or black beans, about 3 cups

1 onion, chopped

1 tomato, chopped

2 whole garlic cloves, peeled

2 tablespoons chopped cilantro

2 whole serrano chiles

Salt to taste

Optional: Some kind of meaty flavoring, such as salt pork, soup bone, ham, bacon, or a couple of bouillon cubes for a low-fat pot of beans

Pick over beans; rinse well. Place in large pot and cover with water (at least five times the depth of the dried beans.) Add onion, tomato, garlic, meat flavoring, cilantro, chiles, and salt. Bring to a boil, then lower heat to simmer and cook until tender, about 3 hours. Let cool fully before storing in refrigerator.

To refry, add 2 tablespoons oil to a skillet and heat. Add cooked beans and mash with a potato masher. Simmer, then serve hot.

*The Texas Provincial Kitchen Cookbook*

# Mexican-Style Rice

2 cups chicken broth or water

1 tomato

1 to 2 garlic cloves, peeled

2 tablespoons vegetable oil

½ onion, chopped

1 cup white rice

2 whole serrano chiles

Salt to taste

½ cup minced carrots or peas, or a combination of the two (optional)

Pinch of ground cumin

Pinch of ground black pepper

In a blender, puree the chicken broth, tomato, and garlic. Set aside. Sauté the onion in the oil until transparent in a heavy, lidded skillet. Add raw rice; sauté until rice turns opaque, without browning. Add puree, chiles, salt, carrots, cumin, and pepper. Add salt to taste. Allow rice to boil. Lower heat to a simmer, cover tightly and simmer for 25 to 30 minutes. Do not remove lid during cooking process. Serves 4.

*The Texas Provincial Kitchen Cookbook*

# Arroz Roja *(Red Rice)*

4 cups chicken broth

3 or 4 saffron threads

2 cups white long-grain rice

2½ tablespoons canola oil

1 large onion, chopped

1 (15-ounce) can plum tomatoes, drained
  and chopped

½ teaspoon chili powder

½ teaspoon ground cumin

Salt to taste

Combine the chicken stock and saffron threads in a heavy-bottomed 4-quart saucepan over high heat. Bring the stock to a boil and stir in the rice. Cover pan and turn heat to lowest setting. Cook for exactly 15 minutes; remove pan from heat and set aside.

While rice is cooking, heat the canola oil in a heavy 12-inch skillet over medium heat. Sauté the onion until it is wilted, about 6 minutes. Stir in the tomatoes, chili powder, and ground cumin. Cook until mixture is very wilted, about 8 minutes. Remove from heat.

When the rice is done, stir onion and tomato mixture into the rice, blending well. Serve hot. Serves 4 to 6.

*Texas on the Plate*

# Fideo *(Mexican Pasta)*

1 (10-ounce) package vermicelli pasta

¼ cup cooking oil

1 can whole tomatoes

2 garlic cloves, minced or pressed

3 cups boiling water

½ teaspoon cumin

½ teaspoon freshly ground black pepper

¼ cup chopped green bell pepper

2 teaspoons salt

Fry vermicelli in oil until golden brown. Add tomatoes, garlic, water, spices, bell pepper, and salt. Simmer 15 to 20 minutes. Serves 4 to 6.

**VARIATIONS:** Cooked chicken, ground beef, or pork may be added to make this a main dish.

*The San Antonio Tex-Mex Cookbook*

# Casseroles & Stews

Casseroles and stews are the perfect solution for the working person who needs to provide a wholesome, filling meal to a family. Casseroles can be assembled quickly using precut vegetables, shredded cheeses, cubed or sliced meats, canned broth, etc., purchased from the supermarket. Same with stews. Once assembled, they can cook happily away on their own with little supervision "until browned and bubbly." In the meantime you can tend to other household chores and the kids. When it's done, put the pot on the table, add a salad and some bread, and you've got yourself a nice little meal in a very short time.

I've selected several recipes for this chapter. Use them as is, or experiment with adding different meats or fish or shellfish. Vary the vegetables, cheeses, and seasonings to suit your family's preferences. I like to think of casseroles and stews as blank canvases on which you can create your own flavor combinations. And, if you wish, you can substitute lower-fat ingredients.

# Hill Country Goulash

1 pound beef, cut into bite-size pieces

1 tablespoon olive oil

2 medium onions, diced

¼ teaspoon dry mustard

½ teaspoon paprika

2 tablespoons brown sugar

1¼ teaspoons salt

2 to 3 tablespoons Worcestershire sauce

¾ teaspoon apple cider vinegar

6 tablespoons ketchup

1 (12-ounce) can beer, divided

3 tablespoons flour

1 (12-ounce) package egg noodles

Brown meat in olive oil in a large skillet. Add onions and sauté until wilted and transparent. Combine mustard, paprika, sugar, salt, Worcestershire, vinegar, and ketchup; add to the skillet. Stir and add 1 cup of the beer. Stir, covered, and cook on low heat for 2½ hours, or until meat is fork-tender. Blend ½ cup of the remaining beer with flour and add to meat, stirring to blend well. Increase heat to medium and stir until thickened. Serve over cooked egg noodles. Serves 4.

> **HINT:** You may use nonalcoholic beer, if desired. This recipe can be doubled, as it freezes well.

*Texas Blossoms*

# The Wiz's Red Beans and Rice

2 tablespoons bacon drippings or oil

4 green onions with tops, chopped

1 bell pepper, chopped

3 celery stalks, chopped

½ cup minced carrots

Fresh oregano, rosemary, and thyme, minced, or 1 tablespoon Italian seasoning

3 bay leaves

3 tablespoons chopped parsley

2 garlic cloves, minced

Salt and pepper to taste

Tabasco sauce to taste

¼ teaspoon Worcestershire sauce

1 (15-ounce) can chicken broth

1 pound dry red kidney beans, rinsed and sorted

1 pound ham, cut in chunks

1 link sausage, sliced

Cooked white rice

In a heavy stockpot, sauté vegetables and seasonings in bacon drippings. Add broth, beans, and remaining ingredients. Add enough water to cover by 1 inch or more. Bring to a boil, cover, and simmer over low heat for about 3 hours, stirring often. Remove about ½ cup of the beans and mash until smooth. Return to pot to thicken gravy. Continue cooking until meat is tender, about ½ hour. Adjust seasonings as needed and serve over hot rice. Serves 6 to 8.

*¡Viva! Tradiciones*

# Homemade Chicken Pot Pie

1 fryer, cut up

1 onion, sliced thin

½ cup chopped celery

1½ teaspoons salt

1½ teaspoons pepper

2 cups water

1 cup small pearl onions

1 cup cubed raw potatoes

1 cup cubed raw carrots

¼ cup flour

½ cup milk

1 cup English peas

Unbaked pie crust

Boil chicken with onion, celery, salt, pepper, and water. Remove chicken from broth; reserve broth. Remove skin and bones; cut chicken into chunks.

In a saucepan, heat 2 cups broth and add pearl onions, potatoes, and carrots. Cover and cook until tender but crisp. Remove vegetables with a slotted spoon. To the saucepan add additional broth to make 2 cups. Blend flour with milk and stir into broth; bring to a boil. Add cooked vegetables, English peas, and chicken. Pour into a large baking dish and top with pie crust. Cook at 425 degrees about 25 to 30 minutes, or until crust is golden brown. Serves 6.

Ann Kimbrough, Grand Saline, Texas
*Texas Country Reporter Cookbook*

# King Ranch Chicken Casserole

1 large fryer, boiled in water seasoned with salt and pepper

1 onion, chopped

1 green bell pepper, chopped

1 garlic clove, minced or pressed

1 can cream of mushroom soup

1 can cream of chicken soup

1 cup reserved chicken broth

1 can Ro-Tel diced tomatoes with green chiles

2 cups shredded Cheddar and/or Monterey Jack cheese

1 dozen corn or flour tortillas, sliced in 1-inch strips

Drain chicken, reserving 1 cup of the broth. Debone the chicken and shred with fingers into bite-size pieces. Set aside.

Sauté onion, pepper, and garlic until tender.

Combine soups, chicken broth, and Ro-Tel tomatoes to make a sauce.

In a large, oiled casserole dish, layer the chicken, sauce, tortillas, sautéed vegetables, and cheese. Repeat layers, ending with cheese. Bake at 350 degrees for 30 minutes, or until bubbly. Serves 6 to 8.

*The San Antonio Tex-Mex Cookbook*

# Quick Casserole

1 pound ground beef

1 small onion, chopped

1 package macaroni and cheese mix

1 (17-ounce) can whole-kernel corn, drained

2 (8-ounce) cans tomato sauce

Salt and pepper to taste

1 cup Velveeta cheese or more

In a skillet, cook ground beef and onion until lightly browned. Drain off grease. Meanwhile, prepare the macaroni and cheese according to package directions. Stir the meat into the macaroni. Transfer ground beef mixture and macaroni and cheese to a 3-quart casserole dish. Add corn and tomato sauce and mix well. Top with cheese. Bake covered at 350 degrees for 30 minutes, or until bubbly. Serves 4 or more.

Teresa Iraggi, Victoria, Texas
*Texas Country Reporter Cookbook*

# Corn and Sausage Skillet Bake

1 pound bulk-style sausage

1 (17-ounce) can cream-style corn

1 tablespoon diced onion

1 tablespoon butter

½ teaspoon salt

½ teaspoon pepper

1 small jar chopped pimientos

1 (7½-ounce) package yellow corn bread mix

Cook sausage in a 10-inch cast-iron skillet until crumbly and well done. Add remaining ingredients except corn bread mix. Simmer 10 minutes. Set aside. Prepare the batter for the corn bread mix as directed on package. Spread evenly on top of corn mixture. Bake at 400 degrees for 20 to 25 minutes, or until golden brown and corn bread is cooked. Serves 4 to 6.

Sue Richie McSpadden, Frankston, Texas
*The Texas Country Reporter Cookbook*

# Round Steak Casserole

1 tablespoon flour

1 round steak, cut ½ inch thick

Salt and black pepper

1 tablespoon butter

2 onions, sliced into rings

1 cup dry white wine

Rub flour, salt, and pepper into both sides of steak. Melt butter in a frying pan and brown the steak on both sides. Remove from skillet and cut meat into bite-size pieces. In an ovenproof casserole, alternately layer meat and onions. Pour wine over the top. Cover and bake at 350 degrees for 1½ hours.

*Great German Recipes*

# Tamale Pie

1 dozen tamales, shucked

3 chicken breasts, poached, boned, and shredded

1 onion, chopped

1 garlic clove, minced or pressed

1 green bell pepper, seeded and chopped

1 tablespoon olive oil

1 (15-ounce) can tomato sauce

1 (4-ounce) can sliced black olives

2 tablespoons ground chiles or chili powder

1 (14½-ounce) can cream-style corn

8 ounces shredded Cheddar cheese

Oil a 9 × 13-inch casserole dish. Line the bottom with tamales. Layer the chicken on top. Sauté onion, garlic, and bell pepper in olive oil, Add tomato sauce, olives, ground chiles, and corn. Blend well and pour over chicken. Sprinkle cheese on top. Bake at 350 degrees for 1 hour, or until bubbly. Serves 6 to 8.

*The San Antonio Tex-Mex Cookbook*

# Side Dishes

**W**hat you serve alongside your main dish is as important as that main meat or fish. When creating a meal, it's necessary to think of the combination of everything that will be on the plate. Does the combination please your mind's tongue when you consider the flavors together? Is there a balance between the heavier starches and the vegetables? If you're serving a heavy red meat, you should plan to accompany it with a simple starch like oven-roasted potatoes or a simple rice pilaf or couscous or another grain dish and a simple roasted or steamed vegetable like asparagus. Avoid serving more than one heavy casserole-type side dish on one plate. For instance, don't serve potatoes au gratin and a cheese-laden squash casserole together. If you serve the potatoes, then pair them with something like quickly sautéed spinach and mushrooms with a little garlic or blanched and sautéed green beans.

Consider how the seasonings in your side dishes will work together—or not. You probably wouldn't want to serve two dishes on the same plate that contained bold-flavored herbs like tarragon or marjoram. They will compete for domination on the palate, and the result is not a harmonious taste experience!

Get adventurous with vegetables. Make it a habit each week to try one you've not cooked before. Or try an old standby cooked in an entirely different manner. Hate those boiled rutabagas that your mother tried to make you eat? Well, try them peeled and boiled in vegetable stock until fork-tender, then mashed with butter, salt, and pepper for an entirely new flavor. Parsnips are very tasty, as are mashed turnips seasoned with a little horseradish.

Branch outside the mashed-potato routine. Try oven-roasted tiny red new potatoes with olive oil, garlic, and rosemary. Wow! What a flavor sensation. Or get beyond potatoes totally a few times a week and try some grain side dishes like quinoa or amaranth. Go to your local health food store or specialty market and peruse the grains. Couscous can be combined with just about any seasoning to make a great side. Rice offers limitless possibilities. Experiment with the aromatic rice strains like basmati with its hint of nuts, or jasmine with its floral notes. Make risotto using Italian Arborio rice. Brown rice and wild rice add a rich depth to winter plates. And don't forget the small pasta varieties like elbow macaroni or orzo, which can be used with any type of sauce or seasoning, or simply tossed with minced herbs and a little olive oil after cooking.

Get creative with your sides. Remember, they're limited only by your imagination. But whenever possible, cook with fresh, seasonal vegetables. Become a regular at the closest farmers' market and get to know the farmers. What a secure feeling it is to know where your food comes from and the person who grew it!

# Grandmother's Favorite Dressing

4 cups day-old bread crumbs

4 cups crumbled corn bread

4 cups crumbled biscuits

¼ cup chopped green onions, with tops

¾ cup chopped onion

1 cup chopped celery

¼ cup minced parsley

1½ teaspoons rubbed sage

1 teaspoon salt

¼ teaspoon pepper

½ cup butter or margarine, melted

2 eggs, slightly beaten

2 to 4 cups defatted turkey broth or chicken broth

Parsley (optional)

In a large bowl, combine first 10 ingredients, toss well. Add butter, eggs, and broth (mixture should be extra moist, just this side of soupy). Mix well, but toss lightly.

Place dressing in a well-greased 2½-quart baking dish. Bake uncovered at 325 degrees about 30 minutes, or until browned. Garnish with parsley, if desired. Yields about 12 cups.

> **NOTE:** To cook dressing with turkey, loosely stuff body cavity with dressing before roasting turkey according to directions. Place remaining dressing in a well-greased baking dish, refrigerate, and then bake during last 30 minutes of turkey-roasting time. Before serving, blend dressing from turkey with that baked separately.

Ann Criswell
*Cooking with Texas Highways*

# Shiner Bock Rice Pilaf

1 dried ancho chile, seeds and veins removed

2 tablespoons olive oil

1 small onion, chopped

1 tablespoon minced parsley

1½ teaspoons minced fresh thyme

1½ cups long-grain white rice

2½ cups chicken stock

½ cup Shiner Bock beer

1 teaspoon minced lime zest

Toasted sliced almonds as garnish

Place the ancho chile in bowl of hot water; set aside for 15 to 20 minutes, or until chile is soft and pliable. Coarsely chop the chile and puree with a little of the water in which it soaked; set aside. Heat the olive oil in a heavy sauté pan over medium heat. When oil is hot, add the onion, parsley, and thyme.

*(Continued)*

Sauté until onions are very wilted and lightly browned, about 5 minutes. Add the raw rice and cook, stirring often, to lightly brown the rice. Add the chicken stock, beer, the reserved chile puree, and lime zest. Cook, covered, for about 30 minutes, or until rice is cooked through but not overcooked. (It should not be sticky.) Garnish with toasted almonds and serve hot. Serves 4 to 6.

Terry Thompson-Anderson

# Almond Rice Pilaf

4 cups beef or chicken stock, depending on entrée

1 tablespoon unsalted butter

Pinch of salt

2 cups long-grain white rice

2 tablespoons additional unsalted butter

2 small carrots, peeled and minced

3 green onions, minced, including green tops

2 tablespoons wheat germ

3 tablespoons chopped, sliced, skin-on almonds

2 teaspoons minced flat-leaf parsley

1 teaspoon minced fresh sage

¼ teaspoon curry powder

½ teaspoon sugar

Salt and freshly ground black pepper to taste.

Combine stock, 1 tablespoon butter, and pinch of salt in a 3-quart saucepan and bring to a rapid boil. Add the rice, stir, cover, and reduce heat to lowest setting. Cook for 15 minutes, then remove pan from heat and set aside.

Melt the 2 tablespoons additional butter in a heavy 10-inch skillet over medium heat. Add remaining ingredients except salt and pepper. Sauté until green onions are wilted, about 8 minutes, stirring often. Stir the vegetables into the cooked rice, blending well. Season to taste with salt and freshly ground black pepper. Serve hot. Serves 4 to 6.

*Texas on the Plate*

## EDITOR'S NOTE ON COOKING RICE

Rice production accounts for a good portion of the South Texas economy, with rice farms stretching southward from Anahuac in Chambers County and Katy in Waller County to Brazoria, Fort Bend, and Matagorda counties. Cooking perfect rice, with slightly firm grains that don't stick together (even when reheated), is easy.

Here are a few handy pointers about cooking rice. Always use one part rice to two parts liquid. The liquid can be any liquid. If you're serving rice with a chicken dish, use chicken stock as the cooking liquid, beef stock for a beef dish, etc. Adding a little white wine can produce an interesting taste, as can adding an assertively flavored beer, such as a bock, as part of the cooking liquid. Add a little salt and melted butter to the cooking liquid.

When you come across a recipe that calls for a certain amount of *cooked* rice and you need to know how much raw rice to start with, use this simple formula: divide the amount of cooked rice indicated in the recipe by three. This will give you the amount of raw rice that you need. The remaining portion will be your liquid. For example:

> A recipe calls for 6 cups of cooked rice.
>
> Divide 6 by 3 (6 ÷ 3 = 2). You need 2 cups of raw rice
>
> Subtract the 2 cups from the total of 6 cups.
>
> 6 – 2 = 4. You need 4 cups of liquid.

Now test yourself: 2 cups of raw rice + 4 cups liquid = 6 cups cooked rice, or 1 part rice to 2 parts liquid.

When estimating the quantity of rice you need to cook, use the following guideline: Each cup of raw rice will produce 3 cups of cooked rice. The following recipe will cook 3 cups of perfect rice.

2 cups liquid, such as water or stock

1 tablespoon unsalted butter

½ teaspoon salt

1 cup long-grain white rice

Combine the liquid, butter, and salt in a heavy, 2-quart saucepan over high heat. Bring to a full boil, and then stir in the rice. Cover the pan and reduce heat to the lowest setting. Set a timer for exactly 15 minutes. When the timer goes off, transfer the rice to a serving dish and cover until ready to serve, *even if there is still a small portion of liquid remaining.* By the time you have put the rest of the meal together, the rice will be perfect.

Use the same procedure for brown rice, except that it will cook for 45 minutes. Allow 50 minutes for wild rice. (Wild rice is done just when the kernels show a tiny slit of white beneath the dark brown hull. Don't cook wild rice until it completely opens up to reveal the whole white inner grain.) The "aromatic" strains of rice—such as basmati, Texmati, pecan rice, popcorn rice, jasmine rice, etc.—are actually long-grain white rice strains. They are very flavorful, and it's great to experiment with them. They should be cooked the same as for plain long-grain white rice.

# Southwestern Risotto

½ cup chopped onion

2 garlic cloves, minced

2 tablespoons butter, melted

1 cup Arborio rice

½ cup dry white wine

6 cups chicken broth, divided

½ cup whipping cream

2 medium tomatoes, peeled, seeded, and chopped

1 jalapeño chile, seeded and minced

½ cup sliced green onions

½ cup grated Parmesan cheese

2 to 3 tablespoons minced cilantro

Fresh cilantro sprigs and cubed tomatoes (optional)

Cook onion and garlic in butter in a large skillet or saucepan over medium heat, stirring constantly, until tender. Add the rice and cook 2 to 3 minutes, stirring frequently. Add white wine and cook, uncovered, until liquid is absorbed. Add 1 cup chicken broth; cook, stirring constantly, over medium-high heat 5 minutes, or until broth is absorbed. Continue adding broth, 1 cup at a time, cooking and stirring constantly until each cup is absorbed, about 25 to 30 minutes. (Rice will be tender and have a creamy consistency.)

Stir in the whipping cream, tomatoes, jalapeño, green onions, Parmesan cheese, and cilantro; cook 2 minutes. Garnish with cilantro sprigs and cubed tomatoes, if desired, and serve immediately. Serves 6.

*Seasoned with Fun*

# Red Pepper Rice

2 tablespoons olive oil

½ cup finely chopped red bell pepper

¼ cup finely chopped green onion

½ teaspoon ground cumin

1 cup white rice

1½ cups vegetable broth

Salt and pepper to taste

Sauté red bell pepper and onion in oil until soft. Add cumin and rice; cook over low heat until rice is lightly browned. Add broth, salt, and pepper. Bring to a boil, cover, and lower heat. Simmer for 17 minutes, fluff with fork, and serve. Serves 4.

*¡Viva! Tradiciones*

# Quinoa with Lentils and Curry

1 cup quinoa

2 tablespoons unsalted butter

½ cup finely chopped onion

2 cups hot chicken stock

1 teaspoon curry powder

½ teaspoon ground cumin

1 tablespoon minced cilantro

⅔ cup hot cooked lentils

Rinse the quinoa under running water. Shake to expel water. Place the quinoa in a dry cast-iron skillet over medium-high heat. Toast, shaking the pan back and forth constantly, until the quinoa gives off a fragrant aroma. Do not allow it to burn. Turn out into a small bowl and set aside.

Melt the butter in a heavy 3-quart saucepan over medium heat. Sauté the onion until wilted and transparent, about 5 minutes. Pour in the hot chicken stock, curry powder, cumin, and quinoa. Bring to a rapid boil. Reduce heat to medium-low, cover pan, and cook until liquid is absorbed, about 12 to 15 minutes. Remove from heat and stir in the cilantro and lentils. Serve hot. Serves 4 to 6.

**NOTE:** For a special presentation, serve this dish in a baked winter squash.

*Texas on the Plate*

# French Fries

1½ pounds russet potatoes, peeled and
  cut into ½-inch cubes

Vegetable oil for frying

Fine sea salt to taste

Soak the potatoes in cold water for 1 hour to remove some starch.

Preheat vegetable oil to 330 degrees in a large saucepan, about 4 to 5 inches deep.

Remove the potatoes from the water, dry off completely, and fry in the oil, being careful not to splatter. Fry the potatoes for about 4 minutes, or until limp and about halfway cooked.

Remove from the oil and drain on paper towels. You may need to do this in two batches. Set the cooking oil aside, covered for future use.

Lay the potatoes out on a sheet pan and refrigerate for 2 hours or overnight until completely chilled. At this point, you may also freeze them if you wish and cook later.

Just before serving, reheat the oil to 365 degrees and fry the chilled potatoes for 2 to 3 minutes, or until golden brown and crisp. Drain on a paper-towel-lined sheet pan and season with salt while still hot. Serve immediately. Serves 4.

*Ciao Y'All*

# Spicy Steak Fries

2 egg whites

2 tablespoons water

1 (18-ounce) package frozen potato
    wedges

½ cup seasoned dry bread crumbs

1 tablespoon paprika

1 teaspoon salt

½ teaspoon garlic powder

½ teaspoon ground cayenne pepper

Preheat oven according to directions on potato package. In large bowl whisk together egg whites and water. Toss potato wedges in mixture until coated. In plastic bag mix the remaining ingredients. Add the potatoes and shake well. Bake on greased baking sheet in a single layer. Serves 6 to 8.

Cindy Etier
*Hullabaloo in the Kitchen II*

# Rosemary Roasted Potatoes

3 pounds Yellow Finn or Yukon Gold
    potatoes, cut into 6 wedges each

2 tablespoons olive oil

Kosher salt and freshly ground black
    pepper

1 large yellow onion, peeled and julienned

2 tablespoons coarsely chopped fresh
    rosemary

Preheat oven to 450 degrees and place an ovenproof shallow pan or cookie sheet with sides in the oven for 10 minutes.

Toss all of the ingredients together in a large bowl and set aside.

Once the pan or cookie sheet is hot, pull it out of the oven and spread the potatoes and onions evenly on the pan. Return to the oven and cook for 20 minutes.

Carefully turn the potatoes with a metal spatula, and cook another 20 to 30 minutes, or until potatoes are cooked through and golden brown. Serves 6 to 8.

*Ciao Y'All*

# Roasted New Potatoes Royale

¼ cup olive oil

8 extra-large garlic cloves, smashed

20 new potatoes, cut in half

1 tablespoon minced fresh rosemary

1½ teaspoons minced fresh thyme

Salt and coarsely ground pepper to taste

Sprigs of fresh rosemary (optional)

Mix the olive oil and garlic in a bowl. Let stand for at least 1 hour to allow the flavors to blend.

Place the potatoes in a baking dish. Pour the olive oil mixture over the potatoes and toss to coat well. Scatter the minced herbs over the potatoes and season to taste with salt and pepper.

Bake at 400 degrees for 45 minutes, or until the potatoes are tender and crusty, stirring occasionally. Garnish with sprigs of fresh rosemary. Serves 6 to 8.

*Dining without Reservations*

# Romano Potatoes

5 pounds new potatoes

¼ pound cooked and chopped bacon

½ bunch green onions, green part only, chopped

¼ pound melted butter

1 cup shredded Monterey Jack cheese

1½ cups shredded Cheddar cheese

1 cup heavy whipping cream

1 tablespoon Lawry's Seasoned Salt

1 teaspoon cracked black pepper

1 teaspoon white pepper

½ tablespoon paprika

¼ cup Romano cheese

Boil the potatoes until tender, about 20 minutes, and allow to cool. Once the potatoes have cooled, cut into quarters. Mix the potatoes, bacon, green onions, and cheeses. In a separate bowl, mix the whipping cream, melted butter, Lawry's Seasoned Salt, cracked black pepper, and paprika. Add this mixture to the potato mixture and mix well. Pour into a greased baking pan. Sprinkle the top with the Romano cheese. Bake uncovered at 350 degrees for approximately 15 minutes, or until heated throughout. Serve hot.

Saltgrass Steakhouse, Houston, Dallas, and San Antonio
*Gruene General Store Cookbook*

# Kartoffelpuffer *(Potato Pancakes)*

3 cups grated potatoes, drained well

1 small onion, grated and drained well

2 eggs, well beaten

2 tablespoons all-purpose flour

⅛ teaspoon salt

½ cup vegetable oil

Sugar

Cranberry sauce or cinnamon-flavored applesauce (optional)

Combine first 5 ingredients, mixing well. Form into patties and fry in hot oil in a shallow skillet until evenly browned, turning once. Drain well on paper towels and sprinkle with sugar. Serve with cranberry sauce or cinnamon-flavored applesauce, if desired. Yields 6 to 8 pancakes.

*Georgia Mae Smith Ericson, Aunt Hank's Rock House Kitchen*
*Cooking with Texas Highways*

# Potato Soufflé

8 large baking potatoes (4½ to 5 pounds)

1 (8-ounce) package cream cheese at room temperature

1 cup sour cream

2 teaspoons garlic salt

½ teaspoon pepper

2 teaspoons chopped green chives

4 tablespoons butter

Paprika

Peel potatoes and cook, covered, in 5-quart pan in boiling water for 40 minutes, or until potatoes are tender. Drain, then mash well. With electric mixer, beat together cream cheese and sour cream. Gradually add mashed potatoes and continue beating until smooth. Beat in garlic salt, pepper, and chives. Turn into buttered 3-quart soufflé dish. Dot with butter and sprinkle lightly with paprika. Bake at 400 degrees for 1 hour, or until hot and crusty.

*Eileen Buis*
*Hullabaloo in the Kitchen II*

# Boerne Blackened Potatoes

1 pound thin-skinned potatoes, quartered

1 teaspoon salt

1 tablespoon butter

1 tablespoon olive oil

4 garlic cloves, minced

1 medium onion, diced

1 jalapeño pepper, minced

¼ cup chopped fresh rosemary or dill

Salt and pepper to taste

In a large pot, add potatoes, salt, and enough water to cover. Boil 20 minutes, or until tender; drain. In a large nonstick skillet over medium-high heat, add butter and olive oil; heat and add potatoes, breaking them into smaller pieces. The potatoes will soak up the butter and oil as they cook; add more as needed to keep the skillet well greased. Sauté 15 to 20 minutes, turning occasionally, or until potatoes begin to brown. Add garlic, onions, and jalapeño pepper; cook 15 more minutes, or until the mixture is browned and crispy. Add herbs, salt, and pepper, tossing well. Cook 1 to 2 more minutes and serve warm.

*Cooking with Texas Peppers*

# Cilantro and Goat Cheese Mashed Potatoes

1 pound small new potatoes, unpeeled and quartered

2 tablespoons unsalted butter

1 small onion, cut into tiny dice (about ½ cup)

4 ounces Pure Luck Texas Plain Chèvre or other brand of goat cheese

1 heaping tablespoon minced cilantro

¼ teaspoon freshly ground black pepper

¾ teaspoon sea salt

Place potatoes in a heavy 3-quart saucepan. Add cold water to cover. Bring to a full, rolling boil over medium-high heat and cook for 20 minutes, or until potatoes are very soft.

While potatoes are cooking, melt butter in a heavy 8-inch skillet over medium heat. Add onions and sauté, stirring often, until wilted and transparent, about 5 minutes. Remove from heat and set aside.

Drain potatoes in a colander and transfer to a medium bowl. Add the sautéed onions and any residual butter in the skillet, chèvre, cilantro, salt, and pepper. Mash the potatoes with a potato masher, incorporating the other ingredients. Leave them slightly lumpy. Serve hot. Serves 4.

*The Texas Hill Country*

# Green Chile and Mexican Crème Smashed Potatoes

### Smashed Potatoes

**1 bottle Shiner Bock beer**

**6 large Idaho baking potatoes**

**1 cup Hatch green chiles, fire-roasted and peeled (canned or frozen are fine)**

**1 bunch cilantro, chopped**

**1 cup Mexican Crème (see recipe below)**

**½ pound butter at room temperature**

**Salt and pepper to taste**

### Mexican Crème

**1 cup heavy cream**

**¼ cup buttermilk (not ultra-pasteurized)**

Make the Mexican Crème the day before. Mix the heavy cream and buttermilk together. Let the mixture sit out overnight in a glass (nonreactive) bowl covered with plastic wrap. This is much like making yogurt.

Pour beer in a saucepan and reduce to ½ cup; keep warm. Peel and boil the potatoes in salted water until tender. Drain the water and smash the potatoes with a ricer. Combine the potatoes with the remaining ingredients, including the Mexican Crème and reduced beer. Smash them together. Serve at once or keep warm until served. Serves 8.

*Fired Up!*

# Cilantro-Seasoned Potatoes with Garlic-Lime Butter

**2 pounds medium new potatoes, washed and quartered**

**2 tablespoons butter**

**3 tablespoons olive oil**

**4 large garlic cloves, minced**

**4 tablespoons fresh lime juice**

**2 teaspoons coriander seeds, freshly ground**

**1 bunch green onions, with some tops, chopped**

**¾ to 1 cup fresh cilantro sprigs, loosely chopped**

**1 tablespoon pure mild New Mexico chili powder**

**Salt and freshly ground black pepper**

**¼ cup shredded Parmesan cheese**

Cover the potatoes with cold salted water and bring to a boil; reduce heat and simmer about 12 minutes, but do not overcook.

Meanwhile, in a small saucepan, melt the butter and olive oil along with the garlic, lime juice, and ground coriander. Drain the cooked potatoes and toss gently with the garlic butter, adding the chopped onions, cilantro, chili powder, salt, and pepper. Serve potatoes warm or at room temperature, generously sprinkled with shredded Parmesan and chili powder prior to serving.

*The Herb Garden Cookbook*

# Hudson's Nutmeg Scalloped Potatoes

6 large Idaho potatoes

1 pound bacon, chopped

2 large yellow onions, peeled and julienned

1 quart whipping cream

1½ teaspoons black pepper

1½ teaspoons white pepper

1 tablespoon freshly grated nutmeg

4 tablespoons cornstarch mixed with 3 to 4 tablespoons water

Salt to taste

1 tablespoon butter

½ cup grated Parmesan cheese

Put potatoes in a large saucepan with cold water to cover. Bring to a boil. Boil potatoes in skin until done but still firm. Cool potatoes and remove skin. Cut potatoes in half lengthwise and then cut across into ½-inch slices.

Place potatoes in buttered baking dish or casserole, overlapping rows of slices like shingles on a roof.

Brown the bacon and drain well, reserving drippings. Sauté onion in 2 tablespoons of the bacon drippings in the same pan. Combine with bacon.

Combine the cream, peppers, and nutmeg in a clean saucepan over medium heat. Bring to a boil and add cornstarch slurry to make the sauce. It's better for it to be too thick than too thin. Stir well and adjust seasonings as needed.

Sprinkle bacon-onion mixture over potatoes. Top with sauce and sprinkle with Parmesan cheese. Bake at 400 degrees for 30 to 45 minutes, or until bubbling and browned. Serves 12.

*Cooking Fearlessly*

# Yippee! Yams

1 to 3 tablespoons olive oil

4 large yams (sweet potatoes), peeled and cubed

2 tablespoons brown sugar

½ teaspoon salt

½ to 1 teaspoon cayenne pepper, according to taste

Preheat oven to 450 degrees. Coat potatoes and a 9 × 13-inch baking dish with olive oil. Place baking dish in oven for 5 minutes. Add the potatoes to the hot dish and roast for 25 minutes, tossing occasionally until well browned. Remove from oven and scatter with a mixture of sugar, salt, and cayenne. Toss to coat all potatoes with seasoning and serve. Serves 6.

*And Roses for the Table*

# Sweet Potato Pone

3 large sweet potatoes, about 27 to 30 ounces total

¾ cup unsalted butter, softened and cut into ½-inch cubes

¾ cup sugar

3 eggs, beaten

½ cup evaporated milk

1 tablespoon vanilla extract

½ teaspoon cinnamon

### Topping

¾ cup firmly packed light brown sugar

¼ cup unsalted butter, softened and cut into ½-inch cubes

¼ cup all-purpose flour

½ cup chopped pecans

Preheat oven to 400 degrees. Lightly butter a 13 × 9-inch baking dish; set aside.

Place the sweet potatoes in a second baking dish and bake in preheated oven for about 40 to 45 minutes, or until a fork can be inserted into the flesh with ease. Remove the sweet potatoes and set them aside for a few minutes until they are cool enough to handle. Lower oven temperature to 375 degrees. Peel the potatoes, place them in a large bowl, and mash thoroughly. Add butter, sugar, eggs, evaporated milk, vanilla, and cinnamon, then stir to blend well and melt the butter. Turn mixture out into prepared baking dish.

To make the topping, combine brown sugar, butter, and flour in work bowl of food processor fitted with steel blade. Process until smooth and fluffy. Add the pecans and process just to blend, using the pulse feature and leaving the pecan pieces fairly intact.

Spread topping over potato mixture. Bake in preheated oven until set and lightly browned on top, about 45 minutes. Serve hot. Serves 6 to 8.

*Texas on the Plate*

# Sweet Potato Crunch

4 cups grated raw sweet potatoes

½ teaspoon ground ginger

¼ teaspoon ground cloves

1 cup brown sugar, firmly packed

¾ cup butter, melted

1 teaspoon grated lemon zest

1 teaspoon ground cinnamon

½ teaspoon salt

5 beaten eggs

2 cups chopped pecans

Preheat oven to 325 degrees. Place grated potatoes on a tea towel and wring out excess moisture. Combine all ingredients except pecans. Mix well. Pour mixture into a greased 1½-quart baking dish. Top with pecans. Bake 40 to 45 minutes, or until bubbly. Serves 6 to 8.

*Necessities and Temptations*

# Annie J's Sweet Potatoes

4 to 5 medium sweet potatoes, peeled and cut into chunks

¾ cup sugar

¼ cup (½ stick) butter

½ teaspoon ground cinnamon

½ teaspoon freshly grated nutmeg

1 teaspoon vanilla

⅓ cup bourbon whiskey

2 eggs, beaten

Small marshmallows

Cook sweet potatoes in water to cover until tender; drain well. Mash the potatoes and add all remaining ingredients except marshmallows. Blend well. Turn mixture out into 9 × 13-inch Pyrex baking dish. Put small marshmallows on top. Bake at 375 degrees for about 20 to 30 minutes, or until marshmallows are browned. Serves 6 to 8.

Annie J. Todd, HK Ranch, Placedo, Texas
*Stolen Recipes*

# Southern Baked Yams

4 pounds sweet potatoes, peeled and cut into wedges

Kosher salt and freshly ground black pepper

¼ cup bourbon

1 cup orange juice

½ cup brown sugar

⅓ cup flour

¾ cup chopped pecans

4 tablespoons butter, cut into cubes

Preheat oven to 400 degrees.

Place the sweet potatoes into a buttered 9 × 9-inch casserole dish and season with salt and pepper to taste. Drizzle with the bourbon and orange juice. Cover with foil and bake for 35 to 45 minutes, or until tender.

Remove from oven and take off the foil. In a medium bowl, mix together the brown sugar, flour, and pecans.

Sprinkle the mixture evenly over the top of the cooked yams, dot with butter, and return to the oven for 10 to 15 minutes, or until brown and bubbly. Serves 6.

*Ciao Y'All*

# Chile Corn Pudding

1 (10-ounce) can whole green chiles,
    drained

1 (17-ounce) can cream-style corn

1 tablespoon all-purpose flour

2 eggs, well beaten

¼ cup butter, melted

⅓ cup milk

½ teaspoon salt

Pepper and savory salt to taste

Shredded cheese

Preheat oven to 350 degrees. Split chiles and line bottom of greased ovenproof baking dish. Mix other ingredients except cheese and pour over chiles. Top generously with cheese. Bake 30 minutes, or until set. Serve hot. Serves 4.

*Seasoned with Sun*

# Creamed Summer Corn

10 ears of fresh corn, boiled until tender

1 cup heavy cream

1 cup milk

1 to 2 tablespoons sugar

1 teaspoon kosher salt

½ teaspoon pepper

½ teaspoon granulated garlic

½ teaspoon dried thyme

½ cup (1 stick) salted butter

1 tablespoon all-purpose flour

Cut the tops off the corn kernels into a stockpot using a sharp knife. Add the heavy cream, milk, sugar, salt, pepper, garlic and thyme; mix well. Bring to a boil gradually, stirring frequently. Reduce the heat and simmer for 3 minutes, stirring occasionally.

Bring the butter to a boil in a saucepan and reduce the heat to simmer. Add the flour and cook until blended, stirring constantly. Stir the butter mixture into the corn mixture and simmer for 3 minutes, stirring frequently. Serve warm. Serves 8.

*Dallas Dish*

# Corn Custard

4 eggs, beaten

4 cans (8 cups) cream-style corn

1½ cups cornmeal

1½ teaspoons salt

1 garlic clove, minced or pressed

1 teaspoon baking powder

¾ cup melted butter

2 (4-ounce) cans diced green chiles

1 tablespoon sugar

1½ cups shredded Cheddar cheese

Preheat oven to 375 degrees. Combine all ingredients, blending well. Pour into a greased large casserole dish. Bake for 1 hour, or until a knife inserted in the center comes out clean. Serves 10 to 12.

*The San Antonio Tex-Mex Cookbook*

# Grilled Sweet Corn on the Cob with Jalapeño-Lime Butter

8 ears of unhusked corn

Jalapeño-Lime Butter (see recipe below)

### Jalapeño-Lime Butter

2 jalapeño chiles, roasted, peeled, and seeded

2 teaspoons minced garlic

2 sticks unsalted butter, softened and cut into 1-inch cubes

1½ teaspoons salt

2 teaspoons grated lime zest

Make the Jalapeño-Lime Butter. Process the jalapeño and garlic in food processor until minced. Add the butter, salt, and lime zest. Process until smooth.

Shape the butter into a log and wrap in plastic wrap. Refrigerate until ready to use. May be prepared 2 to 3 days in advance, or frozen for up to 2 months.

To grill the corn, pull the corn husks back, leaving the husks attached at the base of the cobs. Remove the silk and reposition the husks to cover the corn. Soak the ears of corn in a large container of chilled water for 1 to 2 hours. Drain.

Preheat the grill to low to medium. Pull back the corn husks and generously coat the corn kernels with the Jalapeño-Lime Butter. Reposition the husks and secure with kitchen twine. Grill for 20 to 25 minutes, turning 4 or 5 times. Remove the twine, pull back the husks, and cut off the stem end with the husks, discarding them. Coat corn with additional Jalapeño-Lime Butter and serve immediately. Serves 8.

*Dallas Dish*

# Mexican Hominy

1 medium onion, chopped

2 garlic cloves, minced or pressed

½ pound bacon

2 (16-ounce) cans white hominy

1 (14½-ounce) can chopped tomatoes

3 tablespoons chili powder

1 cup shredded Cheddar cheese

Sauté onion, garlic, and bacon until bacon is crisp and onions are clear. Drain off the fat. Crumble bacon. Return to pan.

Add hominy, tomatoes, and chili powder. Cook over low heat until creamy. Pour into a 9 × 13-inch casserole and top with shredded cheese. Bake at 350 degrees for 30 minutes, or until heated through. Serves 10 to 12.

*The San Antonio Tex-Mex Cookbook*

# Mexican Grits Casserole

2 cups quick grits

2 cups shredded Cheddar cheese

1 stick (½ cup) butter

3 eggs, well beaten

2 jalapeños, seeded and minced fine

2 dashes Tabasco sauce

1 teaspoon garlic salt

1 (4-ounce) can diced green chiles

Cook grits according to package directions. Remove from heat and add remaining ingredients, blending well. Pour into oiled 9 × 13-inch casserole pan. Bake at 350 degrees for 1 hour.

*The San Antonio Tex-Mex Cookbook*

# Fried Grits

Prepare grits according to the directions on the package, then season well with salt and butter. Pour into a loaf pan and refrigerate overnight to set.

When ready to serve, cut the grits into slices or squares; dredge in seasoned flour, and fry in butter until crisp and brown.

For spicier grits to accompany a mild fish dish, add grated cheese and chopped jalapeño or bell peppers to grits during cooking.

*Gulf Coast Cooking*

# Spinach Madeleine

2 packages frozen chopped spinach

4 tablespoons butter

2 tablespoons flour

2 tablespoons chopped onion

½ cup evaporated milk (low-fat works well)

½ cup reserved spinach liquor

½ teaspoon black pepper

¾ teaspoon celery salt

¾ teaspoon garlic salt

½ teaspoon salt

1 (6-ounce) roll jalapeño cheese, cut into small pieces (or substitute 6 ounces Velveeta plus ¼ cayenne pepper)

1 teaspoon Worcestershire sauce

Cayenne pepper to taste

Cook spinach according to directions on package. Drain, reserving the cooking liquid. Melt butter in a saucepan, add flour and onion, and cook on low heat until onion is soft. Add milk and spinach liquor slowly, stirring constantly. Cook until smooth and thick; add seasonings, cheese, and Worcestershire. Stir until cheese is melted. Combine with cooked spinach. Pour into greased casserole and bake at 350 degrees for 30 minutes, or until hot and bubbly.

*Gruene General Store Cookbook*

# Sensational Spinach

3 (10-ounce) packages frozen spinach

1 pint sour cream

1 package dry onion soup mix

Cook spinach and drain well. Toss spinach with sour cream and onion soup mix, blending well. Warm to serving temperature. Do not boil! You may substitute broccoli for the spinach. Serves 6 to 8.

Kelly Carroll, Rockin C, Victoria, Texas
*Stolen Recipes*

# Spinach Sauté

2 tablespoons olive oil

1 garlic clove, minced

¼ cup chopped onion

4 to 5 large mushrooms, sliced

¼ cup white wine

1 (10-ounce) package frozen chopped spinach, cooked and drained well

¾ cup grated Parmesan cheese

Salt and pepper to taste

Sauté garlic, onion, and mushrooms in olive oil until onions are wilted and transparent. Stir in wine and cooked spinach. Add cheese, salt, and pepper; heat through. Serves 3 to 4.

*And Roses for the Table*

# Stewed Green Beans and New Potatoes

2 tablespoons extra-virgin olive oil

2 slices pancetta or bacon, cut into medium slices

¼ cup peeled and finely chopped yellow onion

1 garlic clove, peeled and chopped fine

1 cup crushed canned tomatoes with juice

Kosher salt and freshly ground black pepper

1 pound green beans, ends trimmed

16 very small new potatoes

Heat the oil and pancetta in a medium pot over medium heat until the pancetta starts to render its fat. Add the onion and cook until soft and starting to caramelize. Add the garlic and cook 1 minute more.

Add the tomatoes and bring to a boil. Season with salt and pepper to taste. Add the beans and potatoes and stir to coat.

Reduce the heat, cover the pan, and cook until beans and potatoes are tender, about 20 minutes. Adjust the seasonings to taste. Serves 8.

*Ciao Y'All*

# Fresh Steamed Green Beans with Wasabi Dipping Sauce

3 pounds green beans, trimmed

1 cup mayonnaise-based salad dressing

4 teaspoons soy sauce

1½ teaspoons sugar

2 teaspoons freshly squeezed lemon juice

2 teaspoons wasabi paste

Steam the green beans in a small amount of water in a large saucepan or electric steamer to desired degree of doneness. Drain into a colander and rinse under cold running water to stop the cooking process. Drain and pat dry.

Whisk the salad dressing, soy sauce, sugar, lemon juice, and wasabi paste in a bowl until the sugar is dissolved. Serve drizzled over the green beans. Serves 6 to 8.

*Dining without Reservations*

# Green Beans with Feta and Pecans

⅓ cup white vinegar

½ teaspoon minced garlic

1 teaspoon dill weed

¼ teaspoon salt

¼ teaspoon freshly ground black pepper

⅔ cup olive oil

2 pounds green beans

½ cup chopped red onion

1 cup (4 ounces) crumbled feta cheese

1 cup pecans, toasted and coarsely chopped

Combine the vinegar, garlic, dill weed, salt, and pepper in a bowl and mix well. Drizzle in the olive oil, whisking constantly, to blend well.

Trim the green beans and cut into 1-inch pieces. Cook in water in a saucepan just until tender-crisp; drain. Immerse in cold water, drain, and pat dry. Place in a shallow serving bowl and sprinkle the onion, feta cheese, and pecans over the beans. Add the vinegar and oil mixture at serving time and toss gently to coat well. Serves 4 to 6.

*Lone Star to Five Star*

# Green Bean Bundles

1 pound fresh green beans, trimmed

4 bacon slices

½ cup packed brown sugar

¼ cup (½ stick) butter, melted

½ garlic clove, crushed

Blanch the beans in boiling water in a saucepan for 3 minutes; drain. Plunge the beans into a bowl of ice water to stop the cooking process; drain.

Divide the beans into 4 equal portions. Wrap each portion with 1 slice of bacon and secure with a wooden pick. Arrange the bundles in a 1½-quart baking dish. Combine the brown sugar, melted butter, and garlic in a bowl and mix well. Drizzle over the beans. Bake at 350 degrees for 30 minutes. Serves 4.

*Austin Entertains*

# Tomatoes Florentine

½ green bell pepper, finely chopped

½ cup finely chopped onions

2 celery stalks, finely chopped

1 tablespoon butter

2 (10-ounce) packages frozen chopped
   spinach

2 hard-boiled eggs, chopped

Salt and pepper to taste

¼ cup mayonnaise

1 teaspoon lemon juice

4 to 5 large tomatoes (2 pounds each)

1 lemon

Sauté finely chopped vegetables in butter. Mix with cooked, drained spinach and eggs. Season. Stir in lemon juice and mayonnaise. Slice tomatoes ½ inch thick and arrange slices on baking sheet. Spoon spinach on each slice. Warm in 350-degree oven for 5 minutes, or until spinach is hot. Top with thinly sliced lemon curl. Serves 8 to 10.

*Lagniappe*

# Fried Green Tomatoes

2 cups peanut oil or other vegetable oil

1 cup finely ground cornmeal

Salt and ground white pepper to taste

2 eggs, beaten with 2 tablespoons of water

4 green tomatoes, thickly sliced

In a heavy-bottomed pot, heat the oil to 350 degrees. Place the cornmeal on a plate and season with salt and white pepper. Place the beaten egg mixture in a shallow dish, such as a pie plate. Drop the green tomato slices in the egg mixture and pat them in the cornmeal to coat. Place the tomato slices in the hot oil in batches and fry for 2 to 3 minutes, turning over once during the frying. Remove the slices from the fryer and allow to cool slightly on a wire mesh rack. Serve immediately. Makes about 12 tomato slices.

*Legends of Texas Barbecue Cookbook*

# Roasted Parsnips, Turnips, and Carrots

2 medium carrots, peeled and sliced into 1-inch pieces

2 medium parsnips, peeled and sliced into 1-inch pieces

4 small turnips, peeled and cut into bite-size wedges

4 large garlic cloves, peeled and sliced lengthwise

3 tablespoons extra-virgin olive oil

2 tablespoons maple syrup

Kosher salt and freshly ground black pepper

Preheat oven to 425 degrees. Combine the carrots, parsnips, turnips, and garlic cloves in a 13 × 9-inch baking dish. Whisk the olive oil and maple syrup together in a small bowl. Pour the mixture over the vegetables and toss to coat well. Season to taste with salt and pepper.

Place the baking dish in the preheated oven and cook for 10 minutes without stirring. Toss the vegetables again and roast for another 10 minutes. Check for doneness by piercing the turnips with a paring knife. The knife should slide easily into the turnips. If they are still hard, continue to cook, checking every 5 minutes for doneness. Do not stir the vegetables again (too much tossing can break them apart). Serve hot. Serves 4.

Terry Thompson-Anderson

# Turnip Greens

3 large batches turnip greens

3 bacon slices, chopped

2 teaspoons molasses

Salt to taste

Wash the greens well in water, removing any grit. Chop into 1-inch-wide strips. Boil the greens in a large pot of water with the bacon, molasses, and salt for 25 to 30 minutes. Serve greens with some of the "pot likker" (cooking liquid). Serves 8.

*The Texas Provincial Kitchen Cookbook*

# Zucchini Perini

½ pound ground beef

½ pound hot sausage

1 large onion, diced

Dash of salt

Dash of ground black pepper

1 (28-ounce) can whole tomatoes, mashed and drained

6 ounces tomato paste

¼ cup tomato sauce

2 teaspoons oregano

Dash of garlic powder

2 pounds zucchini, sliced ¼ inch thick

¼ cup freshly grated Parmesan cheese

In an oven-safe pan, brown the ground beef, sausage, and onion. Add salt and pepper to taste. Add the whole tomatoes, tomato paste, and tomato sauce. Add the oregano and garlic powder and simmer 5 minutes. Add the zucchini. Mix thoroughly, then sprinkle with Parmesan cheese. Bake at 350 degrees until cheese melts and starts to brown, about 10 minutes. Serves 10.

Martha Pender, Abilene, Texas
*Texas Cowboy Cooking*

# Squash Dressing

3 cups chopped yellow squash, cooked

3 cups corn bread, crumbled

3 eggs, beaten

⅓ cup chopped celery

⅓ cup chopped onion

2 teaspoons poultry seasoning

Salt and pepper to taste

1 can cream of chicken soup

¼ cup (½ stick) butter

A little milk or water if dressing is too dry

Mix all ingredients except butter and place in greased baking dish. Dot top with small pats of butter, Bake at 350 degrees for 1 hour.

*Texas Cookoff*

# Mamma's Squash Casserole

¼ cup extra-virgin olive oil

1 medium onion, peeled and chopped

1 large celery stalk, thinly sliced

4 garlic cloves, peeled and chopped fine

2 pounds yellow squash, ends trimmed, sliced ¼ inch thick

1 cup store-bought seasoned bread crumbs

2 tablespoons chopped fresh parsley

2 green onions, sliced into small rings

Kosher salt and freshly ground black pepper

¼ cup finely grated Pecorino Romano cheese

2 eggs

½ cup unseasoned bread crumbs

¼ stick butter for dotting

Preheat oven to 400 degrees. Lightly butter an 8-inch glass pie pan or gratin pan.

Heat olive oil in a 12-inch skillet, add onion, and cook until it starts to turn golden brown. Add celery, garlic, and sliced squash. Cook until squash is very soft and pan juices are almost dry. Transfer mixture to a bowl and let cool.

To the bowl of cooled squash, add seasoned bread crumbs, parsley, green onions, salt, pepper, cheese, and eggs. Mix well.

Spread the squash mixture evenly in the prepared pie pan or gratin pan. Sprinkle with the unseasoned bread crumbs. Dot with butter. Bake 20 minutes, or until lightly browned. Serves 4 to 6.

*Ciao Y'All*

# Southwestern Squash

5 yellow squash, peeled and sliced

1 tablespoon minced onion

½ teaspoon salt

¼ cup (½ stick) butter

¾ of an 11-ounce can diced tomatoes with green chiles

1 cup (4 ounces) shredded sharp Cheddar cheese

2 tablespoons melted butter

⅓ cup butter cracker crumbs

Preheat the oven to 350 degrees. Sauté the squash, onion, and salt in ¼ cup butter in a skillet until tender; drain. Stir in the tomatoes with green chiles and cheese.

Spoon the squash mixture into a buttered 1½ quart baking dish. Drizzle with 2 tablespoons melted butter. Sprinkle with the cracker crumbs and bake for 30 minutes, or until bubbly. Serves 4 to 6.

*Dallas Dish*

# Black-Eyed Peas

3 cups dried black-eyed peas, picked over

1 onion, chopped

1 tomato, chopped

2 whole garlic cloves

2 tablespoons chopped cilantro

2 whole serrano chiles

3 bacon slices, chopped, or ham

Salt to taste

Rinse the peas well. Place in large pot and cover with water (at least five times the depth of the amount of dried peas). Add onion, tomato, garlic, bacon or ham, cilantro, chiles, and salt. Bring to a boil, then lower heat to simmer until tender, about 1 hour. Let cool fully before storing in refrigerator. Serves 8 to 12.

*The Texas Provincial Kitchen Cookbook*

# Southern Succotash

6 cups fresh lima beans

6 cups fresh corn kernels

1½ cups chopped red bell pepper

3 tablespoons butter, softened

1 cup plus 2 tablespoons whipping cream

¾ teaspoon sugar

Salt and freshly ground pepper to taste

3 tablespoons minced fresh parsley

Combine the lima beans with enough water to cover in a saucepan. Bring to a boil; reduce heat. Cook until tender-crisp. Stir in the corn. Simmer for 2 minutes, stirring occasionally. Add the red peppers and mix well. Cook for 3 minutes, stirring occasionally; drain in a colander, shaking to remove all water, and turn out into a bowl. Add the butter, tossing to coat. May be prepared to this point one day in advance, covered, and stored in the refrigerator until just before serving. When ready to serve, stir in the whipping cream. Cook over medium heat until thickened, stirring occasionally. Add the sugar and mix well. Season with salt and pepper. Spoon into a serving bowl. Sprinkle with the minced parsley. Serves 10.

*Texas Ties*

# Raspberry Carrots

4 to 5 carrots, peeled and sliced thin

¼ cup butter

½ cup water

Pinch of salt

2 to 4 teaspoons raspberry vinegar

2 teaspoons brown sugar

Chopped parsley

In a large covered saucepan, simmer carrots in butter, water, and salt until tender. Add raspberry vinegar and sugar. Cook, uncovered, another 1 to 2 minutes. Garnish with chopped parsley and serve. Serves 3 to 4.

*Necessities and Temptations*

# Maple-Glazed Carrots with Rosemary

3 quarts water

½ tablespoon salt

1 pound baby carrots, peeled

2 tablespoons unsalted butter

6 tablespoons maple syrup or sorghum

2 teaspoons finely chopped fresh rosemary

Salt and white pepper to taste

Bring water and salt to a boil in a large saucepan over medium-high heat. Add carrots and blanch about 4 to 6 minutes; drain and reserve.

Melt butter in a large skillet over medium heat. Add maple syrup and rosemary; simmer about 1 minute. Add reserved carrots and sauté until hot. Season with salt and pepper; serve immediately. Serves 4.

*Brennan's of Houston in Your Kitchen*

# Simple and Elegant Cognac Carrots

2 cups slivered carrots

1 tablespoon sugar

½ cup (1 stick) melted butter

4 tablespoons Cognac

Combine all ingredients and place in covered baking dish. Bake at 350 degrees for 30 minutes. Serves 4.

Laura Lee Planche Graber
*Lagniappe*

# Okra Gumbo

2 slices bacon, chopped

½ cup chopped onion

1 (10-ounce) package frozen sliced okra

1 (14½-ounce) can diced tomatoes

Salt and black pepper to taste

Sauté bacon until fairly crisp. Add onion to the pan and brown. Add okra and tomatoes. Cook over low heat until okra is tender. Season with salt and pepper. Serves 4 to 6.

Marie Livingston, Seven L Ranch, El Paso
*Stolen Recipes*

# Sweet-Sour Red Cabbage *(Süßsauer Rotkohl)*

4 cups shredded red cabbage

2 medium apples, peeled, cored, and sliced

1 cup water

4 tablespoons vinegar

4 tablespoons sugar

1 tablespoon butter

½ teaspoon salt

¼ teaspoon black pepper

Cook the cabbage and apples in the water until tender, about 15 to 20 minutes. Add the vinegar, sugar, butter, salt, and pepper; cook a few minutes more. Reheats well. Best with roast chicken or pork.

Connie Zuber, Bill Zuber's Restaurant, Homestead, Amana Colonies, Iowa
*German-Style Recipes*

# Red Cabbage Supreme

1 tablespoon butter

1 large yellow onion, finely chopped

1 head red cabbage, cored and thinly sliced

1 Golden Delicious apple, peeled, cored,

and thinly sliced

½ teaspoon salt

1 tablespoon dark brown sugar

1 cup water

1 tablespoon red wine vinegar

Melt butter in a large skillet and sauté onions about 2 minutes. Add cabbage and apple and continue cooking for 5 minutes, stirring often. Add the salt, brown sugar, water, and vinegar and cook, covered, over low heat for about 30 minutes, or until cabbage is tender. Stir once or twice and check to see if more water is needed. Serves 3 to 4.

*Texas Blossoms*

# Braised Red Cabbage with Apples, Onions, and Sausage

1 small head of red cabbage

2 small Granny Smith apples, peeled, cored, and sliced

1 teaspoon salt or to taste

1 tablespoon freshly squeezed lemon juice

1½ teaspoons light brown sugar

¾ cup chicken stock

2 tablespoons bacon drippings

1 small onion, chopped

¼ teaspoon freshly ground black pepper

1 tablespoon red wine vinegar

8 ounces kielbasa sausage, sliced into bite-size pieces, or another smoked pork sausage

Quarter the cabbage. With a sharp knife, shred it coarsely, discarding tough center. Rinse the cabbage and place it in a 6-quart pot with the diced apples, salt, lemon juice, brown sugar, and chicken stock. Bring to a boil, lower heat, and cover the pan. Simmer for 15 minutes, stirring occasionally.

Meanwhile, heat the bacon drippings in a heavy 10-inch skillet over medium-high heat. Sauté the onion until lightly browned, about 10 minutes. Add the onion to the cabbage along with the pepper, vinegar, and sausage pieces. Cook, covered, for about 20 minutes, or until sausage is cooked through. Serve hot. Serves 4 to 6.

*Texas on the Plate*

# Sweet-Sour Rutabagas

4 medium rutabagas, peeled

½ cup bacon drippings

1 large onion, chopped

1 teaspoon salt

½ teaspoon freshly ground black pepper

1 tablespoon sugar

¼ cup cider vinegar

6 green onions, chopped

Fill a 5-quart saucepan half full of water; bring to a boil over medium-high heat. Add rutabagas; cook until almost tender, about 10 minutes. Drain and cool to room temperature. Dice cooked rutabagas into ½-inch cubes; set aside. Heat bacon drippings in a heavy 12-inch skillet over medium heat. Add rutabaga cubes and onion; cook, stirring often, until onion is wilted and golden brown, about 15 minutes. Add salt, pepper, and sugar; cook 5 minutes. Add vinegar; stir quickly, scraping up browned bits from bottom of pan. Cook until liquid has evaporated to a glaze, 6 to 7 minutes. Stir in green onions. Serve hot. Serves 4 to 6.

*Cajun-Creole Cooking*

# Baked Eggplant

2 medium eggplants

Salt to taste

½ medium white onion, chopped

2 eggs, beaten

1 cup (4 ounces) grated Parmesan cheese

Pepper to taste

2 cups fine bread crumbs

3 to 4 tablespoons melted butter

Peel and chop the eggplants. Cook in a small amount of salted water in a saucepan until tender; drain. Place the eggplant in a bowl and add the onion, eggs, Parmesan cheese, and pepper; toss gently to mix.

Toss the bread crumbs with the melted butter in a bowl. Add half the bread crumbs to the eggplant mixture and mix gently.

Spoon the eggplant mixture into a greased 2-quart baking dish. Top with the remaining buttered bread crumbs. Bake at 350 degrees for 30 to 45 minutes, or until bubbly and lightly browned. Serves 8 to 10.

*Lone Star to Five Star*

# Grilled Portabella Mushrooms

4 large portabella mushrooms

2 tablespoons olive oil

1 teaspoon chopped fresh rosemary

1 tablespoon minced garlic

Salt and pepper to taste

Balsamic vinegar

Rub the mushrooms with the olive oil and sprinkle with rosemary, garlic, salt, and pepper. Place in a roasting pan. Roast at 375 degrees for 20 minutes. Remove from the oven and keep warm.

Heat a grill to medium-hot and brush the rack with a small amount of olive oil. Place the mushrooms on the rack and grill for 6 minutes, or until tender, rotating every 2 minutes. Sprinkle with balsamic vinegar to serve. Serves 4.

Chamberlain's Steak and Chop House, Dallas
*Lone Star to Five Star*

# Parmesan Broccoli Bake

1 egg white

¼ cup mayonnaise

3 tablespoons grated Parmesan cheese

2 tablespoons chopped parsley

Grated zest of ½ lemon

2 pounds fresh or 2 (10-ounce) packages frozen broccoli spears, cooked and drained

2 tablespoons butter, melted

Sesame seeds

Paprika

Beat egg white until soft peaks form. Fold in mayonnaise. Stir in cheese, parsley, and lemon zest. Set aside.

Arrange the cooked broccoli in an ovenproof serving dish. Pour melted butter over broccoli. Top with egg white mixture, spreading evenly. Scatter sesame seeds and paprika over the top. Bake for 5 minutes at 450 degrees, or until puffy and lightly browned. Serves 4 to 6.

*Necessities and Temptations*

# Broccoli Casserole

½ cup (1 stick) butter

½ cup diced yellow onions

1 pound frozen broccoli florets

1 (10¾-ounce) can cream of mushroom soup

2 cups cooked white rice

1 teaspoon granulated garlic

1 teaspoon kosher salt

1 teaspoon freshly ground black pepper

2 cups (8 ounces) shredded Cheddar cheese

4 fresh broccoli florets, blanched

Preheat oven to 350 degrees. Melt butter in a large skillet over medium-high heat. Add onions and cook about 3 minutes. Stir in broccoli and cook until almost thawed. Add soup, rice, garlic, salt, and pepper; bring to a simmer, stirring often. Remove from heat and add half of the cheese. Fold together. Place mixture into an 11 × 7-inch casserole dish, top with remaining cheese, and bake in oven about 20 minutes, or until cheese is browned and casserole is hot. Remove and let rest about 20 minutes before serving. Garnish with fresh blanched broccoli florets. Serves 8.

> **TIP:** Let this casserole rest to help bring all of the flavors together and give it the proper texture.

*Luby's Recipes & Memories*

# Ellen's Ratatouille Gratin

Salt

1 medium eggplant, peeled and thinly sliced

4 tablespoons olive oil, divided

1 large onion, thinly sliced

1¼ cups grated Parmesan cheese, divided

3 medium tomatoes, peeled and sliced

1 large garlic clove, minced

Juice of 1 lemon

2 tablespoons chopped fresh basil

2 small zucchini, thinly sliced

1 large bell pepper, cut in 1-inch strips

Salt eggplant slices and place in a colander. Drain for 1 hour, pressing out excess moisture. Coat a large skillet with half of the oil. Cover bottom with a layer of eggplant. Layer onion and scatter with some of the Parmesan cheese. Add tomatoes and ½ of the garlic, ½ of the lemon juice, and all of the basil. Next, layer zucchini, sprinkle with Parmesan cheese, and top with remaining eggplant. Finish with a layer of onions, tomatoes, garlic, and lemon juice. Place bell pepper strips around edge of the skillet. Scatter with a bit more of the Parmesan cheese. Cover and simmer over low to medium heat for 20 minutes. Remove from heat and pour off any liquid. Place remaining cheese on top and drizzle with remaining olive oil. Place under preheated broiler until cheese is lightly browned and top is bubbly. Serves 4.

*¡Viva! Tradiciones*

# Ratatouille Supreme

½ cup olive oil

4 cups cubed, peeled eggplant

4 cups cubed zucchini

½ cup diced green bell pepper

½ cup diced red bell pepper

½ cup chopped onions

2 tablespoons chopped garlic

½ cup dry white wine

4 fresh tomatoes, peeled and quartered

Pinch dried thyme

1 bay leaf

1 teaspoon dried sweet basil

Pinch dried rosemary

1 tablespoon salt or to taste

1 teaspoon white pepper

½ cup pitted small black olives

2 tablespoons minced fresh parsley

Heat oil in a large skillet. Sauté the eggplant and zucchini in hot oil for 8 minutes. Add the bell peppers and onion and simmer, uncovered, for another 6 minutes. Add the garlic and simmer for 2 minutes. Add wine, tomatoes, herbs, salt, pepper, and black olives. Transfer to a 3-quart casserole and bake, covered, at 350 degrees for 20 minutes, or until eggplant is tender. Sprinkle with parsley and serve. Serves 16 to 18.

*Lagniappe*

# Cajun Cauliflower

1 head cauliflower, cut into florets

½ bunch green onions, chopped

3 tablespoons butter

2 tablespoons flour

1 teaspoon salt

1½ cups milk

4 ounces sharp Cheddar cheese, grated

½ roll garlic cheese, cubed

½ cup Ro-Tel tomatoes with chiles, drained

Buttered Italian bread crumbs

Steam cauliflower until crisp-tender. Drain well and place in a 2-quart casserole. In a saucepan, sauté onions in butter until soft. Stir in flour and salt, blending flour well. Add milk and stir until thick. Place in a blender with cheeses, tomatoes, and onions. Blend until smooth. Pour over cauliflower and top with bread crumbs. Bake at 350 degrees for about 20 minutes, or until browned and bubbly. Serves 6 to 8.

*¡Viva! Tradiciones*

# Best Baked Beans

4 slices bacon

2 onions, chopped

1 cup green bell pepper, chopped

1 cup parsley, chopped

1 cup celery, chopped

2 garlic cloves, minced

2 large cans pork and beans

1 can Ro-Tel tomatoes with diced chiles

1 can pimiento, chopped

1 tablespoon prepared mustard

1 teaspoon chili powder

Salt and black pepper to taste

Fry the bacon strips until crisp, remove from drippings, and set aside. Sauté all of the fresh vegetables in the bacon drippings until tender. Add beans, tomatoes, pimientos, seasonings, and crumbled bacon. Place in a casserole or bean pot and bake at 300 degrees for 1½ hours. Serves 10 to 12.

*Of Magnolia and Mesquite*

# Black Beans with Sour Cream

1 pound dried black beans

1½ cups onion, coarsely chopped

2 large garlic cloves, minced

3 celery stalks, coarsely chopped

1 medium carrot, scraped and coarsely chopped

1½ tablespoons salt

½ teaspoon freshly ground black pepper

2 bay leaves

¼ teaspoon oregano

1 tablespoon parsley, chopped

Dash cayenne pepper

4 tablespoons butter

4 ounces dark rum

Sour cream

Rinse beans and pick over. Place in large kettle; add water to cover. Cover and bring quickly to a full boil. Remove from heat and let stand, covered, for 1 hour. Add next 9 ingredients and more water to cover. Return to a boil and simmer, covered, over low heat for 2 hours, stirring occasionally. Correct seasoning; if desired, a bit of cayenne pepper can be added.

Remove bay leaves and turn bean mixture out into a 3-quart casserole. Stir in butter and 2 ounces dark rum. Mix thoroughly. Cover and bake in preheated 350-degree oven for 1 hour or more, until beans are thoroughly tender. Remove from oven and stir in remaining 2 ounces rum. Serve with side dish of sour cream as topping. Serves 12.

*Of Magnolia and Mesquite*

# Desserts

Desserts—now there's a subject that will get the attention of everybody in Texas! We do love our desserts. "Life is short. Eat dessert first." I first heard that witty maxim from Chef Carl Walker at Brennan's of Houston. No one is sure who first coined the phrase, but no matter. We all agree: dessert is a must!

Dessert can be as simple as a bowl of ice cream, preferably homemade, or a rich and gooey concoction that takes hours to bake and assemble. You'll find a bit of everything included in this chapter.

Baking cookies is a great way to spend time with your children, and everybody gets to enjoy the results. Remember that cake layers freeze well, so you can make a couple of varieties of cake layers and freeze them. When you need a cake, simply thaw and frost the layers. Voilà! Almost instant cake.

Same with pie pastries. Make several, roll them out, shape them in pie pans, wrap, and freeze. You can pull out a frozen pastry, add your desired fillings, and bake according to recipe instructions.

When serving dessert at the end of a nice meal for company, try upping the ante on the dessert course by serving a good Texas dessert wine with it. Muscat Canelli, a sweet white, is always a good choice, as is a Texas port-style wine with anything chocolate. I also love to serve our big bold Texas cabernet sauvignons, or a big, fruity Meritage with seriously sinful chocolate desserts.

# Peanut Brittle

1 cup light corn syrup

3 cups sugar

½ cup water

3 cups raw peanuts

3 tablespoons butter

½ teaspoon salt

2 teaspoons baking soda

Combine corn syrup, sugar, and water in a saucepan; bring to a boil. Boil until mixture will spin a thread. Add peanuts; cook and stir until peanuts are golden brown. Remove from heat; stir in butter, salt, and baking soda. Pour on 2 greased cookie sheets. Cool; break into pieces. Yields 2½ to 3 pounds.

**EDITOR'S NOTE:** A sugar mixture will spin a thread when it reaches 230–235 degrees on a candy thermometer.

Alma Jewel Westerman
*Flavor Favorites*

# Microwave Peanut Brittle

1 cup sugar

1 cup raw peanuts

½ cup light corn syrup

1 tablespoon butter

1 teaspoon vanilla

1 teaspoon baking soda

Combine sugar, peanuts, and syrup in a 2-quart microwave-safe bowl. Cook on high power for 8 minutes. Stir in butter and vanilla and microwave for 1 additional minute. Add baking soda and stir, then pour quickly onto a greased cookie sheet. Spread in a very thin layer. Let cool completely, then break into pieces and store in an airtight container. (Do not attempt to make this candy when the weather is damp, as it will be sticky.)

Wylene Taft, Garland, Texas
*Texas Country Reporter Cookbook*

# Pralines

2 cups sugar

½ cup milk

½ cup light corn syrup

¼ teaspoon baking soda

¼ cup butter

1 teaspoon vanilla extract

2 to 4 cups pecan halves

Combine sugar, milk, syrup, and baking soda in a saucepan; blend well. Cook, stirring frequently, over medium heat to soft-ball stage (232 degrees on a candy thermometer). Remove from heat. Add butter and vanilla; beat with a portable electric mixer until creamy. Stir in pecans. Working quickly, drop by tablespoons onto a waxed-paper-covered baking sheet. Let stand until firm. Yields about 3 dozen.

Frances Dean Herr
*Flavor Favorites*

# Microwave Pralines

1 pound brown sugar

1 cup whipping cream

2 cups pecans

2 tablespoons butter

2 teaspoons vanilla

In a microwave-safe mixing bowl, combine cream and brown sugar. Microwave on high for 7 minutes. Stir, and microwave for 7 more minutes. Add butter, nuts, and vanilla. Stir and return to microwave for 1½ minutes. Using two spoons, one to spoon and one to push, drop pralines by spoonfuls on a wax-paper-lined baking sheet. Cool. Makes 24 pralines.

Mimi Kerr
*Perennial Favorites*

# Jack Daniel's Whiskey Balls

1½ cups vanilla wafer crumbs

1 cup powdered sugar

1 cup finely chopped pecans

2 tablespoons unsweetened cocoa powder

2 tablespoons light corn syrup

¼ cup Jack Daniel's whiskey

Powdered sugar

Combine cookie crumbs, powdered sugar, pecans, cocoa powder, corn syrup, and whiskey in medium bowl, blending well. Roll into 24 balls and dredge in powdered sugar to coat well; shake off excess sugar. Cover and refrigerate until ready to serve. Makes about 24 pieces.

**NOTE:** These make great hostess gifts to take to holiday parties. Pack in small tins lined with brightly colored tissue paper.

*Texas on the Plate*

# Dream Bars

½ cup (1 stick) butter, softened

½ cup firmly packed brown sugar

1 cup flour

2 eggs

1 teaspoon vanilla

½ teaspoon baking powder

½ teaspoon salt

1½ cups coconut

1 cup chopped pecans

Preheat oven to 350 degrees. Blend together the butter, brown sugar, and flour, leaving no traces of unblended ingredients. Press evenly into the bottom of a 9 × 13-inch baking pan. Bake the crust for 10 minutes; set aside.

Make the filling by combining all remaining ingredients and blending well. Pour on top of crust and bake an additional 20 minutes, or until filling is completely set. Cool on wire rack. Cut into squares to serve.

Virginia Henderson Winston, Winston 8 Ranch, Lufkin, Texas
*Stolen Recipes*

# Black Velvet

## Crust

**2 cups crushed chocolate wafers**

**½ cup melted butter**

## Filling

**1 pound semisweet chocolate morsels**

**⅔ cup cold water**

**2 tablespoons instant coffee**

**10 eggs, separated**

**¼ cup light rum**

## Topping

**2 cups whipping cream**

**2 tablespoons powdered sugar**

**4 tablespoons dark crème de cacao**

## Garnish

**Sliced, skin-on almonds, toasted**

**Chocolate wafers**

To make the crust, mix ingredients together well and press into a 3-quart glass casserole. Bake 10 minutes at 350 degrees.

To make the filling, combine chocolate, water, and instant coffee in top of double boiler. Melt over boiling water. Beat egg yolks into chocolate mixture. Beat in the rum and allow mixture to cool slightly. In a separate bowl, beat egg whites to soft peaks. Fold whites gently but thoroughly into the chocolate mixture. Pour into crust. Refrigerate until set.

To make the topping, whip the cream with powdered sugar and liqueur until stiff enough to hold a shape. Cut the chilled dessert into 18 pieces and place on glass serving plates. Top each with a portion of the whipped cream. Garnish with toasted almonds and a chocolate wafer. Makes 18 servings.

*Lagniappe*

# Lemon Bars

1 cup (2 sticks) butter, softened

¼ teaspoon salt

½ cup powdered sugar

2 cups flour

4 eggs, beaten

4 tablespoons lemon juice

2 cups sugar

4 tablespoons flour

Grated zest of 1 lemon

Powdered sugar in shaker can

Blend the first 4 ingredients well and press into a greased 9 × 13-inch baking dish. Bake at 350 degrees for 20 to 30 minutes. Mix remaining 5 ingredients together and pour over the crust. Bake for 20 to 30 minutes at 325 degrees, or until firm. Dust with powdered sugar and cut into 1½-inch squares when cool. Keep in refrigerator. Makes about 4 dozen bars.

Mrs. Alan Schoellkopf
*The Dallas Junior League Cookbook*

# Ginger Snaps

¾ cup shortening

1 cup sugar

1 egg

¼ cup molasses

2 cups all-purpose flour

1 tablespoon ground ginger

2 teaspoons baking soda

1 teaspoon cinnamon

1 teaspoon salt

½ teaspoon ground cloves

Cream shortening and sugar. Beat in egg and molasses. Sift and add dry ingredients. Form into balls; roll in sugar. Bake at 350 degrees for 12 to 15 minutes.

Sue Duncan
*Hullabaloo in the Kitchen II*

# Snickerdoodles

1 cup vegetable shortening

1½ cups sugar

2 eggs

2¾ cups flour

1 teaspoon baking soda

½ teaspoon salt

¼ teaspoon cream of tartar

2 tablespoons sugar

2 teaspoons ground cinnamon

Cream shortening with sugar in bowl of electric mixer until light and fluffy. Add eggs and beat well. Sift together all remaining dry ingredients, except 2 tablespoons sugar and cinnamon. Beat into the creamed sugar and egg mixture. Chill the dough for 1 hour.

Toss the cinnamon and sugar together in a small bowl; set aside. After chilling, roll the dough into small balls. Roll balls in the sugar-cinnamon mixture. Place the balls about 2 inches apart on an ungreased cookie sheet and bake at 400 degrees for 8 to 10 minutes. Yields 5 dozen cookies.

Mrs. Ken Moyer (Bonnie)
*Lone Star Legacy*

# Hello Dolly Cookies

6 tablespoons butter, melted

1 cup crushed vanilla wafers

1 package semisweet chocolate chips

1 cup angel flake coconut

1 cup chopped pecans

1 can sweetened condensed milk

Preheat oven to 325 degrees. Pour the melted butter into a 9 × 13-inch baking pan. Add the crushed vanilla wafers and press flat. Layer the remaining ingredients except condensed milk. Drizzle the milk over the top evenly. Bake in preheated oven for 30 minutes. Cool on wire rack before cutting into squares.

Virginia Henderson Winston, Winston 8 Ranch, Lufkin, Texas
*Stolen Recipes*

# Cocoa Kiss Cookies

1 cup (2 sticks) butter, softened

⅔ cup sugar

1 teaspoon vanilla extract

1⅔ cups flour

¼ cup Hershey's baking cocoa

1 cup chopped pecans

1 (9-ounce) package chocolate kisses

Confectioners' sugar for rolling

Beat the butter, sugar, and vanilla in a mixing bowl until light and fluffy. Combine the flour and baking cocoa in a small bowl, tossing to mix well. Add to the butter mixture and beat until well blended. Add the pecans and beat on low until well mixed. Chill the dough for 1 hour. Shape 1 tablespoon of dough around each chocolate kiss, forming a ball and covering the candy completely. Place on ungreased cookie sheets. Bake at 375 degrees for 10 to 12 minutes. Let cool slightly and roll the cookies in confectioner's sugar. Cool completely before serving. Makes about 3 dozen cookies.

*Dining without Reservations*

# Chocolate Chunk Cookies

1⅛ cups flour

1¼ teaspoons baking soda

½ teaspoon salt

½ cup vegetable shortening

¼ cup brown sugar

½ cup granulated sugar

1 tablespoon honey

1 teaspoon Grand Marnier

1 egg, beaten

1 teaspoon vanilla extract

½ pound semisweet chocolate, cut into chunks

Stir together flour, baking soda, and salt; set aside.

In a separate bowl, cream together shortening and sugars. Add honey, Grand Marnier, egg, and vanilla extract, beating thoroughly. Add the dry ingredients and fold in the chocolate.

Drop from a teaspoon onto a buttered cookie sheet. Preheat oven to 350 degrees and bake for about 10 minutes. Remove from cookie sheet and cool on a rack. Makes about 4 dozen cookies.

Henry Douglas, Radisson Admiral Semmes Hotel, Mobile, Alabama
*Gulf Coast Cooking*

# Buffalo Chips

2 cups (4 sticks) butter

2 cups brown sugar

2 cups white sugar

4 eggs, well beaten

4 cups flour

2 teaspoons baking powder

2 teaspoons baking soda

2 teaspoons vanilla

1 cup chopped pecans

2 cups oats

3 cups Post Toasties

1 cup coconut

1 (6-ounce) package semisweet chocolate chips

1 (6-ounce) package milk chocolate chips

1 (6-ounce) package butterscotch chips

Cream butter and sugars. Add eggs, flour, baking powder, baking soda, and vanilla. Mix well. Add remaining ingredients and blend well. Chill in refrigerator for 2 hours. Drop by tablespoons onto ungreased cookie sheet. Bake at 350 degrees for 10 to 12 minutes, or until slightly browned.

Saundra Perry, Dallas
*Texas Country Reporter Cookbook*

# Lunitas de Fresca

1 (8-ounce) package cream cheese, softened

1 cup (2 sticks) butter, softened

3 cups flour

1 small jar strawberry preserves

Powdered sugar

Combine cream cheese, butter, and flour with hands to form dough. Shape dough into 1-inch balls and flatten with a small flat-bottomed glass dipped in flour. Put a small dollop of strawberry preserves in the middle of each round and fold dough over preserves. Press edges with a fork to seal.

Place cookies on a cookie sheet and bake at 350 degrees for 15 to 20 minutes, or until lightly browned. Transfer cookies to a wire rack and sprinkle with powdered sugar. Cool before serving. Yields 50 small cookies.

*Seasoned with Fun*

# Polvorones de Tequila *(Tequila Sugar Cookies)*

### Cookies

**5 cups flour**

**1¼ cups sugar**

**¾ cup tequila**

**1 tablespoon ground cinnamon (freshly ground, if possible)**

**1½ teaspoons baking powder**

**2¾ cups solid shortening**

### Sugar Topping

**1 cup sugar**

**1 tablespoon ground cinnamon (freshly ground, if possible)**

Preheat oven to 350 degrees. Combine cookie ingredients in a large mixing bowl. Knead dough together with hands. When the dough is well mixed, allow to rest for 15 minutes. Combine topping ingredients in a shallow dish.

On a floured surface, roll cookie dough out to a thickness of ¼ inch. Cut into 2-inch rounds with a cookie cutter or a small glass. Arrange on an ungreased cookie sheet and bake for 12 to 15 minutes, or until pale golden in color and firm to the touch. Roll in sugar topping while hot. Makes 12 dozen cookies.

*The Texas Provincial Kitchen Cookbook*

# Sour Cream Chocolate Chip Cookies

**2 cups sugar**

**1 cup solid shortening**

**2 large eggs**

**1 cup sour cream**

**½ teaspoon vanilla**

**½ teaspoon baking soda**

**4 teaspoons baking powder**

**4½ cups flour**

**¼ teaspoon salt**

**1 (12-ounce) package semisweet chocolate chips**

**½ cup chopped Texas pecans**

Preheat oven to 350 degrees. Grease 2 large cookie sheets; set aside.

Cream sugar and shortening. Add eggs, one at a time, beating well after each addition. Stir in sour cream and vanilla; blend well. Sift baking soda, baking powder, flour, and salt. Stir into butter-egg mixture. Blend in chocolate chips.

Drop by tablespoons onto prepared cookie sheets. Sprinkle with nuts. Bake in preheated oven for 20 minutes. Cookies should be large, soft, and fairly thick. Cool on wire rack. Makes 3½ dozen cookies.

*Under the Texan Sun*

# Smokehouse Cowboy Cookies

1 cup oatmeal

½ cup chopped pecans

½ cup coconut

8 ounces milk chocolate chips

1 cup brown sugar

1 cup white sugar

½ cup butter, softened

½ cup shortening

2 eggs

1 teaspoon vanilla

2 cups flour

1 teaspoon baking powder

1 teaspoon baking soda

¼ teaspoon salt

1 cup corn flakes

In a large bowl, mix oatmeal, pecans, coconut, and chocolate chips. With a mixer, cream together the brown sugar, white sugar, butter, and shortening. Add eggs, one at a time, mixing well after each addition. Next, add vanilla, flour, baking powder, baking soda, and salt to the creamed mixture. Mix well. Add creamed mixture to oatmeal mixture. Stir well. Add corn flakes and gently toss.

Drop cookie dough by the spoonful onto an ungreased cookie sheet and bake at 325 degrees for approximately 15 minutes, or until lightly browned. Makes about 3 dozen cookies.

*New Braunfels Smokehouse*

# Crème de Menthe Brownies

1 box of your favorite plain chocolate brownie mix

⅔ cup chopped pecans

¾ cup semisweet chocolate chips

## Topping

2 cups powdered sugar

½ cup (1 stick) unsalted butter, softened and cut into small chunks

3 tablespoons green crème de menthe

## Glaze

1 cup semisweet chocolate chips

6 tablespoons unsalted butter

Prepare the brownies according to package directions, adding the pecans and chocolate chips to the batter before baking. Bake and set aside to cool completely.

To prepare the topping, cream the powdered sugar and butter in bowl of electric mixer at medium speed until light and fluffy, about 4 to 5 minutes. Add the crème de menthe and beat just to blend. Spread the topping evenly over the cooled brownies. Refrigerate.

To prepare the glaze, combine the chocolate chips and butter in a heavy 1-quart saucepan over medium-low heat. Cook, stirring often, until chocolate has melted and mixture is smooth. Remove pan from heat and allow to cool until slightly thickened, about 20 minutes. Pour the glaze evenly over the brownies and refrigerate just until the chocolate is set, about 1 hour. Don't allow the glaze to harden completely, or it will crack unevenly when the brownies are sliced. Cut into 1½-inch squares. Makes about 20 pieces.

*Texas on the Plate*

# Chocolate Cream Cheese Brownies

### First Layer

½ cup butter

1 box chocolate cake mix

1 egg, beaten

1 cup chopped pecans

### Second Layer

8 ounces cream cheese

1 (16-ounce) box powdered sugar

2 eggs

Preheat oven to 350 degrees.

For the first layer, melt butter in a 9 × 13-inch metal pan. Sprinkle cake mix over butter. Add egg and pecans. Stir ingredients together in pan and pat down evenly.

For the second layer  cream together cream cheese, powdered sugar, and eggs until well blended and fluffy. Spread over the chocolate mixture in pan.

Bake for 45 minutes. Cool to lukewarm and slice into squares. Yields 24 to 36 squares.

*Necessities and Temptations*

# Cabernet Cupcakes

6 tablespoons cocoa

2 cups flour

1½ cups sugar

1 teaspoon baking soda

⅛ teaspoon salt

2 eggs, well beaten

¾ cup butter, melted

½ cup milk

½ cup of your favorite Texas cabernet sauvignon

1 teaspoon vanilla

Prepared chocolate or vanilla frosting

Preheat oven to 375 degrees. Place paper muffin tin liners in muffin pans. Set aside.

Mix the first 5 ingredients in mixing bowl. In a separate bowl, mix melted butter, milk, vanilla, wine, and eggs. Add to flour mixture, but do not stir until all of the ingredients are in the bowl, then beat well.

Pour into lined muffin tins. Bake 20 minutes in preheated oven. Frost with your favorite chocolate or vanilla frosting. Makes 12 cupcakes.

*Under the Texan Sun*

# Bread Pudding with Whiskey Sauce

1 cup sugar

½ cup (1 stick) butter, softened

5 eggs, beaten

2 cups heavy cream

¼ cup raisins

1 tablespoon vanilla extract

⅛ teaspoon ground cinnamon

12 slices fresh potato bread or cinnamon raisin bread

Whiskey Sauce (see recipe below)

## Whiskey Sauce

1 cup sugar

1 cup heavy cream

1 tablespoon unsalted butter

1 cinnamon stick, or ⅛ teaspoon ground cinnamon

¼ cup water

½ teaspoon cornstarch

1 tablespoon bourbon

Beat the sugar and butter in a mixing bowl until creamy, scraping the bowl occasionally. Add the eggs, heavy cream, raisins, vanilla, and cinnamon and beat until mixed well. Pour the mixture into a 9 × 13-inch baking dish; set aside.

Preheat the oven to 350 degrees. Arrange the bread slices in a single layer over the egg mixture and let stand for 5 minutes to soak up some of the liquid. Turn the bread slices and let stand for 10 minutes longer. Carefully press the slices down into the egg mixture until almost covered, being careful not to tear the slices.

Place the baking dish in a larger baking pan and add enough water to the larger baking pan to come within ½ inch of the top of the smaller baking dish. Bake, covered with foil, for 35 to 40 minutes; remove the foil. Bake for 10 minutes longer, or until the top is browned and the custard is set but still soft, not firm. Spoon the pudding onto dessert plates. Pass the Whiskey Sauce separately. Serves 6.

To make the Whiskey Sauce, mix the sugar, heavy cream, butter, and cinnamon stick in a saucepan and bring to a boil, stirring occasionally. Mix the water and cornstarch in a bowl and add to the cream mixture.

Cook until clear and thickened, stirring constantly. Remove from the heat and stir in the bourbon. Discard the cinnamon stick.

*Dallas Dish*

# Fredericksburg Peach Bread Pudding with Peach and Whiskey Sauce and Chantilly Cream

8 ounces white chocolate, cut into small chunks

2 cups half-and-half

¼ pound (1 stick) unsalted butter, softened

½ teaspoon ground cinnamon

10 ounces day-old croissants, cut into ½-inch pieces

3 eggs

¾ cup sugar

7 medium fresh Fredericksburg peaches, peeled and chopped into bite-size pieces (about 3 cups)

½ cup toasted chopped pecans

1 tablespoon vanilla extract

## Peach and Whiskey Sauce

½ pound (2 sticks) unsalted butter, softened

1½ cups sugar

2 eggs, beaten until frothy

⅓ cup peach schnapps

3 tablespoons good-quality sour mash whiskey

## Chantilly Cream

1 cup whipping cream, well chilled

2 tablespoons sour cream

2 tablespoons powdered sugar

1 tablespoon vanilla extract

Preheat oven to 350 degrees. Butter a 13 × 9-inch baking dish; set aside. In a 2-quart saucepan, combine the white chocolate, half-and-half, butter, and cinnamon. Cook over medium-low heat, stirring often, until smooth. Remove from heat and set aside. Place croissant pieces in a large bowl and stir in the white chocolate mixture, blending well and breaking up the croissants. In bowl of electric mixer, combine the eggs and sugar; beat at medium speed until thickened, about 7 minutes. Add the peaches, pecans, and vanilla; beat just to blend. Fold egg mixture into the croissants, blending well. Turn out into prepared baking dish and bake in preheated oven for 45 to 55 minutes, or until a knife inserted in center comes out clean. Set aside to cool.

To make the Peach and Whiskey Sauce, cream butter and sugar in bowl of electric mixer until very light and fluffy, about 7 minutes. Transfer to top of a double boiler over simmering water. Cook for 20 minutes, whisking often, until the mixture is silky smooth and comes away from the side of the pan when whisked. Whisk ½ cup of the hot butter mixture into the beaten eggs, then another ¼ cup. Whisk the egg mixture slowly into the remaining butter mixture over the heat. Cook until thickened, about 4 to 5 minutes, whisking constantly. Whisk in the schnapps and whiskey; whisk to blend. Keep warm over low heat.

Make the Chantilly Cream by combining all ingredients in bowl of electric mixer. Beat at medium speed until the mixture forms loose, floppy peaks. Refrigerate, tightly covered with plastic wrap, until ready to serve.

To serve, slice the warm pudding into squares. Place a portion of the Peach and Whiskey Sauce in the bottom of each serving bowl and set a square of pudding in the center. Top with a large dollop of Chantilly Cream. Serves 12.

*The Texas Hill Country*

# Turtle Cheesecake

## Crumb Crust

2 cups vanilla wafer crumbs

6 tablespoons (¾ stick) butter, melted

## Filling

1 (14-ounce) package caramels

1 (5-ounce) can evaporated milk

1 cup chopped pecans

16 ounces cream cheese, softened

½ cup sugar

1 teaspoon vanilla extract

2 eggs

½ cup (3 ounces) semisweet chocolate chips

To prepare the crust, mix the vanilla wafer crumbs and butter in a bowl. Press over the bottom and sides of a 9-inch springform pan. Bake at 350 degrees for 10 minutes. Refrigerate while preparing the filling.

To prepare the filling, melt the caramels with the evaporated milk in a saucepan over low heat, stirring to blend well. Spread over the baked crust and scatter the pecans over the top. Combine the cream cheese, sugar, and vanilla in a mixing bowl and beat until smooth. Beat in the eggs, one at a time. Stir in the chocolate chips. Spoon into the springform pan.

Bake at 350 degrees for 40 minutes. Place on a wire rack to cool. Chill in the refrigerator. Place on a serving plate and remove the sides of the springform pan to serve. Serves 12.

*Lone Star to Five Star*

# Oreo Cheesecake

### Oreo Crust

1½ cups Oreo cookie crumbs

⅓ cup butter, melted

### Oreo Filling

2 pounds cream cheese at room
temperature

1½ cups sugar, divided

2 tablespoons all-purpose flour

4 extra-large eggs

2 large egg yolks

⅓ cup whipping cream

2 teaspoons vanilla, divided

1½ cups coarsely chopped Oreo cookies

1 cup sour cream

### Fudge Glaze

1 cup whipping cream

8 ounces semisweet chocolate, chopped

1 teaspoon vanilla

To make the crust, blend all ingredients in bowl, then press onto bottom and sides of a 10-inch spring-form pan. Refrigerate crust until firm, about 30 minutes.

To make the filling, preheat oven to 425 degrees. Beat cream cheese in large bowl of electric mixer on lowest speed until smooth. Beat in 1¼ cups sugar and flour until well blended. Beat in eggs and yolks until mixture is smooth. Stir in cream and 1 teaspoon vanilla. Pour half of batter into prepared crust. Sprinkle with chopped Oreos. Pour remaining batter over, smoothing with spatula. Bake 15 minutes. Reduce oven temperature to 225 degrees. Bake 50 minutes, covering top loosely with foil if browning too quickly. Remove from oven. Increase temperature to 350 degrees. Blend sour cream, remaining ¼ cup sugar, and remaining 1 teaspoon vanilla in small bowl. Spread over cake. Bake 7 minutes. Refrigerate cake immediately. Cover cake with plastic wrap and chill overnight.

To make the glaze, scald cream in heavy saucepan over high heat. Add chocolate and vanilla and stir 1 minute. Remove from heat and stir until all chocolate is melted. Refrigerate glaze for 10 minutes. Set cake on platter and remove springform. Pour glaze over top of cake. Using pastry brush, smooth top and sides. Refrigerate cake until ready to serve.

*Of Magnolia and Mesquite*

# Jalapeño Cheesecake

## Crust

2 cups graham cracker crumbs

½ cup pecans

½ cup sugar

1 stick butter at room temperature

## Filling

1½ pounds cream cheese

½ cup sugar

1 tablespoon lemon juice

1 teaspoon vanilla

3 eggs

1 jalapeño, seeded and coarsely chopped

## Glaze

1 cup sour cream

1 tablespoon sugar

1 tablespoon lemon juice

## Jalapeño Sauce

*(Makes 4 cups.)*

6 cups sugar

1½ cups finely chopped green bell pepper

¼ cup finely chopped fresh jalapeño

1½ cups vinegar

1 package Certo or other brand of fruit pectin

To make the crust, combine the graham cracker crumbs, pecans, and sugar in a food processor and pulse until smooth. Add the butter and mix well until combined. Line the bottom and sides of a spring-form pan with the crumb mixture.

To make the filling, preheat oven to 350 degrees. Combine the cream cheese, sugar, lemon juice, and vanilla in a food processor until smooth. Add the eggs and jalapeño and process until well blended. Pour into the crumb-lined pan. Bake for 1 hour and remove from oven. The top of the cheesecake will have shallow cracks.

Make the glaze by mixing together the sour cream, sugar, and lemon juice. Spoon the glaze over the top of the hot cheesecake and bake an additional 15 to 20 minutes. Remove from oven, cool completely at room temperature, and chill for several hours in the refrigerator. Serve with warm Jalapeño Sauce. Serves 12.

To make the Jalapeño Sauce, bring the sugar, peppers, and vinegar to a boil, stirring constantly. Remove from heat and stir in Certo. Pour what you are not going to use within a few days into hot sterilized jars and seal with paraffin. This can also be served as a spread over cream cheese, or as a substitute for mint jelly on brisket, venison, baked chicken, or lamb.

*Texas Cowboy Cooking*

# Mocha Cheesecake

### Chocolate-Pecan Crust

1½ cups chocolate wafer crumbs

1½ cups ground toasted pecans

6 tablespoons (¾ stick) butter, melted

4 ounces semisweet chocolate, melted

### Filling

16 ounces cream cheese, softened

1 cup packed brown sugar

4 eggs

2 teaspoons vanilla extract

8 ounces semisweet chocolate, melted

⅓ cup brewed strong coffee

1 cup sour cream

### Chocolate Glaze

4 ounces semisweet chocolate chips

⅓ cup heavy cream

2 tablespoons sugar

To prepare the crust, combine the chocolate wafer crumbs, pecans, and butter in a bowl and mix well. Press over the bottom and sides of a 9-inch springform pan. Drizzle with the melted chocolate. Chill until the chocolate is firm.

To prepare the filling, combine the cream cheese and brown sugar in a mixing bowl and beat until fluffy. Add the eggs, one at a time, beating for 1 minute after each addition. Beat in the vanilla and melted chocolate. Add the coffee and then the sour cream, mixing well.

Spoon into the prepared crust. Place in a 300-degree oven on middle rack; place a pan of water on a lower oven rack. Bake for 1 hour. Reduce the oven temperature to 275 degrees and bake for 1 hour. Reduce the oven temperature 250 degrees and bake for 30 minutes longer. Turn off the oven and let stand with the oven door ajar for 30 minutes. Chill in the refrigerator for 4 hours.

To prepare the glaze, melt the chocolate chips in a saucepan. Add the cream and sugar and mix well. Cook until sugar has dissolved. Cool to lukewarm. Pour over the cheesecake. Chill for 1 hour, or until topping is set.

Place the cheesecake on a serving plate and remove the sides of the springform pan. Serves 12.

*Lone Star to Five Star*

# The Best Gingerbread

3 eggs

1 cup sugar

1 cup molasses

1 teaspoon ground cloves

1 teaspoon ground ginger

1 teaspoon ground cinnamon

1 cup canola oil

2 teaspoons baking soda

2 tablespoons hot water

2 cups all-purpose flour

1 cup boiling water

Preheat oven to 350 degrees. Spray a 9 × 13-inch baking pan with nonstick cooking spray; set aside. Place eggs, sugar, molasses, cloves, ginger, cinnamon, and canola oil in a bowl and beat well. Dissolve the 2 teaspoons of baking soda in the 2 tablespoons of hot water and add to the bowl. Sift in the flour and beat well. Add the boiling water; beat quickly and lightly. The batter will seem thin. Turn the batter out into prepared pan and bake in preheated oven for 45 minutes, or until a wooden pick inserted in center of cake comes out clean. Cool on wire rack.

Marianne Crain
*Perennial Favorites*

# Tiramisu

4 egg yolks

½ cup sugar

2 tablespoons sweet Italian Marsala wine

8 ounces mascarpone cheese, softened

4 egg whites at room temperature

½ cup heavy whipping cream

3 cups Italian espresso, chilled

¼ cup rum

¼ cup Kahlúa

48 ladyfingers

Bittersweet baking cocoa to taste

Whisk the egg yolks, sugar, and wine in a bowl for 2 minutes and fold in the mascarpone cheese. Beat the egg whites in a mixing bowl until soft peaks form. Beat the heavy whipping cream in a bowl until very stiff peaks form. Fold the egg whites and whipped cream into the cheese mixture with a spatula until the mixture has a soft, light, creamy texture and is well blended. Mix the espresso, rum, and Kahlúa in a bowl.

Arrange 24 of the ladyfingers in a tight rectangle shape on a large serving plate. Brush lightly with the espresso mixture. Spread the mascarpone cheese mixture over the top. Arrange the remaining ladyfingers over the cheese layer and brush the top with the remaining espresso mixture. Chill, covered, for about 4 hours. Sprinkle with baking cocoa just before serving. If you are concerned about using raw eggs, use eggs pasteurized in their shells, which are sold at some specialty food stores, or use an equivalent amount of pasteurized egg substitute. Serves 6.

Arcodoro & Pomodoro, Dallas
*Dallas Dish*

# Toffee Pound Cake

## Cake

**2½ cups all-purpose flour**

**1½ cups sugar**

**1 teaspoon baking soda**

**½ teaspoon salt**

**½ cup butter, softened**

**¼ cup shortening**

**1½ cups buttermilk**

**1½ teaspoons vanilla**

**3 eggs**

**1 (7.8-ounce) package almond brickle baking chips**

## Frosting

**⅓ cup butter**

**2 cups powdered sugar, sifted**

**1 teaspoon vanilla**

**2 to 3 tablespoons water**

Preheat oven to 350 degrees. Grease and flour a 12-cup fluted tube pan. In large bowl, blend all cake ingredients except brickle chips at low speed until moistened. Beat 3 minutes at medium speed. By hand, stir in brickle chips. Pour into prepared pan. Bake in preheated oven for 50 to 60 minutes, or until a toothpick inserted in center comes out clean. Cool upright in pan for 10 minutes, then invert onto serving plate. Cool completely.

In medium saucepan, heat butter until light golden brown; remove from heat. Blend in powdered sugar and 1 teaspoon vanilla; add water, 1 tablespoon at a time, as needed to make frosting. Immediately spoon over top of cake, allowing some to run down sides. Freezes well.

*Of Magnolia and Mesquite*

# Pineapple Upside-Down Cake

1¼ cups sifted cake flour

¼ teaspoon salt

1 teaspoon baking powder

½ cup sugar

½ cup milk

1 egg

1 teaspoon vanilla extract

⅓ cup butter, melted

4 tablespoons butter

½ cup brown sugar

6 pineapple slices

12 maraschino cherries

1 cup heavy cream, whipped

Sift together flour, salt, baking powder, and sugar. In a separate bowl, beat together milk, egg, and vanilla extract. Gradually add to flour mixture. Add melted butter and beat well until batter is creamy and smooth. Set aside.

Melt 4 tablespoons butter in a heavy, ovenproof skillet. Add brown sugar and stir until dissolved. Spread evenly over the bottom of the skillet.

Arrange pineapple and cherries in skillet to make a decorative pattern. Top with the reserved batter.

Preheat oven to 350 degrees and bake for about 50 minutes, or until a toothpick comes out clean. Cool for about 10 minutes, then turn out onto a cake plate. The topping should come out clean, but if the worst has happened, rearrange the fruit on top of the cake, spooning the sugar in between as needed.

Serve warm, topped with whipped cream. Serves 6 to 8.

*Gulf Coast Cooking*

# Pineapple Upside-Down Cake II

½ cup butter

⅔ cup brown sugar

1 can pineapple slices, drained

Maraschino cherries

⅓ cup butter

½ cup granulated sugar

1 egg

1 teaspoon vanilla

1¼ cups sifted flour

1½ teaspoons baking powder

½ teaspoon salt

½ cup milk

Melt the butter in a large cast-iron skillet. When completely melted, crumble in the brown sugar. Arrange drained pineapple slices in a decorative fashion over the brown sugar. Place a cherry in the center of each slice; set aside.

Make the cake batter. Cream the butter and sugar until light and fluffy. Add egg and vanilla, beating well. Sift the flour with the baking powder and salt. Add flour mixture alternately with the milk, mixing until smooth.

Pour cake batter over pineapple slices and bake in 350-degree oven for 55 minutes, or until done. Let cake stand in skillet about 5 to 10 minutes before turning out upside down onto a platter.

*Tales from Texas Tables*

# Sam Houston White Cake

¾ cup (1½ sticks) butter or margarine, softened

2 cups sugar

3 cups all-purpose flour

1 teaspoon baking powder

½ teaspoon salt

½ cup milk

½ cup water

1 teaspoon almond extract

6 egg whites at room temperature

## Frosting

3 (1-ounce) squares unsweetened chocolate

4 cups sifted powdered sugar

⅛ teaspoon salt

¼ cup hot water

3 egg yolks

¼ cup (½ stick) butter or margarine, melted

1 teaspoon vanilla extract

Cream butter and gradually add sugar, beating well. Combine flour, baking powder, and salt. Combine milk and water. Add flour mixture to butter mixture alternately with milk mixture, beginning and ending with flour mixture. Mix well after each addition. Stir in almond extract. In a separate bowl, beat egg whites until stiff peaks form and fold into batter. Pour batter into 3 greased and floured 9-inch round cake pans. Bake at 350 degrees for 25 minutes. Cool before frosting.

To make frosting, melt chocolate in top of double boiler over boiling water. Remove from heat. Add powdered sugar, salt, and hot water. Beat on medium speed of electric mixer until thoroughly blended. Add egg yolks, one at a time, stirring well after each addition. Add butter and vanilla, beating until frosting reaches spreading consistency.

Diana M. Weise, Yorktown, Texas
*Texas Country Reporter Cookbook*

# Quatro Leches Cake with Kahlua Mousse

## Cake

1 cup flour

⅓ cup cocoa

1 teaspoon baking powder

½ teaspoon salt

1 cup sugar

5 eggs

¼ cup water

1 tablespoon vanilla

## Quatro Leches

2 tablespoons cocoa

1 tablespoon instant coffee

¼ cup sugar

½ cup Kahlúa

½ cup goat's milk

1 cup heavy cream

1 (14-ounce) can condensed milk

1 (12-ounce) can evaporated milk

## Kahlúa Mousse

1 cup Kahlúa

2 tablespoons instant coffee

4 ounces semisweet chocolate

2 cups heavy cream

½ cup granulated sugar

Begin by making Kahlúa Mousse. Combine Kahlúa and instant coffee in a saucepan and reduce until ½ cup remains. Cool and reserve.

Melt chocolate over a simmering water bath or in a double boiler covered with plastic wrap. Stir until smooth and transfer to metal bowl. Cool at room temperature.

Whip the heavy cream and sugar in a well-chilled bowl with an electric mixer, slowly adding the cooled Kahlúa-coffee mixture into the cream. It will begin to form soft peaks. Stop mixing at medium-firm peaks. Take 1 cup of the whipped cream mixture and, using a whisk, vigorously whip it into the bowl with the chocolate until the two are well blended. This will keep the chocolate from seizing up when blending with cold whipped cream. Gently fold in the rest of the whipped cream until smooth. Chill for 2 hours.

Bake the cake. Preheat oven to 400 degrees. Butter a 9 × 9 × 2-inch baking pan and set aside. Sift flour, cocoa, baking powder, and salt together in bowl; set aside.

In a mixer, blend sugar and eggs about 3 minutes, or until light and frothy. Add vanilla and water. Mix on high until fluffy and about twice the original size in volume, approximately 10 minutes. Quickly fold in the dry ingredients and pour into prepared cake pan. Bake 12 to 15 minutes, or until tester comes out clean. Remove and cool on wire rack.

Make the Quatro Leches. Whisk cocoa, instant coffee, sugar, and Kahlúa together in a saucepan and simmer for 3 minutes. Set aside to cool.

Blend the 4 milks in a mixing bowl. Add cooled coffee mixture and whisk together.

Slide a knife around the cake pan and poke several dozen holes in the cake with a cake tester toothpick. Pour milk mixture slowly over the cake until it can't absorb any more. You may have a little milk mixture left over. (Add a couple of scoops of ice cream and blend to make the world's best milk shake.)

Cut the cake into squares and top with Kahlúa Mousse. A dollop is dandy, but if you want to get fancy, put the mousse into a pastry bag with a star tip and make a rosette on the squares. Serves 10.

*Cooking Fearlessly*

# Schwartzwälder Kirschtorte *(Black Forest Cherry Cake)*

## Cake

**10 eggs, separated**

**1 cup sugar**

**2 teaspoons vanilla extract**

**2 tablespoons rum**

**⅔ cup unsweetened cocoa**

**1½ cups flour**

## Fillings

**1 large can cherry pie filling**

**5 tablespoons Kirschwasser**

**1 quart whipping cream**

**3 tablespoons powdered sugar**

**1 teaspoon vanilla extract**

**10 to 15 maraschino cherries**

**2 ounces chocolate, grated**

For cake, beat the egg whites in a large mixing bowl until stiff. Gradually add sugar, vanilla, and rum. Beat in egg yolks, one at a time. Sift the flour and cocoa together and gradually fold into the batter. Pour into 2 greased 10-inch springform pans or 4 greased 9-inch round cake pans. Preheat oven to 400 degrees and bake for 15 to 25 minutes, or until cake tests done. Cool 5 minutes before removing from pans. When completely cool, cut cakes into 2 layers horizontally if springforms are used.

For fillings, stir the cherry pie filling and Kirschwasser together. Whip cream in a large mixing bowl, adding powdered sugar and vanilla just before stiff peaks form.

To assemble, place 1 cake layer on cake plate. Spread with ½-inch layer of whipped cream mixture. Top with second cake layer. Spread with all of cherry pie filling. Top with third cake layer and again spread with whipped cream mixture. Place final layer on cake and spread remaining whipped cream on top and sides. Decorate cake with maraschino cherries and grated chocolate. Do not make cake too far in advance, as whipped cream does not hold its shape very long.

*Great German Recipes*

# Banana Cake

⅔ cup shortening or oil

1⅔ cup sugar

2 egg yolks plus 1 whole egg

1¼ cups mashed bananas

2½ cups sifted flour

1¼ teaspoons baking powder

1 teaspoon salt

1 teaspoon baking soda

⅔ cup buttermilk

### Frosting

1 pint whipping cream

2 egg whites

1 tablespoon vanilla

¾ cup powdered sugar

Bananas, sliced

Stir shortening until softened, then cream together with sugar. Add eggs and mix well. Stir in bananas. In a separate bowl, sift together all dry ingredients. Slowly add dry ingredients to shortening mixture, alternating with buttermilk. Beat vigorously for 2 minutes. Bake in parchment-paper-lined cake pans at 350 degrees for about 35 minutes. Cool 10 minutes before removing from pan.

To make frosting, beat whipping cream and egg whites until stiff peaks form. While still beating, add vanilla and powdered sugar. Continue to beat until mixed well, but before butter begins to form. Sprinkle banana slices over top of first layer, then top with frosting. Cover with second layer, sprinkle with bananas, and top with frosting. Cover sides of cake with frosting. Refrigerate until ready to serve.

Mrs. R. M. Parks, Dallas
*Texas Country Reporter Cookbook*

# Brown Sugar Cake with Caramel Sauce

### Butter Cake

2 cups (4 sticks) butter at room temperature

2 cups firmly packed light brown sugar

6 eggs

4 cups all-purpose flour, sifted

1 teaspoon baking powder

¼ teaspoon salt

⅔ cup milk

2 cups pecans, chopped

### Caramel Sauce

1 cup firmly packed light brown sugar

½ cup (1 stick) butter

½ cup whipping cream

To prepare cake, preheat oven to 325 degrees. Grease and flour a 10-inch tube pan. Beat 2 cups butter and sugar in large bowl until smooth and creamy. Add eggs, beating well after each addition. Mix in flour, baking powder, and salt. Gradually blend in milk. Add pecans. Pour batter into prepared pan, smoothing top with spatula. Bake until top is cracked and no longer moist, about 1½ hours. Invert cake onto rack and cool completely in pan.

Meanwhile, to prepare sauce, combine sugar, butter, and cream in heavy-bottomed small saucepan over low heat. Cook, stirring constantly, until sugar is dissolved. Remove from heat and whisk for 1 minute. Store caramel in jar with tight-fitting lid until ready to serve.

To serve, cut cake into wedges. Spoon some sauce over each piece. Pass remaining sauce separately.

*Of Magnolia and Mesquite*

# Buttermilk Spice Cake

¾ cup (1½ sticks) butter, softened

¾ cup sugar

¾ cup firmly packed brown sugar

3 eggs

1 teaspoon vanilla

2¾ cups flour

2 tablespoons baking powder

1 teaspoon baking soda

½ teaspoon ground cinnamon

½ teaspoon nutmeg

¼ teaspoon ground cloves

1¼ cups buttermilk

1 cup chopped pecans or walnuts

### Icing

1 (3-ounce) package cream cheese, softened

¼ cup (½ stick) butter, softened

1½ teaspoons instant coffee

3 cups sifted powdered sugar

Cream butter and sugars. Add eggs and vanilla, and beat for 5 minutes at high speed. Sift dry ingredients together. Add to creamed mixture alternately with buttermilk, stopping to scrape down sides of bowl after each addition. Stir in nuts. Pour batter into 2 greased and floured 9-inch cake pans. Bake at 350 degrees for 30 minutes, or until cakes test done. Cool and frost.

To make the icing, cream the cream cheese and butter together, blending well. Add the coffee and powdered sugar. Beat until smooth and fluffy.

Mrs. Peter M. Tart
*The Dallas Junior League Cookbook*

# German Chocolate Cake

2½ cups cake flour, sifted

1 teaspoon baking soda

½ teaspoon salt

4 ounces German's Sweet Chocolate

½ cup boiling water

2 cups sugar

1 cup butter, softened

4 egg yolks

1 teaspoon vanilla extract

1 cup buttermilk

4 egg whites

Coconut-Pecan Frosting (see recipe
   below)

## Coconut-Pecan Frosting

1 cup evaporated milk

1 cup sugar

½ cup (1 stick) butter

3 egg yolks, lightly beaten

1 teaspoon vanilla extract

1⅓ cups shredded coconut

1 cup chopped pecans

To make the cake, line three 8- or 9-inch cake pans with waxed paper or parchment paper. Preheat oven to 350 degrees.

Sift the cake flour, baking soda, and salt into a bowl and mix well.

Combine the chocolate and boiling water in a bowl, stirring until the chocolate melts. Let stand until cool.

Beat the sugar and butter in a mixer bowl until light and fluffy, scraping the bowl occasionally, about 5 minutes. Add the egg yolks, one at a time, beating well after each addition and scraping down the bowl. Add the vanilla and chocolate mixture and mix well. Add the dry ingredients alternately with the buttermilk, beating well after each addition and scraping the sides of the bowl.

Beat the egg whites in a chilled mixer bowl until stiff peaks form. Fold into the chocolate batter. Spoon into the prepared cake pans.

Bake in preheated oven for 35 to 40 minutes, or until the layers test done. Invert onto wire racks to cool.

Spread the Coconut-Pecan Frosting between each layer and over the top and sides. Serves 12.

To make the Coconut-Pecan Frosting, combine the evaporated milk, sugar, butter, egg yolks, and vanilla in a 2-quart saucepan. Cook over medium heat for 12 minutes, or until thickened, stirring constantly. Remove from heat. Stir in the coconut and pecans. Let stand until the frosting is of spreading consistency, stirring occasionally.

*Texas Ties*

**HINT:** When alternating the addition of liquids and dry ingredients, always begin and end with dry ingredients.

# Chocolate Lava Cakes with Whiskey Sauce

Softened unsalted butter for greasing ramekins

¼ cup cocoa powder, blended with ¼ cup raw sugar

1½ sticks unsalted butter

9 ounces bittersweet chocolate

3 eggs

3 egg yolks

⅓ cup sugar

⅛ teaspoon salt

3 tablespoons all-purpose flour

Whiskey Sauce (see recipe below)

Sweetened whipped cream

## Whiskey Sauce

1 cup (2 sticks) unsalted butter, softened

1½ cups firmly packed dark brown sugar

2 eggs, beaten until frothy

½ cup Jack Daniel's whiskey

Mint sprigs or small edible flowers as garnish

Begin by making the Whiskey Sauce. Using an electric mixer, cream the butter and sugar until it is very light and fluffy, about 7 minutes. Transfer the mixture to the top of a double boiler over simmering water. Cook for 20 minutes, whisking often, or until the mixture is silky smooth and comes away from the sides of the pan cleanly when whisked. Whisk ¼ cup of the hot butter mixture into the beaten eggs, then another ¼ cup. Whisk the egg mixture slowly into the remaining butter mixture over the heat. Cook until thickened, about 4 to 5 minutes, whisking constantly. Whisk in the whiskey, blending well. The sauce may be kept warm over hot water until ready to serve, or it can be stored in the refrigerator. Gently reheat, whisking vigorously 3 or 4 times, before serving to restore the smooth consistency.

Preheat the oven to 450 degrees. Line a baking sheet with parchment paper; set aside. Butter 6 (6-ounce) ramekins on bottom and sides. Coat with the raw sugar-cocoa mixture. Tap out excess on the side of the sink. Place ramekins on prepared baking sheet and set aside.

Combine the butter and chocolate in the top of a double boiler over simmering water. In a separate bowl, beat the eggs and extra egg yolks with sugar and salt at medium-high speed until thickened and light lemon yellow in color, about 5 minutes.

Whisk the chocolate and butter mixture until smooth. Whisk the flour into the chocolate, blending well. Turn the chocolate mixture into the egg and sugar mixture, beating just to blend. Spoon the batter into the prepared ramekins, smoothing the tops. Bake in preheated oven to 11 to 12 minutes, or just until the sides of the cakes are firm. The centers will still be soft. Reheat the whiskey sauce in the double boiler while cakes are baking. Remove baking sheet from the oven and allow cakes to cool in the ramekins for 2 minutes, then invert onto individual serving plates, letting them stand for about 1 minute before unmolding. Spoon some of the whiskey sauce around each cake and top with a generous dollop of the sweetened whipped cream. Garnish with mint sprigs or edible flower and serve at once. Serves 6.

Terry Thompson-Anderson

# Texas Chocolate Cake

½ pound (2 sticks) butter

4 tablespoons cocoa

1 cup water

2 cups sugar

2 cups flour

1 teaspoon baking soda

2 eggs, beaten

½ cup buttermilk

1 teaspoon ground cinnamon

1 teaspoon vanilla

¼ teaspoon salt

## Icing

½ cup (1 stick) butter

4 tablespoons cocoa

8 tablespoons milk

1 (16-ounce) box powdered sugar

1 cup chopped pecans

Preheat oven to 325 degrees.

To make the cake, melt the butter in a heavy saucepan. Add the cocoa and water. Bring to a boil. Combine sugar, flour, and soda. Pour in boiled mixture and whisk vigorously to combine. Add eggs, buttermilk, cinnamon, vanilla, and salt; beat well. Pour into a prepared 9 × 13-inch baking pan. Bake at 325 degrees for 30 minutes. Cool cake about 15 minutes and pour freshly made icing over the top.

To make the icing, melt the butter in a heavy saucepan, then add the cocoa and milk, whisking to blend well. Bring to a boil. Place the powdered sugar in a bowl. Pour the cocoa mixture over the powdered sugar and whisk to blend well. Stir in the pecans. Pour over the cake.

*It's a Long Way to Guacamole*

# Classic Carrot Cake

## Cake

2 cups flour

2 teaspoons baking soda

2½ teaspoons cinnamon

1 teaspoon salt

2 cups sugar

1½ cups vegetable oil

4 eggs

3 cups grated carrots

2 teaspoons vanilla extract

## Cream Cheese Frosting

½ cup (1 stick) butter, softened

8 ounces cream cheese, softened

1 (16-ounce) package confectioners' sugar

2 teaspoons vanilla extract

Milk

To prepare the cake, sift the flour, baking soda, cinnamon, and salt together. Combine the sugar, vegetable oil, and eggs in a bowl and beat until smooth. Add the flour mixture and mix well. Fold in the carrots and vanilla.

Spoon the batter into 3 greased and floured 8-inch cake pans. Bake at 325 degrees for 45 minutes. Cool in the pans for 5 minutes, then remove to wire racks to cool completely.

To prepare the frosting, combine the butter and cream cheese in a bowl and beat until light. Add the confectioners' sugar and vanilla and beat until fluffy. Add enough milk as needed for the desired consistency, beating until smooth. Spread between the layers and over the top and sides of the cake. Serves 12.

*Lone Star to Five Star*

# Creole Fudge Cake

## Cake

**4 ounces unsweetened chocolate**

**1 cup firmly packed light brown sugar**

**½ cup water**

**1 tablespoon instant coffee granules**

**1 cup sugar**

**8 tablespoons butter, softened**

**3 eggs**

**2½ cups sifted cake flour**

**2 teaspoons baking powder**

**½ teaspoon baking soda**

**¼ teaspoon salt**

**1 cup milk**

**Cocoa**

## Coffee Buttercream Icing

**2 tablespoons instant coffee granules**

**¼ cup hot water**

**1 cup butter, softened**

**2 egg yolks**

**6 cups sifted powdered sugar**

**Chocolate shavings (optional)**

To make the cake, combine chocolate, brown sugar, water, and coffee in top of double boiler. Heat over simmering water until well blended. Cool. In bowl of electric mixer, add sugar slowly to butter, beating at medium speed until well blended. Add eggs, one at a time, beating well after each addition; continue beating until mixture is light and fluffy. Beat in cooled chocolate mixture. Sift together cake flour, baking powder, baking soda, and salt. Add alternately with milk to creamed mixture. Divide batter among 3 (8-inch) round cake pans that have been greased and dusted with cocoa. Stagger pans in oven; bake in a preheated 350-degree oven for 25 to 30 minutes, or until cakes test done. Cool 10 minutes in pans. Turn onto racks; refrigerate until cold. Frost between layers and on sides and top with Coffee Buttercream Icing. Scatter chocolate shavings on top, if desired.

To make the icing, dissolve coffee granules in hot water. Cool. In bowl of electric mixer, blend butter and egg yolks at medium speed. Add the powdered sugar and coffee mixture; blend until smooth.

*Texas Blossoms*

# Chocolate Cayenne Cake

2 cups sugar

½ cup cocoa powder

2 cups all-purpose flour

2 teaspoons baking soda

1 teaspoon baking powder

½ teaspoon red (cayenne) pepper

1 cup vegetable oil

1 cup buttermilk

1 cup water

2 teaspoons vanilla extract

2 eggs, beaten

Cream cheese frosting with anise (your favorite recipe with 1 teaspoon toasted and crushed anise seeds added)

## Chocolate Ganache

1½ cups bittersweet chocolate chips

3 tablespoons unsalted butter

2 tablespoons whipping cream

Preheat oven to 350 degrees. Generously grease two 9-inch cake pans and set aside.

Combine the sugar, cocoa, flour, baking soda, baking powder, and cayenne pepper, stirring to blend well. In a separate bowl, combine the vegetable oil, buttermilk, water, vanilla extract, and beaten eggs. Add to the dry ingredients, beating to blend well. Divide the batter between the prepared cake pans; bake in preheated oven for 30 minutes, or until a toothpick inserted in the center comes out clean. Remove from oven and cool in pans on wire racks for 10 minutes. Turn the layers out onto the racks, allow to cool completely, and refrigerate until chilled.

To make the Chocolate Ganache, melt the chocolate chips and butter in a double boiler over simmering water; stir until smooth. Add the cream slowly, stirring until smooth and spreadable.

To assemble the cake, place one layer on a serving plate and spread with the cream cheese frosting, all the way to the edge. Place the second layer on top of the frosting. Frost the top and sides of the cake with the Chocolate Ganache. Allow the ganache to set before slicing. Makes one 9-inch double-layer cake.

Elaine's Table, Hunt, Texas
*The Texas Hill Country*

# Mayonnaise Cake

2 cups flour

1 cup sugar

1½ teaspoons baking soda

1½ teaspoons baking powder

4 tablespoons cocoa

1 cup mayonnaise

1 cup cold water

2 teaspoons vanilla extract

### Icing

1 cup sugar

½ cup cocoa

¼ cup butter

¼ cup milk

2 teaspoons vanilla extract

Sift flour, sugar, soda, baking powder, and cocoa together. Add mayonnaise, cold water, and vanilla. Beat just to blend ingredients. Pour batter into a greased 9 × 13-inch baking dish or two 8- or 9-inch greased cake pans. Bake at 350 degrees for 30 to 35 minutes, or until cake tests done. Cool on wire rack and spread icing over the top if baked in one layer, or between layers and on top and sides if baked in round cake pans.

To make the icing, combine all ingredients, except vanilla, in a saucepan and boil for 1 minute. Cool slightly, then stir in vanilla. Cool completely before icing cake.

Betty Littlejohn
*Through Our Kitchen Door*

# Flan Cake

1 (12-ounce) can evaporated milk

1 (14-ounce) can sweetened condensed milk

3 eggs

1 tablespoon vanilla extract

Vegetable cooking spray

½ cup cajeta (Mexican caramel) or caramel ice cream topping

1 box butter cake mix

In large bowl, mix evaporated milk, sweetened condensed milk, eggs, and vanilla extract with a spoon; set aside. Spray a 12-cup Bundt pan very liberally with vegetable cooking spray. Spread cajeta into bottom of Bundt pan. Microwave the caramel on high for 30 seconds to make it easier to spread.

Prepare cake mix as directed on box. Pour cake batter on top of cajeta in Bundt pan. Slowly pour the flan mixture over cake batter (flan mixture will sink to the bottom of the pan). Bake at 325 degrees for 45 to 50 minutes. Cool in pan for 15 minutes; invert onto serving platter and cool completely. Serves 12 to 14.

*Seasoned with Fun*

# Fresh Apple Cake

1 cup sugar

½ cup vegetable oil

2 eggs

1½ cups all-purpose flour

½ teaspoon salt

1 teaspoon baking soda

2 tablespoons hot water

2 cups chopped apples (2 large apples), unpeeled

1 teaspoon vanilla

1½ cups chopped pecans, divided

½ cup firmly packed brown sugar

Lady apple (or small apple), sliced in half (optional)

Grapes (optional)

Mint leaves (optional)

Combine sugar, oil, and eggs; beat well. Sift together flour, salt, and baking soda; add to egg mixture along with 2 tablespoons hot water. Mix well. Add chopped apples, vanilla, and 1 cup chopped pecans; mix well. Pour into two 8-inch greased and floured deep quiche pans or 8-inch round cake pans, or one greased and floured 12-cup Bundt pan.

Combine brown sugar and remaining pecans and sprinkle half the mixture on top of each cake (if using a Bundt pan, sprinkle all on top). Bake at 325 degrees for 30 to 35 minutes (if using a Bundt pan, bake 50 to 60 minutes). Cool in pan 10 minutes, remove from pan, and let cool completely on a wire rack. Garnish with apple halves, grapes, and mint leaves, if desired. Yields two 8-inch cakes or one large Bundt cake.

Institute of Texan Cultures, *The Melting Pot: Ethnic Cuisine in Texas*
*Cooking with Texas Highways*

# Hot Apple Cake with Caramel Rum Sauce

## Cake

1 cup (2 sticks) butter, room temperature

1 cup sugar

2 eggs, beaten

1½ cups all-purpose flour

1 teaspoon freshly grated nutmeg

1 teaspoon cinnamon

1 teaspoon baking soda

½ teaspoon salt

3 medium-size tart apples, cored and finely chopped

¾ cup chopped walnuts

1 teaspoon vanilla

Vanilla ice cream (optional)

Preheat oven to 350 degrees. Grease two 10-inch pie plates and set aside. Cream butter with sugar in large bowl. Add eggs and beat well. Sift flour, spices, baking soda, and salt. Blend into butter mixture. Add apple, nuts, and vanilla and mix thoroughly. Pour into prepared pie plates. Bake until lightly browned, about 45 minutes. Serve warm, topped with vanilla ice cream and Caramel Rum Sauce. Makes 2 cakes (12 servings).

## Caramel Rum Sauce

*(Makes 1 cup.)*

½ cup sugar

½ cup firmly packed brown sugar

½ cup whipping cream

½ cup (1 stick) butter

¼ cup rum

Combine sugars and cream in top of double boiler set over gently simmering water; cook 1½ hours, replenishing water in bottom of double boiler as necessary. Add butter and continue cooking 30 minutes. Remove from heat and beat well. Add rum and blend thoroughly. Serve warm. Cake and sauce can be prepared ahead and reheated before serving.

*Of Magnolia and Mesquite*

# Hummingbird Cake

## Cake

3 cups flour

2 cups sugar

1 teaspoon baking soda

1 teaspoon cinnamon

1 teaspoon salt

3 eggs, beaten

1½ cups vegetable oil

1 (8-ounce) can crushed pineapple

2 cups chopped bananas (about 4 bananas)

2 cups chopped pecans

1½ teaspoons vanilla extract

## Fluffy Cream Cheese Frosting

1 cup (2 sticks) butter, softened

16 ounces cream cheese, softened

2 (16-ounce) packages confectioners' sugar

2 teaspoons vanilla extract

Salt to taste

1 cup chopped pecans

To prepare the cake, mix the flour, sugar, baking soda, cinnamon, and salt in a large bowl. Add the eggs and vegetable oil and mix until moistened. Stir in the undrained pineapple, bananas, pecans, and vanilla.

Spoon the batter into 3 greased and floured 9-inch cake pans. Bake at 350 degrees for 25 minutes, or until a wooden pick comes out clean. Cool in the pans for 10 minutes, then remove to a wire rack to cool completely.

To prepare the frosting, beat the butter and cream cheese in a mixing bowl until light. Add the confectioners' sugar gradually and beat until fluffy. Stir in the vanilla and salt. Spread between the layers and over the top and sides of the cake. Top with the pecans. Serves 8 to 10.

*Lone Star to Five Star*

# Kahlúa Cake

1 box Devil's Food cake mix

1 cup Kahlúa (use as a substitute for the 1 cup water)

⅓ cup water

½ cup canola oil

3 eggs

½ to 1 package Semisweet Chocolate Mini-Morsels

### Icing

½ cup whipping cream

6 ounces cream cheese

¼ pound butter, softened

1 teaspoon vanilla

1 box powdered sugar

Follow mixing directions on cake mix box, substituting 1 cup Kahlúa for 1 cup water. Fold chocolate morsels into mix before baking. Follow baking instructions on box.

To make the icing, mix whipping cream, cream cheese, and butter together; let come to room temperature. Mix powdered sugar and vanilla into whipping cream mixture; beat until thick and smooth. Spread on cooled cake.

Bill Cone
*Gruene General Store Cookbook*

# Mexican Chocolate Cake

1 stick butter

½ cup oil

2 ounces (2 squares) unsweetened chocolate

1 cup water

2 cups all-purpose flour

1 teaspoon baking powder

2 cups sugar

½ cup buttermilk

2 eggs, beaten

1 teaspoon ground cinnamon

1 teaspoon vanilla

Preheat oven to 350 degrees. In a small saucepan, combine butter, oil, chocolate, and water and heat until chocolate is melted. Combine remaining ingredients in a mixing bowl. Blend in the chocolate mixture. Pour into a greased 9 × 13-inch pan. Bake for 20 to 25 minutes. Ice with Mexican Chocolate Icing (recipe on page 338).

*(Continued)*

### Mexican Chocolate Icing

1 stick butter, softened

2 squares (2 ounces) unsweetened chocolate

¼ cup milk

1 pound powdered sugar

1 teaspoon vanilla

½ cup chopped pecans

Combine butter, chocolate, and milk in a small saucepan. Heat until butter and chocolate melt. Remove from heat and gradually add powdered sugar, vanilla, and pecans. Blend thoroughly and ice cake while still warm.

*The San Antonio Tex-Mex Cookbook*

# Milky Way Cake

6 Milky Way candy bars

1 stick butter

2 cups sugar

1 cup vegetable shortening

4 eggs

2½ cups sifted flour

½ teaspoon baking soda

1½ cups buttermilk

2 teaspoons vanilla

Combine and melt candy bars and butter. Let cool. Cream sugar and shortening, then add eggs, one at a time. Combine flour, baking soda, and buttermilk alternately. Add candy mixture and vanilla. Bake in 3 greased and floured cake pans at 350 degrees for 30 minutes. Cool completely before icing.

### Chocolate Marshmallow Cream Icing

2½ cups sugar

1 small can evaporated milk

1 stick butter

1 (6-ounce) package chocolate chips

1 pint jar marshmallow creme

½ teaspoon vanilla

½ cup pecans

Cook sugar, evaporated milk, and butter in saucepan for 5 minutes, stirring constantly, until sugar and butter have melted. Add remaining ingredients and blend. Spread between layers and on top and sides of cake.

*Gruene General Store Cookbook*

# Way South of the Border Ancho Pepper Pecan Pie

1 (9-inch) deep-dish pie shell from the dairy case in your grocery store

7 egg yolks

½ cup light corn syrup

1 cup granulated sugar

½ cup unsweetened cocoa

1 cup dark brown sugar, firmly packed

½ stick butter, melted

3 cups Southern Comfort or Jack Daniel's bourbon

2 cups pecan halves

1 cup Ancho Pepper Puree (see recipe below)

Pinch of salt

4 tablespoons all-purpose flour

2 tablespoons vanilla bean paste

## Ancho Pepper Puree

6 ancho chile peppers, seeds removed

2 cups hot water

To make the puree, soak the chiles in water for 30 minutes, or until very soft. Puree in blender with a little of the chile water.

To make the pie, preheat oven to 300 degrees. In a saucepan over high heat, reduce the bourbon to ¼ cup. Caution: When heating alcohol, a 3-foot flame can result.

In a sauté pan, add both sugars and corn syrup and bring to a boil. Add the reduced bourbon, Ancho Pepper Puree, cocoa, salt, vanilla bean paste, and butter to the boiling sugars and continue to boil.

Whisk the egg yolks in a bowl. Slowly add the bubbling sugar mixture to the eggs. Do this very slowly, adding just a small amount at a time, as you will scramble the eggs if done too quickly.

Remove from heat and whisk in the flour. Place pecan halves in bottom of pie shell. Pour filling into pie shell. Place on a sheet tray and bake for 40 minutes in preheated oven. Serves 8.

*Fired Up!*

# Key Lime Pie

## Crust

1¼ cups finely ground graham cracker crumbs

2 tablespoons plus 1½ teaspoons granulated sugar

¼ cup melted butter

## Filling

3 egg yolks

8 ounces cream cheese at room temperature

1 (14-ounce) can sweetened condensed milk

½ cup fresh Key lime juice, or substitute regular lime juice

Sweetened whipped cream for garnish, if desired

Preheat oven to 350 degrees. Mix the graham cracker crumbs and sugar together, tossing to blend. Stir in the melted butter, coating well. Turn the mixture out into a 10-inch pie pan. Using the back of a spoon, press mixture against the sides of the pan to a thickness of ¼ inch, taking care to follow the slope of the pan. Spread the mixture in the bottom of the pan and press down with a flat surface like the bottom of a measuring cup. Bake in preheated oven for 10 minutes. Remove from oven and allow to cool. (The crust can also be frozen for later use.)

While the crust is cooling, make the filling. Place the egg yolks in bowl of electric stand mixer and beat until light lemon yellow in color and very thick and "ribbonlike" in texture, about 5 minutes. Using a rubber spatula, scrape the thickened yolks into a separate bowl and set aside. Put the cream cheese in the mixer bowl and beat at medium speed until light and fluffy, scraping down the sides of the bowl often.

Return the yolks to the mixer bowl and beat at high speed for 3 minutes, scraping the sides of the bowl as needed. Add the sweetened condensed milk and mix at high speed for 3 minutes, scraping the bowl as needed. Add the lime juice and beat at medium speed for 3 minutes, scraping the bowl as needed. The mixture should begin to thicken slightly as you beat in the lime juice.

Pour the filling into the cooled pie crust and bake in 350-degree oven for 7 minutes. Allow the pie to rest for 30 minutes at room temperature, then place in an airtight container or carefully wrap in plastic wrap and refrigerate overnight before slicing. (This pie freezes quite well.)

Before serving, top each slice with a generous dollop of sweetened whipped cream, if desired. Makes one 10-inch pie.

Wimberley Pie Company, Wimberley, Texas
*The Texas Hill Country*

# Key Lime Pie II

2 egg yolks

2 (14-ounce) cans sweetened condensed milk

1 cup Key lime juice, fresh or frozen

1 (9-inch) graham cracker pie shell

1 cup sour cream

½ cup sugar

Pinch of salt

Lime slices

Beat the egg yolks, sweetened condensed milk, and lime juice in a large mixing bowl for 5 minutes. Pour into the pie shell. Bake at 350 degrees for 15 minutes, or until the edge is set. Place in the refrigerator. Beat the sour cream, sugar, and salt in a small mixing bowl for 3 to 6 minutes, or until the sugar is dissolved. Spread the topping evenly over the filling, sealing to the edge. Bake at 350 degrees for 15 minutes, or until the top is set. Do not allow the top to brown. Chill for 24 hours before serving. Serves 6 to 8.

*Dining without Reservations*

# Amish Lemon Pie

4 eggs, separated

1 cup sugar

1 teaspoon grated lemon rind

3 tablespoons flour

1 tablespoon butter, softened

⅓ cup freshly squeezed lemon juice

1 cup milk

1 (9-inch) baked pie crust, cooled

Beat the egg whites until stiff. Set aside. Combine the sugar, lemon zest, flour, butter, and egg yolks in mixer bowl. Beat until well blended. Add the lemon juice and milk, blending well. Fold this mixture gently but thoroughly into the egg whites. Pour into the crust and bake at 325 degrees for 35 to 40 minutes, or until a knife inserted into the center comes out clean. Cool completely before serving. If desired, garnish with fresh strawberries or other fruit in season. This custard-like pie will have a sponge-like topping.

*German-Style Recipes*

# Banana Caramel Pie

1 (14-ounce) can sweetened condensed milk

1 baked and cooled pie crust

4 medium bananas (may vary)

½ pint whipping cream, whipped and lightly sweetened

3 small Heath candy bars, frozen and chopped

Place unopened can of condensed milk in saucepan (remove the label). Cover the can with water and simmer for 4 to 5 hours. Add more water as needed. Remove and let can cool.

Line the pie crust with sliced bananas (a lot of bananas will balance the caramel, which is very sweet). Pour caramelized milk over the bananas. Spread the whipped cream on top. Sprinkle the candy bars over the whipped cream.

Verna Richards
*The Peach Tree Family Cookbook*

# Peanut Butter Pie

1 (8-ounce) package cream cheese, softened

1 cup chunky peanut butter

⅔ cup powdered sugar

⅓ cup half-and-half

1 (8-ounce) carton whipped topping

1 graham cracker crust

½ cup heavy cream

1 tablespoon powdered sugar

Beat cream cheese, peanut butter, and powdered sugar together until smooth. Gradually add half-and-half, beating until well blended. Stir in whipped topping. Spoon into graham cracker crust. Whip cream, gradually adding powdered sugar until soft peaks form. Spoon or pipe around edge of pie. Freeze. Slice while frozen. Let stand 20 minutes before serving.

Mary Lauderdale, Greenville, Texas
*Texas Country Reporter Cookbook*

# Raspberry Cream Pie

1 cup sugar

⅔ cup flour, divided

2 large eggs, lightly beaten

1⅓ cups sour cream

1 teaspoon vanilla extract

3 cups fresh or frozen raspberries, thawed
    if frozen

1 (9-inch) pie pastry

⅓ cup firmly packed brown sugar

⅓ cup chopped pecans

3 tablespoons butter, softened

Whipped cream and fresh raspberries
    (optional)

Combine sugar, ⅓ cup flour, eggs, sour cream, and vanilla in a large bowl, stirring until smooth. Gradually fold in the raspberries. Spoon into pie pastry. Bake at 400 degrees for 40 to 45 minutes, or until center is set.

Combine remaining ⅓ cup flour, brown sugar, pecans, and butter; sprinkle over hot pie. Bake at 400 degrees for 10 minutes, or until golden, shielding edges of pastry with foil, if necessary, to prevent excessive browning. Garnish with whipped cream and fresh raspberries, if desired. Yields 8 servings.

*Seasoned with Fun*

# Shoofly Pie

1½ cups flour

½ cup sugar

½ teaspoon baking soda, divided

4 tablespoons butter

½ cup molasses

½ cup hot water

1 (8-inch) pastry shell, unbaked

Preheat oven to 375 degrees.

Thoroughly mix together flour, sugar, and ¼ teaspoon baking soda. Cut in the butter until crumbly. Set aside. Combine molasses, remaining ¼ teaspoon baking soda, and water. Pour ⅓ of the liquid into unbaked pastry shell; sprinkle with ⅓ of the flour mixture. Repeat layers, ending with flour mixture. Bake for 40 minutes. Cool before slicing.

Betty Ann Sheffloe, Nebraska
*Kickin' Back in the Kitchen Cookbook*

# Pecan Fudge Pie with Raspberry Puree

## Fudge Pie

½ cup (1 stick) butter

2 ounces unsweetened chocolate squares

1 cup sugar

½ cup flour

¼ teaspoon salt

⅓ cup toasted, chopped pecans

2 large eggs

1 teaspoon vanilla

## Raspberry Puree

2 cups fresh raspberries, divided

3 tablespoons real maple syrup

2 tablespoons sugar

To make the pie, preheat oven to 350 degrees. Butter a 9-inch pie pan; set aside. In a small saucepan, melt the butter and chocolate over low heat. Turn off heat and add sugar.

Combine the flour, salt, and pecans. Blend into butter, chocolate, and sugar mixture. Whisk the eggs into the chocolate and flour mixture. Add vanilla. Turn mixture out into prepared pie pan. Bake in preheated oven for about 25 minutes, or until a wooden pick inserted in center of pie comes out clean.

Make the Raspberry Purée. Simmer 1½ cups of the raspberries, maple syrup, and sugar until thickened. Pour through a fine strainer, pressing down on berries to extract all liquid. Discard berries.

To serve, pool a portion of the Raspberry Puree on each serving plate. Place a slice of the pie on top. Garnish with remaining raspberries. Serves 8.

Susan Auler, Fall Creek Vineyards, Tow, Texas
*Under the Texan Sun*

# Brownie Pecan Pie

⅔ cup sugar

⅛ teaspoon salt

1 cup light corn syrup

1 (4-ounce) package German's Sweet
 Chocolate, broken into pieces

3 tablespoons butter

3 eggs, beaten

1 teaspoon vanilla

1 cup coarsely chopped pecans

1 (9-inch) unbaked pie shell

Whipped cream as garnish

Combine sugar, salt, and corn syrup in a 3-quart saucepan over medium heat. Bring to a boil, stirring until sugar dissolves. Boil for 2 minutes. Remove from heat. Add chocolate and butter and stir until both have melted. Set aside and allow to cool. Place the beaten eggs in a medium bowl. While whisking the eggs, gradually add the corn syrup mixture, blending thoroughly. Add the vanilla and pecans. Pour into pie shell and bake at 350 degrees for 50 minutes. Cool before serving. Top each serving with whipped cream. Serves 6 to 8.

Mrs. Joe Bowles (Mary)
*Lone Star Legacy*

# Blue Bonnet's German Chocolate Pie

1 (9-inch) baked pie crust

1 cup sugar

¼ cup cornstarch

¼ teaspoon salt

3 cups milk

4 eggs, separated

¼ cup cocoa

3 tablespoons butter

1½ teaspoons vanilla

1 cup pecans

1 cup coconut

Whipped cream for topping

Separate egg yolks from the whites; reserve whites for another use. Combine sugar, cornstarch, salt, milk, and cocoa. Cook mixture over medium to low heat, stirring constantly. After mixture bubbles up and thickens, cook an additional 2 minutes. Remove from heat.

Beat yolks slightly. Gradually stir 1 cup of the hot mixture into the yolks. Return egg mixture to saucepan; bring to a gentle boil. Cook 2 minutes more. Remove from heat. Add butter and vanilla. Stir until butter melts. Add ¾ cup each of pecans and coconut to pie filling; stir well.

Pour into baked pie crust and cool. Combine the remaining pecans and coconut and toast lightly in the oven. Top cooled pie with whipped cream and sprinkle with toasted pecans and coconut.

*What's Cooking at the Blue Bonnet Café*

# Buttermilk Pecan Pie

1 cup granulated sugar

⅓ cup all-purpose flour

⅛ teaspoon salt

⅔ cup butter, melted

1⅓ cups buttermilk

½ teaspoon vanilla extract

½ cup chopped pecans

½ cup raisins

¼ cup sweetened coconut flakes

1 (9-inch) unbaked pie shell

Preheat oven to 350 degrees. In a large bowl, combine sugar, flour, and salt. Whisk in melted butter, buttermilk, and vanilla extract. In a small bowl, toss together pecan pieces, raisins, and coconut. Place pie shell on a large foil-lined baking sheet. Spread pecan mixture into bottom of pie shell, then pour in buttermilk mixture. Bake 1 hour and 20 minutes, or until pie is set in center and golden brown. Remove from oven and cool to room temperature. Makes one 9-inch pie.

*Luby's Recipes & Memories*

# Butterscotch Cream Pie

6 tablespoons flour

¾ cup brown sugar

½ teaspoon salt

½ cup sugar

⅓ cup hot water

2 cups milk

4 tablespoons butter, melted

2 eggs

1 (9-inch) pie shell, baked

1 cup heavy cream, whipped until stiff

Toasted skin-on, sliced almonds

Combine first 3 ingredients and set aside. Place white sugar in a heavy saucepan and cook over medium heat, without stirring, until melted and golden brown. Remove from heat and slowly add to hot water. Stir until sugar dissolves. Add milk and heat to almost boiling; remove from heat. In top of double boiler, melt butter. Add flour mixture and stir well. Beat in eggs. Slowly add caramel mixture and cook over boiling water until thickened, stirring constantly. Cover and cook 10 additional minutes, stirring occasionally. Cool to room temperature and pour into prepared pie shell. Chill for several hours, or until firmly set. Top with whipped cream and scatter the toasted nuts over the top. Serves 8.

*¡Viva! Tradiciones*

# Chocolate Ice Box Pie

2½ cups milk

1⅓ cups granulated sugar

¼ cup unsweetened cocoa

1 tablespoon butter or margarine

7 tablespoons cornstarch

3 extra-large egg yolks

1 teaspoon vanilla extract

1 cup miniature marshmallows

1 baked 9-inch pie shell

Sweetened whipped cream, as needed

Chocolate curls or shavings, as needed

In a medium saucepan, combine 2 cups of milk, sugar, cocoa, and butter. Bring just to a boil over medium heat. In a medium bowl, mix together cornstarch and remaining ½ cup of milk until cornstarch is completely dissolved. Then whisk in egg yolks and vanilla extract until well blended. Whisking constantly, gradually add egg and milk mixture to saucepan. Cook, stirring constantly, about 2 minutes, or until mixture is thickened and smooth. Remove from heat. Stir in marshmallows until melted. Pour into pie shell. Press plastic wrap directly onto filling and refrigerate at least 4 hours. To serve, remove plastic wrap, top pie with whipped cream, and garnish with chocolate curls. Makes one 9-inch pie.

**TIP:** Pressing plastic wrap directly onto the top of the hot pie filling prevents the formation of a tough, dry "skin" while the filling cools. To make decorative chocolate curls or shavings from a chocolate candy bar, use a vegetable peeler.

*Luby's Recipes & Memories*

# Dutch Apple Pie

6 Golden or Red Delicious apples

1 cup sugar

3 tablespoons flour

1 teaspoon cinnamon

⅛ teaspoon freshly grated nutmeg

1 unbaked 9-inch pie shell

⅓ cup packed light brown sugar

½ cup (1 stick) butter, cut into small cubes

1 cup flour

Peel, core, and slice the apples and place in a large bowl. Combine the sugar, 3 tablespoons flour, cinnamon, and nutmeg in a bowl. Add to the apples and toss to mix well. Pour into the pie shell. Combine the brown sugar, butter, and 1 cup flour in a bowl and mix until crumbly. Scatter the mixture over the apples, patting down lightly. Place the pie on a baking sheet to prevent spills inside the oven. Bake at 350 degrees for 1 hour and 10 minutes, or until golden brown and apples are tender. Let cool before serving. Serves 6 to 8.

*Dining without Reservations*

# Mendy's Favorite Apple Pie

1 cup sugar

2 tablespoons flour

1 teaspoon cinnamon

Dash of salt

6 apples, peeled, cored, and thinly sliced

½ cup flour

¼ cup sugar

½ cup grated Cheddar cheese (packed)

¼ cup butter, melted

1 (9-inch) unbaked pie crust

Sour cream (optional)

Mix the sugar, 2 tablespoons flour, cinnamon, and salt. Sprinkle over the apple slices and place in pie crust. Mix the ½ cup flour, ¼ cup sugar, cheese, and melted butter. Crumble the mixture over the apples. Bake at 400 degrees for 30 to 35 minutes. Serve warm with sour cream spread over the top, if desired.

*Of Magnolia and Mesquite*

# Sweet Potato–Pecan Pie

## Pastry

**1 cup all-purpose flour**

**½ cup (1 stick) well-chilled unsalted
    butter, cut into 1-inch cubes**

**Pinch of salt**

**½ teaspoon sugar**

**3 to 4 tablespoons ice water**

## Filling

**2 tablespoons unsalted butter, melted**

**1 cup hot mashed sweet potatoes**

**2 eggs, beaten**

**¾ cup firmly packed light brown sugar**

**1 teaspoon ground ginger**

**½ teaspoon ground cinnamon**

**½ teaspoon freshly grated nutmeg**

**1 tablespoon vanilla extract**

**½ teaspoon salt**

**½ cup dark corn syrup**

**1 cup evaporated milk**

**1½ cups chopped pecans**

## Topping

**1 cup whipping cream**

**2 tablespoons powdered sugar**

**2 tablespoons praline liqueur**

To make the pastry, combine flour, butter, and salt in work bowl of food processor fitted with steel blade. Using the pulse button, pulse just until butter is broken into pea-size chunks. With processor running, add just enough of the water to form a soft, moist dough. Do not process until the mixture forms a ball. Turn dough out onto lightly floured work surface (it will be crumbly) and knead 2 or 3 times by hand. Spray a 9-inch pie pan with nonstick vegetable spray. Roll the pastry out on floured work surface to form a circle about ¹⁄₁₆ inch thick. Loosely roll the pastry around the rolling pin and unroll into pie pan. Lift the edges of the pastry, allowing it to fall to the bottom of the pan. Do not stretch the pastry, or it will shrink while baking. Press onto the bottom and sides of the pan. Cut off excess pastry at the edge, leaving a ½-inch overhang. Turn the pastry under and flute the edge, or press the pastry against the pan rim with the tines of a fork. Refrigerate the pastry while making the filling. Preheat oven to 350 degrees.

In a large bowl, stir the butter into the hot sweet potatoes. Add all remaining filling ingredients except pecans; blend well.

Pour the sweet potato filling into prepared pie shell; scatter the pecans evenly over the top. Bake in preheated oven for about 40 to 45 minutes, or until filling is set and knife inserted into center comes out clean. Cool in pan on wire rack before slicing.

To prepare topping, combine the whipping cream, powdered sugar, and praline liqueur in bowl of electric mixer. Beat with wire whisk until stiff peaks form. Refrigerate, tightly covered, until ready to serve.

To serve, slice pie into 8 wedges. Serve each slice with a large dollop of the topping. Makes one 9-inch pie.

*Texas on the Plate*

# Pumpkin Pie

1 unbaked 9-inch pie crust

2 cups pumpkin meat, peeled and cut into 1-inch dice

¾ cup brown sugar

½ teaspoon salt

1 teaspoon cinnamon

½ teaspoon ground ginger

¼ teaspoon freshly grated nutmeg

3 eggs, beaten

1½ cups milk

Combine pumpkin, sugar, salt, and spices in a medium saucepan. Cook until sugar melts. Mash the pumpkin until smooth. Slowly add beaten eggs, mixed with milk, to the pumpkin mixture. Pour into pie shell. Bake at 350 degrees for 35 to 40 minutes, or until set. When done, there will be a small amount of moisture in the center of the pie.

Betty Stripling
*Through Our Kitchen Door*

# Kahlúa Pecan Pie

3 eggs, well beaten

1 cup sugar

¾ cup light corn syrup

½ cup butter

1 teaspoon vanilla extract

2 tablespoons Kahlúa

½ cup semisweet chocolate morsels, melted and cooled

⅔ cup pecans

1 (9-inch) unbaked pie shell

Preheat oven to 350 degrees. Combine the first 6 ingredients; add cooled chocolate morsels and pecans; stir to blend well. Pour into pie shell. Bake for 55 minutes, or until set. Chill well before slicing. Serves 6 to 8.

*And Roses for the Table*

# Pecan Tassies

## Pastry

3 ounces cream cheese, softened

½ cup butter, softened

1 cup flour

## Filling

1 egg, beaten

¾ cup brown sugar

1 teaspoon vanilla

Pinch of salt

1 cup chopped pecans

With an electric mixer, combine the pastry ingredients until you have a soft dough. Chill the dough for 1 hour.

Heat oven to 325 degrees. Divide dough into 24 portions. Roll into balls, then press balls into miniature muffin pans (2 inches in diameter). Use a little flour on your fingers if the dough gets sticky.

Whisk together the egg, brown sugar, vanilla, and salt. Stir in the pecans. Pour the filling into the prepared pastries. Bake for 20 to 25 minutes. Make 24 pastries.

*The Texas Provincial Kitchen Cookbook*

# Angel's Peach Cobbler

8 cups sliced peaches

2 cups packed brown sugar

6 tablespoons butter

2 tablespoons lemon juice

1 cup Messina Hof Angel Riesling

4 teaspoons cornstarch

½ cup cold water

## Topping

2 cups all-purpose flour

1 cup sugar

2 teaspoons baking powder

Pinch salt

1 cup butter, softened

½ cup cold water

In a large saucepan, combine the peaches, brown sugar, butter, and lemon juice. Cook until fruit is soft. Add wine. Dissolve cornstarch in cold water; add enough of the cornstarch mixture to the peaches to thicken. Pour into a greased 3-quart baking dish or individual baking dishes.

To make topping, combine flour, sugar, baking powder, and salt in a bowl. Mix in softened butter. Slowly add water until mixture is a loose batter. Spoon over fruit. Bake at 350 degrees, or until cobbler is set and topping is golden brown. Serve warm with a scoop of homemade vanilla ice cream. Serves 10 to 12.

*Vineyard Cuisine*

# Stonewall Peach Cobbler

## Filling

2 to 2½ cups sugar

½ cup cornstarch

8 cups sliced fresh peaches

½ teaspoon almond extract

¼ cup (½ stick) melted butter

## Pastry

2 cups flour

2 tablespoons sugar

Pinch of salt

½ cup shortening

4 tablespoons ice water

½ cup (1 stick) melted butter

Additional ¼ cup sugar

To make filling, combine sugar and cornstarch and toss with peaches. Add almond extract and butter and set aside.

To make pastry, combine flour, sugar, and salt. Cut shortening into flour until mixture is the consistency of cornmeal. Gradually add ice water until dough holds its shape. Roll out on a floured board and cut into strips. Pour peach filling into a buttered 9 × 13-inch baking pan. Crisscross dough strips over filling. Brush pastry with melted butter and sprinkle with additional sugar. Bake at 400 degrees for 30 minutes, or until crust is brown.

Matthew Kast, Fredericksburg, Texas
*Texas Country Reporter Cookbook*


# Flamed Bananas

⅓ cup butter

½ cup brown sugar

6 slightly green bananas, peeled and
    halved lengthwise

Cinnamon to taste

½ cup rum

¼ cup liqueur, brandy, Grand Marnier, etc.

Melt the butter and sugar in a shallow skillet. Sprinkle the sliced bananas with desired amount of cinnamon. Sauté the bananas for 1 minute in the butter and sugar. Pour in the rum and liqueur; ignite. Serve at once with ice cream and/or whipped cream. Drizzle the pan juices over the top.

*It's a Long Way to Guacamole*

# Figs in Madeira

36 large figs

2 cups sweet Madeira

1 cup heavy cream

1 teaspoon vanilla extract

½ cup toasted slivered almonds

In a large saucepan combine figs and Madeira; bring to a boil, reduce heat, and simmer, covered, for 5 minutes. Remove from heat and allow to stand for at least 30 minutes, or until figs have absorbed Madeira and are very tender.

Whip cream to form soft peaks. Add vanilla extract.

Garnish figs with whipped cream and almonds and serve with Madeira syrup. Serves 6.

*Gulf Coast Cooking*

# Death by Chocolate

2 cups butter

1 cup sugar

1 cup water

2⅔ cups semisweet chocolate chips

8 eggs

Raspberry Coulis (see recipe below)

Chocolate shavings for garnish

## Raspberry Coulis

3 pints fresh raspberries

1½ cups red currant jelly

1½ cups sugar

1½ teaspoons cornstarch

Salt to taste

Line a 9-inch springform pan with foil. Preheat oven to 350 degrees.

Bring the butter, sugar, and water to a boil in a saucepan. Remove from heat. Add the chocolate chips, stirring until blended and melted. Add the eggs, one at a time, beating well after each addition. The batter will be very thin. Pour into the prepared pan.

Bake in preheated oven for 1 hour. Chill for several hours before serving. Garnish each serving with chocolate shavings. Serve with Raspberry Coulis. Serves 8.

To make Raspberry Coulis, combine the raspberries and red currant jelly in a saucepan and bring to a boil, stirring occasionally. Reduce heat and stir in the sugar, cornstarch, and salt. Cook over low heat until thickened and clear, stirring constantly. Remove from heat and strain; let stand until cool. Chill, covered, until serving time.

**NOTE**: The coulis is also great served over ice cream or pound cake.

*Texas Ties*

# Lemon Curd

2 whole eggs

2 egg yolks

1 cup sugar

⅔ cup fresh lemon juice

1 cup (2 sticks) butter

Mix all ingredients in blender or mixer. Cook in stainless or ceramic double boiler until thickened, stirring constantly. Serve warm. Refrigerate leftover sauce and reheat in double boiler to serve. Yields about 2 cups.

**NOTE:** This excellent sauce has a multitude of uses—ice cream topping, pie filling, pudding garnish, cake frosting, to mention a few—and keeps well in the refrigerator.

**VARIATION:** Once sauce is thickened, stir in chopped sweet herbs—rose geranium, mints, lemon verbena, or rosemary.

*Southern Herb Growing*

# Banana Pudding

½ cup sugar

⅓ cup flour

¼ teaspoon salt

2 cups milk, scalded

2 egg yolks

1 teaspoon vanilla

3 bananas, sliced

18 vanilla wafers

2 egg whites

⅓ cup sugar

½ teaspoon cornstarch

Blend sugar, flour, salt, and milk. Cook over hot water or in double boiler until thick, stirring constantly. Cover and cook for 15 minutes. Beat egg yolks slightly, then add custard gradually. Return to double boiler and cook 2 minutes. Cover and cool, then add vanilla. Line a baking dish with vanilla wafers and sliced bananas, alternately. Cover with custard. Beat egg whites until stiff, adding cornstarch and sugar gradually until thick, then spread over custard. Make peaks in meringue with bottom of spoon. Bake at 325 degrees for 20 minutes. Serves 6.

Gordon Lee, Smithville, Texas
*Texas Country Reporter Cookbook*

# Persimmon Pudding

2 cups persimmon pulp

2 cups sugar

3 eggs, beaten

1¼ cups buttermilk

2 cups flour

1 teaspoon baking powder

1 teaspoon baking soda

½ teaspoon cinnamon

3 tablespoons butter, melted

Mix all ingredients except butter, then add butter to mixture. Pour into a 9 × 13-inch pan. Bake at 350 degrees for 30 to 35 minutes. Serve warm with whipped topping.

Juanita Seagraves, Somerville, Texas
*Texas Country Reporter Cookbook*

# Coffee Bavarian

1 cup fine graham cracker crumbs

¼ cup melted butter

1 envelope unflavored gelatin

½ cup cold water

½ cup sugar

1 tablespoon instant coffee

¼ teaspoon salt

1⅔ cups evaporated milk

1 cup shaved chocolate

Mix cracker crumbs and melted butter. Line bottom of an 8-inch springform pan with mixture and chill. In a 1-quart saucepan, soften gelatin in cold water. Add sugar, coffee, and salt. Stir over low heat until sugar and gelatin dissolve. Remove from heat. Stir in 1 cup of the evaporated milk. Pour into small bowl of electric mixer and chill until firm. Beat at low speed until mixture is just broken up. Add ⅔ cup of evaporated milk. Beat at high speed until mixture fills bowl, then pour it over crumbs in pan. Sprinkle shaved chocolate over top and chill until firm. To serve, cut into wedges of desired size. This may be prepared several days ahead.

*Gruene General Store Cookbook*

# Mississippi Mud

1 cup (2 sticks) butter

2 cups sugar

4 eggs

2 tablespoons cocoa

2 teaspoons vanilla

1½ cups flour

1⅓ cups (4 ounces) coconut

1½ cups chopped pecans

1 large jar marshmallow cream

### Frosting

1 pound powdered sugar

½ cup (1 stick) butter, softened

½ cup evaporated milk

⅓ cup cocoa

1 teaspoon vanilla

Cream butter and sugar. Add eggs, cocoa, and vanilla. Beat until light and fluffy, about 5 minutes. Add flour, beating until blended. Fold in coconut and turn out into a greased and floured 9 × 13-inch baking pan. Bake at 350 degrees for 30 to 40 minutes, or until the brownie layer tests done. Spread the top with the marshmallow cream and let cool completely before frosting.

To make the frosting, beat all ingredients together until smooth. Spread over top of brownies and marshmallow cream. Cut into 1- to 1½-inch squares. Makes 4 to 5 dozen.

Mrs. Larry M. Nobles
*The Dallas Junior League Cookbook*

# Peaches and Cream Kuchen

2 cups flour

1 cup sugar, divided

½ teaspoon salt

¼ teaspoon baking powder

½ cup (1 stick) butter

1½ pounds fresh ripe peaches

Lemon juice

1 teaspoon cinnamon

1 teaspoon ground mace

2 egg yolks

1 cup heavy cream

Combine flour, 2 tablespoons of the sugar, salt, baking powder, and butter. Blend with pastry blender. Turn into a buttered shallow pan; pat down to a smooth crust.

Peel, pit, and slice peaches. Dip in lemon juice. Arrange peaches on flour mixture in pan. Combine remaining sugar and spices; sprinkle over peaches. Bake at 400 degrees for 15 minutes. Remove from oven and reduce temperature to 325 degrees.

Beat egg yolks with cream until smooth. Pour evenly over peaches and bake about 30 minutes, or until golden brown and custard is set in center. Remove and cool 15 to 20 minutes. Serve warm. Reheats nicely in 5 to 6 minutes in hot oven.

*Southern Herb Growing*

# Warm Apple Crisp

### Filling

**6 Granny Smith apples**

**Juice of 1 lemon**

**¼ cup flour**

**½ cup sugar**

**2 teaspoons cinnamon**

**2 tablespoons brandy (optional)**

### Topping

**¾ cup butter, softened**

**1 cup flour**

**1 cup rolled oats**

**1 teaspoon cinnamon**

**1 cup sugar**

Preheat oven to 350 degrees. Peel, core, and slice apples into a bowl with the lemon juice. Add remaining filling ingredients. Toss to coat apples evenly. Place mixture in a 2-quart baking dish.

Combine topping ingredients in a separate bowl. Mixture should resemble small peas. Scatter topping over apples. Bake for 45 minutes, or until top is golden brown. Serves 8.

*The Texas Provincial Kitchen Cookbook*

# Chocolate Pâté

**1½ pounds semisweet chocolate, chopped**

**1¾ pounds butter, cubed**

**½ pound confectioners' sugar**

**½ cup Messina Hof Papa Paulo Texas Port**

**9 eggs beaten**

In the top of a double boiler, melt chocolate and butter. Whisk in confectioners' sugar and wine. Slowly add eggs, whisking constantly. Pour into buttered miniature loaf pans; cool. Store in the refrigerator. Slice like pâté to serve.

*Vineyard Cuisine*

# Vanilla Crème Brûlée

4 cups heavy whipping cream, chilled

⅔ cup granulated sugar

1/16 teaspoon salt

12 egg yolks

1 teaspoon vanilla extract

½ cup turbinado sugar or large-grain sugar

Adjust the oven rack to the lower-middle position and preheat the oven to 300 degrees. Place a tea towel in the bottom of a large, shallow baking dish and arrange twelve 4-ounce ramekins on the towel. Bring a large saucepan of water to a boil.

Combine 2 cups of the heavy cream, the granulated sugar, and salt in a saucepan and scald over medium heat to about 155 degrees, stirring occasionally to dissolve the sugar. Remove pan from the heat and stir in the remaining 2 cups of heavy cream. Whisk the egg yolks in a bowl until blended. Add the warm cream mixture to the egg yolks, whisking constantly until blended. Whisk in the vanilla.

Pour the cream mixture evenly into the ramekins and place the baking dish on the oven rack. Add enough boiling water to the baking dish to reach ⅔ of the way up the sides of the ramekins. Bake for 30 to 45 minutes, or until the centers of the custards are set and an instant-read thermometer inserted in the center registers 180 degrees.

Remove the ramekins to a wire rack and cool to room temperature. Arrange the ramekins on a baking sheet. Cover tightly with plastic wrap and chill until serving time. Just before serving, remove the plastic wrap and blot any condensation with paper towels. Sprinkle each with 1 teaspoon of the turbinado sugar and caramelize the sugar with a kitchen blowtorch or under the broiler, watching carefully to prevent scorching. Serve immediately. Serves 12.

## White Chocolate Crème Brûlée

8 ounces white chocolate, chopped

Prepare the recipe above as directed, adding the white chocolate to the scalded cream mixture after removing it from the heat. Stir until the chocolate is melted and proceed as directed.

## Praline Crème Brûlée

1½ tablespoons praline liqueur

12 pecan halves, toasted

Prepare the recipe above as directed, substituting the liqueur for the vanilla. Garnish each custard by placing a toasted pecan half in the center of the warm caramelized sugar.

*Dallas Dish*

# Chocolate and Goat Cheese Crème Brûlée

⅓ cup light brown sugar

2¼ cups whipping cream

4½ tablespoons sugar

3 ounces bittersweet chocolate

2 tablespoons Dutch-process cocoa

4 egg yolks

2½ teaspoons vanilla extract

7½ ounces goat cheese at room temperature

Preheat oven to 250 degrees. Spread the brown sugar in a thin layer on a baking sheet and place in preheated oven for about 10 minutes. Do not allow the sugar to melt. Remove baking sheet to cooling rack while preparing custard. Increase oven temperature to 325 degrees. Lightly butter bottom and sides of six (6-ounce) ramekins; set aside.

Combine the whipping cream, sugar, chocolate, and cocoa in a heavy 2-quart saucepan over medium heat. Whisking often, cook until chocolate is melted and sugar has dissolved. Remove from heat and set aside to cool.

Combine the egg yolks, vanilla extract, and softened goat cheese in work bowl of food processor fitted with steel blade. Process until smooth and well blended. Turn the egg mixture out into a medium bowl and whisk in the chocolate mixture until smooth. Divide the mixture among the prepared ramekins and place the ramekins in a baking dish. Add hot water to reach halfway up the sides of the ramekins. Bake in preheated oven for 1 hour. Remove ramekins from baking dish and refrigerate until the custard is well chilled, at least 6 hours.

Put the cooled brown sugar in work bowl of food processor fitted with steel blade or an electric coffee grinder and process until the sugar is very fine. Set aside.

When the crème brûlée is well chilled, place the ramekins on a baking sheet and divide the brown sugar among the ramekins, spreading a thin layer on top of each one. Using a culinary blowtorch, caramelize the sugar, taking care not to burn it. (Or preheat the broiler and place oven rack 3 inches under heat source. Place the baking sheet under broiler and cook just until sugar has caramelized.) Allow the sugar to harden for a few minutes and then serve. Makes six (6-ounce) ramekins.

*The Texas Hill Country*

# Remarkable Reese's Torte

1 (16-ounce) frozen pound cake, thawed

2 pints vanilla ice cream, softened

1⅓ cups hot fudge topping at room temperature

4 (2-cup) packages Reese's Peanut Butter Cups, frozen and chopped

1 cup chilled whipping cream

2 tablespoons sugar

Chocolate curls as garnish

Cut the pound cake into ⅓-inch-thick slices. Cut each slice diagonally into triangles. Line the bottom of a 9-inch springform pan with some of the cake triangles, arranging them with the points facing toward the center of the pan. Fill in the center with additional triangles, then cut additional pieces to fill in any remaining spaces. Spread half of the ice cream over the cake. Freeze for 1 hour, or until firm.

Spread half of the fudge topping over the ice cream and scatter half of the candy evenly over the fudge. Repeat the layering with the remaining cake, ice cream, fudge topping, and candy, freezing after the ice cream layer. Freeze, covered, until firm. Beat the whipping cream and sugar in a mixing bowl until stiff peaks form. Remove the sides of the springform pan. Place the torte on a serving platter. Spread the whipped cream over the sides of the torte. Garnish with chocolate curls. Serves 8.

*Dining without Reservations*

# Martinez Foster with Peaches

3 tablespoons butter

1 tablespoon flour

3 fresh peaches, peeled and halved, pits removed

2 tablespoons brown sugar

¼ teaspoon cinnamon

⅛ teaspoon cayenne pepper

1 ounce peach or apricot brandy

Vanilla ice cream

Melt butter in a skillet on low heat; stir in flour. Keep on low heat for the entire cooking process. Place the peaches, cut side down, in the buttery flour and cook for 3 to 4 minutes.

Flip the peach halves over; mix the brown sugar, cinnamon, and cayenne together, then sprinkle over the peaches (mostly into the pit holes). Stir the brandy into the butter/flour mixture. Cook for 3 to 4 minutes, basting the peaches during the last minute. Serve with vanilla ice cream and drizzle the pan drippings over the top. Makes 4 to 6 servings.

**VARIATION:** You can use Jack Daniel's instead of peach or apricot brandy.

*Matt Martinez MexTex*

# Himbeerschnee *(Raspberry Snow)*

1 quart fresh raspberries

½ cup sugar

2 tablespoons sweet white wine, such as Muscat Canelli

2 egg whites

Reserve 8 to 10 raspberries for garnish. Puree the remaining raspberries or rub through a sieve. Add sugar and wine, stirring well. Beat egg whites until stiff and fold into the raspberry mixture. Pour into a serving dish and freeze until firm. Garnish with whole raspberries and serve with whipped cream.

*Great German Recipes*

# Hill Country Peach Ice Cream

2¼ cups sugar

⅓ cup flour

⅛ teaspoon salt

4 cups half-and-half

2 (12-ounce) cans evaporated milk

6 eggs, lightly beaten

4 to 6 cups peeled and sliced fresh peaches

¾ cup sugar

3 tablespoons vanilla extract

2 teaspoons almond extract

Combine 2½ cups sugar, flour, and salt in a large saucepan and mix well. Stir in the half-and-half, evaporated milk, and eggs. Cook over medium heat until the mixture is hot and begins to thicken, stirring constantly. Remove from heat. Let stand until cool. You may prepare up to this point and store, covered, in the refrigerator for 8 to 10 hours.

Combine the peaches and ¾ cup sugar in a food processor. Process just until the peaches are finely chopped. Let stand for 30 minutes. Stir the peach mixture and flavorings into the milk mixture. Pour into a 5-quart ice cream freezer container. Freeze according to manufacturer's directions. Serves 15 to 20.

**POINTERS FOR PEELING PEACHES**: Place up to 3 medium peaches in a stockpot or large saucepan of boiling water. Let stand for 30 seconds. Remove the peaches with a slotted spoon to a bowl of ice water. Cool slightly. The peel should then slip off easily. If the peaches are not quite ripe, the process may take longer. This procedure also works well with tomatoes.

*Austin Entertains*

# Adult Banana Split

½ cup (1 stick) butter

½ cup plus 2 tablespoons firmly packed brown sugar

2 medium bananas, peeled and sliced into rounds

Juice of ½ medium orange, strained (2 generous tablespoons)

Juice of ½ medium lemon, strained (2 generous tablespoons)

½ tablespoon Grand Marnier

½ tablespoon orange liqueur

½ tablespoon banana liqueur

½ quart vanilla ice cream

Unsweetened whipped cream

2 to 3 tablespoons coarsely chopped toasted macadamia nuts

Melt butter in medium saucepan over medium heat. Add brown sugar and stir until smooth. Add banana slices and stir until coated. Blend in juices and liqueurs and bring to a simmer. Let simmer for 2 minutes. Divide ice cream among individual dishes. Spoon hot sauce over. Top with whipped cream and sprinkle with nuts. Serve at once.

*Of Magnolia and Mesquite*

# Strawberry Sorbet

1 quart fresh strawberries, cleaned and hulled

½ cup sugar (adjust amount according to sweetness of berries)

1 tablespoon freshly squeezed lemon juice

½ cup water

Using a blender, blend berries into a purée. Add the sugar, lemon juice, and water. Blend until all the ingredients are combined. Pour mixture into a metal ice cube tray or other similar metal pan. Freeze several hours or until solid. Break the solid mixture into chunks and blend to a soft slush with either a hand mixer or food processor. Place in a covered container and return to the freezer. Allow sorbet to sit out a few minutes for easier serving. Makes 4 servings.

**NOTE:** Mango sorbet can easily be made with this recipe. Use about 4 cups sliced mango, ⅓ cup sugar, 1½ tablespoons lime juice and ½ cup water.

*It's a Long Way to Guacamole*

# Hot Fudge Sauce

¼ cup butter

2 ounces unsweetened chocolate

1 cup sugar

½ cup evaporated milk

Melt butter and chocolate in double boiler. Stir in sugar and evaporated milk. Cook in double boiler for 10 minutes. Makes 1½ cups.

Kay Ebert
*Perennial Favorites*

# Recipe Sources

## AND ROSES FOR THE TABLE
### A Garden of Recipes

By the Junior League of Tyler

A book for entertaining, for gracious, thoughtful eating, and for special meals that take time to plan and prepare. The recipes are about special occasions and presentations, each unique and delicious. The photography is stunning, and the "roseology" is most interesting.

Junior League of Tyler • 1919 South Donnybrook • Tyler, TX 75701 • 903-595-5426 • www.juniorleagueoftyler.org

## AUSTIN ENTERTAINS

By the Junior League of Austin

*Austin Entertains* has been honored as "The Official Cookbook of the City of Austin" and features 250 menu-driven recipes with color photos and trivia about the Austin area.

The Junior League of Austin • 5416 Parkcrest, Suite 100 Austin, TX 78731 • 512-467-8982 • www.jlaustin.org

## BLUE BONNET CAFÉ
## Still Cookin' 80th Anniversary Cookbook

By Blue Bonnet Café

A collection of recipes we use in our 80-year-old café, along with those of friends and family.

Blue Bonnet Café • 211 Hwy. 281 • Marble Falls, TX 78654 • 830-693-2344 • www.bluebonnetcafe.net

## BRENNAN'S OF HOUSTON IN YOUR KITCHEN

By Carl Walker

Brennan's of Houston general manager Carl Walker reveals recipes, tips, and techniques from his kitchen.

Bright Sky Press • 2365 Rice Blvd., Suite 202 • Houston, TX 77005 • 866-933-6133 • www.brightskypress.com

## CAJUN-CREOLE COOKING

By Terry-Thompson Anderson

Combining the best of classic French cuisine with authentic Louisiana cooking, Chef Terry Thompson Anderson brings the rich culinary heritage of New Orleans and the bayous to a new generation of home cooks eager to discover the pleasures of the Cajun-Creole table.

www.thetexasfoodandwine gourmet.com

## CHINESE CUISINE MADE SIMPLE

By Dorothy Huang

This beautiful book contains 160 mouth-watering recipes that emphasize nutritional value, easy preparation, and taste appeal. Gorgeous photographs appear throughout the book. The pictures of Chinese condiments, ingredients, and vegetables are especially helpful to beginners. It's a great shopping guide.

Pinewood Press • 755 Last Arrow • Houston, TX 77079 • 281-493-0885

## CIAO Y'ALL

By Johnny Carrabba and Damian Mandola

Over 150 recipes from the popular hosts of *Cucina Amore!* Italian cooking influenced by Louisiana Cajun and Creole cuisines and American Southern cooking culture.

Bright Sky Press • 2365 Rice Blvd., Suite 202 • Houston, TX 77005 • 866-933-6133 • www.brightskypress.com

## COOKING FEARLESSLY
## Recipes and Other Adventures from Hudson's on the Bend

By Jeff Blank and Jay Moore with Deborah Harter

Spirited recipes that reflect Chef Jeff Blank's bold approach at the acclaimed Austin restaurant Hudson's on the Bend.

Hudson's on the Bend • 3509 RR 620 North • Austin, TX 78734 • 512-266-1369 • www.hudsonsonthebend.com

### COOKING WITH TEXAS HIGHWAYS

By Nola McKey

More than 250 recipes that sample all the major ethnic cuisines of Texas, with stories about the food, tips on cooking techniques, and sources for ingredients. Beautiful color photos from *Texas Highways* accompany the recipes. Also included is a special chapter on Dutch-oven cooking.

**University of Texas Press •** P.O. Box 7819 • Austin, TX 78713 • 800-252-3206 • www.utexaspress.com

### COOKING WITH TEXAS PEPPERS

By Peggy Struble

More than 100 quality, tested recipes using jalapeños and a variety of other peppers to create fun, flavorful dishes that capture the true essence of Texas cuisine. Also includes a "Heat Chart" of peppers and cooking times for grilling perfect meats.

**Tastebud Adventures • 101 Turtle Creek Circle •** Huntsville, TX 77340 • 936-294-9117 • www.tastebud adventures.com

### DALLAS DISH

By the Junior League of Dallas

A collection of more than 280 innovative recipes contributed by Junior League members, their relatives and friends, and famous chefs from the Dallas area. Each recipe reflects the character of Dallas life and its rich cultures.

**Junior League of Dallas • 8003 Inwood Road • Dallas, TX** 75209 • 214-352-8822 • www.jld.net

### THE DALLAS JUNIOR LEAGUE COOKBOOK

By the Junior League of Dallas

Fondly referred to as the "Blue Book," *The Dallas Junior League Cookbook* has become a classic since its debut in 1976. From Mushroom Turnovers to Cold Raspberry Soup, there are over 400 pages of truly mouthwatering recipes, menus, and food gift ideas between its covers.

**Junior League of Dallas • 8003 Inwood Road • Dallas, TX** 75209-3399 • (214) 357-8822 • www.jld.net

### DINING WITHOUT RESERVATIONS

By the Junior League of Beaumont

*Dining without Reservations* continues the tradition of cooking for the pure joy of it. Whether preparing a sophisticated dinner party, a casual feast for friends, or the everyday family meal, you will find a variety of recipes to tempt every palate.

**Junior League of Beaumont •** 2388 McFaddin • Beaumont, TX 77702 • 409-832-0873 • www.juniorleaguebeaumont.org

### DOWN-HOME TEXAS COOKING

By James Stroman

Treat yourself to a genuine taste of Texas with this collection of authentic and savory dishes as broad as the Texas sky and as hearty as a cowboy's laugh. James Stroman traveled the Lone Star State and collected the special recipes that have become traditional mealtime favorites with Texas families.

**National Book Network • 15200 NBN Way • Blue Ridge Summit, PA 17214 •** 800-462-6420

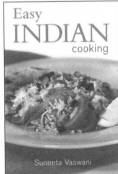

### EASY INDIAN COOKING

By Suneeta Vaswani

User-friendly recipes that work well, taste incredible, and introduce you to Indian culture and history. Stunning full-color photography throughout.

**Robert Rose, Inc. • 190 Eglinton Ave. East •** Toronto, Ontario Canada M4P 1E2

### FIRED UP!
### More Adventures & Recipes from Hudson's on the Bend

By Jeff Blank with Sara Courington

Recipes for adventurous dishes as big and robust as the Lone Star State, reflecting Chef Jeff Blank's no-holds-barred approach.

**Fearless Press • 3509 RR 620 North • Austin, TX 78734 •** 512-266-1369 • www.hudsonsonthebend.com

### FLAVOR FAVORITES
### A Collection of Treasured Recipes from the Kitchens of Baylor Alumni

By the Baylor Alumni Association

A compilation of recipes submitted by Baylor University alumni.

Baylor Alumni Association
One Bear Place, No. 97116
Waco, TX 76798 • 888-710-1859 • www.bayloralumni
association.com

### FLAVORS OF FREDERICKSBURG

By St. Barnabas Episcopal Church Women

This book is a compilation of recipes by members of St. Barnabas Episcopal Church. The illustrations of Fredericksburg scenes are from the original art of church member Lee Ethel.

St. Barnabas Episcopal Church • 601 West Creek • Fredericksburg, TX 78624 • 830-997-5762

### FONDA SAN MIGUEL
### Thirty Years of Food and Art

By Tom Gilliland and Miguel Ravago

Text by Virginia B. Wood

In celebration of three decades of success, *Fonda San Miguel: Thirty Years of Food and Art* presents more than 100 recipes from the restaurant's menus over the years, including many of the signature dishes that have made it one of the Southwest's top restaurants.

Shearer Publishing • 406 Post Oak Road • Fredericksburg, TX 78624 • 800-458-3808 • www.shearerpub.com

### GERMAN-STYLE RECIPES

By Karen Gottier

This volume is packed full of more than 100 recipes, plus tidbits about German culture. Try iced coffee, ham and cheese toast, vegetable broth with dumplings, German-style potato salad, pretzels, German rye bread, Sauerbraten, cod in herbed sauce, apple streusel pie, honey cookies, and more.

Penfield Books • 215 Brown Street • Iowa City, IA 52245 • 800-728-9998 • www.penfieldbooks.com

### GRAZING ACROSS TEXAS
### Rod, Gun & Ranch Cooking

By Tosh Brown

From the accomplished chef to the casual cook, *Grazing across Texas* offers recipes for any level of culinary expertise. If you know your way around a kitchen, you can try dishes from some of the state's finest game and fish chefs. If down-home camp cooking is more your style, there are plenty of recipes that use basic tools and ingredients.

Collectors Covey • 5550 Lovers Lane • Dallas, TX 75209 • www.collectorscovey.com

### GREAT GERMAN RECIPES

By Lynn Hattery-Beyer

Recipes include Berlin punch, German coleslaw, hearty barley soup, raisin bread, sauerbraten, cauliflower in white sauce, and Black Forest cherry cake. The book also contains information about German-American sites, folk art designs, table blessings, traditions, and familiar German words.

Penfield Books • 215 Brown Street • Iowa City, IA 52245 • 800-728-9998 • www.penfieldbooks.com

### GRUENE GENERAL STORE COOKBOOK
### Tried and True Recipes from the Heart of the Hill Country

By Virginia K. Hughes

Step back in time for recipes like your mother and grandmother used to make. These tried and true recipes from the Texas Hill Country will make you nostalgic for home cooking.

Hughes Interests • 1610 Hunter Road • New Braunfels, TX 78130 • 830-629-5990 • www.gruenegeneralstore.com

### GULF COAST COOKING
### Seafood from the Florida Keys to the Yucatan Peninsula

By Virginia Elverson

In this collection of over 300 mouth-watering recipes, based on the finfish and shellfish of the Gulf of Mexico, culinary professional Virginia Elverson has skimmed the cream of her own recipe files and those of other food professionals from the Florida Keys to the Yucatan Peninsula.

Shearer Publishing • 406 Post Oak Road • Fredericksburg, TX 78624 • 800-458-3808 • www.shearerpub.com

### THE HERB GARDEN COOKBOOK
### The Complete Gardening and Gourmet Guide

By Lucinda Hutson

*The Herb Garden Cookbook* provides full instructions for growing robust and flavorful herbs using organic gardening techniques, harvesting and storing herbs, and preparing more than 150 delicious recipes, with valuable information on exotic herbs from Mexico and Southeast Asia, menu planning, and sources for plants, seeds, and gourmet products.

University of Texas Press • P.O. Box 7819 • Austin, TX 78713 • 800-252-3206 • www.utexaspress.com

### JIM PEYTON'S THE VERY BEST OF TEX-MEX COOKING
### Plus Texas Barbecue and Texas Chile

By James W. Peyton

Brings culinary sophistication to American kitchens with a collection of outstanding recipes and the lore surrounding the most popular dishes ordered in Tex-Mex restaurants. Tex-Mex, barbecue, and chile are important aspects of Texas regional cooking developed over many years of trial and error by thousands of remarkable cooks.

Maverick Publishing Co. • P.O. Box 6355 • San Antonio, TX 78209 • 210-828-7874 • www.maverickpub.com

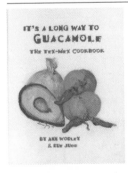

### HULLABALOO IN THE KITCHEN II

By the Dallas County A&M University Mothers' Club

A collection of favorite recipes from Aggie Moms members, friends, and celebrities. Interspersed throughout are pictures of the Texas A&M University campus and its traditions.

Dallas County A&M University Mothers' Club • P.O. Box 600182 • Dallas, TX 75360 • 214-349-3336 • www.dallasaggiemoms.org

### KICKIN' BACK IN THE KITCHEN COOKBOOK
### A Collection of Family Recipes from Sun City, Texas

By P&P Publishing

A collection of over 400 recipes from the residents of Sun City, Texas. Dishes include everything from family fare to international taste treats gathered during world travels.

Newman Marketing • 3802 Antelope Trail • Temple, TX 76504 • 254-774-9141

### THE KITCHEN TABLE

By Randy Evans

Details the experience of dining in Brennan's of Houston's private dining room within the kitchen. Customers tell of what they saw and tasted, and the seven courses served at the famous restaurant—from lagniappe through dessert and cheese—are described.

Bright Sky Press • 2365 Rice Blvd., Suite 202 • Houston, TX 77005 • 866-933-6133 • www.brightskypress.com

### IT'S A LONG WAY TO GUACAMOLE
### The Tex-Mex Cookbook

By Ann Worley and Rue Judd

A collection of recipes drawn from several Texas couples transplanted to Washington, D.C., who began meeting for informal Mexican-food dinners. Basic techniques, ingredients, sauces, and fillings take the mystery out of Tex-Mex and make tacos, chili suppers, covered-dish suppers, or elegant brunches understandable, easy, and simply delicious.

Newman Marketing • 3802 Antelope Trail • Temple, TX 76504 • 254-774-9141

### LAGNIAPPE
### A Little Something Extra

By the Junior League of Beaumont

A collection of polished, yet practical recipes. The book is seasoned with hospitality hints, special how-tos, menu extras for entertaining, and even some secret family recipes.

Junior League of Beaumont • 2388 McFaddin • Beaumont, TX 77702 • 409-832-0873 • www.juniorleaguebeaumont.org

## LEGENDS OF TEXAS BARBECUE COOKBOOK
**Recipes and Recollections from the Pit Bosses**

### By Robb Walsh

Welcome to Texas barbecue. They love to make it. They love to eat it. And they love to argue about it, igniting as many feuds as fires from Houston to El Paso. *Legends of Texas Barbecue Cookbook* delivers both practical recipes and a guided tour of Texas barbecue lore, giving readers straightforward advice right from the pit masters themselves.

Chronicle Books • 690 Second Street • San Francisco, CA 94102 • www.chroniclebooks.com

## LICENSE TO COOK TEXAS STYLE

### By Dianna Stevens

This book celebrates the many cultures that contribute to the variety of flavors and tastes in the art of food and cooking, along with historical sites to see. Recipes include frosty Texas citrus refresher, poppers, bleeding armadillo bread, campfire chili, Tex-Mex enchiladas, rum-marinated rib-eye steaks, shrimp fajitas, Texas sheet cake, and caramel custard.

Penfield Books • 215 Brown Street • Iowa City, IA 52245 • 800-728-9998 • www.penfieldbooks.com

## LONE STAR LEGACY
**A Texas Cookbook**

### By the Austin Junior Forum, Inc.

This book, Austin Junior Forum's original cookbook, has become a classic. It was the first Texas cookbook selected for the Walter S. McIlhenny Community Cookbook Hall of Fame. Over 800 recipes are seasoned with cooking tips, spiced with Texas trivia, and frosted with breathtaking photos of Texas landmarks and landscapes.

Austin Junior Forum • 1401 West Avenue • Austin, TX 78701 • 512-472-0779 • www.austinjuniorforum.org

## LONE STAR TO FIVE STAR
**Culinary Creations for Every Occasion**

### By the Junior League of Plano, Inc.

Features a collection of recipes designed to enhance every occasion. In addition to over 250 recipes extensively tested in home kitchens, the book contains signature recipes from more than a dozen of the most lauded chefs in North Texas.

Junior League of Plano, Inc. • 5805 Coit Road, Suite 301 • Plano, TX 75093 • 972-769-0557 • www.jlplano.org

## LUBY'S RECIPES & MEMORIES
**A Collection of Our Favorite Dishes and Heartwarming Stories**

### By Luby's, Inc.

Celebrates a milestone as well as pays tribute to our loyal customers. Included are 120 of our guests' favorite recipes plus stories and pictures highlighting our devoted patrons who have helped make Luby's a success.

Luby's, Inc. • 13111 NW Freeway, Suite 600 • Houston, TX 77040 • 877-GoLubys • www.lubys.com

## MATT MARTINEZ MEX-TEX
**Traditional Tex-Mex Taste**

### By Matt Martinez

Matt Martinez of El Rancho restaurant brings his "prairie/range" style of cooking to the reader, using traditional methods and native ingredients.

Bright Sky Press • 2365 Rice Blvd., Suite 202 • Houston, TX 77005 • 866-933-6133 • www.brightskypress.com

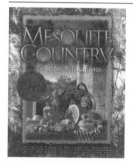

## MESQUITE COUNTRY
**Tastes & Traditions from the Tip of Texas**

### By the Museum of South Texas History

*Mesquite Country* was created in keeping with the Museum of South Texas History's mission of preserving and presenting the borderland heritage of South Texas and northeastern Mexico. It represents not only a unique blend of cultures through recipes but also an album of the region with historical photographs and information.

Museum of South Texas History • 200 N. Closner • Edinburg, TX 78541 • 956-383-6911 • www.mosthistory.org

## NECESSITIES AND TEMPTATIONS

### By the Junior League of Austin

*Necessities and Temptations* is two books in one—a cookbook and a reference guide. A must for every kitchen with over 400 pages of recipes and useful hints, including ingredient substitutions, table setting guidelines, and definitions of cooking terms.

The Junior League of Austin • 5416 Parkcrest, Suite 100 • Austin, TX 78731 • 512-467-8982 • www.jlaustin.org

## NEW BRAUNFELS SMOKEHOUSE
### Our Favorite Recipes

By Susan Dunbar Snyder

Features recipes we include on our menu in our popular New Braunfels restaurant. Established in 1952, the New Braunfels Smokehouse has served comfort food to customers from all over the world. Our cookbook also includes favorite recipes from family, friends, and employees

Treeline Publishing • P.O. Box 311159 • New Braunfels, TX 78131 • 800-537-6932 • www.nbsmokehouse.com

## NUEVO TEX-MEX
### Festive New Recipes from Just North of the Border

By David Garrido and Robb Walsh

Nuevo Tex-Mex cooking, the hottest new trend in Nuevo Latino cuisine, embraces and celebrates both its zesty Latin American flavors and no-nonsense Texas personality.

Chronicle Books • 680 Second Street • San Francisco, CA 94107 • www.chroniclebooks.com

## OF MAGNOLIA AND MESQUITE
### A Menu Cookbook of Simple Elegance

By Suzanne Corder and Gay Thompson

A unique collection of family-inspired recipes presented in menu form. The menus include Breakfast and Brunch, Luncheons, Dinners, and Special Occasions. Each menu is designed to serve a specific number—from 2 to 200—and the recipes have been adjusted to generously serve the suggested numbers.

www.amazon.com

## THE PEACH TREE FAMILY COOKBOOK

By Cynthia Collins Pedregon

Like its companion volumes, this cookbook was printed in response to customer requests for recipes from the Peach Tree Tea Room in Fredericksburg. The emphasis is on straightforward instructions and fresh, seasonal, easy-to-find ingredients.

The Peach Tree Collection • 210 South Adams • Fredericksburg, TX 78624 • 830-997-9527 • www.peach-tree.com

## THE PEACH TREE TEA ROOM COOKBOOK

By Cynthia Collins Pedregon

The first of three cookbooks featuring recipes from Fredericksburg's Peach Tree restaurant, established in 1972. Many of these dishes, developed from 1984 through 1990, are still served daily. Some favorite recipes from this book are Cynthia's Chicken Salad, Chilled Avocado Soup, Monterey Quiche, and a variety of ice cream pies.

The Peach Tree Collection • 210 South Adams • Fredericksburg, TX 78624 • 830-997-9527 • www.peach-tree.com

## PERENNIAL FAVORITES
### Portable Food from the Garden Club of Houston Bulb and Plant Mart

By the Garden Club of Houston's Bulb and Plant Mart

Offers easy recipes for food that you can pack up and take to the ranch, tailgate party, casual potluck, or elegant dinner. It includes recipes for comfort food that can become a mainstay at your family reunion.

Bright Sky Press • 2365 Rice Blvd, Suite 202 • Houston, TX 77005 • 866-933-6133 • www.brightskypress.com

## REMEMBER THE FLAVORS OF AUSTIN
### A Restaurant Guide & Recipe Sampler

By Barbara Allen

Recipes from a wide range of Austin restaurants along with a locator map.

Bazaar Barbara Press • 7711 Broadway, Suite 19-B • San Antonio, TX 78209 • 210-805-8255

## THE SAN ANTONIO TEX-MEX COOKBOOK

By Elizabeth Blakeley

A complete collection of the Alamo City's authentic Tex-Mex recipes using local ingredients and presented with easy-to-follow instructions.

San Antonio Tex-Mex • P.O. Box 15345 • San Antonio, TX 78212 • 210-325-3601 • www.satexmex.com

## SEASONED WITH FUN
### Cooking and Entertaining with Pizzazz

By the Junior League of El Paso

More than 200 tested recipes ranging from appetizers to desserts, along with entertaining and decorating tips as well as helpful information about cooking techniques.

Junior League of El Paso • 520 Thunderbird • El Paso, TX 79912 • 915-584-3511 • www.JLEP.org

## SEASONED WITH SUN
### Recipes from the Corner of Texas and Old Mexico

By the Junior League of El Paso

A collection of 400 authentic recipes from the region, including many from noted El Paso and Juarez restaurants. They represent the rich heritage of the Southwest, Mexico, and the Rio Grande, which all blend to make El Paso.

Junior League of El Paso • 520 Thunderbird • El Paso, TX 79912 • 915-584-3511 • www.JLEP.org

## SETTINGS, SUNRISE TO SUNSET:
### A Medley of Flavors, Tastes, and Styles from the Texas Gulf Coast

By the Assistance League of the Bay Area

Recipes chosen to spotlight local favorites, members' family treasures, and area restaurants, while appealing to all levels of gourmets.

Assistance League of the Bay Area • P.O. Box 590153 • Houston, TX 77259 • 877-277-3452 • www.bayarea.assistanceleague.org

## SOUTHERN HERB GROWING

By Madalene Hill and Gwen Barclay with Jean Hardy

A comprehensive guide to growing more than 130 herbs in the challenging climate of the American South, illustrated by approximately 300 color photographs. Written by the experienced former herb growers of Hilltop Herb Farm near Cleveland, Texas, the book includes a treasury of appetizing, herb-flavored dishes from the menu of the Hilltop Herb Farm Restaurant.

Shearer Publishing • 406 Post Oak Road • Fredericksburg, TX 78624 • 800-458-3808 • www.shearerpub.com

## STOLEN RECIPES
### Recipes Stolen from Only the Finest of Texas Cooks Living on Only the Finest of Texas Ranches

By Mary Sue Koontz Nelson

A unique collection of 345 recipes from 111 ranch cooks around the state.

Stolen Recipes • P.O. Box 235 • Placedo, TX 77977 • 361-575-0855

## TALES FROM TEXAS TABLES
### Recipes and More

By Carol Blakely

This book explores the roots of Texas cooking, which resulted from an unusual mix of climate and cultures. It includes recipes from old Texas cookbooks as well as unrecorded recipes passed down from one generation of Texans to another. Recipes include dill pickles, tea cakes, kolaches, German potato salad, poke salad, jumbo soup, chicken-fried steak, calabacitas, and chocolate fudge cake.

Penfield Books • 215 Brown Street • Iowa City, IA 52245 • 800-728-9998 • www.penfieldbooks.com

## TEXAS BLOSSOMS
### Food, Flowers & Friendship

By the Richardson Woman's Club, Inc.

This beautiful spiral hardbound book contains 500 tested recipes, many of which are Texas specialties, as well as suggested menus for special occasions. In addition to breathtaking photography of Texas landscapes and wildflowers, there is an introduction by Liz Carpenter, press secretary for Lady Bird Johnson, as well as Mrs. Johnson's personal recipe for Spiced Tea.

Richardson Woman's Club • P.O. Box 831963 • Richardson, TX 75083-1963 • 972-238-0841 • www.richardsonwomansclub.com

## TEXAS COOKOFF
### Recipes from *Stewing in Texas* and More

By Carol Blakely

This collection of the all-time best Texas recipes was compiled by Carol Blakely, one of the leading authorities on Southwestern cooking. The classic recipes include such favorites as Pico de Gallo, Easy Skillet Fajitas, Prairie Fire, Cheese Wafers from Lady Bird Johnson, Armadillo Eggs, Perfect Guacamole, Poo Poos, and Pioneer Jailhouse Chili.

Penfield Books • 215 Brown Street • Iowa City, IA 52245 • 800-728-9998 • www.penfieldbooks.com

### THE TEXAS COUNTRY REPORTER COOKBOOK
**Recipes from the Viewers of "Texas Country Reporter"**

By Phillips Productions, Inc.

In traveling the backroads to gather material for his television show *Texas Country Reporter,* Bob Phillips has tasted some of the best in Texas Cooking—from crawfish in Mauriceville to chili in Terlingua to sautéed tumbleweeds in Clint. This cookbook contains the favorite recipes of viewers from across the state, along with colorful anecdotes about the history of the dish.

Shearer Publishing • 406 Post Oak Road • Fredericksburg, TX 78624 • 800-458-3808 • www.shearerpub.com

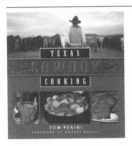

### TEXAS COWBOY COOKING

By Tom Perini

Reflecting Tom Perini's love of ranch life and his unique cooking style, this book features 75 favorites served at his Perini Ranch Steakhouse, a world-famous destination for regional cuisine. In addition to his signature recipes, Tom serves a generous helping of cowboy lore and humor.

Comanche Moon Publishing • P.O. Box 728 • Buffalo Gap, TX 79508 • 800-367-1721 • www.periniranch.com

### THE TEXAS HILL COUNTRY: A Food and Wine Lover's Paradise

By Terry Thompson-Anderson, photography by Sandy Wilson

This book celebrates the agricultural bounty of the Texas Hill Country and highlights 100 notable food finds: farm stands, cheese and sausage makers, artisan bakeries, breweries and wineries, and unique eateries. Included in the book are recipes gathered from proprietors or developed by the author to highlight the local food products.

Shearer Publishing • 406 Post Oak Road • Fredericksburg, TX 78624 • 800-458-3808 • www.shearerpub.com

### TEXAS ON THE PLATE

By Terry Thompson-Anderson

Chef and cookbook author Terry Thompson-Anderson demonstrates her flair for combining unusual flavors and diverse ethnic cooking styles to exemplify the new Texas Cuisine. Among the more than 150 recipes are upscale interpretations of traditional favorites as well as adventurous new dishes. In addition to professional cooking tips, the book includes wine lists and tasting notes highlighting award-winning Texas wines.

Shearer Publishing • 406 Post Oak Road • Fredericksburg, TX 78624 • 800-458-3808 • www.shearerpub.com

### TEXAS PEPPERS
**The Jalapeño Cookbook**

By Peggy Struble

Over 100 quality, tested recipes using the jalapeño pepper. Many are very easy to prepare, with only four or five ingredients. Also includes a list of festivals in Texas that celebrate the jalapeño, a "Heat Chart" of peppers, and a history of the jalapeño.

Tastebud Adventures • 101 Turtle Creek Circle • Huntsville, TX 77340 • 936-294-9117 • www.tastebudadventures.com

### THE TEXAS PROVINCIAL KITCHEN COOKBOOK

By Melissa Guerra

An eighth-generation Texan and a native of South Texas, Melissa Guerra presents 190 authentic recipes from her family kitchen as well as 52 exciting menus that blend the tastes of Mexico and Texas. This has become the classic Texas Border cookbook.

Melissa Guerra • P.O. Box 3789 • Edinburg, TX 78540 • 877-875-2665 • www.melissaguerra.com

### TEXAS TIES
**Recipes and Remembrances from the Junior League of North Harris County, Inc.**

By the Junior League of North Harris County, Inc.

Celebrates both the Epicurean and emotional ingredients of great food. It contains over 350 recipes peppered with personal essays and short recollections of family, food, and traditions. *Texas Ties* is also a Tabasco award-winning cookbook.

Junior League of North Harris County • 21021 Springbrook Plaza Dr. Suite 175 • Spring, TX 77379 • 888-839-8437 • www.jlnhsmc.org

### THROUGH OUR KITCHEN DOOR

By the Dallas County Heritage Society

A collection of some of the most fondly remembered dishes that have been passed down through many generations of the families of the Heritage Society and our many friends.

**Dallas County Heritage Society • 1515 South Harwood • Dallas, TX 75215 • wwwDallasheritagevillage.org**

### UNDER THE TEXAN SUN
### The Best Recipes from Lone Star Wineries

By Rhonda Cloos

A collection of innovative recipes from nearly 30 wineries, showcasing dishes that either contain wine or pair well with wine. There are also chapters on wine recipes developed by Texas chefs, wine and cheese combinations, and the challenge of pairing wine with chocolate.

**National Book Network • 15200 NBN Way • Blue Ridge Summit, PA 17214 • 800-462-6420**

### VINEYARD CUISINE
### Meals & Memories from Messina Hof

By Merrill and Paul Bonarrigo

A historic journal about wine, food, and 30 years of love and laughter. It is a collection of recipes that all include wine.

**Bright Sky Press • 2365 Rice Blvd., Suite 202 • Houston, TX 77005 • 866-933-6133 • www.brightskypress.com**

### ¡VIVA! TRADICIONES
### South Texas Cooks from Brush to Bay

By the Junior League of Corpus Christi, Inc.

Long live our traditions, our communities, and our families! The Junior League of Corpus Christi is proud to bring you a cookbook that reveals the riches of our varied ethnic heritage, the bounty of the gulf waters, and the treasures of our farms and ranches.

**Junior League of Corpus Christi • 4050 Weber Road • Corpus Christi, TX 78411 • 361-884-3000 • www.jlcc.org**

### WITH LOVE, FROM CYNTHIA
### A Collection of Recipes & Remembrances

By Cynthia Collins Pedregon

A collection of lovingly developed recipes and some shared recipes from close friends. Written to encourage fellowship and good times, this book reflects the spirit of hospitality that permeates the soul of the author's writings.

**The Peach Tree Collection • 210 South Adams • Fredericksburg, TX 78624 • 830-997-9527 • www.peach-tree.com**

## Copyright Information

*Gulf Coast Cooking: Seafood from the Florida Keys to the Yucatán Peninsula* Text © 1991 Virginia Elverson

*The Herb Garden Cookbook: The Complete Gardening and Gourmet Guide* © 1987, 1992, 1998, 2003 Lucinda Hutson

*Hullabaloo in the Kitchen II* © 1998 Dallas County A&M University Mothers' Club

*It's A Long Way to Guacamole: The Tex-Mex Cookbook* © 1978, 2003 J&W Tex-Mex Publications

*Jim Peyton's The Very Best of Tex-Mex Cooking: Plus Texas Barbecue and Texas Chile* © 2005 James W. Peyton

*Kickin' Back in the Kitchen Cookbook: A Collection of Family Recipes from Sun City, Texas* © 2005 P&P Publishing

*The Kitchen Table* © 2006 Brennan's of Houston, Inc.

*Lagniappe: A Little Something Extra* © 1982 The Junior League of Beaumont, Inc.

*Legends of Texas Barbecue Cookbook: Recipes and Recollections from the Pit Bosses* © 2002 Robb Walsh; used with permission of Chronicle Books, San Francisco

*License to Cook Texas Style* © 2002 Penfield Books

*Lone Star Legacy: A Texas Cookbook* © 1981 Austin Junior Forum, Inc.

*Lone Star to Five Star: Culinary Creations for Every Occasion* © 2004 The Junior League of Plano

*Luby's Recipes & Memories: A Collection of Our Favorite Dishes and Heartwarming Stories* © 2006 LUBCO, Inc.

*Matt Martinez MexTex: Traditional Tex-Mex Taste* Text © 2006 by Matt G. Martinez Jr.

*Mesquite Country: Tastes & Traditions from the Tip of Texas* © 1996 Museum of South Texas History

*Necessities and Temptations* © 1987 The Junior League of Austin, Inc.

*New Braunfels Smokehouse: Our Favorite Recipes* © 2007 Susan Dunbar Snyder

*Nuevo Tex-Mex: Festive New Recipes from Just North of the Border* Text © 1998 Robb Walsh, David Garrido, and Manny Rodriguez; used with permission of Chronicle Books, San Francisco

*Of Magnolia and Mesquite: A Menu Cookbook of Simple Elegance* © 1985 Su-Ga Publications

*The Peach Tree Family Cookbook* © 1994 Peach Tree Gift Gallery & Tea Room

*The Peach Tree Tea Room Cookbook* © 1990 Peach Tree Gift Gallery & Tea Room

*Perennial Favorites: Portable Food from the Garden Club of Houston Bulb and Plant Mart* © 2007 The Garden Club of Houston

*Remember the Flavors of Austin: A Restaurant Guide & Recipe Sampler* © 1998 Bazaar Barbara Press

*The San Antonio Tex-Mex Cookbook* © 2000 Elizabeth Blakely

*Seasoned with Fun: Cooking and Entertaining with Pizzazz* © 2000 The Junior League of El Paso, Inc.

*Seasoned with Sun: Recipes from the Corner of Texas and Old Mexico* © 1989 The Junior League of El Paso, Inc.

*Settings, Sunrise to Sunset: A Medley of Flavors, Tastes, and Styles from the Texas Gulf Coast* Text © 2007 Assistance League of the Bay Area

*Southern Herb Growing* © 1987, 1997 Gwen Barclay, Jean Hardy, and Madalene Hill

*Stolen Recipes: Recipes Stolen from Only the Finest of Texas Cooks Living on Only the Finest of Texas Ranches* © 2000 Mary Sue Koontz Nelson

*Tales from Texas Tables: Recipes and More* © 2003 Carol Blakely

*Texas Blossoms: Food, Flowers & Friendship* © 2002 Richardson Woman's Club, Inc.

*Texas Cookoff: Recipes from Stewing in Texas and More* © 2007 Penfield Books

*The Texas Country Reporter Cookbook: Recipes from the Viewers of "Texas Country Reporter"* © 1990 Phillips Productions, Inc.

*Texas Cowboy Cooking* © 2000 Tom Perini

*The Texas Hill Country: A Food and Wine Lover's Paradise* Text © 2008, 2010 Terry Thompson-Anderson

*Texas on the Plate* Text © 2002 Terry Thompson-Anderson

*Texas Peppers: The Jalapeño Cookbook* © 2001 Peggy Struble

*The Texas Provincial Kitchen Cookbook* Text © 1997 Melissa Guerra

*Texas Ties: Recipes and Remembrances from the Junior League of North Harris County, Inc.* © 1997 Junior League of North Harris and South Montgomery Counties, Inc.

*Through Our Kitchen Door* © 1978 Dallas County Heritage Society, Inc.

*Under the Texan Sun: The Best Recipes from Lone Star Wineries* © 2005 Rhonda Cloos

*Vineyard Cuisine: Meals & Memories from Messina Hof* © 2007 Merrill and Paul Bonarrigo

*¡Viva! Tradiciones: South Texas Cooks from Brush to Bay* © 1996 The Junior League of Corpus Christi, Inc.

*What's Cooking at the Blue Bonnet Café* © 2007 Morris Press Cookbooks

*With Love, From Cynthia: A Collection of Recipes & Remembrances* © 1999 Peach Tree Gift Gallery & Tea Room

# Index